THE MOSAIC OF
ECONOMIC GROWTH

❖

EDITED BY RALPH LANDAU,
TIMOTHY TAYLOR, AND GAVIN WRIGHT

STANFORD UNIVERSITY PRESS

Stanford, California 1996

Stanford University Press
Stanford, California

© 1996 by the Board of Trustees of the
Leland Stanford Junior University

Printed in the United States of America

CIP data are at the end of the book

Stanford University Press publications are distributed
exclusively by Stanford University Press within the
United States, Canada, Mexico, and Central America;
they are distributed exclusively by Cambridge University Press throughout the rest of the world

Preface

The occasion for the papers collected in this volume was the opening of the Donald L. Lucas Conference Center, located in the new Ralph Landau Center for Economics and Policy Research. The building was dedicated here on the Stanford University campus on May 4, 1994; the conference took place on June 3–4, 1994. The spirit of the occasion was for the Stanford economics community to baptize the new home for the economics department. Thus, all of the single authors in the volume are Stanford professors, and in the jointly authored papers, at least one of the authors is a Stanford faculty member. While most of the authors are affiliated with the Department of Economics, the papers that follow also draw upon many other centers of economic insight at Stanford: the Graduate School of Business, the Hoover Institution, the Center for Economic Policy Research, the engineering schools, the Law School, the Food Research Institute, and the Institute for International Studies.

The subject—the mosaic of economic growth—is a hot one in both academic and political circles these days. But years before it became a hot topic, the community of economists at Stanford University had already been asking about the forces that produce technological change, and what these forces imply for growth-generating public policies. For example, Stanford researchers have collaborated on two earlier books, *The Positive Sum Strategy* in 1986 and *Technology and the Wealth of Nations* in 1992.

The conference organizers were Ralph Landau and Gavin Wright. They wish to thank Deborah Carvahlo for her indispensable assistance in organizing the logistics of the conference. The papers in this volume have been revised and edited since the conference, in response to comments presented at the time as well as the urgings of the editors. Timothy Taylor took the lead in this process of editing and revision, with administrative assistance from Donna Holm.

For their contributions as moderators and commenters at the conference, the editors would like to thank Janet Alexander, Donald Brown, Gordon Cain, Clive Crook, Walter P. Falcon, Lawrence Goulder, Robert Hall, Grant Heidrich, Dale Jorgenson, Donald Kennedy, Fumio Kodama, Gordon Moore, James Morgan, David Mowery, Richard Nelson, John Pencavel, Gottfried Plumpe, James Poterba, Condoleeza Rice, Albert D. Richards, Paul Romer, Richard Rosenbloom, David Rowe, William Spencer, David Starrett, James Sweeney, and Frank Wolak. Special thanks go to Michael Boskin, who delivered a dinner address (not included in this volume) on the subject of "Economic Policy and Economic Growth." We would also like to thank the economists, business people, and journalists who attended the conference, many of whom contributed mightily in the informal discussions and feedback, which are such a large part of what make this sort of conference worthwhile.

The subject of economic growth deserves the concentrated attention of scholars, policy makers, and interested citizens. We hope that this book can play a role in stimulating greater interest in and awareness of these issues.

R.L.
T.T.
G.W.

Contents

RALPH LANDAU

Contributors

MOSES ABRAMOVITZ is the Coe Professor of American Economic History (Emeritus) at Stanford University.

MASAHIKO AOKI is the Henri and Tomoye Takahashi Professor of Japanese Studies and Professor of Economics, Stanford University.

TIMOTHY F. BRESNAHAN is Professor of Economics (by Courtesy) in the Graduate School of Business, and Professor of Economics, Stanford University.

THOMAS J. CAMPBELL is a California State Senator and a Professor of Law at the Stanford Law School.

LINDA R. COHEN is Associate Professor of Economics at the University of California, Irvine.

PAUL A. DAVID is quondam Coe Professor of American Economic History at Stanford University, and Senior Research Fellow, All Souls College, Oxford University.

SHANE GREENSTEIN is Assistant Professor at the University of Illinois, Urbana-Champaign.

DANIEL P. KESSLER is Assistant Professor of Economics, Law, and Policy in the Graduate School of Business, Stanford University.

ANNE O. KRUEGER is Professor of Economics, Stanford University.

RALPH LANDAU is former chairman and cofounder of the Halcon SD Group, Inc., and Consulting Professor of Economics at Stanford University.

LAWRENCE J. LAU is Co-Director of the Asia Pacific Research Center and the Kwoh-Ting Li Professor of Economic Development in the Department of Economics, Stanford University.

RONALD I. MCKINNON is the William Eberle Professor of Economics at Stanford University.

ROGER G. NOLL is the Director of the Public Policy Program, Professor (by Courtesy) in the Department of Political Science and Graduate School of Business, and the Morris M. Doyle Centennial Professor of Economics, Stanford University.

NATHAN ROSENBERG is the Fairleigh S. Dickinson, Jr., Professor of Public Policy and Professor of Economics in the Department of Economics, Stanford University.

HENRY S. ROWEN is Senior Fellow at the Hoover Institution, and the Edward B. Rust Professor of Public Management in the Graduate School of Business, Stanford University.

SYLVESTER J. SCHIEBER is Director of The Wyatt Company's Research and Information Center in Washington, D.C.

MYRON S. SCHOLES is a principal and limited partner at Long-Term Capital Management, L.P., an investment management firm based in Greenwich, Connecticut. He is also Senior Research Fellow at the Hoover Institution and is currently on leave as Professor of Law, Stanford Law School. He is the Frank E. Buck Professor of Finance in the Graduate School of Business, Stanford University.

GEORGE B. SHEPHERD is a former practicing lawyer and is currently a senior-level graduate student in economics at Stanford University.

JOHN B. SHOVEN is the Charles R. Schwab Professor of Economics and Dean of the School of Humanities and Sciences, Stanford University.

A. MICHAEL SPENCE is the Philip H. Knight Professor of Economics and Management and Dean of the Graduate School of Business, Stanford University.

JOHN B. TAYLOR is the Mary and Robert Raymond Professor of Economics and Director of the Center for Economic Policy Research, Stanford University.

TIMOTHY TAYLOR is the Managing Editor of the *Journal of Economic Perspectives* at the Humphrey Institute of Public Affairs at the University of Minnesota.

GAVIN WRIGHT is the Pitt Professor of Economic History at Cambridge University, and the William Robertson Coe Professor of American Economic History at Stanford University.

THE MOSAIC OF
ECONOMIC GROWTH

Introduction

RALPH LANDAU, TIMOTHY TAYLOR,
AND GAVIN WRIGHT

During most of human history, countries seeking more rapid economic advancement have resorted to plundering or seizing their neighbors. Competitiveness meant better armies and weapons, and one nation's gain was another's loss. As this Hobbesian society gave way to the expanding markets celebrated by Adam Smith in the eighteenth century, and again to the robust industrial innovations of the nineteenth century and the science-based technologies of the twentieth, the prospects for sustained progress on a global scale have brightened considerably. Economic thinkers through the ages, from Adam Smith to Alfred Marshall to Joseph Schumpeter, have pondered the forces that contribute to economic growth. However, it is only since the end of the Second World War that economic growth has emerged as an explicit objective of government policy, and even during the postwar era, understanding the economics of growth has not been the top priority of the economics profession.

This situation is fast changing. As countries around the world struggle to restructure their economic institutions, long-submerged issues about the detailed design of market economies are rising to the surface. Indeed, in the light of concerns about the performance of the U.S. economy over the past quarter-century, the analysis of long-term growth is emerging as the central topic of the 21st century. Economists who differ widely over short-run priorities, such as inflation-unemployment trade-offs or welfare reform, are in strong agreement about the importance of productivity growth over longer periods. Consider, for example, the following two statements from recent annual reports of the President's Council of Economic Advisers:

The fundamental challenge facing the American economy is the slowdown in the rate of productivity growth, which began in the late 1960s and worsened in the early 1970s. Even small differences in the rate of productivity growth compounded over long periods of time can lead to dramatic differences in future standards of living. With its productivity growing half a percentage point less rapidly than that of the United States, the United Kingdom went from the highest standard of living in the world in the late 19th century to a standard of living only two-thirds that of the United States today. . . . Responding to economic challenges to enhance the Nation's long-term economic growth in an open world trading system is the single most important thing Americans can do to enhance the prosperity of future generations. (CEA, 1993, pp. 27–28, 34)

America's long-run average productivity growth rate over the century leading up to 1973 was slightly above 2 percent per year; since 1973 it has averaged about 1 percent. At 2 percent growth, productivity doubles in 35 years; at 1 percent growth, doubling takes 70 years. Even seemingly modest changes in productivity can have dramatic effects on living standards in the long run. . . . Nothing is more important to the long-run well-being of the U.S. economy than accelerating productivity growth. (CEA, 1994, pp. 24–25)

The underlying theme here—the extraordinary importance of growth in the long run—is identical. However, the messages come from different, partisan sources: the first passage is from the last economic report of the council during the Bush administration, while the second is the first report of the council during the Clinton administration. The extent to which actual policies of either administration have lived up to these expressions of concern is, of course, another question.

In the next few pages, we offer a brief survey of recent research trends and thinking on the subject of economic growth, highlighting what we believe to be the emerging issues for the 21st century. This introduction reflects the thinking of the editors of this volume, and does not necessarily represent the views of individual contributors.

The Theory of Economic Growth

The modern study of the sources of economic growth dates from the late 1950s and early 1960s, when Robert Solow of MIT (1956, 1957), Moses Abramovitz of Stanford (1956), and Dale Jorgenson of Harvard (see papers in Jorgenson, Gollop, and Fraumeni, 1987) identified the basic inputs to a growing economy as labor, capital, and technology. They demonstrated that the first two of these basic inputs (labor and capital), taken alone, could not account for most of the aggregate steady-state growth of the economy. Some other factor, which they labeled "technological change," was responsible for up to three-quarters of all growth. Notice that this method could not measure technology directly, but instead inferred it as a residual, leading Abramovitz to call it "a measure of our ignorance," a phrase that seems to have resonated through the decades.

Several strong mathematical assumptions were then needed to build a growth model on this foundation. For example, the early models used the neoclassical economic assumption that markets are perfectly competitive and that all firms maximize profits. Moreover, the models of economic growth formulated by Solow at that time postulated that this growth in technology was exogenous; in other words, it came as "manna from heaven," not from within the system of economic activity. Paul Romer (1990) of the University of California at Berkeley stated the resulting dilemma of this growth theory as follows: "The [neoclassical] assumptions of [diminishing returns to increasing investment] and perfect competition placed the accumulation of new technologies at the center of the growth process and simultaneously denied the possibility that economic analysis could have anything to say about this process." In other words, while these early versions of growth theory convincingly demonstrated the importance of studying the subject, the aggregate macroeconomic models that were used offered little room for analysis of the sources of invention or innovation, new and improved products or processes, or organizational or structural change.

These early neoclassical models should be viewed in context. In the 1950s, they helped to focus attention on long-term growth as opposed to stabilization, which was becoming a major concern of the economics profession. They permitted economists to examine the "big picture" of what was happening in the overall economy without being confused by obscure details that they could not measure or model. As Solow (1994, p. 48) observes, the treatment of technology as an exogenous constant was not meant to be taken literally. In the tradition of landmark intellectual work, even as the growth theory of the 1950s answered questions about the importance of technological change, it posed a fundamental new question: how to interpret the finding that "technology," in some sense, was the primary source of economic growth since the Civil War.

In considering the analytical issues posed by this approach to the study of growth, Ralph Landau has proposed a useful analogy based on the physics of gases. Scientists have long known that gases contain very large numbers of molecules that move randomly but constantly against each other and the walls of their containers. By assuming that gases obeyed certain "perfect gas" laws, an observer needed to know only the temperature and the amount of gas to calculate the pressure of that gas. In effect, the molecules in this model did not react with one another, but bounced off each other like billiard balls. Although this model served scientists well in many cases, it was soon observed that in reality, heavier or more complex molecules tended not to bounce away from an encounter but to adhere to one another, or cluster, at least for a while. These interactions would result in deviations from the perfect gas laws. As the complexity of the gas and the severity of the conditions increased, it became necessary to develop tables of such deviations that engineers could use in designing their equipment. In many instances, these deviations were substantial, even involving chemical reactions which changed the nature of the gas system itself. As their analytical tools grew more refined, scientists were able to examine directly the interacting molecules and clusters.

Only in the past few years have economists' modeling techniques and richer data from several industrial countries accumulated to the point that many of the strong assumptions of the early Solow-style growth theory could be relaxed. These approaches offered more realistic models that could consider how events at the microeconomic level (like the molecular level of gas interactions) affect the long-term growth and behavior of the macroeconomic system. Instead of viewing technology as a sort of magic, or relying on assumptions of perfectly competitive markets, it is now possible to explore the incentives and implications behind technological change. Scholarly interest in this area has increased rapidly.[1] This work has suggested a number of ways in which the assumptions of early growth theory can be modified to allow interactions with many other branches of the discipline of economics.

A first modification is that early growth theory did not differentiate among firms (like the billiard-ball molecules); the emphasis was on aggregate macroeconomic causes, not on what happens at individual companies. How firms learn from experience, how good management differs from bad, how firms differ in the ways they gather and transmit information internally, how some firms compete successfully in international markets and others do not: these issues did not arise in the early models. But the empirical evidence, indeed the entire business literature, suggests that firms do persistently differ in their characteristics, behavior, performance, and

---

1. The interested reader might begin with the "Symposium on New Growth Theory," with articles by Romer, Solow, Gene Grossman and Elhanan Helpman, and Howard Pack, appearing in the Winter 1994 issue of the *Journal of Economic Perspectives*. Also, Zvi Griliches (1994) devoted his recent presidential address to the American Economic Association to the econometric analysis of the recent productivity slowdown.

problem-solving abilities and strategies. In a capitalist economy, what firms do vis-à-vis their competitors is where dynamic comparative advantage really occurs. Michael Porter (1990) and Alfred Chandler (1992) of Harvard have contributed to the understanding of what makes for competitive advantage at the level of the firm.

A second area where early models can now be improved is the assumption of perfect competition. In a perfectly competitive world, firms would never be able to justify doing research and development, because successful innovations would be immediately copied, and no firm could ever recoup its R&D costs. Schumpeter (1943) and Arrow (1962) identified the problem of appropriability as key to investments in research. Today's growth models, building on Dixit and Stiglitz (1977), employ the more realistic assumption of monopolistic competition. Companies with some market power invest in R&D to gain an advantage and to earn profits by selling at high prices for as long as possible before the competition catches up. But market power is only one of the vehicles by which firms cope with the appropriability problem. Today's growth economists study a wide range of other devices by which firms hold on to their intellectual property, ranging from taking out patents to developing idiosyncratic firm-specific work environments.

A third implication of the early growth theory is that because the secrets of technical progress are available to all and therefore common to all, productivity should converge, at the steady state, to the levels implied by best-practice technology. Baumol (1986) has found evidence for such a process among the advanced countries of the world, but it is clear that convergence is not the general rule for the world as a whole (Lucas, 1988, 1990; Baumol, Nelson, and Wolff, 1994; Lau's chapter in this volume). Clearly national, organizational, and firm efficiencies—what Abramovitz (1989) calls the "social capability" to gain the advantages of advanced technologies—vary greatly among nations. Robert Putnam (1993) advances a similar notion of "social capital" as a factor of production. These and other difficult-to-measure factors probably account for a large part of the productivity growth of nations, and technology in the narrow sense used by engineers may well be only a minor fraction of the total.

A fourth unstated implication of the early growth models was that because all firms were undifferentiated, all industries were of equal importance. But is it true, after all, that in terms of economic growth, $100 worth of potato chips are worth the same as $100 worth of semiconductor chips? It seems clear that some industries are more important to long-run productivity growth than others; in economists' terms, investment in some industries (whether in physical capital, knowledge, labor skills, or some other way) offers a broader social return that will not be captured by the private investor. Historical studies suggest that the major beneficiaries of breakthrough innovations may be in economic sectors far removed from the originator: modern information technologies, for example, have had revolutionary effects on such "low tech" industries as clothing and forest products (Rosenberg, 1994, p. 233). Other industries may offer the possibility of increasing returns to scale; in the chemical industry, for example, a 60 percent increase in capital can double the capacity of a plant. Some industries may be more important to international trade. Other industries may be key to job formation, or to encouraging investment by other firms. Jorgenson et al. (1990) have studied such interindustry differences among several countries, and stress that no aggregate theory of growth captures the detail required for an understanding of the growth process. The study of disaggregation and reaggregation is now going forward, though there is as yet no consensus with respect to the policy implications of these findings.

A fifth implication of the early growth theory, one which many students have found counterintuitive, was that the long-term steady-state rate of growth was independent of the rate of savings and investment. An increase in savings and investment could provide a temporary boost to the level of economic productivity, but the economy would then gradually revert to the steady-state rate of growth determined by the exogenous rise in the quality and quantity of labor. However, economists have believed that the process of accumulation and investment was a fundamental force for productivity growth. Michael Boskin and Lawrence Lau of Stanford University (1992) show by cross-country comparisons that technology is capital augmenting, which means the higher the capital stock, the more technology can increase productivity. Instead of a one-time boost to productivity, higher rates of saving and capital investment increase the rate at which productivity rises. *There is no steady state of growth*. Dynamic economies are always in transition. Policy makers looking to the intermediate future, a generation or two away, must recognize that the key inputs of growth—skilled labor, sophisticated capital, new forms of technology— are not independent of each other but are positively interdependent. Of course, these effects are present only where market incentives are appropriate. The collapse of the Soviet Union despite high capital investment rates shows that more is involved in growth than inefficiently pouring money into obsolete plants run by unmotivated workers in the absence of market competition.

Savings, Investment, and International Competition

Since Adam Smith, economists have linked the progress of nations to expansion of markets and trade. Smith emphasized that the wealth of nations is properly measured by the standard of living of the population, not the gold accumulated in the treasuries of monarchs. David Ricardo built upon these ideas to formulate the principle of comparative advantage. It holds that even if one country is more efficient than another in *every* area of production, both countries can still benefit from trading with each other. The theory holds that each nation should produce those goods where its productivity advantage is greatest, or where its productivity disadvantage is least. Although the formal theory advanced by Ricardo and his successors was static, they clearly pictured international trade as a source of dynamic energies as well as static efficiency gains. Modern theories pioneered by Helpman and Krugman (1985) build on the notions of monopolistic competition and product specialization to explain the high volume of two-way trade within conventional industry categories. Since these specializations grow out of investments in R&D, and other forms of learning, there is a certain parallel between the modern theories of trade and endogenous growth; together, they support the venerable economic view that growing trade is a stimulus to innovation and progress. As Anne Krueger's paper in this volume emphasizes, virtually all periods of accelerated world growth have also been periods of expanding international trade.

This perception of comparative advantage as dynamic and changing offers an image where industries and firms, aided by a government-sustained macroeconomic business climate favoring innovation and commercialization of new technology, search continually for new and improved products and services for customers. Science and technology harnessed by an enlightened capitalistic democratic system can improve the standard of living through higher growth rates, without requiring revolutions, wars of conquest, or colonization. It took Germany two costly world war losses to realize this, and the Japanese one, but their experience underlines the conclusion that a non-militaristic technology-based economy is the key to growth.

Much of the recent concern about U.S. performance does have an international focus, but often with a different slant. Flying the banner of "competitiveness," many observers portray the United States as engaged in head-to-head economic competition with Japan and other nations; judging from the state of the trade balance, they reason, America is losing the race. This view is truly anachronistic, a throwback to mercantilism. Once

we escape from the notion that the purpose of economic growth is to pre-
pare for military combat, then economic exchange between nations is not
rivalrous, and progress abroad does not harm the United States. In this
respect, the perspective of the nation as a whole may differ from that of
particular industries or groups of workers, who may indeed be threatened
by tougher competition, whether it comes from abroad or from innovative
domestic firms. Their concerns may be legitimate, but it is important not
to confuse the national interest with the sum total of particular industry
interests, a classic example of the "fallacy of composition." Trade is not a
zero-sum game. As Paul Krugman (1994a) argues, "economic growth in
the Third World is an opportunity, not a threat."

When the concept of competitiveness is used appropriately, the definition amounts to this: the ability to sustain an acceptable rate of growth
in the real standard of living of the population, while avoiding social costs
such as high unemployment, excessive environmental damage, or extremes
of inequality in the distribution of income. Furthermore, current growth
must be achieved without reducing the growth potential in the standard of
living of future generations. This last condition constrains borrowing from
abroad or incurring excessive future tax or spending obligations to pay for
the present generation's higher standard of living. Accordingly, the most
promising way to increase the U.S. standard of living is a healthy annual
increase in the productivity of labor. Indeed, productivity is a more fundamental concept than competitiveness. We have in mind a notion of productivity that is broadly defined and that, in addition to the normal expansion and improvement of facilities, also reflects the continuing flow of new
products and quality improvements that are prominent features of today's
technology-based industries, such as computers and semiconducters. As
Griliches (1994) shows, a fair portion of the pessimism regarding recent
productivity trends may be attributed to the difficult problems of output
measurement in high-tech industries and in services.

There are a number of reasons for the popular exaggeration of the significance of foreign competition for American economic growth. First,
although U.S. workers remain the most productive in the industrialized
world, other advanced countries have been steadily gaining in relative
terms since World War II, as shown in Figure 1. One reason is that American firms no longer possess the unrivaled technological leadership over foreign rivals that they enjoyed in the early postwar era. New products and
equipment embodying new technologies now flow in both directions, and
patents issued to foreign firms imply comparable levels of quality and technical sophistication (Frame and Narin, 1990). For the most part, these developments do not reflect a failure on the part of the American economy;

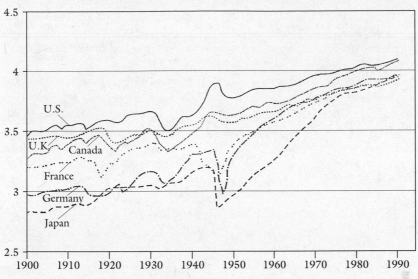

Figure 1. Per capita income, in logs of U.S. dollars. Source: Personal communication, Steven N. Durlauf, University of Wisconsin (1992).

they are the inevitable consequence of a global process of catching up to the leader. "Convergence" has not just happened through some automatic equilibration process, but through investments in physical capital and in advanced training and research by many other countries, taking advantage of the increased international mobility of today's science-based technologies (Nelson and Wright, 1992). From a global perspective, this is all to the good, but it is not a situation to which Americans are accustomed.

A second problem is the trade deficit, which too many observers persist in viewing as a kind of scorecard of economic performance. It is not. In fact, the country's research-intensive, high-technology sectors have generally had strong export performance in recent years; but the aggregate trade deficit[2] has been overwhelmingly driven by macroeconomic forces,

2. The most commonly cited trade figure is the U.S. imbalance in merchandise trade, that is, the excess of imports over exports. However, a broader and more useful measure is the current account balance, which includes not only imports and exports of merchandise, but also sales and purchases of services (where the U.S. competitive position is quite strong) and net returns on investments abroad. Both measures show the trade balance moving from near balance in the late 1970s and early 1980s to an enormous deficit in the neighborhood of $160 billion, depending on the measure, by 1987. Both trade deficits have fallen since then but remained greater than $100 billion in 1993. Historical figures for both measures of trade and their components are readily available in the tables at the back of the annual *Economic Report of the President*, from the Council of Economic Advisers.

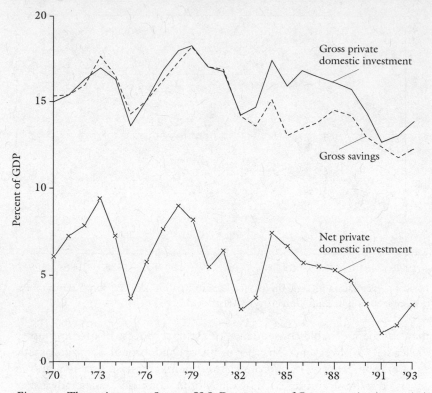

Figure 2. The savings gap. Source: U.S. Department of Commerce (various years).

specifically the national savings rate relative to the level of investment. What the trade figures indicate is that the nation has been consuming (through its imports) more than it has been producing in goods and services. It pays for this consumption with dollars that foreign investors then lend right back to the economy, as Ronald McKinnon's paper in this volume makes clear. This bad news is illustrated in Figure 2, where the gap between the two lines, the current-account deficit, measures the amount of capital that America imported from abroad to cover its surge of consumption.

Those looking for bad news in the trade statistics often focus on Japan, with whom the United States ran a merchandise trade deficit of $50 billion in 1992 and $60 billion in 1993. However, a trade deficit with one country tells literally nothing about a nation's global competitiveness. Even if the United States ran a trade deficit of zero with the world as a whole, it could (and probably would) still run a deficit with Japan, since Japan must sell in the United States and Europe to earn funds for importing raw materials such as oil. Even if Japanese barriers to trade and investment were totally removed, the trade deficit with Japan would still be at least half the present size if not more. Without access to investment funds from Japan (which is to say, without the trade deficit), the performance of the U.S. economy in the 1980s would have been far worse than it was.

Running a trade deficit and borrowing from abroad can benefit economic growth or injure it, depending on whether the money is spent productively. When the United States borrowed from abroad during the nineteenth century to build its railroads, or when South Korea borrowed for industrialization in the 1960s and 1970s, the inflow of capital helped long-run growth. Unfortunately, beginning in the 1980s the United States has in effect been using a substantial proportion of these borrowed funds for consumption. That surge of borrowing from abroad has not been accompanied by an increase in investment and labor productivity. In the 1960s, annual productivity growth averaged 2.4 percent; it was 1.3 percent in the 1970s, and 0.8 percent in the 1980s. During this period, the annual rate of increase of private capital formation per employee dropped from 2.6 percent to 0.6 percent. This drop surely had a depressing effect on output and real hourly earnings. In the last two decades, most of the rise in the standard of living of families has come from the increase in two-earner couples and longer working hours. While these changes raise national output, they do not raise the standard of living that can be earned by a person working a standard work week, and it clearly makes little sense for a nation to pursue "competitiveness" with longer hours and declining or stagnant real wages.

There is thus a grain of truth in the popular link between the trade deficit and poor U.S. economic performance, but the real root of the problem is that the U.S. savings rate is far too low, as Michael Spence's chapter in this volume shows. The recent report of the Board on Science, Technology, and Economic Policy (STEP) of the National Research Council (1994) also stresses the importance of increased savings as a vehicle for raising investment and thereby accelerating the adoption of new technology and raising productivity. Could we accomplish the same goal through imported capital? Perhaps, but detailed studies for the STEP project by George Hatsopoulos of Thermoelectron and James Poterba of MIT (1993) show that for the more risky equity investments, domestic savings are the primary source.

To some extent, all countries are now competing for a world supply of savings. As Harry Rowen's chapter in this volume details, the prospects for greater world growth surely point to increasing capital requirements in the longer run. In a world of low savings and increasing demand for investment, capital will flow where it receives the greatest return, and this will often be in Latin America, China and the rest of East Asia, and perhaps eastern Europe. Although the United States has successfully attracted foreign capital since the mid-1980s, it may have to eventually learn the lesson that foreign capital can become unavailable, or come at a higher price.[3] It has been anomalous, these last few years, for the world's wealthiest nation to finance its investment by borrowing abroad, depleting the world's available savings and accumulating debts for future generations.

Firms, Industries, and the Institutional Setting

The foregoing discussion implies that no single vantage point, or level of aggregation, can encompass the full range of important influences on economic growth. Earlier conceptions of growth have been primarily macroeconomic in nature. The newer approaches recognize the importance of macroeconomic variables such as saving and investment (where aggregate constraints apply), but they also focus on microeconomic dimensions of firms and industries and the climates in which they function. This perspective takes note of the possibility that savings and investment in different industries may have different importance to long-run growth, and a variety of issues arise that the overall macroeconomic view does not address. For example, what should be done about seemingly important firms or industries that face international competition from firms that either seem to or do receive favored treatment by their governments, as in the case of Airbus versus Boeing? When should the U.S. government step in? Should the government act as one of the "high-end" users of technology, whose demand is so critical for cutting-edge technological advances? How can we draw a clear distinction between government support for legal and financial infrastructure and excessive intrusion into the decisions of private firms?

Empirical and theoretical work by Romer (1986, 1990), Durlauf (1992), Robert Barro (1991; with Martin, 1992; with Lee, 1994), Jorgenson, Gollop, and Fraumeni (1987), Nadiri and Bernstein (1988, 1989), Baily, Bartless, and Litan (1992), Joseph Stiglitz (1993), and others con-

---

3. In the last few years, there has been a significant outflow of portfolio investment, amounting to nearly $80 billion in 1993. This is surely a troublesome signal for an economy that is depending on foreign capital to finance an enormous current-account deficit. Indeed, the March 1994 issue of *Bank Credit Analyst* argues that this sort of financing is simply not sustainable. When these fundamental factors show up in the newspapers, they usually do so by provoking trade frictions, or volatility in the foreign exchange markets. These short-term stories will come and go, but their real significance is that they warn of longer-term threats to economic growth.

firms that national, regional, industry, and firm differences leave a legacy. The rate of growth in the future depends somewhat on the rate of growth in the present, which in turn depends on decisions made in the past. History matters. Internal behavior and structures matter. Firm and individual differences matter. Which industries or firms survive in world competition matters. Countries, industries, and firms that pay proper attention to these issues can consistently do better than others. In addressing questions like these, the macroeconomic theory of growth begins to seek to incorporate the extensive findings of the microeconomists of technical change, such as Nathan Rosenberg (1986), Richard Nelson and Sidney Winter (1982), and others, who long ago identified these interactive effects.

However, we are a long way from full understanding. As Howard Pack (1994) has observed, neither old nor new growth theory predicted the meteoric rise of the East Asian economies over the past 25 years. As the historical context changes, confident generalizations about the logic of growth also change. It seems unlikely that any single theoretical model can embrace all of the relevant variables. Perhaps at this time the best guidance comes from cross-country comparisons at various levels of aggregation and for many industries. This is part of the philosophy of the many grants by the Sloan Foundation in recent years, of which two chapters in this volume are examples (Timothy Bresnahan and Shane Greenstein on computers and Ralph Landau on chemicals).

These developments in economic theory hold both a promise and a warning. The promise is that investment in the three-legged stool of physical, intangible, and human capital can stimulate other investment, which can lead—at least in theoretical models—to a sort of virtuous circle of feedbacks that yield increased productivity growth. In such a situation, economic growth need not diminish over time. The corresponding warning is that the policies for achieving this continuing increase in the standard of living are not obvious. Some advocates of "industrial policy" speak as if government can guarantee future prosperity by showering favors on private industry, choosing to ignore or minimize the critical importance of a propitious macroeconomic climate within which all business must work. Some of these point to the supposed Japanese success of such policies; however, a recent study by Beason and Weinstein (1993) demonstrates that Japan's clever bureaucrats picked and supported losers, and suggests that their industrial policy may have hindered Japan's potential growth. It is now becoming more widely recognized that the true power in Japan has been and is its Ministry of Finance, reflecting the savings-investment dominance of Japanese policy (Stokes, 1994). Frequently, the negative consequences of such intervention lie elsewhere in the economy, such as reduced competition or flagging innovation in other industries, or a greater risk of inflation.

The Mosaic of Growth

The chapters in the present volume demonstrate the complexity of real-world growth processes and the diversity of factors that are important not only at the aggregate economy-wide level, but in disaggregating step by step down to the basic functions of firms, where the true determinants of a country's productivity and living standards ultimately reside. Contributors were asked to relate their research to the matrix displayed in Table 1. Thus this volume illustrates a kind of joint enterprise in which each specialized topic is seen as a piece of a larger structure, building what might be called a mosaic of growth.

The first three chapters offer an overview of economic growth and development. In "Convergence and Deferred Catch-up: Productivity Leadership and the Waning of American Exceptionalism," Moses Abramovitz and Paul A. David examine how an interaction between natural endowments and developing technology led to the resurgent U.S. growth of the late nineteenth and early twentieth centuries—and how those same factors have helped other countries to catch up since then. Larry Lau, in his chap-

TABLE 1

Levels of Comparative Advantage

National governance
Socio-political climate
Macro policies
   Fiscal
   Monetary
   Trade
Structural and supportive policies
   Tax
   Regulatory and environmental
   Labor
   Intellectual property
   Education (including university-industry relations)
   Science and technology (including role of engineers and scientists)
Institutional setting
   Legal
   Financial
   Professional bodies
   Corporate governance
   Intermediating institutions
The industry
Companies within the industry

ter "The Sources of Long-Term Economic Growth: Observations from the Experience of Developed and Developing Countries," investigates the sources of the world's most spectacular growth story—the booming economies of East Asia—in comparison with growth in the advanced countries. Lau's conclusion has particular significance for the volume as a whole: "A pro–economic growth policy must therefore have three parts—it should be pro-investment, pro-technology, and pro-education." Henry Rowen offers an upbeat perspective on the factors driving world growth in "World Wealth Expanding: Why a Rich, Democratic, and (Perhaps) Peaceful Era Is Ahead." His discussion identifies the likely hot spots for economic growth in the next few decades, and explains why neither energy shortages, nor environment dangers, nor political turmoil is likely to hold back such growth.[4]

The second part of this volume stresses the domestic macroeconomic context in which growth takes place. John Taylor examines stabilization policy and long-term economic growth. He offers rules of thumb for governing monetary and fiscal policies, and argues that proper use of these tools may be as important as any other policy tool for the pursuit of long-term growth. If based on a credible commitment to reasonably stable responses, he shows, short-term stabilization policies are quite compatible with and favorable to long-term growth. Sylvester J. Schieber and John Shoven focus on the consequences of population aging on saving and asset markets. They raise the alarming prospect that the already-low national savings rate may fall much further when the baby boom generation reaches retirement age, and draw out some implications of this finding. A. Michael Spence, in "Science and Technology Investment and Policy in the Global Economy," discusses the broad macroeconomic problems of savings, investment, and the cost of capital, stressing that these factors have their primary impact on the *deployment* of new technology by the private sector.

---

4. Environmental issues have an important bearing on economic growth, but except for some discussion in Rowen's chapter, they are not represented explicitly in this volume. The conference itself did, however, have a roundtable discussion on environmental regulation and economic growth, chaired by Walter P. Falcon and including as panel members Lawrence Goulder, Donald Kennedy, David Starrett, and James Sweeney. The overall perspective emerging from the session was that contrary to alarmist views often heard, environmental damage is not an inevitable consequence of economic growth; indeed, higher-income countries generally attach a higher value to environmental improvement than do poor countries. Actual implemention of enlightened environmental policies, however, raises many of the same tough issues of policy design and international coordination that occupied much of the rest of the conference. Kennedy, for example, drew upon his experience as chair of the FDA to note that stricter environmental rules tend to favor large established companies over smaller and more innovative firms.

His emphasis on the uncertainties of deployment complements Nathan Rosenberg's chapter (later in this volume) on the inherently unpredictable character of technological trajectories. Spence also suggests that problems of deployment threaten support for basic science, if taxpayers rebel against the prospect of paying for scientific research, only to see the results commercialized in other countries. The way out of this dilemma, in Spence's view, is to build international institutions that will ensure all countries make a reasonable contribution to the growth of scientific knowledge.

The international context is clearly central to issues of economic growth, and is examined in the third part of this book. Anne O. Krueger warns of threats to 21st-century growth in the context of the international trading system. Krueger is concerned that decades of momentum toward free(r) trade seem to be grinding to a halt, and that the United States seems less willing to play its customary leadership role in building and defending multilateral institutions to grease the wheels of international trade. Ronald McKinnon focuses on the financial side of international trade. In "Dollar and Yen: The Problem of Financial Adjustment Between the United States and Japan," he shows that the United States has for two decades been following a policy of driving up the yen. He points out that this policy is unlikely to affect trade deficits—which are determined by macroeconomic imbalances—but is taking a toll on U.S.-Japan relations and the institutions of free trade. Masahiko Aoki tells an evolutionary parable of the gains from international organizational diversity. Rather than focusing on the well-known gains from trading goods, Aoki describes how trade may encourage a spread of different organizational forms, which in turn can stimulate productivity.

The fourth part focuses on the institutional setting for economic growth. In many ways, this can be thought of as defining "technology" more broadly to include a nation's financial and legal structures, which can have a considerable influence on a nation's productivity. Tom Campbell, Daniel Kessler, and George Shepherd investigate the causes and economic impact of liability reforms and demonstrate a correlation between state economic growth and whether states have carried out liability reforms. Myron Scholes discusses financial infrastructure and economic growth. Scholes offers an overview of the evolution in financial markets toward new ways of repackaging financial flows (broadly called "derivatives") and discusses how these new financial instruments will meet the fundamental functional needs of capital markets.

The fifth part focuses on technology issues and the relationship of new technologies to the underlying R&D process that generates them. Linda

Cohen and Roger Noll discuss their concern that America has chosen a competitiveness strategy of privatizing public research. Cohen and Noll fear that rather than following the path discussed by Spence and finding ways to fund research that can be broadly and openly used, America is moving toward making research more and more proprietary and closed. Nathan Rosenberg's chapter helps to explain why openness is so important. In "Uncertainty and Technological Change," he points out that many of the most revolutionary technological innovations have been drastically underestimated, *and that there is no reason to believe that we are getting any better at figuring out what the eventual uses of new technologies will be*. Although Rosenberg does not make the point explicitly, limiting the openness of science and technology institutions will limit the spread of new ideas into unexpected areas, which is often where most of their productivity lies. As Rosenberg writes in this volume, "Government policy ought to be to open many windows and to provide the private sector with financial incentives to explore the technological landscape that can only be faintly discerned from those windows."

Finally, the last part gets down to examining lessons at the level of two particular industries. Timothy Bresnahan and Shane Greenstein tell the tale of the competitive crash in large-scale commercial computing, the story of what factors influence buyers to change over to a new technology, or to remain with the earlier one. Ralph Landau's chapter takes advantage of his long experience in the chemical industry and the fact that chemicals are the oldest science-based industry (about 150 years old) to trace the ebb and flow of dynamic comparative advantage among countries and firms from time to time. In its breadth and sweep, this paper most clearly illustrates the power of the matrix in Table 1 to move through different levels of aggregation, and to examine the many ways in which policies at each level may influence economic growth.

Conclusion

One reason for the recent surge of interest in the economics of growth stems from the recent collapse of the Soviet Union and the end of the cold war. As the military posture of the United States vis-à-vis a single large opponent seemed less important, the relative economic position of the United States—especially with regard to major competitors like Japan and Germany—seemed to take on an added importance. A second reason is the stagnation of U.S. wages over the last two decades. The public in America and other industrialized countries has developed a sense of unease, a fear that the "good jobs" are disappearing, and that unemployment may remain unacceptably high for the indefinite future (Krugman, 1994b). Of course, these fears are sometimes amplified by demagogues, who make little pretense of caring about underlying causes or long-term solutions. But the concern over standards of living is real and valid.

A final reason for the resurgence of interest in the economics of growth is that a number of countries, especially in Asia, have demonstrated that it is at least within the realm of possibility for a less developed country to improve its standard of living quite rapidly. Japan, of course, is the leading success story. But Korea, Taiwan, Singapore, and now China are also demonstrating the power of economic growth. The possible lessons from these models of economic development are being debated and scrutinized around the globe.

These factors, combined with the new tools and data sets that social scientists have developed in the last two decades, lead us to make this (not particularly daring) prediction: In the next half-century, economists, scholars, and policy makers will be far more concerned with long-term growth and development than they have been in the last half-century.

PART I

Overviews of Economic Growth and Development

Convergence and Deferred Catch-up: Productivity Leadership and the Waning of American Exceptionalism

MOSES ABRAMOVITZ AND PAUL A. DAVID

There are two lines of agency visibly at work shaping the habits of thought of [a] people in the complex movements of readjustment and rehabilitation [required by industrialization]. These are the received scheme of use and wont and the new state of the industrial arts; and it is not difficult to see that it is the latter that makes for readjustment; nor should it be any more difficult to see that the readjustment is necessarily made under the surveillance of the received scheme of use and wont.

—Thorstein Veblen (1915)

The comparative productivity experience of nations is commonly viewed as a race. But there is a difference between a runners' race and a productivity race between nations. In a track race, if one runner gets off to a fast start, there is no reason why, on that account alone, her rivals should then be able to run faster than she. A productivity race is different: under certain conditions, being behind gives a productivity laggard the ability to grow faster than the early leader. That is the main contention of the "convergence hypothesis." The most striking example of the convergence to which this hypothesis refers was the experience since World War II, when America's large lead eroded and the productivity levels of the other technologically advanced countries converged.

The convergence hypothesis stands on four sturdy pillars—which in turn float on one large assumption. The assumption is that the countries in the productivity race differ only in their initial levels of productivity but are

We acknowledge with thanks the comments and suggestions of colleagues who read previous drafts of this paper: William J. Baumol, Avner Greif, Alex Inkeles, Dale Jorgenson, R. C. O. Matthews, William N. Parker, Melvin Reder, Bart Verspargen, Herman van de Wee, and Gavin Wright. In preparing this version for publication we have had the additional benefit of Timothy Taylor's extraordinary editorial skills. Deficiencies that have outlasted all this remedial attention are solely ours.

otherwise similar. The four pillars are the four advantages in growth potential that a laggard nation enjoys just because it is behind.

First, when a leader's capital stock is replaced or expands, the improvement in technology embodied in the new plant and equipment is limited by such advances in the efficiency of capital goods as may have been made during the life of a representative asset. In a laggard country, however, the tangible capital is likely to be technologically obsolete. After all, that is one reason the laggard is behind. When such equipment is replaced, the new equipment can embody state-of-the-art technology; so, on that account, the laggard can realize larger improvements in the average efficiency of its productive facilities than are available to the leader. An analogous argument applies to a laggard's potential advance in disembodied technology, that is, in the forms of industrial organization; routines of purchasing, production, and merchandising; and managerial practice generally.

Second, laggard countries tend to suffer from low levels of capital per worker. That condition, especially in view of the chance to modernize capital stock, tends to make marginal returns to capital high and so to encourage rapid rates of capital accumulation.

Third, laggard countries often maintain relatively large numbers of redundant workers in farming and petty trade; so productivity growth can occur by shifting labor from farms to nonfarm jobs and from self-employment and family shops to larger-scale enterprises, even allowing for the cost of the additional capital that might be needed to maintain productivity levels in the new jobs.

Fourth, the relatively rapid growth from the first three sources makes for rapid growth in aggregate output and, therefore, in the scale of markets. This encourages the sort of technical progress which is dependent on larger-scale production.

These, then, are the components of the convergence hypothesis in its elemental form.[1] And if national characteristics were, indeed, to conform

1. Whether the formulation offered here is more or less "elemental" than the neoclassical growth models patterned on Solow's (1956) seminal paper is a matter of taste. In Solow-style models, there exists a unique and globally stable growth path to which the level of labor productivity (and per capita output) will converge, and along which the rate of advance is fixed (exogenously) by the rate of technological progress. A large crop of mutant models of aggregate growth has flowered since the mid-1980s. These have diverged from the pure neoclassical strain of growth theory by rejecting, in one way or another, the assumption that all forms of capital accumulation eventually run into diminishing marginal returns. Consequently, they contest the Solow model's global convergence implications. See Lucas (1988) and Romer (1986, 1990) for seminal contributions in this vein, and the useful recent surveys by Van de Klundert and Smulders (1992),

to the underlying assumption of similarity, we would expect that any national differences in productivity levels which might appear would be eliminated sooner or later, because of the growth advantages inherent in being behind.

The assumption of similarity calls for some explanation here. By it we mean that there are no *persistent* differences in national characteristics that would inhibit a laggard country from exploiting the advantages that being behind would otherwise present. In actual experience, productivity differences among countries stem from both persistent and transient causes. Persistent causes include poverty of natural resources; small scale of domestic markets, coupled with barriers to foreign trade; forms of economic organization or systems of taxation that reduce the rewards for effort, enterprise, or investment; or deeper elements of national culture that limit the responses of people to economic opportunities. Transient causes are occurrences like natural or military disasters, or dysfunctional forms of economic organization and public policy that may have ruled in the past but that have been effectively reformed.[2] The strength of the long-run tendency to convergence depends on a balance of forces: on one side, the advantages in growth potential that are inherent in being behind, and on the other side, the limitations inherent in those persistent causes of backwardness that may originally have caused a country to become a productivity laggard. Therefore, in the limiting case envisaged by the model of unconditional convergence, where differences in productivity levels arise solely from transient "shocks," productivity growth rates in any period would be found to vary inversely with their respective initial levels, so that laggards would tend to catch up with the leaders and differences in levels eventually would be eliminated.

Verspargen (1992), and Amable (1994). Harris (1993) and Dosi and Fabiani (1994) essay thoroughly non-neoclassical approaches to modeling convergence and divergence phenomena.

2. It would be convenient to be able to treat recovery from the effects of war-related destruction and disruption on the productivity of surviving resources as an unambiguous short-run, "rebound" process, in other words, as being clearly distinguishable from the phenomenon of long-run convergence. But in actual experience, the two may be difficult to disentangle. Such is the case when reconstruction provides an opportunity for widespread introduction of structures, capital equipment, and organizational forms that are of much more recent vintage than the economically obsolete facilities that had been destroyed. Dumke (1990), for example, argues that much of western Europe's "supergrowth" after 1948 is attributable to postwar reconstruction; using the ratio of 1948 GDP to 1938 GDP as a measure of the war-related supply shock a country had sustained, he finds from regression analysis that this variable continued to affect growth rates into the 1960s.

For a quarter-century following World War II, as was noted, the growth record of the presently advanced countries was strikingly consistent with this simple formulation of the convergence hypothesis. But not all of the historical experience of economic growth, even for this same group of countries, fits the hypothesis. From 1870 to about 1950, America not only maintained but actually widened its lead over other countries in terms of real GDP per capita and labor productivity. Britain, the world's first industrial nation, had held the lead during the century before that, and the Netherlands did so at a still earlier time when it was a great mercantile power.

The insistent question, therefore, is how to reconcile the convergence hypothesis with the experience of persistent leadership. This involves asking what differences among countries impose limitations on the abilities of laggard countries to profit from the advantages of being backward. We must then ask how and why these limitations changed so as to become less constraining and thus led to the great boom in catch-up and convergence that has marked the era since World War II.[3]

To sharpen the focus of this inquiry, we confine ourselves to a comparison between the United States and a group of presently advanced capitalist countries since 1870. The group consists of sixteen presently industrialized countries of western Europe and North America together with Japan and Australia. (The list of countries appears in the note to Table 1.) They are the countries for which Angus Maddison (1991, p. 196) has compiled estimates of man-hour productivity rendered comparable over time by standard methods of price deflation and across countries by the purchasing-power-parity ratios prepared by Eurostat and the OECD. The next section reviews the broad features of the growth experience of these countries from 1870 to 1990. This is followed by a section in which we

---

3. In the recent literature on the subject of convergence (discussed at greater length below), the term "catch-up" often has been used interchangeably with "convergence." An effort has been made here to eschew that practice. "Catch-up" refers to the long-run process by which productivity laggards close the proportional gaps that separate them from the productivity leader (as reflected in the average measures presented here in Table 1). "Convergence," in our usage, refers to a reduction of a measure of dispersion in the relative productivity levels of the array of countries under examination. Our idea of convergence is associated with the concept that Barro and Sala-i-Martin (1992) have labeled "σ-convergence." This refers to a narrowing of the dispersion within the international cross section of productivity levels over time—as measured by the standard deviation of the logarithm of productivity, or, equivalently here, by the coefficient of variation of the productivity relatives (presented in Table 2). Since it is "quasi-global" σ-convergence, measured for the entire group of advanced countries (including the United States), that we have in mind when speaking simply of "convergence," it is entirely possible for this to occur in the absence of any general catch-up.

identify the kinds of factors other than a low productivity level that may give one or more countries an advantage in growth and, by the same token, operate as limitations on the ability of others to catch up. We then go on to sketch the particular forces that, during the last 120 years, first supported a strong American advantage and inhibited the forces of convergence, and later undermined the basis of that leadership advantage and lent impetus to the catch-up movement among the other industrially developed economies.

The nub of our argument is that in the closing decades of the nineteenth century, the U.S. economy had moved into the position of global productivity leadership, which was to hold for a remarkably long period thereafter, through a fortunate concordance between America's own exceptional economic and social characteristics and the nature of the dominant path of technological progress and labor productivity advances. During the late nineteenth and early twentieth centuries, that path was natural resource–intensive, tangible capital–using, and scale-dependent in its elaboration of mass-production and high-throughput technologies and modes of business organization. Although this trajectory can be traced back to technological and industrial initiatives in both Britain and the United States earlier in the nineteenth century, it found fullest development in the environment provided by the North American continent. And so, during the course of the nineteenth century, it came to provide the United States with a strong productivity leadership advantage. This was so because the historical circumstances of contemporaneously developing economies, particularly those conditions affecting what we refer to as "technological congruence" and their "social capability," imposed limitations on the abilities of the productivity laggards of western Europe and Japan to derive a strong potential for rapid growth simply on the basis of being behind the United States.

Yet America's distinctive advantages did not retain their initially great importance throughout the first half of the twentieth century. The advantage conferred by America's rapid development of its rich endowment of mineral resources gradually dissipated. Some of the peculiar benefits that its industries derived from the larger scale and greater homogeneity of its domestic markets were eroded, partly by the growth of both domestic and foreign markets elsewhere, and partly by a gradual shift of the nature and direction of technological progress. In its global impacts, the course of innovation became less biased towards the ever more intense application of tangible capital and natural resource inputs and, instead, came to favor greater emphasis on intangible capital formation through investments in education and R&D. For these and still other reasons, we contend that the waning of American exceptionalism and the changing trajectory in the development of internationally available technology had the effect of reducing the *comparative* handicaps under which other countries seeking rapid productivity increases formerly were obliged to operate.

With the erosion of these American advantages, the ground was prepared for other countries with broadly similar economic and social institutions to participate in the interconnected processes of "catch-up investment" and "productivity convergence." As we shall see, however, the realization by the laggards among the industrialized countries of that potentiality for differentially faster productivity growth, after having been deferred by the circumstances of the Great Depression of the 1930s and World War II, was fostered by a number of special conditions that obtained internationally during the postwar decades.

The Comparative Productivity Record

In 1870, levels of aggregate labor productivity in the United States and the United Kingdom were apparently quite similar. Maddison's estimates (1991, table 3.4) put the United Kingdom ahead by 4 percent, but given the uncertainties of such calculations, so small a difference can hardly be thought significant. The statistics, however, speak much more clearly about two other matters. First, both the United Kingdom and the United States enjoyed large leads over the other countries that had begun to industrialize by 1870. Second, between 1870 and 1913, the United States established a large lead over the United Kingdom (28 percent) and increased its already large lead over the generality of the other industrializing countries (as shown in Table 1).

Over the course of this long period of general peace and development, there is no sign of a catch-up with the new front-runner by the laggard countries. Among the fifteen advanced countries other than the United States, only America's northern neighbor, Canada, improved its relative productivity position, and only one European country, Germany, was able to maintain its 1870 relative level—which was but half as high as that of the leader. The average level of the fifteen countries other than the United States fell from 62 percent of the American level in 1870 to 54 percent in 1913.[4]

---

4. As the text below points out, however, the speed of convergence within the group of sixteen countries (including the United States) in this period was very slow compared with its pace after 1950, but also compared with the speed of convergence among the

TABLE I

*Mean Labor Productivity Levels in Fifteen Advanced Countries Relative
to United States and in Nine Western European Countries Relative
to United Kingdom and Measures of Rates of Catch-up*

Fifteen advanced countries[a]				Nine western European countries[b]			
Mean level (U.S. = 100)		Rate of catch-up[c] (% per annum)		Mean level (U.K. = 100)		Rate of catch-up[c] (% per annum)	
1870	62	1873–1913	−0.35	1870	57	1870–1913	+0.35
1913	54	1913–1938	−0.30	1913	66	1913–1938	+0.80
1938	50	1938–1950	−1.15	1938	81	1938–1950	−0.67
1950	43	1950–1973	+1.82	1950	74	1950–1973	+1.34
1960	49	1950–1960	+1.28	1960	88	1950–1960	+1.66
1973	66	1960–1973	+2.24	1973	101	1960–1973	+1.09
1987	79	1973–1987	+1.31	1987	103	1973–1987	+0.10

SOURCE: Maddison (1991, Table C-11).

[a] The fifteen advanced countries include the nine western European countries in the following note plus Australia, Austria, Canada, Finland, Japan, and the United Kingdom.

[b] The nine western European countries are Belgium, Denmark, France, Germany, Italy, Netherlands, Norway, Sweden, and Switzerland.

[c] The rate of catch-up is the change per annum in the log of the mean level of productivity relative to that of the United States (or the United Kingdom) times 100.

On the other hand, virtually all the countries of western Europe were closing the proportionate gaps that separated them from Britain, the former productivity leader.[5] This would seem to be quite consistent with the view that in the spread of industrialization during the later nineteenth century, the successful western European "followers" were looking toward Britain, rather than the United States, as the technological and economic leader that it was most relevant for them to attempt to emulate.[6] If that

western European countries. In a recent paper, Taylor and Williamson (1994) estimate that the large population movements during 1870–1913 should have tended to raise the relatively low levels of productivity in Europe and to reduce the relatively high levels in the immigrant-receiving countries, among which the United States was the largest. If one accepts their calculations, the widening relative gap in labor productivity between western European countries and the United States during this same period is even more remarkable: the fall in the ratio of the nine-country western European mean level (see notes to Table 1) vis-à-vis the U.S. level of productivity was from .65 to .53, even more pronounced than the drop shown for the full fifteen-country sample.

5. In describing Britain as "the former productivity leader," we have abstracted from the anomalously high relative level of productivity recorded for Australia in the early twentieth century. Australia's lead at the time rested only on its huge supply of land relative to labor in an economy almost entirely devoted to agriculture and animal ranching.

6. Interestingly enough, Alexander Gerschenkron's classic paper "Economic Backwardness in Historical Perspective"—first published in 1955 and reprinted in Gerschenkron (1962, chap. 3)—took the proposition of British leadership as virtually self-evident, basing it on much less firm empirical foundations than subsequently have been put in place. It now appears that the erosion of British productivity leadership vis-à-vis

view is correct, it suggests another way to frame the central question we are addressing in the present essay: Why did not the industrial latecomers of the European continent follow the lead of America, whose economy was giving visible indications of forging ahead of Britain's?

Between 1913 and 1938, the laggard countries held back by World War I and by the financial disturbances of the 1920s fell back still further. And World War II, which was a great stimulus to U.S. growth as its economy returned to high levels of capacity utilization, was a severe setback to the relative positions of the European countries and Japan. By 1950, after recovery from the most severe aftereffects of the wartime destruction and dislocation, the average relative productivity levels of the other countries had sunk from 54 to 43 percent of the American level.[7]

There then followed the great "catch-up boom" from 1950 to the present.[8] The movement proceeded in two stages. During the first, from 1950 to 1973, the pace of catch-up was relatively fast: the laggards rose toward the American level at a rate of 1.8 percent a year, so that their average

the Continental followers was almost universal; over the 1870–1913 interval, the United Kingdom was able to maintain parity in the growth of real GDP per man-hour only against Belgium (Maddison, 1991, Table 3.4). It would be of interest to try to gauge the extent to which the intra-European convergence observed over the period 1870–1913 was promoted by differentially heavier overseas emigration from the Continent as a whole (vis-à-vis the British Isles), and especially from the Continent's peripheral regions—first Scandinavia, and subsequently southern and eastern Europe. Although Taylor and Williamson (1994) discuss the role of international labor migration in convergence phenomena, their work focuses attention on the potential for altering productivity relationships between sending and receiving regions, not on productivity relationships among the regions that differed in rates of net emigration.

7. The western European productivity catch-up relative to the United Kingdom continued between 1913 and 1938 while losing ground to the United States. All the Continental countries grew at a faster rate than Britain, and their average productivity level rose from 66 to 81 percent of the U.K. level. World War II, however, hit the Continental countries harder than it did the United Kingdom. Only Sweden and Switzerland, the two neutrals, continued their relative rise, and the western European average fell back to 74 percent of Britain's level (Maddison, 1991, Table C.11).

8. In speaking of a "catch-up" movement, we are referring to the rise in the mean of the followers' productivity relatives vis-à-vis the productivity leader, which in this instance is the United States. Throughout the following text, as was forecast in note 3, a distinction is maintained between "catch-up" and "convergence." In the recent macroeconomics literature, reference is often made to a different concept of catch-up that was called "β-convergence" by Barro and Sala-i-Martin (1991, 1992). It is essentially the coefficient on a negative correlation between productivity growth rates and initial levels of productivity (often with additional explanatory variables inserted). However, this kind of catch-up can easily confuse short-run, disequilibrium processes (like recovering from war-related destruction) with long-term convergence. Just as our preferred measures of "catch-up" and of "convergence" can diverge in their movements, σ-convergence is not implied by β-convergence: even though the lower-productivity member of a pair is experiencing faster growth, the size of the absolute gap between them (the dispersion) may nonetheless be widening.

TABLE 2

Measures of Dispersion of Labor Productivity Levels in Sixteen Advanced Countries and in Western Europe, and Rates of Convergence

Sixteen advanced countries[a]				Ten western European countries[b]			
Dispersion $(\sigma/\bar{x})$		Rate of convergence (% per annum)		Dispersion $(\sigma/\bar{x})$		Rate of convergence (% per annum)	
1870	.44	1870–1913	0.36	1870	.31	1870–1913	0.75
1913	.37	1913–1938	0.46	1913	.22	1913–1938	1.73
1938	.33	1938–1950	−2.10	1938	.14	1938–1950	−2.56
1950	.43	1950–1973	4.00	1950	.20	1950–1973	4.51
1960	.34	1950–1960	2.24	1960	.12	1950–1960	4.78
1973	.17	1960–1973	5.35	1973	.07	1960–1973	4.30
1987	.13	1973–1987	1.74	1987	.10	1973–1987	2.88

SOURCE: Maddison (1991, Table C-11).

NOTE: Dispersion is measured by the coefficient of variation $(\sigma/\bar{x})$. The rate of convergence is the negative of the change per annum in the log of $\sigma/\bar{x}$ times 100. Rates of convergence were calculated from unrounded numbers and therefore are not precisely consistent with the rounded measures of dispersion shown above.

[a] The sixteen advanced countries are those listed in note *a* to Table 1, plus the United States.

[b] The ten western European countries are those listed in note *b* to Table 1, plus the United Kingdom.

relative level, which was 43 in 1950, reached 66 in 1973. During this stage, the catch-up was achieved in spite of rapid American productivity growth, which was at least as fast as, and may have been even faster than, in any previous period of comparable duration (Maddison, 1991, Table 3.3). Since 1973, catch-up has been distinctly slower—only 1.3 percent a year—in spite of the severe slowdown in the United States. Growth rates in Europe and Japan fell even more (in percentage points) than in the United States.

There was no general catch-up to the United States before 1950, but it is worth recording that from 1870 to 1938, there was a substantial decline in the dispersion of productivity levels among the laggards, as can be seen from the figures for the western European countries in Table 2. Although for the full sample of sixteen countries the trend rate of convergence was a weak 0.42 percent per annum, the corresponding downward drift of the coefficient of variation among the western European countries including the United Kingdom proceeded at an average rate of 1.11 percent per annum over this 68-year period.[9] Thus, over this long period be-

---

9. In their study of convergence in real GDP per capita levels in Europe during 1850–1990, based on an augmented and revised version of Maddison's (1991) data, Prados de la Escosura, Dabán, and Oliva (1993, p. 11) present the standard deviation of the logs measure of dispersion for the eight countries of the western European core (Belgium, Denmark, France, Germany, Netherlands, Sweden, Switzerland, and the United Kingdom). This shows the same trend rate of decline (1.1 percentage points per annum) over the interval 1860–1938, with a faster rate of convergence during 1860–1913 being interrupted by a sharp rise in the dispersion in the 1913–20 interval.

fore World War II there was "convergence among the followers," without the occurrence of "catch-up" vis-à-vis the newly emerged productivity leader.

During the wartime decade of the 1940s, however, the international dispersion of productivity levels increased markedly; in 1950 the coefficient of variation was larger than its 1938 value by almost two-thirds. From 1950 to 1973 the great "postwar catch-up and convergence movement" proceeded very systematically: the inverse rank-order correlation between countries' initial levels of productivity in 1950 and their subsequent growth rates between 1950 and 1973 was almost perfect—the lower was a country's productivity level in 1950, the higher was its subsequent rate of growth.[10] In company with this, the process of convergence resumed at a pace that was historically unprecedented; the coefficient of variation declined at an average annual rate almost ten times as fast as its pre–World War II trend. Eventually, in the period after 1973, when the postwar growth boom had passed into history and the rate of catch-up vis-à-vis the United States had slowed down appreciably, convergence also became substantially slower.

The general features of the postwar experience of the advanced capitalist economies is consistent with the predictions of a simple convergence hypothesis. Between 1950 and 1973, the gaps separating the productivity levels in the laggard countries from that in the United States were rapidly reduced, and the dispersion of relative levels within this group of econo-

---

10. The Spearman rank correlation coefficient was −0.96, as calculated from the data in Maddison (1989). See also Baumol, Blackman, and Wolff (1989, chap. 5). Prados de la Escosura, Dabán, and Oliva (1993, Table 4) present regression results for the fit of the unconditional convergence specification to real GDP per capita for sixteen European countries over the entire period 1950–90: the estimated regression coefficient on the logarithm of past per capita GDP is highly significant and implies a β-convergence rate of 1.7 percent per annum. Such statistical results, however, are not unproblematic. Abramovitz (1986) pointed out that the measures of inverse rank correlation which he reported and, by the same token, the (β-convergence) results from linear regression analysis of the sort presented by Baumol (1986) would tend to overstate the strength of the negative relationship. DeLong (1988) developed a related point of criticism, noting that inasmuch as the estimates of initial productivity levels were constructed by methods that involved extrapolating backward from later benchmark data, measurement errors in the growth rates would be (negatively) correlated with those in the initial productivity levels. Friedman (1992) presents a systematic treatment of the same classic problem of regression bias due to errors in variables. All the foregoing, it should be noted, do not question the validity of the regression specification of the relationship as being linear in the logarithms of the countries' respective productivity levels, as does Verspargen (1991), for example, to cite a notable exception in the literature. Therefore, whether or not the use of β-convergence-type measures results in the overstatement of the strength of the "true" convergence process post-1950 in comparison with that for the period pre-1938, or pre-1913, is not a matter that has been resolved.

mies declined swiftly. There was catch-up as well as convergence. Since 1973, with productivity gaps reduced, the rate of catch-up has slowed down and the process of convergence has weakened. So far, so good.

But why was there no general catch-up (and only modest convergence) throughout the eight decades from 1870 to 1950? For the period from 1913 to 1950, one may well think (correctly, in our view) that the forces making for catch-up and convergence were overwhelmed by two general wars, by the territorial, political, and financial disturbances that followed, and by the variant impacts of the Great Depression on different countries.[11] Still, what circumstances inhibited catch-up vis-à-vis the United States for more than four decades of peaceful development between 1870 and 1913? And what occurred to release the forces of convergence and catch-up after the Second World War? The next section outlines a framework for study and discussion of these questions.

The Elements of Catch-up Potential and Its Realization

The conditions that govern the abilities of countries to achieve relatively rapid rates of productivity growth may be grouped into two broad classes: those that govern the potential of different countries to raise their productivity levels, and those that influence their abilities to realize that potential.

The convergence hypothesis tells us that one element governing countries' relative growth potentials is the size of the productivity differentials that separate them from the leader. Manifestly, however, the record of growth does not conform consistently to the predictions of the unconditional convergence hypothesis. The assumption that countries are "otherwise similar" is not fulfilled. There are often persistent conditions that have restricted countries' past growth and that continue to limit their ability to

---

11. Actually, the effects of World War I and the Great Depression do not appear to have been sufficient to do more than temporarily interrupt the slow secular reduction of the dispersion in productivity levels that was taking place *within* the core group of western European countries. For compelling evidence on this point, see the study of Prados de la Escosura, Dabán, and Oliva (1993) on the convergence in real GDP per capita levels in Europe from 1850 to 1990. Focusing just on the 1929–1938 interval, we calculate from Maddison's (1991) comparative GDP per man-hour estimates that the coefficient of variation within the group of ten Western European economies (see Table 1) declined by almost 40 percent of its 1929 magnitude. Yet the same measure computed for the entire sample of sixteen advanced countries declined by only some 10 percent. Thus, the Great Depression decade had more of an effect in deferring the convergence of the western European group toward the higher productivity of the United States and other regions of recent settlement than it had in delaying the process at work within the western European "convergence club" itself.

make the technological and organizational leaps that the convergence hypothesis envisages. We divide constraints on the potentials of countries into two categories.

One consists of the limitations of "technological congruence." Such limitations arise because the frontiers of technology do not advance evenly in all dimensions; that is, with equi-proportional impact on the productivities of labor, capital, and natural resource endowments, and with equal effect on the demands for the several factors of production and on the effectiveness of different scales of output. They advance, rather, in an unbalanced, biased fashion, reflecting the direct influence of past science and technology on the evolution of practical knowledge and the complex adaptation of that evolution to factor availabilities, as well as to the scale of markets, consumer demands, and technical capabilities of those relatively advanced countries operating at or near the frontiers of technology.[12]

It can easily occur that the resource availabilities, factor supplies, technical capabilities, market scales, and consumer demands in laggard countries may not conform well to those required by the technologies and organizational arrangements that have emerged in the leading country or countries. Although technological choices do adapt to changes in the economic environment, there are strong forces making for persistence in the effects of past choices and for path-dependence in the evolution of technological and organizational systems. These may render it extremely difficult, if not prohibitively costly, for firms, industries, and economies to switch quickly from an already established regime, with its associated trajectory of technical development, to exploit a quite distinct technological regime that had emerged elsewhere, under a different constellation of economic and social conditions.[13] The laggards, therefore, face varying degrees of difficulty in adopting and adapting the current practice of those who hold the productivity lead.

The second class of constraints on the potential productivity of coun-

12. See David (1975, chap. 1) for an introduction to the theory of "localized" technological progress and its relationship to the global bias of factor-augmenting technical change, and for a synthesis of some of the pertinent historical evidence. Related, more recent studies are noted below. Broadberry (1993) applies this general framework to interpret the historical evidence on manufacturing productivity leadership and technological leadership relationships between the United States and western Europe over the period from 1820 to 1987.

13. On hysteresis effects and path dependence in technological, organizational, and institutional evolution, see, for example, David (1975, 1985, 1988, 1993, 1994a, 1994b). The concept of technological regimes, or "paradigms" and "trajectories," is discussed by Dosi (1982, 1988), extending the work of Nelson and Winter (1977) and Sahal (1981).

tries concerns a more vaguely defined set of matters that has been labeled "social capability." This term was coined by Kazushi Ohkawa and Henry Rosovsky (1972). It covers countries' levels of general education and technical competence; the commercial, industrial, and financial institutions that bear on their abilities to finance and operate modern, large-scale business; and the political and social characteristics that influence the risks, the incentives, and the personal rewards of economic activity, including those rewards in social esteem that go beyond money and wealth.

An illustration may suggest the importance of the social and political constraints to which we refer. The 1989 level of value added per man-hour in Japanese manufacturing was 80 percent of the corresponding value in the United States, according to the careful comparison carried out by Van Ark and Pilat (1993). For the same year, Maddison's estimates (1993, Table 13) show that the overall level of productivity in Japan was only 65 percent of the American level. This difference may reflect many causes, but one important cause is surely the resistance of Japanese politics and society to the substitution of large-scale corporate farming and retailing and of foreign goods for the traditional very small-scale family farms and shops of that country. The productivity gap is especially pronounced in those industries where these influences have been especially strong: Wolff (1994) finds that in 1988, Japanese productivity in agriculture was just 18 percent of the U.S. level; the food, beverage, and tobacco industry's productivity was 35 percent of the American level, and for textiles the figure was 57 percent.

Over time there is a two-way interaction between the evolution of a nation's social capabilities and the articulation of societal conditions required for mastery of production technologies at or close to the prevailing "best practice" frontier. In the short run, a country's ability to exploit the opportunities afforded by currently prevailing best practice techniques will remain limited by its current social capabilities. Over the longer term, however, social capabilities tend to undergo transformations that render them more complementary to the more salient among the emerging technological trajectories. Levels of general and technical education are raised. Curricula and training facilities change. New concepts of business management, including methods of managing personnel and organizing work, supplant traditional approaches. Corporate and financial institutions are established, and people learn their modes of action. Legal codes and even the very concepts of property can be modified. Moreover, experience gained in the practical implementation of a production technique enhances the technical and managerial competencies that serve it, and thus supports further advances along the same path. Such mutually reinforcing interactions impart "positive feedback" to the dynamics of technological evolution. They may for a time solidify a leader's position or, in the case of followers, serve to counter the tendency for their relative growth rates to decline as catch-up proceeds.

On the other hand, the adjustments and adaptations of existing cultural attitudes, social norms, organizational forms, and institutional rules and procedures are not necessarily automatic or smooth. Lack of plasticity in such social structures may retard and even block an otherwise technologically progressive economy's passage to the full exploitation of a particular emergent technology (Freeman and Perez, 1988; Perez and Soete, 1988; David, 1991b). New technologies may give rise to novel forms of productive assets and business activities that find themselves trammeled by features of an inherited jurisprudential and regulatory system that had never contemplated even the possibility of their existence.[14] For laggards, the constraints imposed by entrenched social structures may long circumscribe the opportunities for any sustained catch-up movement.

To summarize our general proposition: countries' *effective* potentials for rapid productivity growth by catch-up are not determined solely by the gaps in levels of technology, capital intensity, and efficient allocation that separate them from the productivity leaders. They are restricted also by their access to primary materials and more generally because their market scales, relative factor supplies, and income-constrained patterns of demand make their technical capabilities and their product structures incongruent in some degree with those that characterize countries that operate at or near the technological frontiers. And they are limited, finally, by those institutional characteristics that restrict their abilities to finance, organize, and operate the kinds of enterprises that are required to exploit the technologies on the frontiers of science and engineering.

Taken together, the foregoing elements determine a country's effective potential for productivity growth. Yet another distinct group of factors governs the ability of countries to realize their respective potentials. One set of issues here involves the extent to which followers can gain access to complete and reliable information about more advanced methods, appraise it, and acquire the artifacts and rights needed to implement that knowledge for commercial purposes. A second set of issues arises because long-term,

---

14. On the problem of adapting intellectual property institutions to changes in the methods of acquiring knowledge of new technologies, and the problems of accommodating the needs of new technology innovations (in computer software and biotechnology, for example) within the existing legal framework of intellectual property, see David (1994a) and references therein.

aggregate productivity growth almost always entails changes in industrial and occupational structure. As a result, the determinants of resource mobility, particularly labor mobility, are also important. And finally, macroeconomic conditions govern the intensity of use of resources and the financing of investment and thereby affect the choices between present and future that control the R&D and investment horizons of businesses. By influencing the volume of gross investment expenditures, they also govern the pace and extent to which technological knowledge becomes embodied in tangible production facilities and the people who work with them.

We are now ready to put this analytical schema into use in a specific historical context: how the United States attained and sustained its productivity lead from 1870 to 1950, and then what changed during these years that released the catch-up and convergence boom of the postwar period.

Bases of the Postwar Potential for Catch-up and Convergence

The dramatic postwar record of western Europe and Japan creates a presumption that they began the period with a strong potential for rapid growth by exploiting American methods of production and organization. The productivity gaps separating the laggard countries from the United States were then larger than they had been in the record since 1870. However, the gains in prospect could only be realized if Europe and Japan could do what they had not been able to do before: take full advantage of America's relatively advanced methods. The insistent question, therefore, is why Europe, itself an old center of technological progress, had proved unable even to keep pace with the United States during the three-quarters of a century following 1870.[15] The answer we propose is that the difficulty lay in the failures of technological congruence and social capability, and that it was the gradual elimination or weakening of these obstacles that opened the way after the war to the strong catch-up and convergence of the postwar years.

---

15. Maddison (1991, Table 1.1) finds that the U.S. productivity advantage may have started well before 1870, perhaps as far back as 1820. But his estimates for these early years are exceedingly rough, and other estimates, at least for the United States, indicate that the American advantage increased little if at all between 1820 and 1870. In any event, industrialization in Canada, Australia, Japan, and several of the European countries had hardly begun before 1870. For that reason, it would be wrong to view all the countries that eventually came to be "industrially advanced" as having been similarly positioned throughout the pre-1870 era in regard to their respective effective potentials for catching up with the productivity leader.

Technological Congruence: Primary Materials

The American advantage stemmed first from America's more abundant and cheap supplies of primary materials.[16] Such supplies had a more important bearing on a country's growth potential in the nineteenth and early twentieth centuries than they have had since that time. This is true because food then constituted a larger share of consumer expenditure and GDP, and resources devoted to agriculture were a larger share of total factor input than they have been since that time. Moreover, America possessed abundant virgin forests and brushlands. In the Age of Wood that preceded the Age of Iron, this profusion of forest resources generated strong incentives to improve methods of production that facilitated their exploitation, to use them extravagantly in the manufacture of finished products (like sawn lumber and musket stocks), and to lower the costs of goods complementary to wood (such as iron nails, to take a humble example).[17]

Beyond that stage, the industrial technology that emerged during the nineteenth and early twentieth centuries, when America rose to productivity leadership and forged farther ahead, was based on minerals: on coal for steam power, on coal and iron ore for steel, and on copper and other non-ferrous metals for still other purposes. American enterprise, reprising its previous performance in rising to "industrial woodworking leadership" by combining technological borrowing from abroad with the induced contributions of indigenous inventors, now embarked upon the exploration of another technological trajectory—one that was premised upon, and in turn fostered, the rapid (and in some respects environmentally profligate) exploitation of the country's vast mineral deposits. In this technology, the costs of coal as a source of steam power, of coal and iron ore for steelmaking, and of copper and still other non-ferrous metals bulked larger in the total costs of finished goods than subsequently came to be true. Cheap supplies of these primary materials thus underlay America's growing comparative advantage as an exporter of natural resource–intensive manufactures during the period 1880–1929 (Wright, 1990, especially Table 6).

16. With some amendment, much of this section and the next follows the argument and evidence of several earlier papers: Rosenberg (1980), Wright (1990), Nelson (1991), David and Wright (1992), Nelson and Wright (1992), and previous work published individually and jointly by the present writers.

17. As Rosenberg (1976, chap. 2) has said, in describing America's rise to woodworking leadership during the period 1800–1850, "It would be difficult to exaggerate the extent of early American dependence upon this natural resource: it was the major source of fuel, it was the primary building material, it was a critical source of chemical inputs (potash and pearlash), and it was an industrial raw material par excellence."

By the eve of the First World War, America had attained world leadership in the production of nearly every major industrial mineral of that era. But this position had been attained only in part because of the nation's abundant natural endowment. Perhaps even more crucial were the nation's successes in rapidly uncovering the existence of its rich sub-surface mineral reserves, in devising new methods of refining and processing that were adapted to their sometimes peculiar chemical characteristics, and in building an efficient network of transportation by water and rail that reached throughout its very large territory.

Government policies and agencies played an active part in all those accomplishments, especially in subsidizing the extension of the railroad network into the American west, and by organizing and funding geological surveys and promoting the beginnings of systematic scientific research on subjects immediately relevant to the mineral industries. So did the newly formed faculties of engineering at the nation's institutions of higher education, both those at the older privately founded universities (like Columbia University's famous School of Mines) and those at the state colleges of more recent establishment under the terms of the 1862 Morrill Act (David and Wright, 1992). The peculiarities of the law of mining in the United States heightened the private, commercial incentives for investments in exploration and development. The federal government claimed no ultimate title to the nation's minerals, not even to those in the public domain. It offered free access to prospectors, and no fees or royalties were assessed against the minerals removed.

Finally, the incentives for minerals exploration and development stemmed even more largely from the demand that appeared as American manufacturing shifted towards the production of minerals-based capital and consumer goods. There was, therefore, a fruitful interaction between the development of primary materials supply, the advance of American technology, and the growth of manufacturing, construction, and transportation (Rosenberg, 1980; Wright, 1990; David and Wright, 1992).

The minerals-based, resource-intensive technology proved to be the dominant path of technical progress in all the presently advanced countries, but America gained substantial advantages in wholeheartedly embarking upon that path by undertaking infrastructural investments to explore, develop, and reduce the costs of access to her mineral resource deposits. Europe as a whole possessed known reserves of a number of the key minerals, such as iron ore, that in 1910 were as large as those identified in North America at the time, and the current rates of production of iron ore, coal, and bauxite in Europe as a whole exceeded those of the United States in 1913.[18] But when it came to petroleum, copper, phosphate, gold, and other minerals, America was out-producing the whole of Europe—even with Russia included. There was no nation in Europe, to say nothing of Japan, which approached the United States in the variety and richness of the mineral resources that actually had been developed, rather than remaining in "reserve" status. Out of fourteen important industrial minerals, America in 1913 accounted for the largest shares of world output of all but two—and for those two it was the runner-up. Given the still high transportation costs of the time and the relative importance of materials in the total costs of finished goods, this translated into a significant cost disadvantage for Europe and Japan vis-à-vis the United States in the production of finished manufactures.[19]

With the passing of time, however, the importance of these inter-country differences declined—for at least six reasons:[20]

First, technological progress reduced the unit labor input requirements in the mining, gas, and oil industries both absolutely and relatively. In the United States, for which the quantitative evidence is most readily available, unit factor costs of minerals production fell relative to unit factor costs in the rest of the economy. Table 3 illustrates these points, with the first panel focusing on absolute costs, and the second panel on relative costs. Compared to the non-extractive (or non-primary production) sector of the domestic economy, the unit costs of labor and capital in minerals decreased by 10 percent between the late nineteenth century and 1919, and then dropped by another 50 percent during the period from 1919 to 1957. Over the same long period, factor productivity in agriculture was merely keeping pace with that in the non-extractive activities as a whole, whereas in the forestry sector relative unit factor costs appear to have risen at an accelerated rate after 1919 (as shown in the second panel).

Second, mineral resources were discovered and developed in many parts of the world where their existence had remained unknown at the end of the nineteenth century, so costs of materials at points of origin and use outside the United States would have tended to fall. Furthermore, technological advance increased the commercial value of mineral resource depos-

18. See David and Wright (1992, Tables 1–2, and Figure 2). The following statements in the text are based on the same source, Figures 3–5, and Wright (1990, Chart 5).

19. For example, Wright (1990, p. 622) cites Foreman-Peck (1982, p. 874) to the effect that as late as the 1920s, "Ford UK faced steel input prices that were higher by 50 percent than those paid by the parent company."

20. These follow and elaborate on the lines of argument in Schultz (1951) and Nelson and Wright (1992).

TABLE 3

*Indicators of Productivity Growth in Production
and Use of Primary Products*

Relative output per worker in 1939 (1902 = 100)[a]	
Mining	280
Gas and oil	444[b]
Mining excluding gas and oil	178
Agriculture	164
Manufacturing	194

Unit costs (labor and capital) of gross product originating
in primary products sectors relative to unit costs of gross domestic
non-primary product[a] in United States

	Minerals	Agriculture	Forestry[d]
1870–1900 (average)	155	97	36
1900	155	94	47
1919	139	97	55
1937	78	91	100
1957	69	97	130

Energy and electricity consumption per dollar of GDP in 1920 prices
(1920 = 100)

	Energy consumption (Btu equivalents per dollar)		Electricity consumption (kwh's per dollar)
	Total[e]	In electricity generation	
1900[f]	86	77	20
1920	100	100	100
1950	64	97	268
1970	63	—	556

SOURCES: Panel A: Barger and Schurr (1944, Table 12). Panel B: Barnett and Morse (1963, Tables 6, 7, 8). Panel C: 1900–50 computed from data in Schurr and Netschert (1960, Tables 52, 58) and from Kendrick (1961, Table A-III) and estimated energy conversion estimates based on data in David (1991a) for 1902; extrapolations for 1950–70 based on Darmstadter (1972, Appendix, Table 1).

[a] Comparisons are for five-year averages centered on 1902 and 1939.
[b] Based on growth rate from 1902 to 1937.
[c] GDP less products of minerals industries, agriculture, forest products, and fishing.
[d] Estimates for sawn logs only; 1937 interpolated from 1930 and 1940 figures.
[e] Mineral fuels, hydropower, and wood for fuel.
[f] Electricity consumption estimates for 1902.

its that previously were neglected, and added new metals and synthetic materials to the available range of primary materials and agricultural products.

Third, petroleum came to be of increasing importance as a source of power for industry and transportation, and also as feedstock for the chemicals industry.

Fourth, transportation costs both by land and by sea declined markedly, which reduced the cost advantages enjoyed by exporters of primary products in the further processing of such materials.

Fifth, crude materials came to be processed more elaborately, and on this account, primary products became a smaller fraction of the final cost of finished goods. The consumption of primary materials declined per unit of final output, which had a similar effect. This is illustrated dramatically by a comparison of energy consumed in generating electric power with the electricity applied in industry and households. While electricity used per dollar of GDP more than quintupled between 1920 and 1970, energy consumed per dollar of GDP declined by a third (as shown in the third panel of Table 3).

Sixth, and finally, services in which the materials component is small became more important, compared with foods and manufactures, in which the materials component is larger.

For all of these reasons, differences in developed natural resource endowments have counted for less in recent decades than they had done earlier. One recent example of these changes deserves special notice. When the postwar period opened, it was widely expected that the well-worked, high-cost coal deposits of Europe and the more general lack of energy sources in Japan would pose serious obstacles to development for both. However, the rapid exploitation of cheap Middle Eastern petroleum and the development of low-cost transport by supertanker changed the picture. Energy problems became much less severe in Europe and Japan, which reduced what had been an important relative advantage of the United States.

Technological Congruence: Capital-Using and Scale-Intensive Technology

The technology that emerged in the nineteenth and persisted into the early twentieth century was not only resource-intensive, but also tangible capital–using and scale-dependent. Exploiting the technical advances of the time demanded heavier use of machinery per worker, especially power-driven machinery in ever more specialized forms. But it required operation on an ever-larger scale to make the use of such structures and equipment economical. Furthermore, it required steam-powered transport by rail and ship, itself a capital-intensive and scale-intensive activity, to assemble materials and to distribute the growing output to wider markets.[21] The im-

---

21. For a general discussion of the trend towards round-aboutness and increasing capital intensity in late-nineteenth-century industrial technology, the interested reader

portance of tangible capital supported by operation on a large scale was the message of all the early economists, beginning with Adam Smith and running through Bohm-Bawerk and Sidgwick to Taussig and Allyn Young. It is also a view supported by the economic history of technology and by statistical studies of American growth in the nineteenth and the early twentieth centuries.[22]

Tangible capital–using and scale-dependent methods again offered a technological path along which the American economy was drawn more strongly, and which the producers in the United States could follow more easily than their European counterparts during the late nineteenth and early twentieth centuries. We have seen how a rich natural endowment had supported American development of the minerals-based technology of the later nineteenth century. In a similar way, the early sparse settlement of America's virgin lands and its abundant forest resources made American wages relatively high and local labor supplies inelastic. And high wages in turn encouraged the development of the era's capital-intensive mechanical technologies. The heavy use of power-driven capital equipment was further supported by the relatively large, rich, and homogeneous domestic market open to American firms.

By 1870, the United States already had a larger aggregate domestic economy than any of its advanced competitors. Moreover, extensive investments in railroads and other transportation infrastructure were helping to realize its potential as an integrated transcontinental product market. Boosted by its comparatively rapid population growth (which was sus-

---

might begin with Abramovitz and David (1973a), Rosenberg (1976), and Hounshell (1984). With regard to the manufacturing industries in the United States and Britain, see the careful quantitative comparisons in James and Skinner (1985) and Broadberry (1993).

22. Growth accounting studies for the U.S. domestic economy in the nineteenth century show that tangible-capital accumulation was then the major source by far of the growth of output per man-hour and of its acceleration. See, for example, Abramovitz and David (1973a), David (1977), and Abramovitz (1993). But statistical analysis also indicates that the importance of capital accumulation in that era rested on a tangible capital–using bias of technological progress. Although a series of studies reports that the elasticity of substitution between tangible capital and labor is less than unity—which by itself would have reduced the income share of capital, which was the faster-growing factor—capital's share of GDP in fact rose markedly in the United States during the nineteenth century and remained stable into the early years of the twentieth century. There is, therefore, a strong presumption that technological progress was tangible capital–using not only at the aggregate level of the domestic economy, but within the industrial and agricultural sectors as well. For quantitative evidence on the elasticity of substitution and the bias of factor-augmenting technical change at the aggregate and industry levels in the United States, see David and van de Klundert (1965), Abramovitz and David (1973b), David (1975, chaps. 1, 4), David (1977), and Cain and Paterson (1981).

tained by a tide of international migration), the U.S. growth rate of real GDP between 1870 and 1913 outstripped those of all other industrializing countries. By 1913, therefore, the size of the American economy was over two and one-half times that of the United Kingdom or Germany, and over four times that of France (Maddison, 1993, Table 3). America's per capita GDP also topped those of the other industrial nations in 1913, exceeding that of the United Kingdom by 20 percent, France by 77 percent, and Germany by 86 percent (Maddison, 1993, Table 1.1). These differences indicate the advantage that the United States enjoyed in markets for automobiles and for the other new, relatively expensive durable goods, to which the techniques of a scale-dependent, capital-using technology (like mass production) especially applied.

The American domestic market was both large and well unified by an extensive transportation network. And it was unified in other ways that Europe at the time could not match. The rapid settlement of the country from a common cultural base in the northeastern and middle-Atlantic seaboards closely circumscribed any regional differences in language, legal systems, local legislation, and popular tastes. In fact, Americans sought consumer goods of unpretentious and functional design in preference to products that tried to emulate the more differentiated, elaborate, and custom-finished look of the old European luxury crafts. This taste structure, which was commented on repeatedly at international expositions where American manufactures were displayed alongside the top-quality wares of the Europeans, owed much to the spirit of democratic egalitarianism that prevailed over large sections of American society, and to the young nation's freedom from a heritage of feudal and aristocratic traditions and aesthetic values. It fostered the entrepreneurial strategy of catering to and actively creating large markets for the standardized products of large-scale production (Rosenberg, 1980; Hounshell, 1984).

The American development of mass-production methods was also encouraged by the country's higher and more widely diffused incomes, which supported an ample domestic market for the new metals-based durable goods. By contrast, Europe's lower and less equally distributed incomes initially restricted the market for such goods to its well-to-do classes, for whom standardized commodities had less appeal in any event, and thereby delayed the full application of American mass-production methods.

Finally, American land abundance and the level, unobstructed terrain of the Midwest and trans-Mississippi prairies were especially well suited to the extensive cultivation of grain and livestock under climatic and topo-

TABLE 4

Comparative Capital-Labor Ratios, 1870–1979

(*U.S.* = *100*)

	Germany	Italy	United Kingdom	Average of three European countries	Japan
1870	73	—	117	—	—
1880	73	26	106	68	12
1913	60	24	59	48	10
1938	42	32	43	39	13
1950	46	31	46	41	13
1970	71	48	53	57	29
1979	105	66	64	78	52

SOURCE: Wolff (1991, pp. 565–79, Table 2).
NOTE: Labor input measured by hours worked, capital by gross fixed non-residential capital stock (Germany by net capital stock, so the German relatives are somewhat understated).

graphical conditions very favorable to the mechanization of field operations. None of these developments could be replicated on anything approaching the same comparative scale within European agriculture at the time. In this way, the "Westward Movement" helped perpetuate conditions of relative labor scarcity, which in turn favored the substitution of machinery (and horsepower) for human effort, and further stimulated technological innovations localized at the capital-intensive end of the spectrum of farming techniques (David, 1975, chaps. 4–5; Parker, 1972). And the recurring shifts of the farming frontier onto virgin soil contributed doubly to boosting nineteenth-century agricultural productivity growth in the still largely agrarian American economy.[23]

The effect of the American advantage in scale, buttressed by high wages relative to the cost of finance, is reflected in comparisons of U.S. capital-labor ratios with those in three large European countries and Japan. Table 4 offers some illustrative figures. In 1870, Britain may still have used more capital per worker than the United States. But by 1913, both the British and German ratios had sunk to about 60 percent of the U.S. fig-

23. Parker (1991, pp. 325–29) addresses the deeper issue of the endogeneity of technical and spatial innovation in the American agrarian context. There were, he suggests, two-way causal influences running between the westward movement and regional agricultural specialization, on the one hand, and technological progress in the development and improvement of farm machinery, on the other hand. This interaction was especially notable in the case of the mechanization of reaping and threshing small grains (which accounted for virtually all of the nineteenth-century American labor productivity growth in wheat and oats), and in the development of improved plows, seed drills, and row cultivators (which accounted for all the productivity growth in corn farming).

ure.[24] European (and Japanese) capital intensity, held back by wars and their aftermath, did not begin to catch up to the United States until after World War II, in conjunction with the postwar catch-up boom.

Again, however, these American advantages gradually waned in importance. As aggregate output expanded in Europe, the markets for more industries and products approached the scale required for most efficient production, with plants embodying technologies that had been developed to suit American conditions. Furthermore, the decline in transportation costs and the more liberal regime of international trade and finance that emerged between 1880 and 1913 encouraged producers to use international markets to achieve the scale required. From 1870 to 1913, the average growth rate of exports in continental Europe was 43 percent greater than GDP growth (Maddison, 1991, Tables 3.2, 3.15). Of course, there was a still greater expansion of trade during the 1950s and 1960s, when the growth of European exports exceeded the growth of their collective GDP (both in constant prices) by 89 percent. In this era, rising per capita incomes also helped assure that scale requirements in the newer mass-production industries producing consumer and producer durables would be satisfied for a widening range of commodities. As larger domestic and foreign markets appeared, laggard countries could begin to switch in a thoroughgoing way to exploit the capital-using and scale-dependent techniques already explored by the United States. This was a path toward catch-up that would prove to be especially important after World War II, even though it had begun to be followed by some large industrial enterprises in Europe and Japan during the interwar period (Denison, 1967, chap. 17; Denison and Chung, 1976, chap. 10).

---

24. Edward Wolff's figures in Table 4, which refer to gross reproducible, fixed, non-residential capital stock per person employed, go back to Maddison (1982). More recent estimates by Maddison, however, based on standardized assumptions regarding asset lives, revise his earlier estimates drastically. They put U.S. stock at a level over twice as high as the United Kingdom's as early as 1890 (Maddison, 1991, Table 3.9). And more recent, still unpublished figures suggest that the United States may already have enjoyed a substantial lead even in 1870.

In manufacturing, however, the capital-labor ratio in the United States was already 94 percent of the U.K. level in 1870, on the evidence of the official (Census) net stock figures. Stephen Broadberry's (1993) adjustments to standardize the service life assumptions underlying the American and British net capital stock figures—carried out by Broadberry for 1950 and later dates—would suggest that the corrected comparison for 1870 would show the capital-labor ratio in the United States to have already been at 150 percent of the U.K. level. One must bear in mind, however, that in 1870, at the end of the golden age of "High Farming" in Britain, heavy reproducible capital formation for drainage and other farm improvements had pushed Britain's agricultural capital-output ratio to a level well above that in the United States.

Still another significant cause of the decline in American advantage was a gradual alteration in the nature of technological progress itself. Towards the end of the nineteenth century, the former bias in the direction of reproducible tangible capital–using, scale-dependent innovations became less pronounced. New capital-augmenting techniques (like the assembly line and automatic railroad signaling, track-switching, and car-coupling devices) were found to increase the throughput rates achievable with fixed production facilities. Even more portentous for the coming century, the growth of the scientific knowledge base relevant to industry encouraged shifts in the direction of innovation that began to favor investment in *intangible* assets (both human and non-human) rather than the further accumulation of conventional, tangible capital goods such as structures and equipment. In other words, the effect of this alteration of the bias of scientific, technological, and organizational innovation, taken by itself, was that of raising the rate of return on intangible capital formation activities— most notably, education and organized R&D—in relation to the rate of return on investments in conventional tangible assets.

This view of the changing general thrust of technological progress at the beginning of the twentieth century finds strong support in the quantitative and qualitative evidence from the American experience (Abramovitz and David, 1973a, b; Kendrick, 1976; David, 1977; Abramovitz, 1993). We believe it applies equally to developments affecting Europe and Japan. One sees this shift reflected, first, in the trend of the share of tangible capital in the factor distribution of GDP. The latter had risen markedly in the middle of the nineteenth century, but then leveled off and declined just as markedly between the early 1900s and the mid-1950s. A second indication is found in the stability of rates of return to education in the face of huge increases during the present century in the proportions of the workforce who had comparatively extended periods of formal schooling. In the absence of some other influence (such as the hypothesized bias of technological change) acting upon the relative productivity and earnings of the more educated, the rising level of educational attainment among the labor force would have driven down the real rate of return on investment in education.

A third indication is to be seen in the rapid rise in organized research and development activities, whether measured as a fraction of corporate revenues or of aggregate output. Overall, according to estimates made by Kendrick (1994, Table 1B) "nonhuman tangible" capital formation— consisting of structures and equipment, utilized land, and civilian and military inventories—represented a secularly decreasing proportion of total real gross investment; the nonhuman tangibles' share declined from 64.9 percent in 1929 to 47.3 percent in 1990.[25] The share of investment devoted to intangible assets such as education, R&D, health, and others rose by a corresponding amount. Kendrick (1994, Table 2) also presents parallel figures showing the growing importance of intangible assets in the total real gross capital stock.

A final manifestation of the rising importance of intangible investment in education is the growth of the number of jobs requiring long years of schooling in relation to the jobs requiring less formal instruction—a trend that was firmly established in the United States during 1900–60, and that has continued unabated during the past three decades (Abramovitz, 1993; Katz and Murphy, 1992). The global dimensions of this trend bear on our contention that there has been an erosion of the part of the American growth advantage which depended upon close congruence between the scale requirements of a tangible capital–using technology and the size of the U.S. domestic market. While western Europe and Japan had lower levels of tangible capital throughout the first half of the twentieth century, they were able quite early to reach levels and trends of schooling more nearly approaching those in the United States, as shown in Table 5. Although the European levels fell back somewhat from their relative position as of 1913—largely because of the more widespread continuation into higher education in the United States—the significance of that limited reversal remains doubtful and uncertain in view of the roughness of the estimates and the differences in the "quality" and intensity of the school year among our small sample of countries. We conclude that the political and social conditions in most of western Europe and Japan were substantially congruent with the new human capital–using bias of technological progress, just as they were in America.[26] Consequently, as intangible capital became more important, America's special advantage waned.

---

25. The technologically driven shift in the structure of relative asset demands, therefore, should be seen to be a significant force that has operated to reduce the conventionally measured gross savings rate (in both real and nominal terms) in the American economy during the twentieth century. The fact that despite the recurrent urging by economists over a number of decades—for example, see Abramovitz and David (1973a), David and Scadding (1974), Eisner (1989), and Kendrick (1976, 1994)—the official national income accounts remain blind to the rising importance of intangible capital formation has been a factor contributing to the misplaced emphasis given forces impinging on the supply of savings in efforts to explain and find policy correctives for the U.S. economy's "declining savings rate" problem.

26. Inkeles (1981, pp. 20, 25) points out that while different countries followed distinctive historical paths towards the complete enrollment of all children in primary school, and eventually in secondary school, too, the industrialized nations arrived quite

TABLE 5

Average Years of Formal Education of Population Aged 1 5 – 64
in Four European Countries and Japan Compared
with United States, 1913 – 89

(*U.S. = 100*)

	1913	1950	1973	1989
France	89	86	85	87
Germany	100	90	82	72
Netherlands	87	78	79	78
United Kingdom	105	99	91	84
Average of four European countries	95	88	84	80
Japan	74	86	90	87

SOURCES: 1913, 1950, 1973 from Maddison (1987, Table A-12); 1989 from Maddison (1991, Table 3.8).

The United States led Europe—with Germany a possible exception—in the late-nineteenth-century development of organized industrial R&D (Mowery and Rosenberg, 1989). Its lead continued to widen until sometime in the 1950s, but thereafter the differential vis-à-vis the R&D efforts of other economically advanced nations began to disappear, and in recent decades the gap in the area of civilian and non–military-related R&D has been essentially closed. Nelson and Wright (1992) attribute the continuing American technological leadership through the period of the 1950s and 1960s to the country's heavy investments in higher education and R&D. There is a distinction, of course, between seizing leadership in technology and managing to catch up in the level of labor productivity. The laggard countries achieved their postwar labor productivity catch-up during 1950–73 mainly by exploiting the production techniques explored by American firms both in earlier times and contemporaneously. European and Japanese capabilities for assessing, acquiring, and adapting existing technology, moreover, were becoming stronger as their R&D investment accumulated. As they approached American levels of efficiency in some lines of production, however, the emphasis of their own innovative efforts gradually shifted towards the exploration of other technological trajecto-

---

rapidly at substantially the same destination in this regard; and ultimately the institutional and administrative structures of their educational systems resembled one another in many broad features. After World War II, all the leading nations of the West increased the proportion of GNP expended on public education, converging on the figure of 6 percent (direct costs) during the period 1955–75, but the national patterns of allocation of educational expenditures among the primary, secondary and tertiary levels remained quite variegated. See also Inkeles and Sirowym (1983).

ries. For example, Broadberry (1993) has suggested that western European industrial firms have been able to reassert a degree of localized technological leadership during the 1970s and 1980s—especially in the development of alternatives to Fordist, fixed-transfer-line, mass-production methods—because they had an advantage in marrying modern information technologies with the small-scale craft organization of production that was traditional in many of their branches of industry.

The Interdependence of Technological Congruence and Technological Progress

The preceding account has often referred to the technology with which American conditions were especially congruent as one that had "emerged" in the nineteenth century. This wording could suggest that we regard the path of nineteenth-century technological progress as exogenously determined. American superiority in making use of the opportunities presented by practical knowledge would then appear as just a happy accident, a fortunate concordance of American conditions with the character or biases of an autonomous path of progress. Was that really so?

It probably was, in some part. The inventions that opened the era of modern industrialization were mechanical inventions, and they drew upon the history of European experiments with labor-saving contrivances that stretched back to medieval times (White, 1968; Mokyr, 1990). That these inventions came first may have been accidental, but some opinion holds otherwise—supposing that the reason they appeared earlier was that they were more readily grasped by people whose everyday observations and experiences had implanted in them intuitions about the laws of mechanics (Parker, 1984, chap. 8). Systematic invention based on electricity, chemistry, solid-state physics, and molecular biology, which required more fundamental and obscure scientific knowledge, had to wait. Meanwhile, the progress of mechanical applications put pressure on the older sources of fuel and primary materials: timber, coal, iron ore, and the other metals. In an era of incomplete geographical exploration and high transport costs, America's natural resource endowment and its early development gave this country an advantage in exploiting the new opportunities.

At the same time, the water-powered and steam-powered mechanical inventions of the time were embodied in tangible and specialized capital equipment and driven by large, factory-sited, central sources of power, transmitted by elaborate and expensive systems of belts. All of this was economical only if operated on a sufficiently large scale. So America's superior market scale gave it another substantial advantage in exploiting the potential of the nineteenth century's path of mechanical progress.

But did the nineteenth-century path of technological progress that favored American productivity growth just "emerge"? Or alternatively, was it the product of a process of exploration, of learning and testing, that was itself shaped by the exceptional, American conditions of resource abundance, high wages, and large market size? After all, when businessmen, craftsmen, and engineers look to reduce costs, they do not search with equal vigor through every possible combination of materials, labor, capital, and scale. Rather, they concentrate on that segment of the spectrum of combinations which has already begun to reveal its economic opportunities and engineering challenges.[27]

In America in the nineteenth and the early twentieth centuries, conditions pointed this search process towards methods that spared the use of expensive labor by accepting intensive use of cheap materials or land, by equipping workers with better tools, and by organizing production on a large scale to spread the overhead of intensive capital use. Many familiar stories of American economic development are consistent with this hypothesis: the country's "wasteful" use of timber; its extensive land cultivation practices (including monoculture) which left soil exhaustion and erosion in the farmers' wake; and its innovative development of machine-made, "interchangeable" parts and later of mass production by assembly-line methods.

The logic of these endogenous mechanisms of technological change suggests that they may not only give direction to the search for progress, but also, in some circumstances, speed up the rate of advance. Insofar as the pace of learning depends on the cumulation of experience, it is influenced by the pace at which engineers and businessmen come into contact with new methods of production and with the capital goods in which they are embodied. Thus, the pace of technical advance may depend on the portion of production activities that involves constructing and installing new capital equipment and related structures, as well as on the growth rate of the cumulative gross stocks that constitute the setting for learning-by-

---

27. See David (1975, chap. 1) for the formulation and historical application of a model of "locally neutral stochastic learning" built on the Atkinson and Stiglitz (1969) concept of localized technical change, the literature of learning by doing following Arrow (1962), and Rosenberg's (1969) notion of "compulsive sequences" of innovation. Antonelli (1994) recently has expanded the concept of localized technological change and shown its applicability in numerous industrial contexts.

doing and learning-by-using capital-embodied technologies.[28] Therefore, if American scale induced larger demand for tangible capital, it would also have supported a rate of technological progress faster than that being endogenously generated in Europe.

Moreover, American scale would have worked to speed up the pace of progress in still another way. The very process of conceiving, designing, testing, and developing new methods and the equipment through which they work is itself an investment, the cost of which is less burdensome when spread over a larger output. It is ideas such as these that are embedded in the "new" growth theories that Paul Romer (1990) and others have put forward recently.

Manifestly, the two views we have sketched are not mutually exclusive. The path of advance that became dominant in the nineteenth century did not become established simply because Americans chose to use it. When Adam Smith wrote in 1776 that the division of labor opened the way to the substitution of tools for labor, and when he proposed his famous dictum that the division of labor is limited by the extent of the market, he did not have before him the American developments that would so thoroughly exploit these principles. The exceptional circumstances of the former colonists, whose Declaration of Independence had coincided with the publication of *The Wealth of Nations*, were propitious in that they so well satisfied the conditions for economic progress envisaged by its author. Thus, the technological investments undertaken by American inventors and entrepreneurs, and the direction in which American business firms pointed their efforts to raise efficiency, lay more directly on the dominant path of nineteenth-century technical progress than was true in the case of Europe; and the results of those investments were embodied in forms of machinery and in a scale of production operations that firms in Europe could not immediately imitate or readily adapt to their own circumstances.

Social Capability

Social capability has to do with those attributes, qualities, and characteristics of people and economic organization that originate in social and political institutions and that influence the responses of people to eco-

---

28. The dependence of the growth rate of efficiency on the growth of the gross stock of (cumulated) investment was hypothesized in Arrow's classic paper (1962) on learning by doing. See Rosenberg (1980) on learning by using in the case of complex production systems. The hypothesis that productivity growth is stimulated particularly by high investment rates in producers' equipment receives some empirical support from DeLong and Summers's study (1991) of international data for the post–World War II period.

nomic opportunity.[29] It includes a society's culture and the priority it assigns to economic attainment. It covers the economic constitutions under which people live, particularly the rights, limitations, and obligations involved with property, and all the incentives and inhibitions that these may create for effort, investment, enterprise, and innovation. It involves those long-term policies that govern particular forms of organization or activity, such as limited liability corporations and financial institutions, and the policies that may support or restrict such organizations. And it covers the policies that provide for the public provision of social services and those that support the accumulation of capital by investments in infrastructure and by public education or research. With all that in mind, we can do no more than suggest how the shifting state of social capability may have worked to inhibit and then release the forces of catch-up and convergence in the group of presently advanced countries.

One thing is clear enough at the outset. The differences in social capability within the group of presently advanced market economies are less important than those between this group and the less developed countries of the present time or those of a century ago. Even in the later nineteenth century, all of the presently advanced group had certain broadly similar features. All had substantially independent national governments at least as early as 1871.[30] Broadly speaking, all the countries except Japan share

---

29. "Social capability" is a subject that has drawn the attention of historians and economists for many years. De Tocqueville (1840) and Veblen (1915) are notable examples of older writings. There was a considerable addition to this literature in the years following World War II, and we depend on these writings in the pages that follow. We refer especially to the essays by Arthur H. Cole, Thomas C. Cochran, and others in the collective volume prepared by the Harvard Entrepreneurial Research Center (1949); to the series of biographies of businessmen edited by Miller (1952); to the essays on France by Sawyer (1951, 1954); to those on France and Germany by Landes (1949, 1951, 1954) and Gerschenkron (1953, 1954b, 1955); and to Wiener's controversial work (1981) on the role of culture and class in Britain's relative decline. In more recent decades the subject has been largely neglected and is only now being taken up again by economic historians, as in Parker (1984, 1991) and Lazonick (1994). An even fuller view of social capability would include the growing literature of public choice, economic organization, and institutions, not only in economics but also in political science and sociology.

30. Some qualifications are in order. Finland was acquired by Russia in 1809 but granted a constitution that gave the country a semi-independent status. Full independence was achieved only in 1917. Denmark has suffered several partitions of Schleswig-Holstein and their transfer between itself and Germany. The unifications of Germany and Italy were completed only in 1871. While Austria itself has survived to the present time, it lost its empire by the Treaty of St. Germain in 1919. Norway did not become fully independent until 1905, but gained substantial control of its internal affairs some decades earlier.

much of the older culture of western Europe. Most important, all the countries, again excepting Japan, have lived during the entire period under basically stable economic constitutions that provide for a system operated mainly by business enterprises coordinated by markets for goods, labor, capital, and land. In Japan, although a middle class of merchants had arisen even under the Shogunate, the country retained much of its older feudal character until the Meiji restoration of 1868. Thereafter, however, it was rapidly transformed and by the turn of the century had established its own form of private-enterprise, market economy (Rosovsky, 1961; Ohkawa and Rosovsky, 1972).

Beyond their economic constitutions, however, certain noteworthy differences worked to impair the ability of European countries to catch up to the United States during the late nineteenth and the early twentieth centuries. Nineteenth-century America presented a contrast with western Europe in its social structure, its people's outlook, and their standards of behavior. In America, plentiful land offered a widespread opportunity to achieve a satisfactory income by the standards of the time. It fostered a relatively equal distribution of income and wealth and an egalitarian spirit. America's Puritan strain in religion tolerated and even encouraged the pursuit of wealth. The older European class structure and feeling did not survive America's wider dispersion of property and opportunity. Americans judged each other more largely on merit, and with the lack of other signs of merit, wealth became the main badge of distinction. America's social and economic circumstances encouraged effort, saving, and enterprise, and gave trade and the commercial life in general a status as high as or higher than that of other occupations (de Tocqueville, 1840, bk. 1, chaps. 5, 8; bk. 2, chaps. 18, 19; Parker, 1991, pp. 24–25, 123, 242–49).

While the social backgrounds of economic life in the countries of nineteenth-century Europe were of course not uniform, there were certain commonalities in their divergence from American conditions of the time. In all the European countries, a traditional class structure—which separated a nobility and gentry from the peasantry, the tradesmen, and an expanding middle class—survived into the twentieth century. Social distinction rested more on birth and the class status it conveyed than on wealth. Insofar as social distinction did turn on wealth, inherited wealth and income counted for more than earned income or the wealth gained by commerce, and landed wealth stood higher than financial wealth and still higher than industrial or commercial wealth. The middle class who aspired to membership in the gentry or nobility bought rural seats and adopted upper-class standards of conspicuous consumption. Class lines were not impassable, but they were hard to cross. Wealth alone was not enough, whereas a step up in the status hierarchy could be gained through the adroit deployment of sufficient wealth in serving the crown or the nobility, or in contracting a socially advantageous marriage, or in purchasing a military or civil commission that entitled one to enter an occupation suitable to a gentleman. In short, the social order of western Europe diluted the characteristic American preoccupation with material success.[31]

These differences in the bases of social distinction—and therefore in the priority assigned to economic attainment—influenced many kinds of behavior that matter for productivity growth. They shaped the occupational choices of both the European gentry and the bourgeoisie. When family income was adequate, sons were pointed towards the occupations that the upper classes regarded as gentlemanly or honorific: the military, the civil service, the church, and, well behind, the professions. Even in the sphere of business, finance held pride of place, all to the detriment of commerce and industry (Landes, 1949, pp. 54–57; Wiener, 1981).

In Europe, a related tradition from pre-industrial times influenced education in a way that reinforced these pre-existing patterns of occupational choice. The curricula in the secondary schools continued to emphasize the time-honored subjects of the classics and mathematics; the faculties of Europe's ancient and most prestigious universities dwelt upon these and also theology, law, and medicine. Throughout Europe, university curricula emphasized what was regarded as proper for gentlemen destined for the clergy, the civil service, and the liberal professions (de Tocqueville, 1840, bk. 1, chap. 10; Wiener, 1981). Although training in engineering did win a place for itself in both France and Germany early in the nineteenth century, its character in both countries was theoretical, concerned with preparing an elite cadre of engineer-candidates to serve the state in administrative and regulatory capacities. In contrast, by the late nineteenth century, engineering schools in America clearly had evolved a more practical, commercial, and industrial bent.[32]

---

31. Note 29 offers citations to works that support what may seem to be a sweeping judgment.

32. See Emmerson (1973) on the intellectual foundations and the contrasting social realities that formed the context for engineering schools in Europe and North America. Especially notable was the contrast with the French *grandes ecoles*, which initially had a strong influence on American engineering education. Ferguson (1992, pp. 72, 208–9) notes that when the U.S. Military Academy was reorganized in 1817, the practical military and civilian engineering curriculum adopted was the one in use at the Ecole Polytechnique in Paris during 1795–1804; the heavily scientific curriculum that had been introduced at the Ecole Polytechnique after 1815 was essentially ignored, and never was widely adopted by American engineering schools. David and Wright (1992) discuss

In a notable series of articles, David Landes (1949, 1951, 1954) and John Sawyer (1951, 1954) argued that the French outlook and social structure, as these had survived from pre-industrial times and then developed after the Revolution, gave the French family a more important role in the new industrial era than was true in America. Together with other factors, mainly the smaller size of the French domestic market, this emphasis on family business restricted the size of French firms. Family-owned businesses assured their family's continuing control by pursuing financial self-sufficiency, which led to a notably cautious policy and resistance to profit seeking by expansion that might require external finance (Landes, 1949, p. 53). This delayed the adoption of the corporate form of organization. Where technology demanded a larger scale than family funds could satisfy, as in steel, the preferred business form for the maintenance of family control was, according to Landes (1951, p. 337, n. 10), the *commandite par actions*, "a form of sleeping partnership" in which ownership is represented by negotiable shares, but in which the "active partners are in sole charge of operations." The *Kommanditgesellschaft auf Aktien*, a similar arrangement, was popular in Germany. Alfred Chandler's great business history (1990, pt. 3) contends that the expansion of British firms and their development of managerial and merchandising capabilities were likewise limited by the desire of British entrepreneurs to keep control within their families.

Survivals of the pre-industrial social structure of France limited the scale of firms in other ways as well. One that we already have noted was an aristocratic taste for quality and individuality in consumer goods, a penchant that may also account for the excessive degree of "finish" and durability that some observers have seen in European tools and machinery. This pursuit of quality and distinction inhibited the development of mass production and supported the extreme fragmentation of retail trade in which tiny boutiques and specialty food stores offered limited lines of merchandise in an individual ambience. Similarly, a business ethos that can be traced back to the medieval guilds discouraged aggressive innovation and price competition, in favor of maintaining a high standard of quality in traditional product lines.

The French social structure and the outlook it inspired were doubtless different in elements and strength from those in other European countries. Yet something of the same character does seem to have been at work throughout western Europe. For example, in M. J. Wiener's picture of En-

---

differences between American and European educational institutions in the case of nineteenth-century mining engineering. In the twentieth century, the long delay in the appearance in Europe of schools of "business administration" and "management" conducted at the university and postgraduate levels is also worth notice in this connection.

glish society (1981), there is the same middle-class yearning to rise on the social ladder to the rungs occupied by the gentry and nobility. There is the same drain of talent from industry and trade into more honorific occupations in the civil service, the military, the clergy, and the law. There is the same pre-modern cast of secondary and higher education, an emphasis on the classical and theoretical as opposed to the practical. Britain was a laggard in the development of curricula in engineering and business, although this probably owes something to a peculiarly British distrust of the educated specialist and a preference in practical life for learning on the job. In addition, class feeling also delayed the spread of mass education at the primary level during the nineteenth century. As one of us (Abramovitz, 1989, p. 59) has written:

The upper class who controlled British politics in the nineteenth century were slow to be persuaded that mass education was needed and that state support was justified. The Church of England resisted the state schools that would be non-denominational. Moreover, when a State system was at last established, British working class feeling gave less than ardent support for its extension. Many workers resisted the view that schooling, at any rate schooling beyond the elementary grades, would be an advantage to their own class-bound children. The net result was that . . . the school system expanded more slowly than in the United States and more slowly also than in some continental countries (for example, Prussia).

Alexander Gerschenkron (1962, p. 64) drew a corresponding parallel between France and Germany:

Most of the factors mentioned by Landes [for France] find their counterpart in the German economy. The strength of preindustrial social values was, if anything, greater in Germany than in France. The family firm remained strong, and the lower entrepreneurial echelons, whose numbers bulked large, behaved in a way which was hardly different from that in France. The pronouncement made at the turn of the century, that modern economic development had transformed the top structure of the German economy while everything beneath it still remained medieval, was, of course, a deliberate exaggeration. But there was some meaning in that exaggeration. Such as it was, it applied to France as much as to Germany.

Evidently, the persistence of pre-industrial social values was widespread in Europe, and its connections with occupational choice, the character of education, the size of firms, the resistance to standardization, and the preference for quality over price suggest that these survivals had, indeed, inhibited European industrial development in the nineteenth century and for some time thereafter.

This conclusion has been disputed. Gerschenkron's main contention, for example (1954a, b; 1962, pp. 63–64), was that the influence of pre-industrial values on the economic development of France was overdrawn by Landes (1954) and Sawyer (1954). Instead, he argued for the importance of differences in natural resource endowment, income levels, and domestic market scale—in short, to differences we have referred to as "technological congruence." Landes and Sawyer, for their part, were careful not to make social structure and outlook the sole or even prime cause of the different pace of French and American development in the nineteenth century. In the face of Gerschenkron's criticism, however, they both strongly rejected his implied conclusion that these social factors were matters of negligible importance. And there the matter rests. Since it is extremely difficult to reduce the notion of "social capabilities" to a meaningful scalar magnitude, such considerations typically are omitted from formal economic models, and assertions as to their effects remain largely untested econometrically, despite the recent wave of interest in international comparative studies such as those surveyed by Fagerberg (1994). Unsatisfactory as this may be, we believe that such factors made some significant contribution to the U.S. pre-eminence in the late nineteenth and the early twentieth centuries. Thus, it would be still more unsatisfactory to leave them wholly out of consideration.

Neither social structure nor outlook, however, remained frozen in its nineteenth-century form. As economic development proceeded, the social status and political power of European business rose. The occupational targets of middle-class youth gradually shifted. Business and the pursuit of wealth as a road to social distinction (as well as material satisfaction) became more appealing. Entrepreneurs became more familiar with public corporations, more receptive to outside capital as a vehicle for expansion, and more experienced in the organization, finance, and administration of large-scale business. The small, specialized retail shop retained much of its old importance into the 1930s. But after World War II, the big, fixed-price chain stores expanded beyond the beachhead that companies like Woolworth and Marks and Spencer previously had established in Britain. The American-style supermarket, aided by the automobile and the home refrigerator, began to transform European retail food distribution.

The timing of this change around World War II is not accidental; the war itself had a profound impact on social structure and outlook. In the aftermath of the war, great steps were taken to democratize education. State-supported secondary schooling and universities were rapidly expanded, literally hundreds of new university campuses were constructed and staffed, and public support for the maintenance of university students was initiated. For virtually all the new students, the mecca became careers in industry, trade, and banking and finance, not the traditional honorific occupations.

In France, even the *polytechniciens* joined industrial firms. Curricula were modified to fit the more practical concerns of this much-expanded student population. Schools of engineering and business administration were founded or enlarged. Even Britain, the perennial laggard in educational reform, responded by opening its new system of comprehensive secondary schools and its new red brick universities and polytechnical colleges.

The most important change of outlook was in the public attitude towards economic growth itself. In the first half of the century, and particularly in the interwar years, the major concerns had been income distribution, trade protection, and unemployment. After World War II, it was growth that gripped people's imagination, and growth became the premier goal of public policy. Throughout Europe and in Japan, programs of public investment were undertaken to modernize and expand the infrastructure of roads, harbors, railroads, electric power, and communications. The demand for output and employment was supported by monetary and fiscal policy. The supply of labor was enlarged by opening borders to immigrants and guest workers. Productivity growth was pursued by expanding mass and technical education, by encouraging R&D, and by providing state support for large-scale firms in newer lines of industry. The expansion of international trade was promoted by successive GATT rounds and by the organization of the Common Market and the European Free Trade Area.

We hold, therefore, that many features of European (and Japanese) social structure and outlook had tended to delay catch-up in the nineteenth century. But these inhibitions weakened in the early twentieth century, and in the new social and political milieu of postwar reconstruction, they crumbled altogether. The traditional upper classes lost their hold on the outlook and aspirations of the growing middle class. The same forces tended to strengthen the political power of business corporations and trade unions, and to shift the directions of public policy accordingly toward institutional reforms and expansionary macroeconomic measures on which both interests could find agreement. In the aftermath of World War II, these developments joined to reinforce the vigorous catch-up process that had been released by the new concordance between the requirements of the forms of technology and organization that had appeared in America and the economic characteristics that now obtained in western Europe and Japan.

Conditions Promoting the Realization of Potential

The postwar period opened with a strong potential for European catch-up. But the actual realization of a strong potential depends on a variety of background conditions that, in the shorter term, govern the responses of businesses, labor, and governments to the opportunities before them. This background may be favorable or unfavorable, and it may persist for an extended span of years. Between 1914 and 1950—counting the difficult years of initial recovery from World War II—these short-term factors doomed the possibility of realizing what might by then have already been a strong potential for rapid growth by catch-up. During the quarter-century following the Second World War, however, the reverse was true. A full exposition of this subject would be a long story. Here, we can do no more than notice some of the important components.

New conditions favored the diffusion of technology. Transport, communications, and travel became faster and cheaper. Multinational corporate operations expanded, creating new channels for the international transfer of technology, management practices, and modes of conducting R&D. Further, heavier investment in R&D was encouraged by a closer connection between basic science and technological applications, while the open, international character of much of the basic science research community fostered the rapid dissemination of information about new and more powerful research techniques and instruments that were equally applicable for the purposes pursued in corporate R&D laboratories.

Industry was able to satisfy a growing demand for labor without creating the tight labor markets that might otherwise have driven wages up unduly and promoted price inflation. Some key factors here were that unions had been weakened by war, unprecedentedly rapid labor productivity growth in agriculture was freeing up workers from that sector, and Europe's borders were opened wider to immigrants and guest workers. U.S. immigration restrictions themselves helped to create more flexible labor-market conditions in Europe (Kindleberger, 1967; Abramovitz, 1979).

Governmental policies at both the national and international levels favored investment, trade, and the spread of technology. The dollar-exchange standard established at Bretton Woods, together with U.S. monetary and fiscal policy and U.S. capital exports, overcame the initial concentration of gold and other monetary reserves in the United States. They sustained a chronic American balance-of-payments deficit that redistributed reserves and ensured an adequate growth of money supply throughout the industrialized world.

These and other matters that bear on the factors supporting "realization" in the post–World War II era deserve more ample description and discussion, which one of us sought to provide on an earlier occasion (Abramovitz, 1979). We must confine this paper largely to the elements of a changing potential for rapid growth by productivity catch-up. Nonetheless, it is important to remember that the rapid and systematic productivity convergence of the postwar years rested on a fortunate historical conjuncture of strong potential for catch-up with the emergence of international and domestic economic conditions that supported its rapid realization.

Many of the elements forming that conjuncture have now weakened or disappeared; most plainly, the large productivity gaps that had separated laggards from the leader have now become very much smaller. The break-up of that favorable constellation of forces has slowed the rate of both catch-up and convergence within the group of advanced countries. The passing of the postwar conjuncture of potential and realization was in large measure the result of developments inherent in the catch-up process itself (Abramovitz, 1994).

Summing Up: Bases of Productivity Leadership and Limits of the Potential for Catch-up

America's position of productivity leadership was gained, and maintained for a remarkably long period, by a fortunate concordance between America's own exceptional economic and social characteristics and the nature of the path of technological progress that emerged and was developed in that region during the course of the nineteenth century. It was a concordance that other countries were not at first able to replicate or match by other means. So their potential ability to catch up or even to keep abreast of American productivity growth was limited.

The nineteenth- and early-twentieth-century path of technological progress was minerals-intensive, tangible capital–using and scale-dependent. America's superior concordance with the nature of this path rested on three elements. One was its superior endowment of natural resources and their early development. A second was its superior market scale. These were the elements of America's technological congruence and so the basis for a more far-reaching exploitation and development of the possibilities of tangible capital–using innovation, including mass production, than the natural resources and scale of European economies could afford in the same period. America's third advantage lay in the sphere of social capability. Its egalitarian and secular outlook made wealth and economic attainment the basis of social distinction, made business a respected occupation, and directed education and science to material ends. In Europe, by contrast, the social outlook was still colored by an aristocratic residue. Talent sought the older honorific occupations, schooling prepared gentlemen for them, and scientific effort was more largely bent towards learning for its own sake. A quest for family status and a reluctance to extend trust and financial control beyond the circle of kinship combined to restrict the size and scope of business enterprises. The persistence of a guild-like ethos, aristocratic standards of taste, and inequality of incomes were still further European obstacles to the standardization of products and the substitution of power and machinery for labor in American-style mass-production factories.

In time, however, the sources of America's exceptional productivity advantage eroded. The region's early superiority in providing cheap access to industrial raw materials and sources of power waned, and the importance of abundant natural resources for production decreased. America's advantage in exploiting the dominant tangible capital–using but scale-dependent character of nineteenth-century technological advance was also undercut. The domestic markets of the laggard countries grew larger. Cheaper transport and more liberal commercial policies opened wider markets, at least until 1913 and again, of course, in the post–World War II period itself. Per capita incomes rose in Europe and Japan and began to provide larger markets for automobiles and the other consumer durables that were especially suitable for mass production. Businessmen in Europe and Japan gradually gained experience with the organization, finance, and operation of large corporations. The bias of technological progress began to shift from its older scale-dependent, tangible capital–using bias to a newer intangible capital–using bias less dependent on scale. Capitalist development gradually weakened the hold of aristocratic values in Europe; the outlook and institutions of European society came to resemble America's more closely.

The post–World War II conjuncture of forces supporting catch-up has now largely done its work. It has brought the labor productivity levels of the advanced, capitalist countries within sight of substantial equality. The significant lags that remain among the advanced economies in the course of catching up are no longer to be found in a marked persistence of backward technology embodied in obsolescent equipment and organizations.[33] Rather, they lie in the remaining differences between American, European, and Japanese capital-labor ratios, and in the sphere of politics and social sentiments that protect unduly low-productivity agricultural sectors and traditional forms of organization in both farming and retail trade. The

---

33. A recent study by Dougherty (1991), applying the refined Tornqvist index procedures developed and implemented by Dale Jorgenson, reaches the following values for relative multifactor productivity (output per combined unit of labor and capital, relative to the United States = 100) in 1989: Canada, 101; Germany, 89; France, 112; United Kingdom, 102; Italy, 101.

great opportunities for rapid growth by modernization now belong to the nations of eastern Europe, South and Southeast Asia, and Latin America. Although it is correct to say that the argument presented here is immediately germane only to the experiences of the group of presently advanced countries during a particular historical epoch, the classes of conditions that figure importantly in the story told here, nevertheless, may have a considerably wider applicability. The work of Barro (1991), DeLong and Summers (1991), Mankiw, Romer, and Weil (1992), and still others, while confined to the post–World War II era, has considered a much wider cultural, political, and economic spectrum than the subset of industrially advanced market economies.[34] The findings of these studies seem to reflect the operation of mechanisms both of "local convergence" among the advanced economies and of "global divergence" between the advanced economies (joined by the few newly industrializing economies) and the remaining low-income countries.[35] Throughout the world, deep-rooted political obstacles and the constraints imposed by social capability, or, to use Veblen's (1915) words, by "the received scheme of use and wont," remain to be overcome.

Among the presently advanced capitalist nations, the question is whether substantial equality in productivity levels will long persist. Will a new bend in the path of technical advance again create a condition of superior technological congruence and social capability for one country? Or will conditions that support the diffusion and application of technical knowledge become even more favorable? Will technology continue to pose demands for "readjustment and rehabilitation" that many countries can meet? For the foreseeable future, convergent tendencies appear to be dominant. But the full potential of the still-emergent Age of Information and Communication is yet to be revealed. The industrialization of the huge populations of South and Southeast Asia may change the worlds of industry and commerce in ways that are now still hidden.

---

34. A considerable body of empirical work on convergence also has been produced using the international database, constructed by Kravis, Heston, and Summers (1982) and extended by Summers and Heston (1988), on GDP constant purchasing power equivalents for more than 100 countries in the period 1950–85. See Fagerberg (1994) for a recent survey. Although the time period covered is briefer, these data offer the advantage of being about a larger and more diverse sample of contemporary countries, within which differences in the degree of technological congruence and in social capabilities are likely to be more pronounced.

35. See Baumol (1986) for the initial suggestion that the international data showed the existence of "convergence clubs" rather than global convergence, and the econometrically rigorous tests for "local" as distinct from global convergence presented by Durlauf and Johnson (1992).

Our treatment of the problems of technological congruence and social capability has been highly general and suggestive. Although it may help us understand the path that we have already traveled, it is not yet able to reveal what lies along the road ahead. When examined more deeply and in greater detail, however, these concepts may yet supply insights into the likely shape of the future, and so a means of preparing for it more effectively.

The Sources of Long-Term Economic Growth: Observations from the Experience of Developed and Developing Countries

LAWRENCE J. LAU

The long-term economic growth of a nation can be attributed to the growth of measured factor inputs, such as physical capital, labor, and human capital, and to technical progress (including improvements in efficiency).[1] The rate of growth of labor is generally constrained by the rate of growth of population. For developed countries, the rate of growth of the labor force is seldom higher than 2 percent per annum, even with international migration. For developing countries, where the rate of growth of the population is generally higher, the annual rate of growth of the labor force is rarely higher than 5 percent. The rate of growth of human capital in the short and intermediate terms is also constrained by the long gestation period required. Consequently, the growth of capital and technical progress, which are not subject to similar limitations, have been found to account for a major proportion of economic growth, especially for countries with high growth rates.

The interesting question, from an economic point of view, is the rela-

In preparing this paper, I have drawn heavily on my joint work with Michael Boskin and Jong-Il Kim, to both of whom I am greatly indebted. I wish to thank the Ford Foundation, the Pine Tree Charitable Trust, and the Technology and Economic Growth Program of the Center for Economic Policy Research, Stanford University, for financial support; Moses Abramovitz, Irma Adelman, Surjit Bhalla, Paul David, Steven Durlauf, Hidekazu Eguchi, Robert Eisner, Harold Furchtgott-Roth, Zvi Griliches, Yujiro Hayami, John Helliwell, Bert Hickman, Dean Jamison, Dale Jorgenson, Lawrence Klein, Ralph Landau, Barry Ma, Paul Romer, Robert Solow, and John Weyant for helpful comments on earlier drafts of this paper. I alone am responsible for any errors.

1. Land is also an important factor input; however, since it does not change over time, the change in the rate of growth of output cannot, in general, be attributed to the change in the rate of growth of the land input. Sometimes, other forms of intangible capital, such as R&D capital and knowledge capital, are also included. See, for example, Boskin and Lau (1994).

tive importance of each of the factor inputs, especially the capital input on one hand, and technical progress on the other. However, technical progress, unlike the quantities of physical capital, labor, and human capital inputs, cannot be directly observed and must be estimated. It is often measured as the "residual," that is, as the growth in output after the effects of the growth of measured inputs have been taken into account. Technical progress thus measured therefore also reflects the effects of changes in omitted and unmeasured inputs such as intangible capital (including R&D capital), and in the methods of organization for production as well as genuine improvements in technology.

Students of economic growth are interested in technical progress for two principal reasons. First, historically, there has always been concern about the ability of the world economy to supply its needs. Land and natural resources being fixed (and diminishing) in supply, given the law of diminishing returns, the marginal products of labor will eventually be driven down by its increased utilization to a point below the average subsistence consumption needs per unit of labor under a static technology. Malthus was an early leading proponent of this view. Capital deepening helps to postpone the arrival of this date, but eventually even the marginal product of capital itself will also be driven down with increased capital accumulation. Technical progress, defined as the increase in output holding inputs constant, is seen as a way out of this difficulty.

Second, many empirical studies, beginning with Abramovitz (1956), have shown that the growth in U.S. aggregate real output since the 1920s cannot be fully accounted for by the growth in the measured inputs—capital and labor—alone. The unexplained growth in real output, which is the "residual" referred to a moment ago, is conventionally attributed to technical progress, which also subsumes more generally the effects of intangible capital such as human capital and R&D capital. Technical progress, or the "residual," has been found to be an important source of the growth of real output for the United States as well as other developed countries over time.[2]

The Endogeneity of Technical Progress

Technical progress is often treated by economists as if it were like manna from heaven—both costless and exogenous.[3] In fact, it has to be

---

2. See, for example, the discussions in Boskin and Lau (1992a).

3. An early exception is Romer (1990). See also the vast literature on induced innovation or technical change.

produced, often through R&D and other innovative activities, which use up real resources in the process. Of course, luck, necessarily exogenous, is also frequently involved, although it is not directly observable. We are interested in measuring how much technical progress there has been, on average, in the developed and developing countries, without trying to determine whether or how much of the technical progress is in fact endogenous or exogenous. On a priori grounds, technical progress, being partly the outcome of purposive activity, must be at least partially endogenous.

Technical progress as a form of intangible capital may have a low marginal productivity in developing countries where the ratio of tangible capital to labor is low, or the ratio of human capital to labor is low, or both—that is, where the complementary factor inputs are lacking. Moreover, to the extent that technical progress is embodied in new gross fixed investment, it must be complementary to physical capital. Without physical capital, the benefits of embodied technical progress cannot be realized. For these reasons, technical progress may be unproductive in certain environments, and it may not be either privately or socially optimal for producers to seek or to invest in the creation of technical progress until a sufficient level in terms of physical capital and human capital per unit of labor is reached.

One may note that to the extent technical progress is embodied, it implies that the average age of the capital stock matters, and the younger the capital stock, the more productive it is, for a given quantity of capital stock. In principle, we should have the best chance of identifying embodied technical progress, if any, in economies in which the capital stock has undergone the most rapid growth. For this reason, the fast-growing developing countries provide the best setting for us to be able to observe the effect of embodied technical progress, if any, on the growth of real output of these countries.

A common hypothesis on technical progress and its diffusion is that the developed countries invest in its original creation and the developing countries can exploit it at little or no marginal cost. Moreover, since the developing countries are likely to operate far within the production possibilities frontier, there is much more room for them to realize an increase in output without increasing inputs, that is, to have a large "residual" or measured rate of technical progress. They should therefore be able to achieve a higher rate of technical progress than the developed countries because of the vast reservoirs of knowledge waiting to be exploited. One interesting empirical question is whether one can actually observe that countries at a lower technological level have a higher rate of technical progress, so that they eventually catch up with the more advanced countries. This is sometimes described as the "late-comer advantage." However, whether there is actual catch-up may also depend on the accessibility of technology, the availability of complementary factor inputs, and the degree of monopoly power in the international market for technology, which in turn affects the appropriability and distribution of rents in the transfer of technologies and the trade in capital goods between developed and developing countries.

In the next section, a summary of the stylized facts based on the recent empirical findings on the long-term economic growth of developed and developing countries by Michael Boskin, Jong-Il Kim, and me is presented. The following section, somewhat more technical in tone, contains a brief discussion of the meta-production function approach utilized in these studies. The empirical findings are then further elaborated, focusing on the similarities and differences between the developed and developing countries. I then present the results of a growth accounting exercise, without the customary assumptions of constant returns to scale, neutrality of technical progress, profit maximization, and complete disembodiment of technical progress. Finally, the catch-up hypothesis is explored via an international and intertemporal comparison of productive efficiency, and some brief conclusions are offered.

Summary of Stylized Facts

In a series of papers, Boskin, Kim, and Lau (Boskin and Lau, 1990, 1991, 1992a, b, 1994; Kim and Lau, 1992a, b, c, 1994a, b, c, d, 1995) have studied the sources of economic growth of developed and developing countries using the aggregate meta-production function framework.[4] They have found:

1. Technical progress in both developed and developing countries

---

4. The term "meta-production function" is due to Hayami and Ruttan (1970, 1985). For an exposition of the meta-production function approach, see Lau and Yotopoulos (1989) and Boskin and Lau (1990). In all of the Boskin, Kim, and Lau studies, the maintained hypotheses of the meta-production function approach cannot be rejected. The two most important maintained hypotheses are: (1) that the aggregate production functions of all countries are identical in terms of "efficiency-equivalent" units of output and inputs; and (2) that technical progress in all countries can be represented in the commodity-augmentation form, with constant geometric augmentation factors. However, the framework does allow the researcher to consider and potentially to reject the maintained hypotheses of traditional growth accounting, for example, the hypotheses (1) constant returns to scale; (2) neutrality of technical progress; and (3) profit maximization.

may be represented as purely capital-augmenting, or, in the case in which vintages of gross fixed investment are explicitly distinguished, as purely capital- and investment-augmenting.[5] In other words, technical progress proceeds as if there were more capital and investment in terms of standardized or "efficiency-equivalent" units over time.

2. Technical progress in both developed and developing countries may also be represented as purely human capital-augmenting.[6] In other words, technical progress also proceeds as if there were more human capital in terms of standardized or "efficiency-equivalent" units over time. However, technical progress can be simultaneously represented as purely capital-augmenting and purely human capital–augmenting if and only if physical capital and human capital together form a Cobb-Douglas aggregate (Kim and Lau, 1992a); that is, the aggregate production function must be representable in the form:

$$Y_{it} = F_i (A_i(t)K_{it}^\lambda H_{it}^{(1-\lambda)}, L_{it}), \ i = 1, \ldots, n,$$

where Y_{it} = quantity of real output of the ith country in the tth period;

   K_{it} = quantity of capital stock of the ith country at the beginning of the tth period;

   L_{it} = quantity of labor employed by the ith country in the tth period;

   H_{it} = quantity of human capital stock of the ith country at the beginning of the tth period;

   t = an index of chronological time;

   λ is a constant; and

   $A_i(t)$ is the augmentation factor of capital (and human capital) of the ith country in the tth period.

This form of the aggregate production function implies that human capital and physical capital together form a separable aggregate quantity index of capital and are complementary to each other as well as to technical progress. Thus, the more physical capital there is, the greater the benefits from human capital and technical progress are and vice versa.

3. Technical progress is the most important source of economic growth for the developed countries in the postwar period; in contrast, capital accumulation is the most important source of economic growth for the East Asian newly industrialized countries, or NICs. Moreover, the hypothesis that there has been no technical progress in these developing countries

---

5. The developed countries analyzed include France, West Germany, Japan, the United Kingdom, and the United States. The developing countries analyzed include Hong Kong, Singapore, South Korea, and Taiwan, and in lesser detail, China, Indonesia, Malaysia, the Philippines, and Thailand.

6. Human capital is measured as the average number of years of education per person of the working age population.

cannot be rejected.[7] This does not mean that labor productivity, or output per unit of labor, has not increased in the East Asian NICs. It has, principally because capital per unit of labor has also increased. Zero technical progress means only that if *both* capital and labor were held constant, output per unit of labor would not have increased over time. In other words, there is no increase in "total factor productivity." Despite their higher rates of economic growth and more rapid capital accumulation, the NICs have actually experienced a significant decline in productive efficiency relative to the developed countries as a group. In Kim and Lau (1994b), another study along these lines with additional developing countries (China, Indonesia, Malaysia, Philippines, and Thailand) included, it is also found that there has been no technical progress in the developing countries in the postwar period, despite their much more rapid rates of economic growth.[8]

4. The effect of human capital on output is positive and statistically significant. The production elasticity of human capital is comparable in magnitude to the elasticities of physical capital and labor. However, because the stock of human capital in an economy changes very gradually, human capital accounts for less than 10 percent of the economic growth in the developed countries and not quite 20 percent of the economic growth in the developing countries.

5. When the analysis is extended to take into account the effects of embodiment of technical progress, which implies that the technical progress occurring in a certain period benefits only the new fixed investment made from that period forward, Kim and Lau (1992b, 1994c) find that technical progress remains the most important source of economic growth in the developed countries. The proportion of the technical progress that is *embodied* in new investment goods is large. However, if the contribution of embodied technical progress is also attributed to capital (since without capital, there is no embodied technical progress), capital accumulation is found once again to be the most important source of economic growth for the developed countries.

6. Given the same measured quantities of inputs, the United States can produce an output that is higher than all of the countries analyzed in our samples by a significant margin. As of 1990, the technologically closest competitor to the United States is able to produce only 80 percent of U.S. output, using the same measured inputs. There is also a large and widening

---

7. The Kim and Lau (1992c, 1994d) results are consistent with those of Tsao (1982, 1985) and Young (1992) for Singapore but not with that of Young (1992) for Hong Kong. Young (1992) finds that there has been technical progress in Hong Kong but not in Singapore in the postwar period.

8. These results reaffirm the findings of Kim and Lau (1992c, 1994d) but are at variance with those of the World Bank (1993).

gap between the productive efficiencies of the developed and the developing countries. In particular, there is to date little or no evidence of catch-up on the part of the developing countries.

The Meta-Production Function Approach

Boskin, Kim, and Lau employ the meta-production function approach in their analysis of the sources of economic growth. The meta-production function approach, introduced by Lau and Yotopoulos (1989), is discussed in some detail in Boskin and Lau (1990) and in Kim and Lau (1992b, 1994a, d). It may be useful here for some readers to give a quick analytic overview of the approach. Readers less interested in this logical structure should be able to skip to the next section of the chapter with only minor loss of continuity. The point of departure is that each country has an aggregate production function, given by:

$$Y_{it} = F_i(K_{it},\ L_{it},\ H_{it},\ t).$$

The meta-production function approach has two basic assumptions. First, all countries have the same underlying aggregate production function F(.) in terms of standardized, or "efficiency-equivalent," quantities of outputs and inputs, that is,

(1) $$Y^*_{it} = F(K^*_{it},\ L^*_{it},\ H^*_{it}),\ i = 1,\ \ldots,\ n;$$

where Y^*_{it}, K^*_{it}, L^*_{it}, and H^*_{it} are the "efficiency-equivalent" quantities of output, capital, labor, and human capital, respectively, of the ith country in the tth year, and n is the number of countries. Second, the measured outputs and inputs of the different countries may be converted into the unobservable standardized, or "efficiency-equivalent," quantities of outputs and inputs by multiplicative country- and output- and input-specific time-varying augmentation factors, $A_{ij}(t)$'s, $i = 1, \ldots, n; j =$ output (O), capital (K), labor (L), and human capital (H):

(2) $$Y^*_{it} = A_{iO}(t)Y_{it};$$

(3) $$K^*_{it} = A_{iK}(t)K_{it};$$

(4) $$L^*_{it} = A_{iL}(t)L_{it};\ \text{and}$$

(5) $$H^*_{it} = A_{iH}(t)H_{it};\ i = 1,\ \ldots,\ n.$$

By substituting equations (2) through (5) into equation (1), we see that technical progress can be represented in the commodity-augmentation form, that is,

$$A_{iO}(t)Y_{it} = F(A_{iK}(t)K_{it},\ A_{iL}(t)L_{it},\ A_{iH}(t)H_{it}),$$

and measured output can be written as a function of measured capital, labor, and human capital inputs and time as:

$$Y_{it} = A_{iO}(t)^{-1} \, F(A_{iK}(t)K_{it}, A_{iL}(t)L_{it}, A_{iH}(t)H_{it}).$$

In other terms,

$$\begin{aligned}Y_{it} &= F_i(K_{it}, L_{it}, H_{it}, t) \\ &= A_{iO}(t)^{-1} \, F(A_{iK}(t)K_{it}, A_{iL}(t)L_{it}, A_{iH}(t)H_{it}).\end{aligned}$$

The reciprocal of the output-augmentation factor, $A_{iO}(t)$, has the interpretation of the possibly time-varying level of the technical efficiency of production in the ith country in the tth period. There are many reasons why these commodity-augmentation factors are not likely to be identical across countries. Differences in climate, natural resources (including land), topography, and infrastructure; differences in definitions and measurements; differences in quality; differences in the composition of outputs; and differences in the technical efficiencies of production are some examples. The commodity-augmentation factors are introduced precisely to capture these differences across countries. One should note that the hypotheses of a single aggregate meta-production function for all countries and the commodity-augmenting representation of technical progress can both be empirically tested.

In the empirical implementation, the commodity-augmentation factors are assumed to have the constant geometric form with respect to time. Thus:

(6) $$Y*_{it} = A_{iO} \, (1 + c_{iO})^t Y_{it};$$

(7) $$K*_{it} = A_{iK} \, (1 + c_{iK})^t K_{it};$$

(8) $$L*_{it} = A_{iL} \, (1 + c_{iL})^t L_{it}; \text{ and}$$

(9) $$H*_{it} = A_{iH} \, (1 + c_{iH})^t H_{it}; \quad i = 1, \ldots, n;$$

where the A_{iO}'s, A_{ij}'s, c_{iO}'s, and c_{ij}'s are constants. We shall refer to the A_{iO}'s and A_{ij}'s as *augmentation level* parameters and c_{iO}'s and c_{ij}'s as *augmentation rate* parameters. For at least one country, say the ith, the constants A_{iO} and A_{ij}'s can be set identically at unity, reflecting the fact that "efficiency-equivalent" outputs and inputs can be measured only relative to some standard. Without loss of generality, we take the A_{iO} and A_{ij}'s for the United States to be identically unity. The most important observation, however, is that subject to such a normalization, the commodity-augmentation level and rate parameters can in fact be estimated simultaneously with the parameters of the aggregate production function from pooled multi-country time-series data on the quantities of *measured* outputs and inputs. There is thus no need to rely on arbitrary assumptions. In fact, it is possible, using the meta-production function approach, to identify the relative efficiencies or qualities of the outputs and inputs of the different nations and their changes over time. For example, it is in principle possible to obtain annual estimates of the "efficiency-equivalent" conversion factors between Japanese and United States labor in the postwar period.

In order to accommodate the wide ranges of variation of the quantities of inputs in the pooled multi-country data, a flexible functional form is chosen for F(.) above. A flexible functional form is also needed to allow for the possibility of non-neutral returns of scale and technical progress. The aggregate meta-production function is specified to be the transcendental logarithmic (translog) functional form introduced by Christensen, Jorgenson, and Lau (1973). With three inputs, capital (K), labor (L), and human capital (H), the translog production function, in terms of "efficiency-equivalent" units of output and inputs, takes the form:

$$(10) \quad \ln Y^*_{it} = \ln Y_O + a_K \ln K^*_{it} + a_L \ln L^*_{it} + a_H \ln H^*_{it}$$
$$+ B_{KK}(\ln K^*_{it})^2/2 + B_{LL}(\ln L^*_{it})^2/2$$
$$+ B_{HH}(\ln H^*_{it})^2/2 + B_{KL}(\ln K^*_{it})(\ln L^*_{it})$$
$$+ B_{KH}(\ln K^*_{it})(\ln H^*_{it}) + B_{LH}(\ln L^*_{it})(\ln H^*_{it}),$$
$$i = 1, \ldots, n.$$

By substituting equations (6) through (9) into equation (10), and simplifying, we obtain equation (11), which is written entirely in terms of observable variables:

$$(11) \quad \ln Y_{it} = \ln Y_O + \ln A^*_{iO} + a^*_{Ki} \ln K_{it} + a^*_{Li} \ln L_{it}$$
$$+ a^*_{Hi} \ln H_{it} + c^*_{iO}t + B_{KK}(\ln K_{it})^2/2$$
$$+ B_{LL}(\ln L_{it})^2/2 + B_{HH}(\ln H_{it})^2/2 + B_{KL}(\ln K_{it})(\ln L_{it})$$
$$+ B_{KH}(\ln K_{it})(\ln H_{it}) + B_{LH}(\ln L_{it})(\ln H_{it})$$
$$+ (B_{KK}\ln(1 + c_{iK}) + B_{KL}\ln(1 + c_{iL})$$
$$+ B_{KH}\ln(1 + c_{iH}))(\ln K_{it})t$$
$$+ (B_{KL}\ln(1 + c_{iK}) + B_{LL}\ln(1 + c_{iL})$$
$$+ B_{LH}\ln(1 + c_{iH}))(\ln L_{it})t$$
$$+ (B_{KH}\ln(1 + c_{iK}) + B_{LH}\ln(1 + c_{iL})$$
$$+ B_{HH}\ln(1 + c_{iH}))(\ln H_{it})t$$
$$+ (B_{KK}(\ln(1 + c_{iK}))^2 + B_{LL}(\ln(1 + c_{iL}))^2$$
$$+ B_{HH}(\ln(1 + c_{iH}))^2 + 2B_{KL}(\ln(1 + c_{iK}))(\ln(1 + c_{iL}))$$
$$+ 2B_{KH}(\ln(1 + c_{iK}))(\ln(1 + c_{iH}))$$
$$+ 2B_{LH}(\ln(1 + c_{iL}))(\ln(1 + c_{iH})))t^2/2,$$
$$i = 1, \ldots, n,$$

where A^*_{iO}, a^*_{ji}'s, c^*_{iO}, and c_{ij}'s, j = K, L, H, are country-specific constants. We note that the parameters B_{KK}, B_{KL}, B_{KH}, B_{LL}, B_{LH}, and B_{HH} are independent of i, that is, of the particular individual country. They must therefore be identical across countries—thus supplying the common link among the aggregate production functions of the different countries. This also provides a basis for testing the first maintained hypothesis of the aggregate meta-production function framework, namely, that there is a single aggregate meta-production function for all the countries. We note further that because of the presence of the three independent parameters c_{iK}, c_{iL}, and c_{iH}, the parameters corresponding to $(\ln K_{it})t$, $(\ln L_{it})t$, and $(\ln H_{it})t$ may be regarded as unrestricted. However, the parameter corresponding to the $t^2/2$ term for each country is not independent but is completely determined given B_{KK}, B_{KL}, B_{KH}, B_{LL}, B_{LH}, B_{HH}, c_{iK}, c_{iL}, and c_{iH}.[9] This provides a basis for testing the second maintained hypothesis of the aggregate meta-production function framework, namely, that technical progress may be represented in the constant geometric commodity-augmentation form.

Equation (11) is the most general specification possible under our maintained hypotheses of a single aggregate meta-production function and constant geometric commodity-augmentation representation of technical progress. In addition to the aggregate meta-production function, we also consider the behavior of the share of labor costs in the value of output—$w_{it}L_{it}/p_{it}Y_{it}$—where w_{it} is the nominal wage rate and p_{it} is the nominal price of output in the ith country in the tth year, as a function of measured capital, labor, human capital, and time:

$$(12) \qquad W_{it}L_{it}/p_{it}Y_{it} = a^*_{Lii} + B_{KLi} \ln K_{it} + B_{LLi} \ln L_{it}$$
$$+ B_{LHi} \ln H_{it} + B_{Lti}\, t,\; i = 1, \ldots, n.$$

Under the hypothesis of profit maximization, the share of labor costs in the value of output is equal to the elasticity of output with respect to labor, $\partial \ln Y_{it}/\partial \ln L_{it}$. The parameters in equation (12) must therefore be equal to the corresponding ones in equation (11), that is:

$$a^*_{Lii} = a^*_{Li};\; B_{KLi} = B_{KL};\; B_{LLi} = B_{LL};\; B_{LHi} = B_{LH};\; \text{and}$$
$$B_{Lti} = (B_{KL} \ln(1 + c_{iK}) + B_{LL} \ln(1 + c_{il}) + B_{LH} \ln(1 + c_{iH})),$$
$$i = 1, \ldots, n.$$

This provides a basis for testing the hypothesis of profit maximization. Alternatively, one may suppose that the share of labor costs in the value of output is equal to the sum of the elasticities of output with respect to labor

---

9. Or, equivalently, the parameters corresponding to $(\ln K_{it})t$, $(\ln L_{it})t$, and $(\ln H_{it})t$.

and human capital, that is, the workers are compensated for both hours worked and for the contribution of their human capital, in which case the restrictions for profit maximization become:

$$a^*{}_{Lii} = a^*{}_{Li} + a^*{}_{Hi}; \quad B_{KLi} = B_{KL} + B_{KH};$$
$$B_{LLi} = B_{LL} + B_{LH}; \quad B_{LHi} = B_{LH} + B_{HH}; \text{ and}$$
$$B_{Lti} = (B_{KL} \ln(1 + c_{iK}) + B_{LL} \ln(1 + c_{iL}) + B_{LH} \ln(1 + c_{iH}))$$
$$+ (B_{KH} \ln(1 + c_{iK}) + B_{LH} \ln(1 + c_{iL}) + B_{HH} \ln(1 + c_{iH})), \quad i = 1, \ldots, n.$$

Equations (11) and (12) constitute the estimating equations for the aggregate meta-production function approach. However, the assumption of profit maximization under competitive output and input markets is not imposed a priori.

It is the essence of the meta-production function approach that countries may differ in the quantities of their factor inputs and intensities and possibly in the qualities and efficiencies of their inputs and outputs, but they do not differ with regard to the technological opportunities; in other words, they are assumed to have equal access to technology.

Common Technology with Distinct Factor Intensities and Efficiencies

One of the maintained hypotheses of the meta-production function approach is that the production functions of all countries, developed and developing, are identical in terms of "efficiency-equivalent" units of output and inputs. What this means is that if somehow we can change the units of measurement to reflect differential efficiencies of the inputs across countries, then all countries will have the same production function. It is remarkable that this hypothesis has not once been rejected in all of the studies that Boskin, Kim, and Lau have made for different sets of countries and with different sets of factor inputs included in the aggregate production function. However, despite this common technology, we also find that there are great variations across countries in factor intensities; that is, countries operate on very different parts of the production function, and in factor efficiencies and their rates of change over time. In this section, we shall analyze these differences in some detail.

First, we briefly review the definitions and measurements of the variables used in our analysis. The aggregate real output (Y) of each country is measured as the real gross domestic product (GDP) in 1980 domestic prices. Labor (L) is measured as the number of person-hours worked. The share of labor in the value of output is estimated by dividing the current labor income (compensation of employees paid by resident producers) by the current GDP of each country. The capital input (K) is measured as the *gross* total (public and private) non-residential fixed capital stock (equipment and structure) in 1980 prices,[10] at the beginning of the period, multiplied by the average capacity utilization rate of the period. However, for the developing countries, data on the benchmark capital stocks are either unavailable or unreliable and have to be separately estimated. Time (t) is measured in years chronologically with the year 1980 being set equal to zero. The data for all countries other than the United States are converted into 1980 U.S. dollars using the period average of market exchange rates between the currencies of the respective countries and the U.S. dollar prevailing in 1980. A detailed explanation of these variables and the data sources are given in Boskin and Lau (1990) and Kim and Lau (1992b, 1994a, b, d, 1995). The human capital variable, defined as the total number of years of education per person of the working age (15–64, inclusive) population at the beginning of the period, is derived from annual time-series data on educational enrollment.[11]

Data on aggregate real outputs and inputs, including physical capital, labor, and human capital, are summarized for five developed and four developing countries in Table 1. The two most striking features of Table 1 are the significantly higher rates of economic growth of the East Asian developing countries compared to the developed countries (only Japan, among the developed countries, came close to the rates of the developing countries) over the periods of analysis, and the significantly higher rates of growth of all the measured inputs—physical capital, labor, and human capital—in the developing countries (again, with the possible exception of Japan in the case of capital input). It should therefore have come as no surprise that the developing countries as a group have grown much faster than the developed countries as a group, because the rates of growth of all measured inputs have been much higher in the former than in the latter. The interesting questions are: How important is the role of technical progress (or improvements in efficiency) compared to the growth of inputs?

---

10. The capital stock is derived as an accumulation of gross fixed investments of different vintages less retirements (but not depreciation). Gross fixed investment is measured as gross fixed capital formation in non-residential assets (equipment and structure) in 1980 prices. Residential assets are not included because the measured gross domestic products of the countries in the sample, with the possible exception of the United States, do not appear to reflect adequately the outputs produced from owner-occupied housing.

11. We use the "perpetual inventory method" for estimating human capital, which was first employed by Jamison and Lau in an unpublished study on sub-Saharan Africa. Subsequent work done by Lau, Jamison, and Louat (1990) used the same method.

TABLE I

Average Annual Rates of Growth of Output and Inputs of Selected Developing and Developed Countries

	Period	Real GDP	Utilized capital	Labor hours	Human capital
Developing countries					
Hong Kong	1966–90	7.8%	8.7%	2.6%	1.8%
Singapore	1964–90	8.9	11.0	4.4	3.5
South Korea	1960–90	8.6	12.4	3.5	4.0
Taiwan	1953–90	8.7	12.1	2.5	2.8
Average		8.5	11.05	3.25	3.025
Developed countries					
France	1957–90	3.7%	4.6%	−0.1%	1.2%
West Germany	1960–90	3.2	4.5	−0.4	1.1
Japan	1957–90	6.7	10.4	0.7	1.0
United Kingdom	1957–90	2.5	3.2	0.2	0.8
United States	1948–90	3.1	2.9	1.6	0.4
Average		3.84	5.12	0.4	0.9

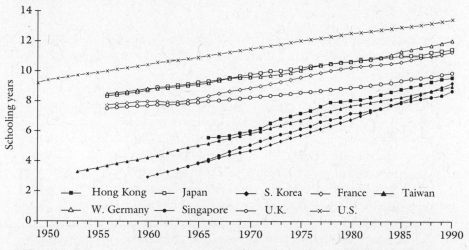

Figure 1. Educational attainment in selected developed and developing countries.

And has one group become relatively more efficient than the other, in terms of the ability of producing real output from given inputs?

In Figure 1, the data on the human capital stocks of the developed and developing countries are presented. It shows that the developed countries are still ahead of the developing countries in terms of the level of the human capital stocks. As of 1990, the United States has still by far the best-educated labor force in the world. However, the gap is being closed rapidly

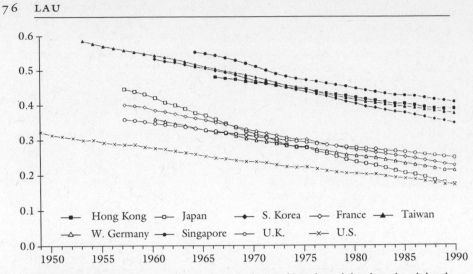

Figure 2. Production elasticities of physical capital in selected developed and developing countries.

by the developing countries, in which the human capital stocks have been growing at more than three times the rate of the developed countries on average.

While the hypothesis that all countries have the same aggregate meta-production function in terms of "efficiency-equivalent" units cannot be rejected, it is also evident that the two groups of countries—developed and developing—operate on very different parts of the production function. In particular, the estimated values of the production elasticities of capital and human capital for the developing countries are much higher and those of the production elasticities of labor much lower than the corresponding elasticities of the developed countries, consistent with the relative factor scarcities.[12]

In Figure 2, the annual estimates of the production elasticity of physical capital of each of the nine countries are plotted against time. The estimated capital elasticities for the developed countries are low compared to those obtained from the more customary factor-share method. It is clear that the production elasticities of physical capital in the developing countries are distinctly higher than those in the developed countries, although

---

12. This is the advantage of using a flexible functional form such as the transcendental logarithmic production function introduced by Christensen, Jorgenson, and Lau (1973), which allows the production elasticities to change with differing relative factor proportions.

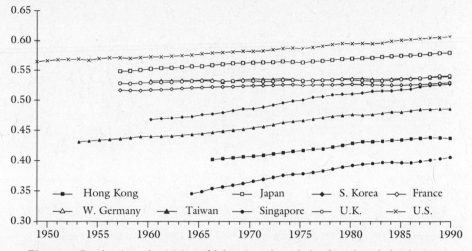

Figure 3. Production elasticities of labor in selected developed and developing countries.

a generally declining trend is evident for both groups of countries. In Figure 3, the annual estimates of the production elasticity of labor of each of the nine countries are plotted against time. The estimated labor elasticities are quite comparable in magnitude to and perhaps slightly lower than those implied by the labor shares for the developed countries.[13] It is clear that the production elasticities of labor in the East Asian developing countries are distinctly lower than those in the developed countries, although a general rising trend is also evident for both groups of countries, mostly on account of a rising capital intensity in the case of the developing countries and on account of technical progress in the case of the developed countries. In Figure 4, the annual estimates of the production elasticity of human capital of each of the nine countries are plotted against time. It is clear that the production elasticities of human capital in the East Asian developing countries are much higher than those in the developed countries. As in Figure 2, a generally declining trend is evident for both groups of countries.

In Figure 5, the annual estimates of the degree of local returns to scale in each of the nine countries are plotted against time. The degree is unity if there are constant returns to scale. It is evident that the estimated degrees of returns to scale are increasing, that is, greater than unity, for most of the

13. Note, however, that our estimate of the production elasticity of labor does not include the effect of human capital on output.

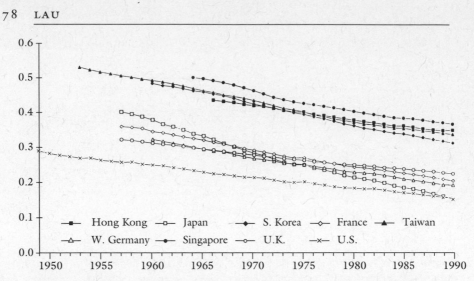

Figure 4. Production elasticities of human capital in selected developed and developing countries.

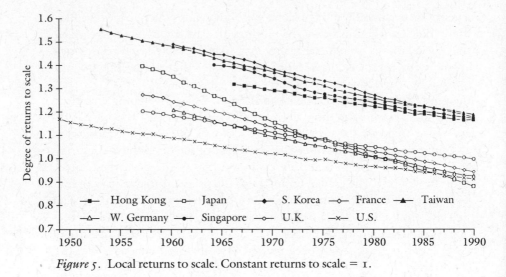

Figure 5. Local returns to scale. Constant returns to scale = 1.

countries and for most of the postwar period, but they are significantly higher for the developing countries, as well as for Japan prior to 1965, than for the developed countries. The degrees of returns to scale, however, decline over time for all of the countries. By 1990, whatever economies of scale there are appear to have been exhausted in the developed countries.

The developed and the developing countries divide naturally into two clusters in terms of the characteristics of the production function. This is most clearly revealed in Figures 1 through 5. Within the developed and the developing countries respectively, there is also remarkable similarity across the different countries, as is also apparent from an examination of the figures. However, Japan, a developed country, has been found to share many characteristics with the developing countries in the early phase of its economic growth, like a relatively high physical and human capital elasticity, as well as a relatively high local degree of returns to scale.

Alternative Growth Accounting

Kim and Lau (1994c) present an alternative growth accounting in which the traditional assumptions of constant returns to scale, neutrality of technical progress, profit maximization, and complete disembodiment are dispensed with.[14] The results are summarized in Table 2. Technical progress, embodied as well as disembodied, remains the most important source of economic growth for the developed countries, as was found in Boskin and Lau (1990, 1994) and Kim and Lau (1994a, b, d), its contribution averaging approximately 50 percent, followed by capital, accounting for approximately 35 percent. In contrast, for the developing countries, capital accumulation remains the most important source of economic growth, contributing more than 60 percent, followed by labor (approximately 20 percent), with human capital in a very close third place. The contrast between the developing countries and the developed countries in the relative importance of the contributions of capital and technical progress is most striking. Technical progress plays no role in the economic growth of the developing countries in the postwar period. Human capital accumulation is a much more important source of economic growth for the developing countries, contributing between 16 and 19 percent, than for the developed countries, where it accounts for less than 10 percent. This may be due to the higher estimated elasticities of the human capital stocks in the developing countries as well as their faster rates of growth.

In Table 3 we present the relative contributions of embodied and disembodied technical progress for the developed countries (bearing in mind that there is no measured technical progress for the developing countries). It is found that approximately 80 percent of the technical progress is of

---

14. For a discussion of the procedure for the decomposition of economic growth into its sources from an estimated aggregate production function, see Boskin and Lau (1990).

the embodied variety. For the developing countries, there is no embodied technical progress. We conclude that technical progress, when it exists, is mostly, but not exclusively, embodied in new capital goods.

However, since embodied technical progress cannot affect aggregate real output in the absence of new gross fixed investment, the contribution of embodied technical progress is also attributable to capital. If this is done (see the lower half of Table 2), the contribution of capital as a source of economic growth becomes overwhelmingly important, with the sum of the contributions of capital and embodied technical progress averaging 75 per-

TABLE 2

Contributions of the Sources of Growth
of Selected Developing and Developed Countries

With embodied technical progress attributed to technical progress

	Capital	Labor	Human capital	Technical progress
Developing countries				
Hong Kong	63%	20%	17%	0%
Singapore	63	19	18	0
South Korea	61	20	19	0
Taiwan	70	14	16	0
Average	64.25	18.25	17.5	0
Developed countries				
France	34%	−1%	8%	58%
Japan	45	6	4	45
United Kingdom	37	4	9	49
United States	24	31	7	36
West Germany	37	−7	9	61
Average	35.4	6.6	7.4	49.8

With embodied technical progress attributed to capital

	Capital	Labor	Human capital	Technical progress
Developing countries				
Hong Kong	63%	20%	17%	0%
Singapore	63	19	18	0
South Korea	61	20	19	0
Taiwan	70	14	16	0
Average	64.25	18.25	17.5	0
Developed countries				
France	86%	−1%	8%	6%
Japan	88	6	4	2
United Kingdom	57	4	9	29
United States	53	31	7	9
West Germany	92	−7	9	6
Average	75.2	6.6	7.4	10.4

SOURCE: Kim and Lau (1994c).

TABLE 3
*Relative Contributions of Embodied and
Disembodied Technical Progress in Selected
Developed Countries*

	Embodied technical progress	Disembodied technical progress
France	90%	10%
Japan	96	4
United Kingdom	41	59
United States	81	19
West Germany	90	10
Average	79.6	20.4

SOURCE: Kim and Lau (1994c).

cent. We conclude that physical capital is by far the most important source of postwar economic growth in the developed countries as well. The other factors of production are relatively unimportant for the developed countries, with the exception of disembodied technical progress for the United Kingdom[15] and labor for the United States. Thus, for different reasons, capital is ultimately the most important source of economic growth for both the developed and the developing countries.

Why is there no *measured* technical progress in the developing countries? This is a paradox inasmuch as the developing countries in our sample are themselves high-growth countries and the "catch-up" hypothesis suggests that they have unexploited technological opportunities created by the developed countries. There are a number of explanations of why measured technical progress is zero in the developing countries, some more plausible than others.

First, it may be argued that since the gross capital stock rather than the net capital stock is used as a factor input in the aggregate production function, allowance has been made only for retirement, but not physical depreciation, of capital. To the extent that physical depreciation is significant, the measured capital stock will overstate the "true" capital stock and the estimated capital augmentation rate may be an underestimate of the "true" capital augmentation rate. Thus, an estimated capital augmentation rate of zero may not necessarily imply a zero "true" rate of capital augmentation—it is also consistent with the interpretation that the "true" rate of

15. The unexpectedly large contribution of disembodied technical progress to the economic growth of the United Kingdom is probably an artifact of its unusually low measured rate of retirement.

capital augmentation is equal to, and hence offset by, the "true" rate of depreciation, resulting in an estimate of zero for the measured capital augmentation rate. However, since the same concept of the gross capital stock is also used for the developed countries, the above argument cannot explain the fact that the estimated rates of capital augmentation are positive and statistically significant for the developed countries but low or negative and statistically insignificant for the developing countries.[16]

Second, as we have seen, there are significant measured economies of scale in all inputs taken together for the developing countries. For economies in which output and inputs are both growing, economies of scale and technical progress provide alternative explanations for the reason why doubling the inputs results in more than doubling the outputs. With data from a single country, it is difficult to distinguish between the existence of economies of scale and technical progress. However, using the meta-production function approach, in which time-series data from several countries are pooled, it is possible to distinguish scale effects from technical progress, because at any given time, production at different scales is observed across countries and the same scale of production is observed in different countries at different times. Empirically, we have found that as far as the developing countries are concerned, it is economies of scale, rather than technical progress, that have been responsible for the good economic performance.

Third, the effects of technical progress in the Boskin-Kim-Lau studies are essentially being captured by the time trend, which is supposed to reflect the influence of omitted or unmeasured variables, such as R&D capital; land, or more generally, the natural endowment of resources; and other intangible "investments," such as software and market development. However, it is likely that such omitted or unmeasured variables are actually relatively unimportant in the developing countries, where there has been, until very recently, little investment in R&D, especially in basic research. Thus the *indigenously* generated improvements in technology must be quite scarce in these countries. By contrast, the developed countries invest a significant percentage of their GDP in R&D and even greater amounts in innovation and other productivity-enhancing activities. Thus, it should not

---

16. Unless one were to assume, in addition, that the "true" depreciation rate is higher in the developing countries than in the developed countries, because of various factors such as the mix of outputs. However, we may also note that Japan, which is supposed to have a high "depreciation" rate, also has a high estimated rate of capital augmentation. In any case, given the magnitudes of the estimated capital augmentation rates of the developed countries, the implied "true" depreciation rates would have to be implausibly high.

be surprising that technical progress, or the "residual," is much larger in the developed countries than in the developing countries. It is also true that despite the very rapid capital deepening in the developing countries, their industries are by and large not knowledge- or technology-intensive, at least until recently. Moreover, the developing countries have been playing "catch-up" in technology—the capital goods installed are likely to be the on-the-shelf variety, and the possibility for indigenous improvements is limited. For all these reasons, the "residual" due to omitted variables is likely to be small, or at least smaller, for the developing countries.

Fourth, the industries in the developing countries typically employ mature technologies with limited innovation possibilities, and the capital goods for these technologies, mostly imported, have been fully priced (that is, the acquisition as well as royalty costs fully reflect the possible efficiency gains and the amortization of R&D and other developmental costs) in the international market, so there is little or no net increase in value-added, over and above the normal returns to the factor inputs. In other words, the "innovation rents" have been largely captured by the foreign inventors, manufacturers, and distributors of the new equipment or intermediate inputs, in markets that are only very imperfectly competitive.[17] The "rents" can also take the form of royalties and fees paid to the foreign technology licensors by the developing countries, which, for some sectors, can constitute a rising share of the output produced, reducing correspondingly the domestic part of the real value-added. Consequently, even if a new technology were adopted, its effect might not be reflected in the form of a higher real value-added, holding measured factor inputs constant.

Fifth, it is possible that whatever technical progress there is in the world is mostly embodied in the capital goods used in the high-technology industries; thus, the developing countries, with a much smaller high-technology sector, would not have been able to take advantage of it to the same extent as the developed countries.

Sixth, it is possible that the growth of the "software" component, broadly defined to include managerial methods and institutional environment as well as supporting infrastructure, lags behind the "hardware" com-

---

17. Another way in which there may be little or no net increase in value added even with the adoption of new equipment and technology is if critical components that are needed as intermediate inputs can be imported only at high monopolistic prices. Thus, the benefits of the new technology are appropriated by the foreign manufacturers and suppliers of the critical components. Examples of such critical components include microprocessors, liquid crystal displays, and MS-DOS® and Microsoft® Windows™ softwares for notebook computers; plastic lenses for cameras; and recording heads for video-camera recorders.

ponent in the developing countries—and hence the capital goods have not been able to realize their full potential productivity, especially in the non-tradable sectors, which are often also the most monopolistic.

Seventh, it is also possible that positive technical progress in certain industries in the developing countries may be offset by rising inefficiency in certain other industries, especially those in the non-tradable sectors, so that the economy as a whole exhibits no measured technical progress. (This is less likely to be true for an open and competitive economy such as Hong Kong's.) Rising inefficiency can persist only in protected markets under monopolistic or oligopolistic conditions. Thus, technical progress at the microeconomic or industrial level may be nullified by the inefficiency caused by the lack of competition in the domestic market.

Eighth, it is also possible that the efficiency of production may be negatively related to the rate of growth of the factor inputs, especially capital inputs, for given levels of the factor inputs, because of costs of adjustments and learning. Essentially, the more rapid the rates of growth of the factor inputs, especially that of capital, the further away is the economy from the steady state, and the productive potential of the new investments may not be fully realized. The rate of growth of the capital input may be taken to be a measure of the amount of disruption or necessary adjustment. If this is the case, the positive effect of any technical progress may be offset in the short term by the negative effect of overly rapid growth of factor inputs until their rates of growth decline to more absorbable, or "steady-state," levels. Thus, as long as a developing country continues in a phase of high input growth, the measured "residual" may be small or negligible.

Finally, it is also possible that improvements in the quality of life, such as a reduction in air pollution or traffic congestion, brought about by increased inputs of both capital and labor, may not be fully reflected in measured real GDP. In other words, not all of the output resulting from the inputs, and its growth over time, is captured by measured real GDP, and hence in the efficiency and productivity measurements.

International and Intertemporal Comparison of Productive Efficiency

To assess the "catch-up" hypothesis and to ascertain whether "convergence in technology" holds, we need to compare productive efficiencies across countries and over time, holding the measured inputs constant. We attempt to net out the effects on output of differences in the rate and pattern of gross fixed investment, both in the rates of growth of labor and human capital inputs, and in scale. Within our framework, in terms of "efficiency-equivalent" quantities of output and inputs, the production functions of the different countries are, by definition, identical. In terms of the measured quantities of output and inputs, however, they are not identical. We therefore pose the hypothetical question: if all countries had had the same quantities of measured inputs of gross fixed investment, labor, and human capital as the United States, what would have been the quantities of their aggregate real outputs and how would they have evolved over time? In other words, we compare their productive efficiencies holding measured inputs constant.

The results of this thought experiment are presented in Figures 6 and 7. The time-series of hypothetical aggregate real outputs are plotted for each country in Figure 6, which shows that in 1949 the United States had the highest level of overall productive efficiency, with Japan in the last place (at less than 40 percent of the productive efficiency of the United States). Over time, Japan has caught up significantly while the United Kingdom has fallen behind the rest of the developed countries. The East Asian developing countries, despite their rapid rate of growth of real output, showed a widening productivity gap not only with the United States but also with the other developed countries, including the United Kingdom, which has the lowest productive efficiency among the developed countries. This is consistent with the finding that economic growth in the developing countries, unlike economic growth in the developed countries, is due mostly to

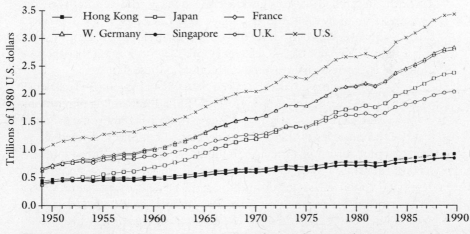

Figure 6. Hypothetical output levels of selected countries, assuming same quantities of measured inputs and human capital as the United States.

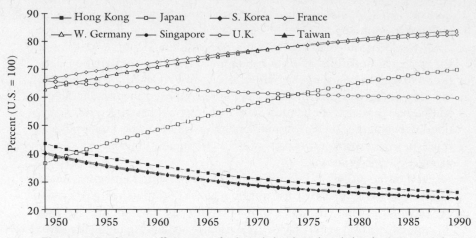

Figure 7. Productive efficiencies of selected developed and developing countries relative to that of the United States.

the increases in the inputs rather than to technical progress or improvements in efficiency.

In Figure 7 the relative productive efficiency of each of the other eight countries is plotted against time, using the United States level as the reference (that is, with U.S. productive efficiency normalized at unity). Figure 7 provides the same picture as Figure 6. The developed countries, with the exception of the United Kingdom, have all closed the productive efficiency gap with the United States significantly. However, the gap between the developing countries and the developed countries has actually widened considerably over this period. As of 1990, the developing countries stand at less than 30 percent of U.S. efficiency. We may note again that the two groups of countries cluster around each other in these figures.

These results show that the United States is still the most "efficient" economy in the world, even though the U.S. "advantage" is diminishing vis-à-vis West Germany, France, and Japan, thus providing some evidence that the technologies of the different developed countries, defined as the ability to produce output from given inputs, appear to be converging (except for the United Kingdom). However, the productive efficiencies of the developed countries as a group and those of the developing countries as a group are clearly diverging over time. The empirical evidence does not appear to support the hypothesis of *convergence in technology*, which would mean that given the same inputs, different countries will over time produce increasingly similar levels of real output. There is also no evidence that the rate of technical progress, or the "residual," is higher in the developing countries, even though they are much further behind the developed countries in terms of their levels of technology.

A simple way to test the "catch-up" hypothesis is to examine the relationship between the level of the technology and the rate of technical progress of a country. If the "catch-up" hypothesis is valid, then the countries with lower technological levels ought to exhibit higher rates of technical progress (in this case, higher rates of capital augmentation). In Figure 8, the estimated rates of capital augmentation are plotted against the corresponding estimated technological levels. Again, there is no clear evidence of any relationship if both groups of countries are simultaneously considered, let alone an inverse relationship. However, if the United Kingdom were excluded, there is some evidence of an inverse association between the rate of capital augmentation and the level of output augmentation of the developed countries alone, lending some support to the "catch-up" hypothesis within the group of developed countries. It is simply not true in general that countries with a lower initial technological *level* have a higher *rate* of technical progress. The "catch-up" phenomenon is not uni-

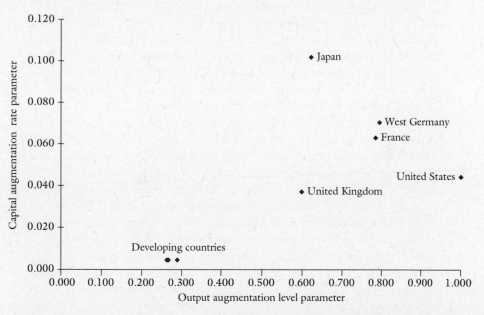

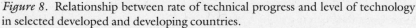

Figure 8. Relationship between rate of technical progress and level of technology in selected developed and developing countries.

versal, and the "late-comer advantage" does not appear to extend to developing countries.

Conclusion

The most striking contrast between the developed and developing countries is revealed in the initially quite surprising empirical finding that while the hypothesis of no technical progress can be decisively rejected for the developed countries, it cannot be rejected for the East Asian developing countries. Consequently, while technical progress, or the "residual," is the most important source of economic growth for the developed countries, it plays no role in the economic growth of the developing countries, which can be attributed in large part to capital accumulation.

While we were surprised to find that there has been no technical progress in the East Asian developing countries, we subsequently discovered that their experience is not unique. Much of the economic growth in the United States in the late nineteenth and the early twentieth centuries can be similarly explained by the growth in tangible capital and labor inputs.[18] Technical progress was not found to be a significant source of U.S. economic growth until the studies of Abramovitz (1956) and Solow (1957) for the period starting in the late 1920s. The same was also true of the Japanese experience. We may therefore reasonably draw the conclusion that physical (or tangible) capital accumulation is most important for countries at an initial phase of economic development. After a certain level of capital intensity has been reached, diminishing marginal productivity of physical capital will inevitably set in, given that land and natural resources are fixed and the labor input can grow only slowly. When that happens, the desirability of intangible capital will increase relative to that of tangible capital; this preference is further reinforced by the complementarity between tangible and intangible capital, which requires a minimal level of the former for the latter to be productive. Technical progress can therefore be expected to assume increasing importance as an economy is transformed from developing to developed status. There is thus a time sequence—with physical capital accumulation being the most important source of economic growth in the initial phase and technical progress assuming an increasingly significant role in the mature phase, after sufficient capital accumulation has taken place. To this extent, technical progress may be considered to be endogenous in the aggregate.

---

18. I owe this point to Professor Moses Abramovitz. See also, for example, Denison (1962) and Kuznets (1971).

The finding that technical progress is simultaneously physical capital–augmenting and human capital–augmenting is enormously significant—it implies that physical capital, human capital, and technical progress are complementary to one another. In other words, each of them increases the efficiency or effectiveness of the other two; a country that has a higher physical capital stock will benefit more from human capital and technical progress than a country with a lower capital stock, other things being equal. Similarly, a country with a higher human capital stock will benefit more from physical capital and technical progress than a country with a lower human capital stock. Technical progress is found to be complementary to physical capital and to human capital.

This complementarity may in fact be one reason why technical progress is not as yet an important source of economic growth in the developing countries. At the prevailing levels of physical capital and human capital, it has not yet become profitable for the developing countries to invest in R&D and other technical progress–creating activities. In time, with diminishing marginal productivity of physical capital and the increase in inputs complementary to technical progress (physical and human capital), the attractiveness of technical progress creation will increase relative to traditional investment in physical capital.[19] In this sense too, technical progress can also be said to be endogenous at the level of the aggregate economy.

The proportion of technical progress that is embodied has been estimated to be approximately 80 percent on average, a rather high figure. Technical progress can thus be said to be mostly, but not exclusively, embodied.[20] This finding provides further support for the complementarity of physical capital and technology. Embodiment also reaffirms the central role of new gross fixed investment in economic growth—without new gross fixed investment, the benefits of technical progress cannot be realized. Thus, because of embodiment, physical capital turns out to be the most important source of economic growth not only for the developing countries in the postwar period, but also for the developed countries as well, although for different reasons.

We find some evidence of catch-up among the developed countries, but no evidence of catch-up as yet by the developing countries. In fact, the gap between the technological levels of the developed and the developing countries appears to be widening. This may be partially explained by the

---

19. For reasons of appropriability, scale, and risk sharing, government intervention may be required in some economies.

20. This finding is consistent with and complementary to that of Delong and Summers (1991), who emphasize the importance of investment in equipment.

distribution of the rents of innovation, with most of them going to the developed countries. The fact that technical progress is mostly embodied rather than disembodied also makes it easier for the creators of new technologies to appropriate the rents. Consequently, the downstream users, consisting mostly of the developing countries, will not realize any significant excess returns to their investment in new plant and equipment imported from abroad.

One important empirical finding is the existence of sharply increasing returns to scale in all inputs in the early phase of economic development. The East Asian developing countries exhibit degrees of increasing returns to scale up to the power of 1.6 (with 1 being constant returns to scale). As economies grow and mature, such economies of scale are gradually exhausted. For the developed countries, returns to scale are approximately constant by 1990. That economies of scale can be exhausted should not in itself be surprising. As the economy grows to be large relative to minimum-efficient-scale plants, it is expected to exhibit approximately constant returns to scale because of the possibility of replication. And as the markets in the economy mature, the coordination externalities that are important in the early phase of economic development are not as critical. The major contrast between the developed and the developing countries is that there is technical progress in the former but little or no economies of scale, and no technical progress in the latter but significant economies of scale.

What policy implications do these empirical findings have? First, the three-way complementarity of physical capital, human capital, and technical progress calls for a three-pronged approach to increasing productivity: one must increase physical capital investment, invest in human capital, and promote technical progress by encouraging and facilitating R&D and other innovative activities. A policy of simultaneous investments in physical capital and intangible capital is likely to be more productive than a policy focusing on physical capital alone. A pro–economic growth policy must therefore have three parts—it should be pro-investment, pro-technology, and pro-education.

The complementarity between human capital and physical capital has additional policy relevance because human capital can be increased only with long lags. This, coupled with increasing returns to scale (at least for the developing countries), suggests that there is room for coordination and public intervention.

Most significantly, our empirical findings have reaffirmed the central importance of capital accumulation for the economic growth of both the developed and the developing countries. Capital accumulation (and deepening) can come about only with high levels of gross fixed investment, which in turn are dependent on domestic savings. This demonstrates the importance of high levels of investment and saving to economic growth and the necessity of pro-saving and pro-investment economic policies.

Finally, our results also show that in the long run, simply having high levels of saving and investment is not enough. As the physical capital stocks of the developing countries continue to grow, their production elasticities will continue to decline because of diminishing marginal productivity. Eventually, increases in the physical capital inputs alone will not be sufficient for the developing countries to maintain their current rates of economic growth. It is therefore troubling to find that despite their high rates of economic growth and rapid capital accumulation, the rates of technical progress (that is, the rates of growth in real output *net* of the growth in the measured capital and labor inputs) have been found to be statistically insignificantly different from zero for all of the developing countries. This finding strongly argues that the developing countries should look ahead and begin to plan to devote greater proportions of their resources to indigenous research and development and other innovative activities, to attain a positive rate of growth in productive efficiency and thus increase the contribution of technical progress to economic growth in the future. This is especially urgent given the long gestation periods for and uncertain returns to such investments in intangible capital. Otherwise, one is not optimistic that the developing countries will ever be able to catch up with the developed countries in terms of productive efficiency.

There are several potentially interesting extensions of this research. First, one can attempt to include as an additional variable in the production function a measure of the quantity of R&D capital. Second, it is possible to study investment in human capital in the vintage-capital framework in a way that is completely symmetric to the vintage-specific treatment of physical capital. In other words, we can incorporate improvements (or deterioration, as some may assert) in successive vintages of school years. Third, it may also be interesting to disaggregate gross fixed investment into its components—structure and equipment—as has been done by Delong and Summers (1991). The conjecture is that the embodiment of technical progress in and the complementarity of human capital and technical progress to physical capital works mostly through fixed investment in equipment rather than structures.

World Wealth Expanding: Why a Rich, Democratic, and (Perhaps) Peaceful Era Is Ahead

HENRY S. ROWEN

A process is under way that promises within a generation to make most of the world's population rich, or much closer to being so than it is today.[1] Moreover, there will likely be substantial convergence of incomes between the inhabitants of the current developing countries and the developed ones. Many important consequences will follow. One is that the world will become more democratic; another is that it might become more peaceful.

This might seem implausible given unsettled conditions from a collapsed empire (the former Soviet Union), high population growth (Africa, Arab world), ethnic and religious conflicts (the Balkans, India, much of the Islamic world, the Caucasus), and economically destructive policies (Ukraine, Nigeria). Furthermore, some local environmental problems are bad and worsening (China) and at least one on a global scale (warming) might become very serious. This is not a story about the imminent, or even distant, arrival of utopia. It is about some fundamentally positive forces at work: better policies and growing social capabilities.

Better Economic Policies

A major reason why there are still poor countries is that their economic policies have produced unstable prices and employment, domestic prices

I am indebted to many people for help and want especially to acknowledge this of my assistants Jeanne Zlotnick, George Wilson, and Bruce Donald. Timothy Taylor gave valuable editorial help.

1. To my knowledge, David Hale (1991) was the first person after the collapse of socialism to suggest that the world might soon become much richer. However, Herman Kahn (Kahn, Brown, and Martel, 1976; Kahn, 1979) also projected a world of "unprecedented affluence."

out of line with world ones, inefficient nationalized and regulated industries, low trade shares, little foreign capital and technology, and obstacles for the creation of new enterprises. Such errors are now widely being corrected. Import-substitution strategies are being replaced by export-oriented ones, countries hitherto hostile to foreign investment are now encouraging it, regulations are being reduced, firms are being privatized, and more. For example, during 1985–90, about 130 state-owned enterprises were sold every year throughout the world (excluding those in East Germany). During 1979–89, 61 countries accepted the liberalizing conditions for at least one structural or sectoral adjustment loan by the Bretton Woods institutions, with an estimated full implementation of 61 percent and at least substantial implementation of 82 percent by the end of the period (Webb and Shariff, 1992). The macroeconomic environment made a substantial difference: countries with low inflation implemented a higher proportion than those with high inflation.

Table 1 shows the direction of change in ten policy variables for the sixteen most populous developing countries from 1980 to 1993. (I have included South Korea in this set of sixteen on the assumption that it will be unified early in the coming generation.) These countries had a total population of 3.3 billion people in 1990, about 75 percent of all people living in non-rich countries. The policy variables are those used by John Williamson (1993).[2] Although this list has omissions (for instance, it omits policy for the acquisition of technologies), most economists would agree that these are of key importance. The ten are: fiscal discipline; public expenditure priorities; tax reform; financial liberalization; exchange rates; trade liberalization; foreign direct investment; privatization; deregulation; property rights.

Of the 160 data points in Table 1, 107 show improvement, modest or strong; 44 show no change; and only 9 show decline or could not be determined. Of the sixteen countries shown in Table 1, none shows a pattern of regression, although it is fair to conclude that Nigeria and Brazil made

---

2. These policy labels are mostly self-explanatory. Public Expenditure Priorities refers to redirection from low economic payoff areas to high ones. Financial Liberalization generally implies abolishing preferential interest rates for privileged borrowers as well as establishing a moderately positive real interest rate. Exchange Rates implies a unified rate (at least for trade) managed so as not to hurt exports. Trade Liberalization implies tariffs replacing non-tariff barriers and being progressively (not necessarily rapidly) lowered. Property Rights includes extending these rights to the informal sector. Policies on capital formation are not explicit in this set, but national savings would be positively affected by three of them: Fiscal Discipline, implying a reduction in budget deficits; Tax Reform, implying a cut in marginal tax rates; and Financial Liberalization.

TABLE I

Trends in Ten Economic Policy Areas, 1980–91/93, in Sixteen Most Populous Developing Nations

	Fiscal discipline	Public expenditure priorities	Tax reform	Financial liberalization	Exchange rates	Trade liberalization	Foreign direct investment	Privatization	Deregulation	Property rights
China	+	+	+	+	++	++	++		+	+
India	−	=	++	+	++	++	++	=	+	=
Indonesia	+	+	++	++	++	+	++	=	++	=
Brazil	−	=	=	++	+	+	=	+	=	=
Russia	−	=	=	++	=	=	++	++	++	+
Nigeria	−	=	=	=	=	+	+	+	+	=
Pakistan	−	=	=	+	++	++	++	+	+	=
Bangladesh	+	=	+	+	+	++	+	++	+	=
Mexico	+	++	++	++	++	++	++	++	++	++
Vietnam	?	=	+	+	++	=	++	+	++	+
South Korea	++	?	+	+	++	+	=	+	=	?
Philippines	+	=	++	+	++	++	++	+	=	=
Turkey	+	=	+	++	++	+	++	=	+	=
Thailand	+	=	+	+	+	=	++	+	=	=
Iran	+	+	+	=	+	+	=	=	+	+
Egypt	+	+	+		+	+	+	=	=	=

SOURCE: Author's estimates.

NOTES: Countries are listed in order from most to least populous. ++ indicates strong improvement; + indicates improvement; = indicates no change; − indicates deterioration; ? indicates that the trend could not be determined.

little progress. The countries that show the strongest patterns of positive change are ones that an attentive observer would expect: China, Russia, India, Indonesia, Mexico, and one that might be a surprise to some, Vietnam. Improvements in South Korea do not show up strongly in Table 1, because policies were already relatively good in the early 1980s. (If North Korea were recorded here, it would show little change from its poverty-producing policies.) The positive assessment of Russia might be questioned given its macro-instability and recent decline in output; but consider where it was in 1980. It is in transition from an inexorably inefficient system with bleak prospects to one that offers the possibility of prosperity; moreover, part of its recorded output loss of the past several years has been a decline in the production of useless goods.

It is natural to ask if these recent changes have resulted in improved overall performance. No robust improvement in various measures of performance (like GDP growth, investment/GDP, savings/GDP, exports/GDP) has been discerned for the 1985–88 period by comparison with the 1970s and early 1980s for countries that had participated intensively in World Bank adjustment programs (Corbo and Rojas, 1992). However, the developing countries faced a hostile environment in the 1980s. There was a world recession at the outset, with the highest real interest rates since the 1930s, declining and volatile terms of trade, and a sudden cut-off from international borrowing for many nations, especially in Africa and Latin America. For the most part, only a set of East Asian countries grew strongly in that environment.

For the smaller sample of countries shown in Table 1, in those with a preponderance of + + and + policy changes that were implemented early enough to affect performance by 1992—that is, China, Indonesia, Korea, Turkey, Iran, Thailand, and Vietnam—there was an average improvement of 1 percent in per capita annual GDP growth between 1973–80 and 1980–92 (Summers and Heston, 1991; World Bank, 1993b). For the entire set of sixteen countries, there was no improvement.[3]

Why did so many countries liberalize after 1980? Although the ideological opposition to economic liberalism began visibly to melt over a decade ago, that alone seems hardly a sufficient reason, given the strength of

---

3. Three negative outliers are Russia, which has only recently made major policy improvements (not including in the area of Fiscal Discipline) and whose output has since fallen; Mexico, which scores very well on policy changes and which grew strongly in the 1970s on oil and borrowing, but in the later period suffered from the debt overhang and the oil price decline; and Indonesia, which similarly improved its policies, but whose performance in the later period compares poorly with the earlier period that also benefited from the oil boom.

interests in the existing arrangements. Large systemic changes, such as entry into radically new trading arrangements or wars and revolutions, seem to be needed to weaken or destroy growth-inhibiting institutions and practices and have a liberating effect (Olson, 1982).

Herein lies an explanation for the changes in many countries—plus a role for chance. Enthusiasm for socialist solutions was waning; interest in liberalism was in the air. Opportunities were created by crises that were abundant. Most Latin American countries had borrowed heavily abroad during the 1970s and had invested less than wisely, and the bills came due in 1982; the resulting crisis triggered policy changes in Mexico and Argentina that have continued while those in Brazil have lagged. After the run-up in the 1970s, producers experienced a fall in the price of oil, an event that encouraged changes in Mexico and Indonesia. The Soviet Union's economic stagnation after the mid-1970s together with the trauma of the Afghan war, the power of modern telecommunications, and the accident of Gorbachev's accession to power produced a revolution. The Chinese leadership by the late 1970s was perhaps moved by fear that a poor China would not be able to stand up against stronger powers; it also had an array of successful models in its neighborhood. In 1980, Turkey was experiencing a foreign debt and foreign exchange crisis, private investment and growth had collapsed, and it had a high level of internal violence; chance provided Turgut Ozal, whose policy changes resulted in a great expansion in exports. Vietnam's economy was failing, its revolutionary spirit was waning, it faced a strategically superior and unfriendly China, and it had been abandoned by the Soviet Union. India's bold program of economic liberalization after 1989 was triggered by a macroeconomic and foreign exchange crisis. As Jagdish Bhagwati (1993) has put it, "It is hard to imagine that the microeconomic reforms now being undertaken would have been attempted with serious resolve unless there had been a compelling crisis."

In these crises, often present was an International Monetary Fund (IMF) / World Bank "adjustment" program (although such a program was neither a sufficient nor necessary condition for reform). The crises had increased the power of these institutions, and they were pushing the liberalizing agenda. Another visible thread in this pattern was the role of economists trained in the United States and Europe who came to play politically active roles—"technopols," as John Williamson (1993) labels them.

The fact that crises played a key and constructive role suggests a caution: will the reforms be sustained and furthered after the crises have passed? Russia is an obvious possibility for regression; there is nervousness about shifts in influence at the top of the Indonesian government; improvements in India might not survive a political change there; and Turkey's macroeconomic policy has been mediocre all along, has recently deteriorated, and is lagging in privatization. Given the past pattern of reforms and regressions, a cyclical process, it would be surprising if there were no setbacks (Krueger, 1993). Much depends on payoffs from the reforms coming without too long a lag. Those in East Asia are impressive, and if reforming countries elsewhere enjoy better performance, a new paradigm will be firmly in place.

Improved Social Capabilities

The term "social capability" has been used by Moses Abramovitz (1989) to mean, broadly, how well things work in a nation, including the level of education and the functioning of political, commercial, industrial, and financial institutions and, consequently, the nation's ability to absorb technology. It has two sub-categories: basic social attitudes and political institutions and the economic characteristics of people and institutions (Abramovitz, 1991). Included in the former are the aims of governors, the stability of the rules governing society, degrees of social mobility, the protection of property rights, and the civic-mindedness of the people (like their propensity voluntarily to cooperate to solve social problems). In the latter are the skills of the workforce; the competency of government and business organizations; and the height of barriers to setting up new businesses. When institutions function poorly and skills are poor, social capability is low. As North (1992) puts it, when the institutions are inappropriate, transactions costs are high and the economy suffers.

The countries of the former Soviet Union starkly display social capability weaknesses and strengths. Deficiencies include unstable political rules, immature political parties, inadequate commercial laws, weak property rights, less than independent judiciaries, underdeveloped accounting systems, poor tax collection, and large gaps in understanding of the requisites of efficient management. On the other hand, Russia and some other Soviet successor states have high levels of educational attainment and have experience with industrial processes.

India also provides an illustration. The caste system, which impedes social mobility and instills contempt for merchants and markets in Hindu society, is dysfunctional (Lal, 1988). The British made legal, educational, and economic contributions, but they changed the underlying structure little. The Gandhian rejection of modernization, along with its support for self-sufficient villages, and, not least, the import of Fabian socialism in this century reinforced the existing incapacities of the society. Perhaps India's greatest social asset is a rooted system of law.

In trying to understand how nations might perform in the next several decades, we are interested not only in current levels of social capability but also in trends insofar as they can be discerned. With a few exceptions, the available measures are imperfect and impressionistic.

Governors' Interests in and Scope of Action for Promoting Growth

Some societies have epitomized the model of near single-minded pursuit of development: Meiji Japan, post–World War II Japan, South Korea, Taiwan, China since 1978, and Singapore are prominent among the small set of nations that have pursued the aim of development with high intensity. To use the phrase once popularized by the mutual fund promoter Bernie Cornfeld, they sincerely wanted to be rich.

States are distributed across a spectrum that includes, at one end, those governors "sincerely" dedicated to the pursuit of national wealth and able to pursue it. It continues through a broad middle set with various sets of governors' aims and objective circumstances that help or hinder development, and on to predator Mobutu's Zaire, the chaos of Lebanon in the 1980s, and today's Rwanda at the other end.

At this latter end, survival is the overarching aim for most people, but almost all governments have to pay some attention to development, if only to secure resources for the rulers (Olson, 1993). The apparent superior ability of authoritarian governments to adhere to a goal, like development, might suggest that their performance should be better in this respect than that of more democratic ones. The fact that the fast-growing East Asian countries were all authoritarian at the onset of their high-speed growth is consistent with this proposition, but a broader body of evidence does not support it.[4]

Internal Divisions and Other Sources of Instability

Many nations are in a poverty equilibrium trap (Londregan and Poole, 1990). Political instability discourages investment, without which poverty, and therefore conditions for continued instability, persists. Most poor countries have authoritarian governments that tend to behave arbitrarily

---

4. The evidence on the association of democracy and growth is mixed. Alesina and Rodrik (1991) distinguish between damaging "kleptocratic" dictatorships and growth-promoting, "technocratic" ones. Helliwell (1992) finds that a prior condition of democracy is neutral for future growth, whereas a prior condition of wealth is positive for later democracy.

and have uncertain tenure; to the extent that this is so, future policies are unpredictable.[5] Reformist governments lack credibility for some time after they are installed, because there is little confidence in their tenure. The prospect of short tenure induces a short-term perspective on economic policies; most such policies entail pain before there is gain. In such a situation some people in power grab what they can for themselves while they can get it, and the need for revenues in a crisis induces short-term policies that damage long-term prospects (Weingast, 1993). All this is bad for business in several ways: the weakness of the rule of law in regulating private business activities causes them to be limited to networks of personal relationships, often family-based, and operating in this way restricts their scope and scale (Borner, Brunetti, and Weber, 1992).[6] Instability also means that property rights are not secured, long-term investments are discouraged, and much capital of wealthy families is held in other countries.

Political instability can have several causes, including the absence of the norm of peacefully turning power over from one group to another. Another is deep internal divisions along ethnic or religious lines. The need to balance among interests and to avoid or cope with violence distracts the attention of leaders and diverts resources from development. In the extreme, internal upheavals can derail a country's progress and sometimes an entire region's. That happened to Russia in 1917, and the Communist Party's takeover in 1949 delayed China's joining the fast-growth bandwagon in East Asia for 30 years. Even the ending of a stultifying system has not brought relief to all; the collapse of the Soviet empire unfroze a host of latent conflicts from the Balkans through the Caucasus to central Asia. There is an abundant supply of such conflicts in South Asia and Africa. Islamic fundamentalists came to power in Iran in 1978, producing a situation that remains unstable; they might soon come to power in Algeria and even all the Maghreb, and the Egyptian government is under attack.

The incidence of such divisions varies widely within the set of sixteen large countries, as shown in Table 2: Nigeria has suffered an ethnically

---

5. How can this observation be reconciled with the one above that there seems to be no growth penalty on the average from having authoritarian governance? One answer is that some authoritarian states are highly growth-focused (notably in East Asia), produce results, and enjoy longer tenure.

6. Variations in the size of the circle of trust are illustrated by southern Italians, overseas Chinese, and Japanese. Banfield (1958), in the mid-1950s, found the inhabitants in a town in Calabria unwilling to extend trust and to cooperate beyond the nuclear family, and Putnam (1993) has recently documented the ancient origins of this behavior pattern in that part of Italy. The overseas Chinese characteristically extend trust relations only to the extended family. The Japanese have reached farther, not only through the custom of adopting talented young males into the family but by conceiving of a firm with unrelated workers as an extended family.

TABLE 2

Selected Social Capability Indicators in Sixteen Most Populous Developing Nations

	Internal ethnic/religious/political divisions	Number of coups and coup attempts (1980–present)	Income distribution[a]	Average years of schooling of those over age 25 (1960)	Average years of schooling of those over age 25 (1985) (* = 1990)	Manufacturing growth[b]	Manufacturing export growth[c]
China	+	0	6.5	n.a.[d]	4.80*	3.1	10.6
India	–	0	4.7	1.43	3.05	0.9	7.0
Indonesia	=	0	4.9	1.11	3.75	1.3	8.4
Brazil	=	0	32	2.64	3.49	1.6	5.7
USSR/Russia	–	2	n.a.	7.21	9.59	n.a.	n.a.
Nigeria	–	4	4.7	n.a.	1.20*	n.a.	0.8
Pakistan	–	0	4.0	0.63	1.92	1.1	6.1
Bangladesh	=	1	14	0.79	1.97	0.2	5.8
Mexico	=	0	n.a.	2.41	4.42	1.0	12.1
Vietnam	=	0	n.a.	n.a.	4.60*	n.a.	n.a.
S. Korea	–	0	n.a.	3.30	7.85	3.1	21.4
Philippines	–	6	7.3	3.78	6.48	0.8	7.5
Turkey	–	1	n.a.	1.95	3.29	1.1	9.0
Thailand	+	3	8.3	3.45	5.08	1.3	19.0
Iran	–	1	n.a.	0.45	3.28	0.4	4.0
Egypt	=	0	n.a.	n.a.	2.80*	n.a.	0.3

SOURCES: World Bank (1992); Barro and Lee (1993a); author's estimates.

NOTES: Countries are listed in order from most to least populous. + indicates that a factor is major, = that it is significant, and – that it is minor.
[a] Ratio of income share of highest 20% of households to that of lowest 20% (varying dates in 1980s–1991).
[b] Growth in manufacturing times 1970 manufacturing share of GDP.
[c] Growth rate in merchandise exports times increase in manufacturing of exports (1970–91).
[d] N.a. means "not available."

based civil war, Pakistan split up (with the surviving part retaining ethnic divisions), and India, Turkey, the Philippines, Iran, Mexico, Egypt, and Russia have ethnically or religiously based troubles of varying degrees of seriousness. Korea is divided on political ideology. But China, Thailand, Brazil, and Bangladesh are relatively free of such divisions. It seems unlikely that many of them will have been healed by 2020; some might have worsened and new ones emerged.

There are other sources of political instability, such as a widespread sense that the regime in power is illegitimate, perhaps because of the way it came to power, or shortcomings in performance or personal failings of leaders. Whatever their sources, Barro (1991) and others have found that the incidence of assassinations, revolutions, and military coups has hurt later growth.[7] Table 2 shows that seven of the sixteen countries have had coups or coup attempts since 1980; only one of the seven (Thailand) has been a high-growth country, while three of the low performers (Nigeria, Bangladesh, and Iran) were so afflicted.

The Distribution of Income and Wealth

A large and persistent difference in income between the rich and the poor is an indicator of a lack of civic-mindedness in the population and imprudence in the elite. Extreme inequalities can hamper growth through efforts by the more numerous to dispossess the rich, the only class capable of substantial investment, giving them an incentive to move their money abroad; through actions to upset regimes that condone such inequalities, actions that tend to sustain poverty; and through the waste of potential human capital.[8]

---

7. Barro (1991) found that political instability, measured by the incidence of coups and assassinations, hurt growth. Alesina, Ozler, Roubini, and Swagel (1992) also found that political instability hurts growth. In addition, "the most common and widespread" problems in a survey of institutional effectiveness in developing countries were political upheavals, wars, and other causes of uncertainty (Israel, 1987). Londregan and Poole (1992) find that a growth inhibitor is non-constitutional rule rather than coups per se, and that non-constitutional rule reduces average growth rates by 0.5 percent a year. Ahmed (1988) notes that three of the four first ("righteous") caliphs of Islam were assassinated while performing prayers, and henceforth "whatever achievements might be made in art, literature and architecture, Muslim politics would display signs of instability."

8. Both Alesina and Rodrik (1991) and Persson and Tabellini (1991) find a negative relationship between income inequality and growth. Persson and Tabellini (1992) also find that a more unequal distribution of income is bad for growth specifically in democracies. Alesina and Perotti (1993) find that income inequality hurts growth by increasing political instability and thereby decreasing investment. Their index of socio-political instability contains, for the period 1960–85, the number of politically motivated assassinations, the number of people killed in domestic mass violence incidents, the number of

A common characteristic of the high-growth countries of East Asia is their relatively equal distribution of income (Birdsall, Ross, and Sabot, 1994), a pattern at variance with the long-accepted view that inequality is necessary at early stages of growth. War had a leveling effect in Japan, South Korea, and Taiwan. Land was then redistributed, with compensation, an action that contributed to social cohesiveness and possibly to their later high growth. This relative equality was reinforced by the rapid and wide extension of educational opportunities. In contrast, Latin America has a much less equal income distribution.[9]

Countries that are providing education universally, increasingly at the secondary level, are laying the basis for more equal incomes in the coming generation. This will pay off in faster productivity growth and probably greater political stability.[10] In contrast, those countries that allocate a larger part of the nation's educational budget to higher education of a small elite, as do some African countries, or that neglect education in parts of the country, as Brazil and India do, invite future slower growth and trouble.

Table 2 presents data on income distribution for nine of the sixteen countries. The negative standout is Brazil. Bangladesh, Thailand, and the Philippines also have more skewed distributions than others.

Level of Education

Barro (1991) gave a boost to the importance of educational attainment in finding a strong association between the initial level of education in 98 countries and later growth rates. The high levels of school enrollment in East Asia in 1960 and the low ones in sub-Saharan Africa and the oil-exporting countries relative to their real incomes in that year predict their later growth.

Human capital, measured in terms of years of schooling, is increasing monotonically in workforces in the developing countries. Between 1960 and 1985, the average years of education (of workers over 25 years of age) in their labor forces increased by nearly two years (to 3.6 in 1985) and will keep increasing steadily while schooling attainment in the rich countries

---

successful and of unsuccessful coups, and a dummy variable for the value of democracy. Among our sixteen countries, they rate eleven of them in increasing order of political stability over that period: Nigeria, Pakistan, Thailand, Bangladesh, Turkey, Egypt, Brazil, Iran, the Philippines, Mexico, and India.

9. The ratio of total incomes of the richest 20 percent of the population to the poorest 20 percent is 4 to 11 times in a set of East Asian countries and 11 to 26 times in a set of Latin American ones.

10. Birdsall, Ross, and Sabot (1994) estimate that the net effect of broadly based educational expansion is to narrow income inequalities and that lower inequalities, controlling for the direct effects of education, have a significant effect on growth.

will grow more slowly (Barro and Lee, 1993; Lau, Jamison, and Jouat, 1991). The trend in school enrollments and the large differences in years of schooling between young and old workers today will add about three years to average years of schooling in the workforces of the developing nations by 2020, bringing this measure of their human capital to nearly seven years. School attainment differences between the OECD nations and the less developed ones should shrink from over five years in 1985 to around three years in 2020.

Many investigators have found both the private and the social returns to investment in education to be high.[11] If an additional year of average schooling in the workforce produces 5 percent more GDP (and this rate of return is sustained as educational levels grow), the projected overall increase of about three years by 2020 should result in 15 percent more output. This amounts to an annual contribution to per capita growth over the period of 0.5 percent. (However, this will not be additive to the past contribution of schooling to growth—possible threshold effects aside—for it continues a trend.)

Although a high level of schooling appears necessary for high incomes, it clearly is not sufficient. The Soviet Union well illustrates this point. At the end of its existence, the average level of schooling of the workforce was well above that of Italy, but it was a much poorer country. The Philippines has an average schooling attainment level close to that of South Korea, but it had one-third the income level in 1990.

Women's education deserves much more attention than it has heretofore received. It has several social benefits: educated women contribute more as workers, have fewer children, and focus their (better educated) talents on a smaller number of children, who are then healthier and build more human capital.[12] In East Asia, the difference between female and male enrollment rates is lower than in other developing regions, although it is converging in all regions, albeit slowly in southern and western Asia and in much of Africa. One consequence is that a mother's time available

11. Barro and Lee (1993b) find that an additional year of secondary schooling for males raises the subsequent growth rate by 1.34 percent. Increasing a year of secondary schooling probably incurs an ongoing annual cost of about 1 percent of GDP (including the opportunity cost to the student); this implies a social rate of return of around 13 percent, a figure consistent with cost-benefit studies on education in less developed countries (Schultz, 1988). Lau, Jamison, Liu, and Rivkin (1993) find a threshold effect of education between three and four years per person in the labor force and that each additional year beyond adds about 5 percent to output.

12. Summers and Thomas (1993) calculate that providing 1,000 Pakistani girls with one extra year of schooling would raise their market productivity 10 to 15 percent and would avert nearly 700 births and close to 50 infant deaths.

per child increased between 1965 and 1985 by 2.5 times in South Korea, 1.4 times in Brazil, and 1.24 times in Kenya, but only 1.04 times in Pakistan (Birdsall, 1993). Overall workforce schooling attainment differences between East Asia and several other regions are small, but perhaps women's education combined with smaller families is contributing an underestimated amount to human capital growth in East Asia (Schultz, 1994).

Table 2 shows the schooling attainment in the workforces of twelve out of the sixteen countries in 1960 and 1985 (with 1990 figures for the four other nations). The standouts in the level of education in 1985 were Russia and South Korea. As to trends, the positive standouts are South Korea, Iran, Indonesia, Mexico, and the Philippines. World Bank data also suggest that China will be among the leaders in educational gains (World Bank, 1993b). The educational laggards in this set are Brazil, Bangladesh, and Turkey.

The return of people from abroad with human capital can be an efficient way to acquire it. Some countries are attracting back the capital and skills of their diasporas even if not always their citizenship. This is happening to Taiwan, China, and Turkey and is likely to happen increasingly with Mexicans and the large and talented Indian expatriate population. The Filipino community overseas could also do much for the Philippines under the right circumstances.

Building Individual and Organizational Competencies by Doing

Managerial capitalism entails learning how to coordinate many activities, work with precision, use complicated accounting systems, do marketing, and so on. Countries like India, China, and the Soviet Union that were long economically isolated denied valuable learning experiences to their people. Now things are changing. Most strikingly, in China, millions of people are learning the rudiments (and more) of managerial capitalism through private enterprises and through the many thousands of town and village collective enterprises that have been created. Fortunately, there are many older Chinese who remember from the period before 1949 how capitalist institutions work, and Chinese from Hong Kong and elsewhere are bringing expertise as well as capital.

Competencies are built in large part through activities that require coordinating many people and things and through learning curve economies (for example, those often gained in manufacturing). Competencies are also gained by exporting; from firms operating abroad, especially in more advanced nations; through inward direct investment by firms based in advanced nations; by the transfer home of skills of members of diasporas (including students educated abroad); and by copying practices in other nations. Advances in information technology and the decreased cost of travel are speeding these processes.

Learning by doing, like schooling, builds human capital.[13] Lucas (1988, 1993) suggests that well-known processes of learning at the factory level can be generalized to an entire economy, with some activities producing a high rate of skill acquisition and others a low rate; therefore, changes in the mix of goods produced will affect the learning rate. For rapid learning to be sustained, new goods must continue to be introduced. In this situation, a powerful motivator is to be an exporter where producers face the great wide world rather than smaller domestic markets. This view is consistent with growth regressions that usually give significant explanatory power to trade shares.

Learning can occur in the conduct of any activity, but the coordination of many different activities is probably greatest in manufacturing (in contrast to most agricultural, mining, and service activities in developing countries). Table 2 shows indices of the growth of manufacturing and of the export of manufactures in most of the sixteen large countries during 1970–91. South Korea and China are at the top on the first measure; South Korea, China, Thailand, Indonesia, Mexico, and Turkey are high on the second one. Of the countries with available data, at the low end are Bangladesh and Iran on both measures and Nigeria and Egypt on exports.

Although foreign direct investment (FDI) comprises a small part of total capital in most countries, it presumably is high-leverage capital because of the associated know-how and technologies that flow with it. In this sense it is a builder of social capability. Although the flow of FDI is still overwhelmingly among the developed countries (about 80 percent), this pattern is changing. In 1991, 34 countries made 82 major changes to their FDI laws, 80 of them less restrictive (World Bank, 1992). Most of the sixteen largest countries reduced barriers to FDI in the past decade, and none raised them. It is safe to predict that the coming decades will see a great increase in FDI to these countries.[14]

The successful East Asian economies have been attentive to building institutions. Several have built competent and honest bureaucracies, sup-

---

13. Inkeles and Smith (1974) judged that the two most important factors in creating "modern man" are education and factory experience.

14. The developing countries' share of world FDI rose to 25 percent in 1991 and possibly to 30 percent in 1992 (*Economist*, Mar. 27, 1993, p. 18). Japan's and South Korea's development shows that a high level of FDI is not necessary for rapid growth, but both made great efforts to study foreign methods and to acquire foreign technology through licensing.

ported the growth of small and medium-sized businesses, created legal and regulatory environments favorable to business, and set up deliberation councils that bring business and government together, thereby helping in the transmission of information (Campos and Root, 1993).[15]

Health

There is a two-way relation between health and development. In one direction, healthy workers lose less work time from disease, healthy children learn more rapidly, and less money is spent on treating avoidable illnesses. So policies to improve health help development. In the other direction, with higher incomes there are more resources for public health measures, and a key source of growth, increased schooling, strongly improves health; this is especially true of the education of women (Summers and Thomas, 1993). Income distribution also matters greatly; the prevalence of poverty and per capita spending on public health account for cross-country variations in life expectancy (World Bank, 1993b).

In the last 30 years, life expectancy in the developing world increased from about 50 to 63 years, and child mortality fell by more than one-half, with the rate of decrease of infant mortality increasing in the 1980s. Despite these improvements, there are still large gaps between the developed countries and most of the underdeveloped ones, especially sub-Saharan Africa, India, the Middle East, and some other parts of Asia. A study of the worldwide distribution of disabilities and early deaths showed that about 35 percent came from communicable and easily preventable diseases in 1990 (60 percent in sub-Saharan Africa).

Continuation of the current trend will bring life expectancies in most of Asia, Latin America, and the Middle East to the level of the developed countries in several decades. The gap in India and sub-Saharan Africa will narrow but will still be large. The burdens of disease will be much reduced, and the economic benefits could be substantial.

The spread of AIDS poses the only serious contrary factor (or at least the only one known now; unknown diseases might emerge). The World Bank estimates "a slowing of growth of income per capita by an average 0.6 percent per year in the ten worst-affected countries in Sub-Saharan Africa" (World Bank, 1993b). It estimates that the number of infected persons outside of the developed and formerly socialist countries will grow

---

15. The World Bank's report (1993a) on the East Asian "miracle" attributes the apparently greater success of industrial policy in the northeast Asian countries and the markedly lower success of such policies in Malaysia, Thailand, and Indonesia to the superior quality of bureaucrats in the former set of countries and their insulation from political and economic interference.

from 7.4 million in 1990 to 25 million in 2000, with a very uneven distribution internationally. (In sub-Saharan Africa, the growth is from 5.8 to 12 million.) Aside from medical advances that would provide a cure and/or a vaccine, much depends on uncertain changes in sexual practices.

AIDS notwithstanding, the continued trajectory of past improvements will result in substantial convergence in the health status of most regions with the developed world in the next several decades.

Population Growth

Population growth can affect economic output both positively and negatively: more people can have a positive effect on output as a complement to abundant land and through economies of scale. But more people can also have a negative effect on output through the dilution of physical capital per worker and the spreading of mothers' attention per child (in effect, a dilution of human capital formation). Although high population growth has often been blamed for the persistence of poverty, on the argument that capital dilution dominates the positive factors, regression analyses of the effect of population growth on economic growth do not consistently support that view (Levine and Renelt, 1992). Probably only when population growth rates are very high do the negatives clearly outweigh the positives. What does this view imply for the world's growth prospect?

To the extent that population growth might have been a negative factor in the past, it will be much less of one virtually everywhere. The fertility rate in the developing world has declined from an average of six children per woman in the mid-1960s to four now (Population Information Program, 1992). The decline has been dramatic in some countries: in ten to fifteen years it plummeted 50 percent in Thailand, 46 percent in Indonesia, 40 percent in Colombia, 31 percent in Morocco, and 21 percent in Turkey. What is even more striking (especially given traditional beliefs) is that fertility over this period declined 26 percent in Botswana, 35 percent in Kenya, and 18 percent in Zimbabwe. These rates of decline are much more rapid than experienced by Europe during its demographic transition. Surveys of the desired number of children show that "in virtually every country outside of sub-Saharan Africa, desired fertility is below three children per woman. In a few countries . . . [it] has reached or fallen below replacement-level fertility of about 2.1 children per woman" (Population Information Program, 1992). However, in Africa, the desired number is above five. "Desired," of course, is not the same as actual, especially in Latin America, but both desired and actual levels are falling everywhere. These observations support lower projections of future population growth (Westhoff, 1991).

The rate of world population growth has shrunk from 2.1 percent per year in the late 1960s to 1.7 percent per year now and in the middle World Bank projection will average 1.4 percent to 2020 (World Bank, 1993b). This would take the world population from 5.3 billion in 1990 to 8.0 billion in 2020, with 90 percent of the increase to take place in sub-Saharan Africa, Asia, and Latin America (World Bank, 1991).

Of the sixteen large-population developing countries, those that stand out with high projected rates are Iran, with well over a doubling of population, and Nigeria and Pakistan, which are expected to double. This is a reason for expecting that their growth will be depressed through the dilution of physical and human capital. The outlook for the other thirteen countries is much better on this score—unless the high absolute (but modest and shrinking relative) increases in China, India, Indonesia, and Bangladesh engender inefficiencies and costs from high population densities. But there is no convincing evidence that high population density hurts growth. Many of the ills often attributed to high density or population growth, such as damage to the environment, are largely a consequence of poverty and the political disorder that often accompanies it.

Social Capability Positives and Negatives

With the exception of population changes and schooling as a proxy for human capital, there is as yet no good analytic way to incorporate social capability variables into growth projections. There is, however, a pattern of clustering: at the positive end are found South Korea, Thailand, China, and Indonesia, countries that on social capability grounds should (continue to) do relatively well, while at the other end are Nigeria, Iran, and Pakistan, countries that one should expect to (continue to) do relatively poorly.

Higher Projected Growth

Some Heuristic Arguments

Over the past 30 years, the mean per capita growth rate in the developing world was 2 percent a year and the standard deviation was also about 2 percent (Easterly, King, Levine, and Rebelo, 1994).[16] This implies that

---

16. *Levels* of GDP are expressed in 1990 purchasing power parity (PPP) units. This measure raises the relative level of less developed countries compared with relative values based on exchange rates because the non-traded services of poor countries are systematically higher in international prices than in their domestic ones. Therefore, a downward adjustment in PPP-based *growth rates* relative to exchange rate–based growth rates is needed.

TABLE 3

Selected Variables for Fast and Slow Growers,
Averages for 1960 –89

Variable	Average for fast growers	Average for slow growers
Share of investment in GDP	0.23	0.17
Secondary school enrollment rate, 1960	0.30	0.10
Primary school enrollment rate, 1960	0.90	0.54
Ratio of government consumption to GDP	0.16	0.12
Inflation rate	12.34	31.13
Black-market exchange rate premium	3.57	57.15
Ratio of exports to GDP	0.32	0.23

SOURCE: Levine and Renelt (1992).

the mean difference between the above-average growers ("fast") and the below-average ones ("slow") was about 2.8 percent a year. Some of the variables that differed between the fast and the slow growers are shown in Table 3.

Looking ahead, it seems hardly possible for the fast growers on the extreme right tail of the distribution to do much better, although some other nations might join (or replace) them in that league.[17] (China remains at such a low level of development that it seems capable of sustaining around 5 percent real growth for several more decades.) Improvement must come from countries in the left and center of the past distribution. My hypothesis is that the improvements posited above will result in a right-ward shift of the mean in the future by an amount equivalent to one-half the standard deviation of the past distribution, that is, a 1 percent increase, to 3 percent a year. This view also implies convergence within the group of developing countries.

The 1991 *World Development Report* (World Bank, 1991) presented an estimate of the differences to be expected in GDP growth rates with variations in domestic policies or in the global economic climate. It is reproduced in Table 4. For the economic climate, the parameters were world trade, capital flows, the health of major financial institutions, the macroeconomic policies of the industrial countries, the prevalence of crises and conflict within and among countries, the course of technology

---

17. Easterly, Kremer, Pritchett, and Summers (1993) find that the correlation of growth rates across successive decades is only 0.2 to 0.3.

TABLE 4

World Bank Projections for Changes in GDP Growth Rates

Domestic policies	Global economic climate		
	Poor	Good	Very good
Very good	1.0%	1.5%	2.0%
Good	−1.0	Central case	0.5
Poor	−3.0	−2.0	−1.0

SOURCE: World Bank (1992, p. 147).

development and its accessibility, oil prices, and environmental hazards. The "central" case assumed moderately favorable values for these parameters. The domestic policies parameters are similar to those discussed here. This assessment is consistent with the hypothesis of a 1 percent improvement in mean growth largely stemming from improvements in domestic factors.

Further support for improvements of this magnitude is provided by a growth model developed by Lau and Kim (1994) and applied to South Korea. Its most salient features are the treatment of macroeconomic stability, the growth of world trade along with the country's openness to trade, the share of exports to total output, the growth in physical capital and R&D capital, changes in the average schooling level in the workforce, and the rate of privatization. It shows the combined effect of changes in all policy parameters in both a positive and a negative direction to be 0.5 percent each way from the past trend, for a difference of 1 percent a year between consistently good and consistently bad policies.

An upper bound for the growth of any nation over the long term is probably the 5 percent a year achieved by the East Asians; at least it has never before been achieved for so long a period. Assume that the currently non-rich countries can average 3 percent annual per capita real growth over the next three decades. This average consists of a set of countries, largely East Asian, with above-average social capabilities, who will probably do better than this, 4 to 5 percent annually, and a set below average, largely in the core part of the Islamic world and in sub-Saharan Africa, who will do worse, perhaps 1 to 2 percent (which would, nonetheless, be an improvement for most of them).

Consider the potential impact of China and a few other high/medium countries that stand a good chance of continuing to do well. China's weight in the world economy is much greater than in the past, and if it grows at 4.5 percent per capita over the next several decades, it *alone* will contribute 1.5 percent a year to the overall growth rate of the non-rich world.[18]

Consider also India. Although its growth prospects do not seem quite as bright as those of China because of more modest social capabilities, if it were to have 3 percent annual per capita growth, it would contribute about 0.5 percent to the per capita growth rate of the entire non-rich world.

The potential growth contribution of these two nations plus other rapidly growing ones in East Asia could contribute nearly 3 percent a year per capita to the overall developing country total. Six nations in East and South Asia now produce nearly one-half of the output of the developing world, a far larger share than earlier. Moreover, as long as they grow faster than the others, they will become progressively weightier in the world economy. Even if their growth rates taper off, as is to be expected as they converge on the leaders, by then their weight in the world economy will be so high that world growth is likely to keep advancing briskly.

A View of the Next Ten Years

The World Bank (1994) has recently published a forecast of world economic growth to 2003 that is consistent with the perspective of this paper. It shows the developing economies increasing their annual rate of growth by 1.3 percent between 1981–90 (when the rate was 3.5 percent) and 1994–2003 (when the Bank projects it will be 4.8 percent). Allowing for declining population growth, this is about a 1.5 percent annual increase per capita. Most of the improvement occurs in sub-Saharan Africa, Latin America, and the Middle East and North Africa, regions that were in the left tail or middle of the past growth distribution.

In sub-Saharan Africa, better policies, better terms of trade, and an assumed recovery in South Africa account for the projected improvement; even so, it only moves the region from a negative 1 percent a year per capita in the 1980s to a positive 1 percent from 1994 to 2003. In Latin America, improved policies, higher exports, and private capital inflows result in about a 1.3 percent per capita improvement between the two periods (from 0.4 percent during 1981–90 to 1.7 percent during 1994–2003). In the Middle East and North Africa, better policies, better petroleum prices, and, perhaps, less conflict in the region are responsible for the gain; all this is very uncertain, but the projection is for a 3 percent per capita improvement (from − 2.2 percent to 0.9 percent).

18. For a growth projection of the Chinese economy to 2020, see Lau (1994). The average of 8 percent annual growth projected in that paper, which is based on exchange rate values, is equivalent to about 5 percent per capita growth in a PPP metric.

In the non-improving regions, East Asia continues on its fast track; eastern Europe/central Asia picks up from its early 1990s trough, but not much from its 1980s average, although its growth rate might reach 4–5 percent a year by the end of the decade; and South Asia continues at a little over 3 percent per year per capita.

This projection is sensitive to the assumed performance of the OECD countries. Their macroeconomic policies and openness to trade, and consequently their growth, strongly influence the developing regions' performance. In an alternative low scenario, there is no aggregate improvement over the 1980s.

Growth Prospects for the Sixteen Large Countries

Based on their performance histories and estimated social capabilities, Table 5 shows a projection of the large-population developing countries' prospects for 2020 (including in 2020 total output adjusted for population

TABLE 5
Growth Prospects for Sixteen Most Populous Developing Nations

Growth category	Per capita level (thousands of dollars)		Total output (billions of 1990 dollars)	
	1990	2020	1990	2020
High (4.5% per capita)				
China	1,950	6,600	2,500	10,000
Indonesia	2,350	8,800	400	2,100
Thailand	4,600	17,000	250	1,300
Vietnam	700	2,600	50	300
Korea (N+S avg.)	5,000	19,000	330	1,600
Medium (3% per capita)				
India	1,150	2,800	1,000	3,600
Brazil	4,800	12,000	720	2,600
Russia (from year 2000)	7,000	13,000	1,000	2,000
Bangladesh	1,050	1,600	120	300
Mexico	6,000	15,000	540	2,000
Philippines	2,300	5,600	140	525
Turkey	5,000	12,000	280	1,000
Egypt	3,100	7,500	150	600
Low (1.5% per capita)				
Pakistan	1,800	4,300	190	900
Nigeria	1,400	2,200	160	500
Iran	4,400	6,800	240	1,000
	Average		Total	
	3,288	8,550	8,070	30,325

SOURCES: World Bank (1992) and author's estimates.

growth increases). Inevitably, there are some debatable growth assumptions and assignments to categories in this table. Some will do better and some worse than is shown here. But there are good reasons for accepting the overall pattern.

Today's rich countries will probably average about 1.5 percent per capita. On this view, the global per capita growth rate will be about 2.1 percent to 2020, about the same as in the past 30 years but with a future bias towards the developing countries. Total world economic output will depend also on population growth. With a workforce growth rate of 1.7 percent a year (and population growth of 1.4 percent), world output growth would then be about 3.8 percent. World gross output should about triple from 1990's level of $22 trillion to about $65 trillion in 2020.

On this projection, the United States, China, and the countries comprising today's European Union will be about tied for first in total output. Less populous Japan will have a smaller total output but might have the highest GDP per capita. Today, the rich countries produce about 60 percent of world output; their share falls to about 40 percent in 2020. The U.S. share falls from about 24 percent to 16 percent.

It is perhaps more illuminating to view this future in a people rather than a country perspective. Today's rich countries have about 800 million people, 15 percent of the world total. In 2020, another 2 billion people, about 25 percent of the world total, then about 8 billion in number, will have crossed today's per capita GDP threshold of about $8,000 a year that distinguishes developed from less developed countries.[19] The share of the world population living in the poorest countries, those with below $2,000 per capita GDP, will decline greatly, and to a lesser degree, so will the absolute number of poor people. About half of 1990's world population lived in countries below this poverty threshold, most of them in China and India. Despite the prediction that there will be many more people in the Islamic core region and sub-Saharan Africa, by 2020 probably only about one-fourth of the world's people will live in countries below the $2,000 threshold.

One might argue that the most relevant measure of such changes is not the *absolute level* of incomes, but *relative* incomes. Both have been addressed here. Not only will billions of people move away from a condition of absolute poverty, but they will gain relative to those in today's rich countries.

---

19. The conventionally accepted income level between rich and non-rich countries will move progressively up from today's $8,000 figure. This analysis retains that threshold throughout.

Potential Obstacles

Like any such social forecast, this future cannot be rigorously demonstrated, and it will certainly be wrong in detail. It might be off the mark more widely not only because bad policies persist and social incapacities are more of a drag than I assume, but also because of internal political instabilities and wars, an impacted world trade regime, or energy or environmental constraints. These are likely "show-slowers," but they seem unlikely to be "show-stoppers."

Energy Supply

A World Bank report says that "under present productivity trends, and given projected population increases, developing country output would rise by 4%–5% a year between 1990 and 2030 and by the end of the period would be about five times what it is today. . . . If environmental pollution and degradation were to rise in step with such a rise in output, the result would be appalling environmental pollution and damage" (World Bank, 1992).

A tripling of world output within 30 years would require a large increase in energy supply, although not a proportional one. World economic output increased 3.5-fold in 1960–90 while world energy consumption increased 2.6-fold, with the difference, about 1 percent per year, reflecting a near-leveling in the use of oil since the 1973 price shock. Is the supply of energy during this period, allowing both for the depletion of resources and for advances in technology, likely to be elastic enough to be compatible with a tripling of world output? With the possible exception of liquid fuels, the cost schedule of energy supply should be fairly flat. The real, delivered price of coal to deep-water ports around the world has been fairly constant; nuclear power costs have risen not because uranium is more costly but because of safety requirements; and natural gas use is expanding rapidly. If energy use continues to grow 1 percent a year less than output it will, on the projection here, about double from 1990 to 2020, from about 340 to 700 quadrillion Btu's. Some combination of coal (environmental constraints permitting), natural gas, nuclear energy, and renewables should be able easily to meet this demand (Starr, Searl, and Alpert, 1992).[20]

---

20. Starr, Searl, and Alpert (1992) project global energy use to 2020 as being about 700 quads on the assumption of "current conversion efficiencies" and a lower level of about 550 quads assuming a "full conservation concept," the latter level being the maximum amount of conservation that could be "implemented without inhibiting economic growth." They see no sharp increases in supply costs until well beyond this period, with the possible exception of oil.

As for oil, its real price (in a weighted basket of the U.S. dollar, deutsche mark, and yen) is now as low as at the time of the first oil shock in 1973. The memory of past crises and economic losses and the possibility of future ones are motivating oil-conserving advances in technology and the continued substitution of other factors of production for oil, even though the price has fallen; these forces will probably keep oil use growing less than output for as long as the Persian Gulf remains a dominant source of supply, which means for a very long time. However, a tripling of total world output would induce a large increase in the demand for transportation fuels. For example, if China's incidence of motorization in 2020 is similar to Europe's when it had China's projected income level for that year ($6,600 per capita), it will have about 250 million vehicles, more than North America or Europe has today.

On the supply side, advances in technology are lowering the cost of producing known oil deposits, but the rate of discovery of major ones has been very low for an unprecedentedly long time. Unless this pattern changes, the world will gradually have to rely more on the large reserves of the Middle East and, at some point, on conversion to liquids from gases and solids (Masters, Root, and Attanasi, 1991).[21] How much more costly synthetic liquid fuels might be in two or three decades is not knowable; today the cost schedule escalates sharply, but it might not then. In any case, oil has a much smaller share of the energy market than it did in 1973 and comprises only a 1.5 percent share of world value-added; the drag on world growth of gradually higher liquid fuel costs would be minuscule.[22]

In sum, there is little reason to believe that energy supplies will be a significant drag on this prospect.

Environment

Environmental impacts stemming from growth are of several kinds: pollution of various media, losses of natural beauty, losses of species, and disruption of some of the earth's protective gases. I do not attempt to assess the net welfare consequences of a world in which billions of people will be better off in many ways, but worse off in some others. That is well beyond my competence. I address a more limited question: From what we

21. There is also reason to believe that reported oil reserves in the Middle East have been exaggerated (Brinegar, 1994).

22. However, in the next decade, world reliance on Middle East oil will increase; therefore, the potential loss to world output from sudden supply disruptions, as happened several times in the 1970s, will grow again. And because marginal uses of oil are of higher value than they were in the oil shocks of the 1970s, losses from potential disruptions have not fallen in proportion to the decline in oil's share in the world economy.

know now, are environmental damages, or rather their mitigation, likely to seriously impede the growth prospect described above?

A useful starting point is to recognize that environmental problems are of two types: local, and wider, including global. As a World Bank report observes (World Bank, 1992), some problems decrease as income increases, like public sanitation services. Some problems worsen and then improve as incomes rise, like air and water pollution, along with deforestation and encroachments on natural habitats. As incomes grow, after some point, as other needs are met, the demand for a cleaner environment grows and countries have the resources and are able to meet these demands. Along these lines, Grossman and Krueger (1994) have found the peak pollution level occurring at a GDP per capita level of $2,700 for dissolved oxygen and $11,600 for cadmium. Finally, some environmental problems continue to get worse as incomes rise, like emissions of carbon, nitrogen oxides, and municipal waste. But such increases are not inevitable. They are amenable to policy actions.

Improvements come at a cost. The World Bank (1992) estimates that the additional cost of local environmental protection could be 2 to 3 percent of GDP for developing countries by the end of the 1990s, about one year's growth for a representative country. It is more likely to be paid by the fast-growers, who will both experience more environmental damage and have more resources with which to control it than the slow-growers. Beyond the end of the 1990s, there will be additional costs of local environmental protection. Perhaps a permanent "tax" rate equivalent to 2 to 3 percent of GDP or more will need to be paid indefinitely.

China, as usual, poses an exceptional challenge. It suffers from severe environmental problems: air pollution, water pollution, and deforestation among them. One estimate is that annual losses from pollution and ecosystem degradation in 1989 were higher than the government's total expenditure on education, culture, science, and health care (Smil, 1993). China is at an income level where damage can be expected to get worse before it gets better. China will have to spend increasing amounts on mitigation, which will slow output growth, but with a growth potential of 4 to 5 percent annually, it will have the needed resources. Its people are better fed, living longer, more educated, and better housed than ever before.

The second type involves problems of wider geographic scope, including global ones. One now receiving much attention is the possible contribution of certain gases, especially carbon dioxide, to global warming via the "greenhouse effect." The biggest carbon contributors today are the developed countries, but those adding the most in the future will be several rapidly growing developing countries, notably China and India. There are many uncertainties, both of physics and economics. The question of concern here is whether actions might have to be taken on environmental grounds that would seriously damage the bright prospects for growth.

Several points are clear: international cooperation would be needed to get effective action; slow adaptation is much less costly than rapid; and the international trading of emissions levels would substantially reduce costs (Weyant, 1993). An analysis conducted by the Energy Modeling Forum concluded that for various control scenarios aimed at stabilizing the emissions rate of carbon by 2040, world GDP would be lowered by about 2.0 to 2.5 percent per year, plus or minus up to 1 percent. "Thus, if climate change turns out to be a very serious problem, it can be controlled without eliminating or even noticeably reducing long-run economic growth" (Weyant, 1993, p. 36).[23] However, these estimates assume that the reductions occur in an efficient way through, for example, a carbon tax in each region.

It is easy to imagine that an efficient process would not be adopted. The Rio formula, which calls on each country to stabilize its emissions, falls relatively lightly on the slow-growing rich countries but much more heavily on the fast-growing developing ones, especially those who use a lot of coal. For China, an OECD estimate of the present value of the loss is around 4 percent of GDP by 2020. This level of spending by China is doubtful. The impacted developing countries would demand compensation, but the process of compensation or assigning emission rights would be formidably difficult (Nordhaus, 1993). An accelerated program using the politicians' favorite command-and-control approach and without international trading of emission rights could result in much more of a drag on growth than these estimates.

The main inference to be drawn from the present state of knowledge is that for there to be a substantial drag on this growth prospect to 2020, global warming would have to require serious action soon and the responses to it would have to be seriously inefficient.

---

23. Manne and Richels (1993) have addressed the uncertainty of the greenhouse effect by conducting a probabilistic analysis based on expert judgments. Using their Global 2000 model, they find the *median* cost of stabilizing global carbon emissions to be 1 percent of gross world product over the next century and the *mean* cost to be 1.5 percent. This is indicative of possible costs in the very long run. Given uncertainty about several parameters, GDP growth rates, elasticity of price-induced substitution, and the rate of autonomous energy efficiency improvements among them, they find that there is a 10 percent probability of the total loss in gross world output being 3 percent of gross world product—less than 1 percent of expected total growth in the next three decades.

Constriction of the International Economic System

Since 1970, world trade has risen an average of 5 percent annually, versus world GDP growth of 3.5 percent. The World Bank projection for the next ten years has world trade growing at almost twice the rate of world output (5.9 percent versus 3.2 percent), a much higher ratio than in the 1974–90 period; this increase is due in large measure to the General Agreement on Tariffs and Trade (GATT) and the North American Free Trade Agreement (NAFTA).

There are, nonetheless, grounds for worrying about the future of trade. Strongly fluctuating exchange rates and the slowdown in world growth since the early 1970s have contributed to the rise of non-tariff barriers. There has been growth of inward-looking forces in many countries, including the United States. Whatever the causes, between 1966 and 1986 the percentage of trade affected by non-tariff measures (not including health- and safety-related ones) increased by 10 percentage points in the United States and Japan and over 30 percentage points in the European Community. It is ironic that this is happening while elites in the developing countries are coming to understand the importance for them of an outward orientation.

The World Bank (1992) estimates that losses from a trade war, compared with a liberal regime, could amount to 3 to 4 percent of world output. In a sensitivity analysis of the international environment for the 1990s (reproduced in Table 4), its "downside scenario" had a higher oil price, GATT not succeeding, financial troubles in the United States and Japan depressing investment and growth in the G-7 countries, and slowed capital flows to the developing countries. It judged the difference between a "very good" and a "poor" global economic climate to imply a 1 to 2 percent a year difference in GDP growth in the 1990s; a poor climate would result in a lower 3 percent a year growth in world output, about 1.5 percent per capita. That difference sustained for long enough could make for a mediocre versus a prosperous world economy.

Beyond ever-present shared benefits, two arguments support the view that the world system will remain relatively open or at least that a major breakdown will be averted. One is the higher ratio of trade to output in virtually all countries, which has raised the stakes in sustaining exports (as rising imports also have for consumers, although they inevitably have greater costs of political organization). The second, more conjecturally, is that most countries want more FDI for the technology and organizational skills that it brings. Because FDI and trade are complements, the rising importance of the former vests more interests in sustaining an open trade regime.

International Conflicts

There seem to be no immediate dangers of major conflict today, but there are many small and costly wars under way from the former Yugoslavia through the Caucasus to central Asia, some of which might lead to larger ones. As for a large war, after a century that saw two devastating ones, it would be foolish to assert that it cannot happen again. One can only observe that the world has not seen a large war in nearly half a century and there are only weak signs of forces that might produce one. But there are potential troubles ahead: Russia is endeavoring, with some successes, to gain influence over the former members of its empire, and no one (including the Russians) can know how far it might try to go. One should not be surprised if a more powerful China presses unsettled territorial grievances—probably later rather than sooner given its focus on getting rich. India already dominates its subcontinent, but when it is more powerful it might endeavor to extend its influence further. Iran is perceived as a danger by Arabs on the other side of the Persian Gulf. And so on.

Wars are tragedies, but do not necessarily derail the economic progress of nations if they have strong social capabilities. This point was amply demonstrated by the recovery of Japan and Germany from the destruction inflicted during World War II. Wider access to nuclear weapons poses the question as to whether some future conflicts might see devastation on a scale never heretofore seen—apart from the destruction of Carthage. That possibility aside, if another major conflict occurs, much would depend on its political aftermath. If it were to be like that after World War I, the projection here would be falsified, but if it were to be like that after World War II, it would be supported.

One development is certain: many newly rich countries will invest significantly in military power. Military investments will occur because of perceived dangers or from tradition, and more resources will be available. It would be most surprising if China, India, and Russia, for example, do not also become major military powers as they become major economic ones. Military spending diverts resources from growth, but if it is no more than a small percentage of GDP, it will not be a large drag, and there is no a priori reason to expect that this sector's share of national income will increase over time.

There will be many profoundly important consequences of a world that experiences something like this economic evolution. Only two are pursued here: implications for democracy and for peace.

Some Implications for Democracy

The fact that several (initially) authoritarian governments in East Asia and Latin America have done well economically has reinforced an old idea that such politics are needed to overcome resistance to growth-favorable policies. But the story on authoritarian versus democratic politics in promoting growth is not simple. Sirowy and Inkeles (1990), surveying the literature on this subject (observing that it has serious shortcomings), found that there was not a well-established tie. In another survey, Przeworski and Limongi (1993) concluded that "we do not know whether democracy fosters or hinders economic growth." However, over a longer span of time the advantage of democracy in securing individual rights to property arguably should result in superior economic peformance (Olson, 1993).

Of more salience for this analysis are the effects of economic growth on politics. The economic gains projected here promise to have enormous political consequences, of which the most important is likely to be the spread and consolidation of democratic forms of government. There are good reasons to expect this. When economic activities are largely independent of political control, the coercive power of government is limited, although government is needed to set and enforce the rules. This effective decentralization of power creates checks to it. As people's livelihoods become independent of the state, as they acquire property, more education, and a level of living beyond that required for subsistence, they have more choices. This limits the capacity of the state and its agents to control their lives. Moreover, as people acquire such means, they want more say on the rules under which they live, and this desire and scope for action enlarges the domain of political freedoms.

Wealth is not a condition for democracy; Bangladesh is proof of this. There are such other correlates as the well-known one involving Protestant societies and perhaps a less well-known one of having been a colony of Great Britain (Lipset, Seong, and Torres, 1993). The perceived link goes far back; Seymour Martin Lipset, whose 1959 book (revised in 1981) *Political Man* first systematically presented data on wealth and democracy, wrote, "From Aristotle down to the present, men have argued that only in a wealthy society in which relatively few citizens lived at the level of real poverty could there be a situation in which the mass of the population intelligently participate in politics and develop the self-restraint necessary to avoid succumbing to the appeals of irresponsible demagogues." Helliwell (1992) has recently investigated the linkage. Starting with 1960 income levels, the effects on later democracy are significant.

The organization Freedom House annually assesses the actual status of two types of democratic rights: political and civil. Political rights include free and fair elections, the opportunity to organize, a real opposition with a realistic chance of coming to power, etc. Civil ones include freedoms of the press, open discussion, and assembly; equal treatment under law; etc. Few people (at least in the West) would disagree that these attributes fairly characterize democracy.

In 1990 there was a 0.96 probability that a randomly selected rich country would be judged "free," rather than "partly free" or "not free." In a combined Freedom House rating system for civil liberties and political rights, only Singapore, out of the 28 countries in 1990 with per capita GDPs over $8,000, was rated less than wholly free (Freedom House, 1993). In recent decades several nations have become politically more pluralistic as they have become wealthier, notably South Korea, Taiwan, Chile, and Mexico.[24]

All the western European countries and those settled by them are free, and almost all are rich. Many non-rich countries are also free or largely so; India, Costa Rica, Uruguay, and Botswana are among them. A regression of income versus democracy that excludes the northwest Europeans and regions of British settlement from the comparison—on the view that the path of history made them both democratic and wealthy—still leaves the wealth-freedom correlation significant at the 5 percent level.[25] The correlation is weakened (remaining significant at the 10 percent level) with the elimination of other former British colonies on the established ground that Britain did a good job of transferring democratic norms and institutions to its colonies.

---

24. Przeworski and Limongi (1993) observe that differential attrition rates of democracies and dictatorships, for instance in their ability to survive crises, present difficulties for statistical analysis and could account for the higher prevalence of democracies among wealthy nations.

25. Lipset (1981) quotes Max Weber as observing that a historically unique concatenation of elements produced both democracy and capitalism in northwest Europe and its English-speaking offspring in America and Australasia. On this reasoning, the northwest Europeans and their English-speaking offspring are removed in this regression. The southern Europeans, notably Spain and Portugal, did not participate in this process, and the later political cultures of their former colonies reflected those of the colonizer at the date of their independence.

Democracies on this analysis have a bright future, but several political analysts, including Huntington (1991), observe that democracy has advanced in waves from the early nineteenth century, with each wave followed by reversals and then new gains. Happily, each reversal did not undo all previous gains; on Huntington's accounting (which differs somewhat from the one used here) the net number of democracies went from zero before 1828 to 59 in 1990. Reversals of democracies can happen again; today, several in the former Soviet Union, Latin America, and Africa look shaky.[26]

The long-term trend, however, is clearly up, and an estimate of future incomes provides a basis for estimating future freedom levels. Given their varying 1990 starting points of income and freedom, and using the 1990 regression between the two conditions, one can project future changes. Assuming a 3 percent average annual growth rate, and assuming that additions to income will add to freedom as much as in the past, the number of "free" countries goes from 67 in 1990 to 85 in 2020, while the number of "not free" shrinks from 53 to 41. (Naturally, if one believes that growth will be slower, but also believes in the wealth/democracy nexus, then this political evolution will take longer.)[27]

In 1990, of the sixteen most populous non-rich nations, only Brazil, South Korea, and Bangladesh were rated as politically "free." In the next generation, allowing for increases in wealth and education, eight of these nations are likely to be rated "free," six as "partly free," and two (down from five in 1990) as "not free."

The Uncertain Implications for Peace

The spread of democracy would have several major consequences, one of which might be a decline in international conflicts.[28] Many scholars have

26. The Freedom House democracy survey for 1993 suggests that the Third Wave is retreating: 42 nations registered a decline in freedom, and 19 registered a gain from the previous year; the proportion of people judged free is the lowest since 1976 (Freedom House, 1993). See also Karatnycky (1993).

27. There is also a strong association of education with democracy. Because education is a major contributor to economic growth as well as presumably directly to democracy, it is difficult to separate out the independent effects of education from those of income growth. But the projected increase in democracies holds given the continued increase in levels of schooling attainment.

28. Insofar as commerce promotes economic growth and therefore democracy and peace, why has trade not shown up in the data more positively? One possibility is that contiguous neighbors both trade more and fight more with each other than noncontiguous ones. However, Polachek (1980) has found evidence that trade and conflict are negatively related.

called attention to the fact that democracies rarely go to war with each other.[29] Doyle (1986) credits Immanuel Kant with the key idea: Republics rest on the consent of citizens; this induces prudence but not abhorrence of war, for wars must be fought for liberal purposes. Liberal states tend to be morally integrated; free speech and communications yield a more accurate perception of foreign peoples and their politics, and this, in turn, leads to understanding and respect. But because non-liberal governments are in a state of aggression with their own people, relations of liberal states with them are suspect. Russett (1993) offers two explanations: The more plausible is that cultural norms of live-and-let-live that operate within democracies are extended internationally to other democracies; the other is that democratic political processes give time to resolve conflicts. In short, democracies have domestic constraints, are cautious about conquest, and have many shared values with other democracies.

This is not a position that holds that democracies are inherently peaceful, for they have had many wars with non-democracies, and a world with both types of societies is not a safe place. However, before World War II, democracies by a modern definition were scarce, often did not share common borders, and therefore had little occasion to come into conflict, whereas today democracies and non-democracies tend to be concentrated geographically. Max Singer and Aaron Wildavsky (1993) have labeled these distinct regional clusters, respectively, "Zones of Peace and Democracy" and "Zones of Turmoil and Development." They define a zone of peace as a region within which international conflict has such a low probability that it can be considered nearly impossible. There are four large ones: North America, western Europe, Australasia, and, marginally, South America (marginal because its democratic norms are not deeply rooted and it contains no rich countries). Zones of turmoil are regions in which few, if any, countries (oil wealth aside) are rich, there are few democracies and those that exist tend not to be deeply rooted, domestic politics are unstable and often violent, and international tensions and hostilities are common. The largest zone of turmoil and development, one predominantly Islamic in culture, stretches from Morocco to central Asia and from southwest Asia

---

29. A starting point here is Babst (1964). Important contributions to this literature have been made by many others, including Rummel (1983) and Doyle (1986). The marginal cases include the War of 1812 between (pre-reform) Britain and the United States (with slavery); the Spanish-American War of 1898 (with Spain nominally democratic); and Germany in 1914 (with some democratic institutions). Civil wars are excluded on the grounds that a common statehood is shared. Britain and several other countries declared war against Finland when it sided with Germany in 1941, but only symbolically; there was no fighting.

to the Balkans. Others are sub-Saharan Africa, the former Soviet Union, South Asia, and East Asia.

Today, three regions might be regarded as nascent zones of peace: north-central Europe, Southeast Asia, and northeast Asia. North-central Europe (Poland, the Czech Republic, Hungary, and Slovakia) has the prospect of becoming an extension of the western European peace zone. Its future seems conditioned on acceptance by the western Europeans and the future character of Russia. Southeast Asia is on a strong growth track, it has experienced decreasing internal and international tensions, and its politics are slowly becoming less authoritarian. Northeast Asia contains two major democracies, Japan and South Korea, and Taiwan has made much progress towards this condition; however, the region also contains the dangerous hermit kingdom North Korea, as well as China and Russia, countries whose future political characters are uncertain and fateful for many peoples.

There are several caveats to the prospect of a more peaceful world. As noted above, many new democracies do not seem stable and might fall back. Another is that the speed with which some nations are becoming rich raises the question as to whether their political character will change as fast as their economic one. Might some countries (China? India?) become powerful while behaving in an atavistic way? This has happened before: Germany became a major industrial power and made much progress towards democracy before Hitler's accession to power; Japan after 75 years of strong economic development and the adoption of many democratic institutions continued to be expansionist and became highly militaristic. And the industrialized Soviet Union remained most undemocratic and aggressive.

The next several decades will see a competition between the forces making for democracy and peace and retrograde forces of instability and conflict. Nations in the zones of internal peace will be safe only from each other; they will not be safe from those in the other zones, who also will not be safe from each other. There are edges to the clusters that make the western and north-central Europeans contiguous with a zone of turmoil to the east and south; similarly, the fate of nations in the nascent peace zones in northeast and Southeast Asia depends not only on developments internal to their regions but on the uncertain future character of their increasingly powerful neighbors.

States in the zones of peace can be hurt in two ways: Direct effects on them, some visible today, include military attack (including with weapons capable of mass destruction that are becoming increasingly accessible), the creation of refugees, terrorism, uncontrolled epidemics, and environmental spillovers—all of which give the wealthy, democratic states a direct interest in influencing developments in the zones of turmoil. There are also indirect effects that can induce responses, on at least moral and perhaps utilitarian grounds, including genocide, natural and government-caused disasters, and the case for supporting shaky democracies.

Conclusion

Although the message presented in this paper is not one of unalloyed optimism, some basic processes are creating a world with expanding zones of prosperity and democracy. This will not happen automatically; the wealthy peoples in zones of peace need to encourage the free flow of goods and capital, to address security threats, and to help fragile democracies and encourage new ones. It would be utopian to hold that everyone will win from this transformation. There will be losers from economic dislocations; sources of technology, the distribution of economic and therefore military power, and the flow of cultural influences will change. Some people will view this prospect with alarm, understandably considering the past behavior of many powerful states. But if anything like the projected economic growth occurs, and has the suggested effects on domestic politics and international behavior, the world will be in a new era. It is hard now to imagine a world in which hundreds of millions more people will have lives like those in the West today, but it is probably not far off.

PART II

The Macroeconomic Context

Stabilization Policy and Long-Term Economic Growth

JOHN B. TAYLOR

Macroeconomic stabilization policy consists of all the actions taken by governments to: (1) keep inflation low and stable; and (2) keep the short-run (business cycle) fluctuations in output and employment small. Stabilization policy includes both monetary policy and fiscal policy. And because no market economy is closed, stabilization policy also includes arrangements for international monetary transactions, that is, exchange rate policy and the international coordination of policy.

In this paper I address the question: What are the effects of stabilization policy on long-term economic growth? By long-term economic growth, I mean the growth of productivity—real GDP per hour of work—over periods longer than the five-year span of the average business cycle. Productivity fluctuates over the business cycle, but it is the long-term trend in productivity growth that is the source of increased living standards and well-being for a nation.

Stabilization policy is not often mentioned as a factor in long-term growth, but this is a serious omission. Stabilization policy is as important as any of the other factors more frequently mentioned, including saving, investment, education, tax policy, technology policy, and regulatory policy. Just as a poorly designed regulatory policy or an inefficient education policy can stifle economic growth, so can a poorly designed fiscal policy. In fact, as shown in this paper, stabilization policy—in particular a deterioration in policy—can explain a large part of a major puzzle about productivity growth in the United States and other advanced countries: the remarkable slowdown in productivity growth from the mid-1960s to the early 1980s and the partial revival in recent years.

I approach the question about the effect of stabilization policy on long-term economic growth in the following way. I first specify a particular stabilization policy which, according to my own research, would work well in achieving the goals of small fluctuations in inflation and small fluctuations in output and employment. I then examine the effects of this policy on long-term growth. Although the policy was explicitly designed to achieve the goals of stabilization policy, its effects on long-run growth are good as well.

The General Rationale for Government Stabilization Policy

Most modern research on stabilization policy is highly technical, involving stochastic simulation of rational expectations models with hundreds of equations (for examples, see Bryant, Hooper, and Mann, 1993; Taylor, 1993b). Much of this research focuses on examining alternative methods of conducting policy. However, the basic economic principles underlying stabilization policy are much less technical. The role of the government in maintaining price stability and keeping the overall economy stable is analogous to the other key roles of government in a market economy: ensuring property rights and enforcing contracts.

Analogy with Property Rights and Contracts

For markets to operate, it is necessary for people to have the ability to buy and sell goods and services. To do so, they must have the property rights to the goods they sell and obtain the property rights to the goods they buy. If there were great uncertainty about the property rights, markets might not even be able to operate. Buyers must also have some assurance that what they buy will actually be delivered as agreed. Agreement to deliver goods or services can be either informal or written down in formal contracts.

The government has a role to play in securing property rights and enforcing contracts. Without this role, markets—at least on the scale we see in modern economies—could not exist. By passing laws and enforcing them through the justice system, the government secures property rights, and thereby creates an environment in which the market can operate efficiently.

Of course, the role of government in establishing and securing property rights did not start overnight. It evolved slowly as feudalism gave way to a market economy and the Industrial Revolution began. Property rights were granted to small farmers on the feudal estates; they were given the right to sell part of the farm products they grew and harvested. Gradually, the courts began to enforce the contracts to deliver food and other goods.

Many less developed countries today still do not adequately enforce contracts for large segments of the population. This is one reason why markets in these economies frequently do not work well. In many formerly centrally planned economies, property rights are still very poorly defined, a fact that became evident when the countries tried to transform to market economies. With no property rights to gain or lose, firms have little incentive to increase profits or minimize losses.

Part of the U.S. government's role in defining and securing property rights is in the U.S. Constitution. For example, Section 8 of Article I says Congress should secure "for limited times to authors and inventors the exclusive right to their respective writings and discoveries." Copyright laws were passed to implement this part of the Constitution. The Fifth Amendment also describes the right to property. However, most laws about property in the United States are state laws and are handled in the state or county court systems.

Inflation Stabilization

As part of its task of maintaining property rights and enforcing contracts, the government stipulates the unit of account for carrying out transactions in markets. In the United States, the unit of account is the U.S. dollar. The contracts to exchange goods and services are written in dollars, and the value of property rights is stated in dollars. For the dollar to be an effective unit of account, however, its value cannot fluctuate wildly over time. Just as a yardstick that increased or decreased in length from year to year would cause havoc to a carpenter, a unit of account whose value fluctuated from year to year would cause problems for those buying and selling in markets.

When the overall price level—the average price of all goods and services in the economy—rises, the value of a dollar falls: it takes more dollars to buy the same amount of goods. Thus, maintaining a stable unit of account means keeping the overall price level stable. If inflation—the percentage increase in the price level from year to year—is positive on average or fluctuating, the dollar is less effective as a unit of account. Of course, the rate of inflation has varied considerably over time. For example, the inflation rate skyrocketed during the American Revolutionary War, averaging more than 50 percent per year from 1776 to 1778 and more than 120 percent from 1778 to 1780. In Germany after World War I, the inflation rate reached more than 50 percent per month, a condition economists call "hyperinflation." Very high inflation has been reached in Brazil in more recent times. In modern times inflation has been less severe in the United

States and other developed countries. However, an unprecedented persistent bout of worldwide inflation—the Great Inflation—occurred in the late 1960s and the 1970s in many countries.

High or variable inflation—a lack of a stable price level—interferes with the functioning of markets. When inflation rises to hyperinflation levels, the price of gasoline and food changes virtually every day in gasoline stations and grocery stores. But the changes are not uniform. Some days the price increase is large, and on other days it is small; and the price of gasoline and food do not always change by the same amount. These changes have little to do with real shifts in the supply and demand for gasoline and food. It is difficult to know what the price is without going around to every store on every day. Inflation adds uncertainty about what the relative prices are. Thus, the informational efficiency of prices is diminished.

Although inflation at lower levels, such as below 10 percent per year, is less of a concern than inflation of 50 percent per month, the change in prices can still add up over time; at 4 percent inflation, for example, the overall price level doubles every 18 years. The cost of a college education could more than double from the time a child is born until freshman year begins. Thus, uncertainty about the price of goods in the future may still be a problem with inflation at 4 percent.

How would one estimate the magnitudes of these effects? According to the Solow growth accounting formula, high rates of inflation would reduce productivity growth if they reduced investment in physical and human capital or if they reduced the rate of technological change (the Solow residual). Why would investment or technological change be affected by inflation? Part of the answer has to do with the common occurrence of high inflation rates and highly volatile inflation rates from year to year, and with the increased volatility of relative prices which is usually associated with inflation.

Investment is negatively related to the interest rate. Higher interest rates reduce the attractiveness of new investment projects which do not have high enough returns. If high inflation rates are associated with highly volatile inflation rates, then high inflation would increase uncertainty about the future returns from investment. A higher rate of inflation than expected would reduce the real cost of borrowing, and a lower rate of inflation than expected would increase the real cost of borrowing. Thus, by increasing uncertainty, high inflation could reduce investment; the resulting lower growth in the capital-to-labor ratio would thus reduce productivity growth.

Higher inflation could reduce the rate of technological change for similar reasons. Investment in human capital and in research and development—both factors in technological change—might therefore be lower.

Quantitative Estimates of the Effects of Inflation on Growth

Observations of economic growth in different countries indicate that inflation is negatively correlated with economic growth. Moreover, technological change as estimated by the growth accounting formula also seems to be negatively correlated with inflation when economists examine different countries.

How large are the effects? Motley (1994) provides a comprehensive set of estimates based on data in both developed and less developed countries. He finds that a reduction in the inflation rate of 1 percentage point would increase the long-run growth rate of productivity by about .06 percentage points per year in developed countries like the United States. If this estimate is correct, then an increase in the inflation rate from 2 percent (close to where it was in the 1950s and early 1960s) to 12 percent (close to where it was in the late 1970s) would lower the annual productivity growth rate by .6 percentage points.

Are these estimates plausible? In Figures 1 and 2, I endeavor to summarize the relevant information for the United States. Figure 1 shows that

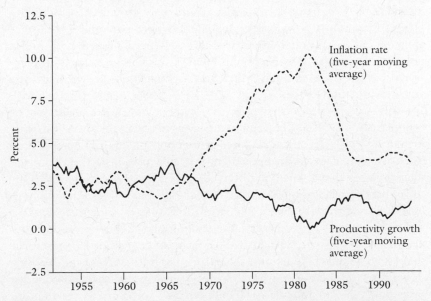

Figure 1. Trends in inflation and productivity growth in the United States, 1952–93.

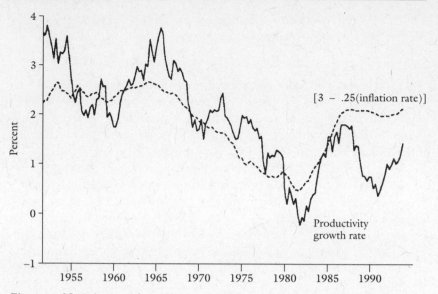

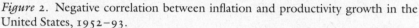

Figure 2. Negative correlation between inflation and productivity growth in the United States, 1952–93.

the start of the Great Inflation in the mid-1960s corresponded very closely in timing to the start of slowdown in productivity growth. Moreover, the productivity growth slowdown ended at about the same time as the Great Inflation ended. Although Figure 1 shows only the United States, similar productivity growth slowdowns and inflation increases occurred in many other countries. And as in the United States, productivity growth increased when the inflation ended.

Although the productivity growth slowdown has ended, the growth of productivity has not yet returned to the levels of the 1950s and 1960s. But neither has the inflation rate. Figure 2 shows how much of a revival in productivity growth would be expected if the simple relationship between productivity growth and inflation observed during these years persisted. Observe that this relationship shows a considerably larger effect of inflation on productivity growth than reported in Motley (1994): in Figure 2 we see a rise in inflation of 1 percentage point leading to a decline in productivity growth of .25 percent. Such an estimate can, of course, be no more than suggestive. People have pointed to many other factors in the productivity slowdown, and there is no reason to expect the .25 coefficient to be stable or to hold outside of the narrow range of observation in Figures 1 and 2.

Nevertheless, Figure 2 clearly shows the plausibility of the Great Infla-

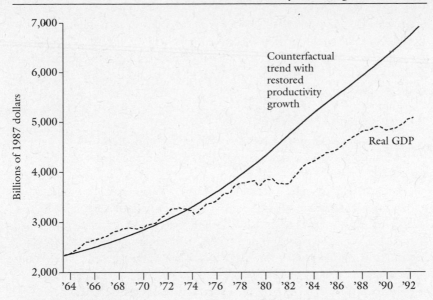

Figure 3. Real GDP versus counterfactual trend with restored productivity growth, 1964–93.

tion as a culprit in the productivity slowdown. It also shows that productivity growth has not yet recovered to levels of the 1950s and 1960s. Despite Figure 2, we can only speculate that lower rates of inflation would help complete the revival.

Figure 3 shows what real GDP might have looked like had the decline in productivity growth, which Figure 2 associates with the Great Inflation, not taken place. It simply restores the productivity shortfall—the difference between the dashed line in Figure 2 and the level of productivity in 1964—to the actual average economic growth rate during the period from 1964 through 1993. By 1993, real GDP might have been 33 percent higher. This gap is about the same as the decline in real GDP during the Great Depression.

While inflation has clearly been correlated with productivity growth during this period, we have not explicitly linked inflation to government policy. However, many historical studies have shown that inflation is ultimately determined by government stabilization policy. In particular, the more governments increase the amount of money in the economy, the higher inflation will be. The more Continentals—the paper currency printed during the American Revolution—were issued by the colonial governments from 1776 to 1780, the higher was the inflation rate. In modern economies, the supply of money is under control of the central bank. In the United States, the role of government in establishing control over the amount of money in the economy is stated explicitly in Section 8 of Article I in the U.S. Constitution, which gives the federal government the right "to coin money."

Is the Optimal Inflation Rate Zero?

If inflation does not lower unemployment and seems to be bad for long-term growth, then why is there debate about the target for the average inflation rate?

Inflation is measured with an upward bias. When measured inflation is about 2 percent, actual inflation is essentially zero (Poole, 1994). The reason for the upward bias in measures of inflation based on a market basket, such as the consumer price index (CPI), is that people tend to consume less of items that increase more rapidly in price. Thus, people would consume fewer wool sweaters and more cotton sweaters as the price of wool rises relative to cotton. However, if the market basket is fixed when computing the CPI, it will appear that people have not reduced wool sweater consumption. Thus, wool sweaters that are increasing in price will be weighted too heavily.

It is hard to estimate how large this bias is, but 2 percent is a common view. If 2 percent is the bias, then the 3 percent inflation seen in America in the early 1990s was actually 1 percent, quite close to zero.

A Trade-off Between Inflation Stability and Output Stability?

Giving the government the role of establishing a stable price level by controlling money also gives the government another power: influencing the ups and downs in total production and employment in the economy. By reducing the amount of money in the economy, the government may temporarily reduce production and employment. Increasing money can temporarily raise production and employment. Large changes in the amount the government spends on goods and services can also affect total production and employment.

The fact that changes in the money supply and government spending can affect production and employment, at least temporarily, gives the government a powerful tool. It is a matter of great controversy among economists how the government should use this tool.

Two points about what is feasible for stabilization policy should be emphasized, however. First, there is no long-term trade-off between infla-

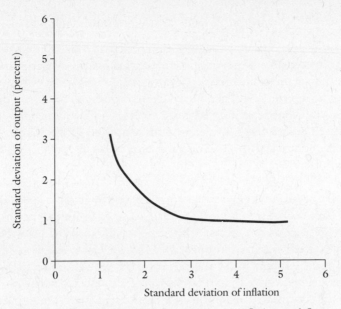

Figure 4. Tradeoff between fluctuations in inflation and fluctuations in real GDP.

tion and unemployment, or between inflation and the deviations of real
GDP from potential GDP. The unemployment rate was almost the same in
1963, 1978, 1987, and 1994—all years that economists would consider
full-employment years—though the inflation rate was higher in 1978 and
1987 than in 1963 and 1994.

But another type of trade-off does seem to exist, as discussed in Taylor
(1979). There is a trade-off between the *fluctuations* in inflation and the
fluctuations in unemployment (or the fluctuations in the cyclical gap between real GDP and potential GDP, since the cyclical GDP gap and the
unemployment rate are nearly perfectly correlated). This trade-off is shown
in Figure 4. For different types of policies, as the variability of inflation
declines, the variability of real output increases. Too much focus on inflation stability could increase the amplitude of the business cycle. This trade-
off raises a question for stabilization policy.

Most feel the government should have a policy that reduces the ups
and downs in the economy. Large fluctuations in the economy are harmful.
They add to uncertainty and cause hardship. Some would say that they are
a sign of market inefficiency.

A Particular Specification of Monetary and Fiscal Policy

To assess the impacts of stabilization policy on long-term growth, it is necessary to consider some specific stabilization policies. What exactly does one mean by stabilization policy? Because stabilization policy involves government action (or lack of action) taken in response to short-run developments in the economy, I need to specify what action would be taken under alternative circumstances. In other words, I need to specify a policy rule. I first consider monetary policy and then fiscal policy.

Monetary Policy

There are different ways that monetary policy can be specified. The central banks could buy and sell securities so as to bring the money supply to a desired level. For example, the policy could keep the growth rate of the money fixed—as in Milton Friedman's k percent rule—or it could adjust the money supply so as to bring real GDP or inflation to some target.

Currently, however, central banks operate monetary policy by buying and selling securities so as to bring the short-term interest rate to a desired level. The reason is that different monetary aggregates have given different signals; for example, recently M1 growth has been strong while M2 growth has been weak. While it is very important to monitor the growth of money and reserves, until these indicators become more reliable, central banks are likely to continue focusing on the interest rates.

In setting interest rates, the central bank must, of course, watch what is happening to inflation. Raising interest rates sufficiently in response to increases in inflation will act to reduce demand and thereby mitigate the increase in inflation. But monetary policy works with a lag, and current inflation—even inflation in sensitive commodity prices—is not a sufficient statistic for future inflation. Therefore, responding to other factors besides inflation is also necessary. The level of GDP in comparison with the normal level of GDP is another factor. If real GDP rises above normal or potential levels, then the central bank should raise interest rates because that will offset inflationary tendencies in the economy.

Table 1 gives a description of such a policy. The federal funds rate is given in the table and is seen to adjust according to what is happening to inflation as well as to the deviations of real GDP from trend, or potential GDP. Higher inflation and increases in real GDP above potential GDP bring about higher interest rates. Similarly, lower inflation and decreases in real GDP below potential GDP bring about lower interest rates.

The policy rule in Table 1 explains the actual behavior of the federal

TABLE I

Federal Reserve Interest Rate Policy

Inflation (percent)	GDP deviation (percent)		
	−2	0	2
0	.5	1	2
2	3	4	5
4	6	7	.8
6	9	10	11
8	12	13	14

NOTE: The table shows the federal funds interest rate for different inflation rates and deviations of real GDP from potential GDP. The formula for the table is r = p + .5y + .5(p−2) + 2 where r is the interest rate, p is the inflation rate, and y is the GDP deviation; see Taylor (1993a).

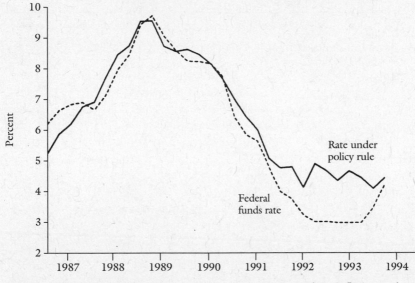

Figure 5. Monetary policy rule in which interest rate responds to inflation and real GDP versus actual policy, 1987–94.

funds rate in recent years quite well, as shown in Figure 5. The level of inflation and the deviation of real GDP from potential GDP, which drive the policy, are shown in Figures 6 and 7. According to the policy rule in Table 1, actual Federal Reserve policy was too easy in much of 1993, but after the tightening moves in 1994, it is again close to the policy rule.

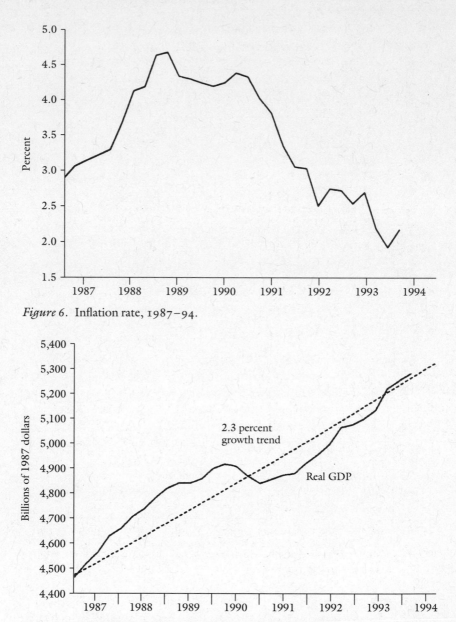

Figure 6. Inflation rate, 1987–94.

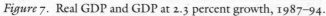

Figure 7. Real GDP and GDP at 2.3 percent growth, 1987–94.

Note that the policy rule leaves some discretion to the central bank. For example, the decline in the federal funds rate at the time of the 1987 stock market crash was an appropriate deviation from the policy rule.

Observe also that the exchange rate is not a factor in the policy rule, and there is no formal attempt to react to developments in other countries. The implication is that the exchange rate is flexible. In other words, the monetary policy rule in Table 1 is one with flexible exchange rates. To the extent that the policy is successful in reducing the fluctuations in inflation and interest rates compared with other policies, the fluctuations in the exchange rate would be small.

If the long-run real interest rate in the economy is 2 percent, then the *implicit target for inflation* is 2 percent in Table 1. For example, if inflation is 2 percent and real GDP is equal to potential GDP, the interest rate is 4 percent.

Fiscal Policy

Fiscal policy also has a role to play in stabilization policy. In a recession, for example, a decrease in taxes can bolster demand and mitigate the downturn. A temporary increase in the deficit can thereby make the recession less severe. Similarly, in a boom, a reduction in the deficit or an increase in the surplus can attenuate the boom and reduce the prospect of future inflation. As with monetary policy, we can distinguish between discretionary policy and rule-like policy. In the case of fiscal policy, the rule-like behavior consists of the automatic stabilizers. In fact, in recent years discretionary fiscal policy has been a very small part of stabilization policy; most of the responses of fiscal policy to the economy have been due to the automatic changes.

Table 2 gives a particular example of a rule for fiscal policy. Analogous to the monetary policy rule, it shows different values of the deficit for different values of the deviation of real GDP from potential GDP. Although in principle one could have fiscal policy responding to inflation, it makes more sense for the Federal Reserve to focus its efforts on inflation.

TABLE 2

A Fiscal Policy Rule

GDP deviation from trend (percent)	−2	−1	0	1	2
Federal budget deficit (percent of GDP)	−1	−.5	0	.5	1

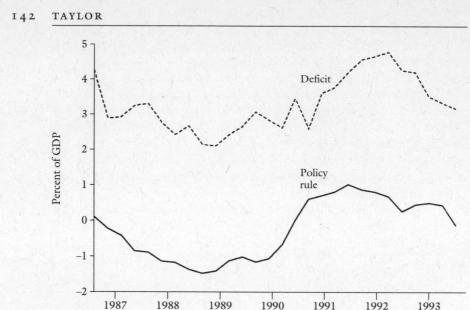

Figure 8. Actual fiscal deficit versus deficit under policy rule in which deficit responds to real GDP, 1987–93.

Figure 8 shows this fiscal policy rule for the deficit in comparison with the actual policy for the deficit. While the cyclical pattern is similar, the level is obviously way off because of the large federal budget deficit. Figure 9 shows what the fiscal policy would look like if the policy rule were shifted up by 3 percent. The response of the deficit to the state of the economy is much like the actual response.

The increase in the deficit in Figure 9 during the recession is due to the reduction in tax revenues that always occurs in recessions and to the increase in government expenditures. During recoveries and booms, tax revenues again rise and expenditures rise less rapidly.

The Automatic Stabilizers in Two Budget Deals

Many have commented on the remarkable similarity between the U.S. budget reduction program of 1990 and the U.S. budget reduction program of 1993. The projected decrease in the deficit was about the same in both, and the proportion devoted to tax increases and spending cuts was about the same in both.

But there is another similarity that has frequently gone unnoticed. As part of the 1990 agreement, several legislative changes were made that al-

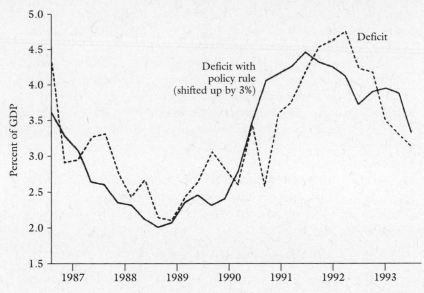

Figure 9. Actual fiscal deficit versus deficit under re-based fiscal policy rule, 1987–93.

tered the automatic response of fiscal policy to the state of the economy. These changes remained in place in the 1993 budget deal. The changes were made recognizing the importance of the automatic stabilizers.

The 1990 budget agreement had special treatment for "discretionary" spending, which consists primarily of military purchases, foreign aid, and domestic purchases of good and services, and "entitlement" spending, which consists largely of transfer payments such as welfare, Medicare, Medicaid, and unemployment insurance. The 1990 budget law put explicit dollar "limits" on discretionary spending for five years and required that any new entitlement program be matched either by reductions in other entitlement programs or by increases in taxes; the latter was called the "pay-as-you-go" rule. Any legislation that violated either the "limit" rule or the "pay-as-you-go" rule would bring about an automatic "seques-ter"—an automatic across-the-board cut in the category of government spending where the violation occurred. The procedures aimed to prevent new government programs from increasing the budget deficit.

However, an increasing budget deficit would be allowed if caused by the automatic stabilizers. For example, if unemployment compensation were to rise as the economy slowed down, then this would be allowed to increase the deficit. But legislated changes in entitlement programs would not be allowed unless they could be offset elsewhere in the budget, or unless an emergency was declared by the president.

In effect, the 1990 act attempted to both reduce the structural deficit through the "limit" and "pay-as-you-go" rules and to allow the automatic stabilizers to increase the budget deficit in a recession. While the new budget law has such features, there is still significant room for improvement. The level of "entitlement" spending, even on existing programs, is still growing rapidly. Additional legislative changes were required to restrain this growth.

The 1993 budget deal preserved these budget rules and extended them to 1998. However, the 1993 budget deal did not consider the major loophole in the 1990 agreement, the continued growth of entitlement programs after the year 2000.

Recent Experience with Discretionary Policy

The fluctuations in taxes and spending have been dominated by these automatic effects in recent years. In fact, in the early 1990s, discretionary policy added virtually nothing to the automatic stabilizers. As in the early 1980s, the increase in the deficit in the early 1990s was mainly due to the automatic stabilizers providing a substantial degree of fiscal stimulus.

In the period after the 1990–91 recession, many proposals were put forth to help speed the recovery. President Bush summarized his proposal in the January 1992 State of the Union address. And soon after he was elected, President Clinton proposed a stimulus package in his 1993 State of the Union address. Both stimulus plans were discretionary, but they should be judged in comparison with the automatic stabilizer effects of fiscal policy shown in Figures 8 and 9.

Table 3 summarizes the Bush fiscal stabilization policy proposals.

TABLE 3

The Bush Discretionary Fiscal Policy Proposals

Shift $10 billion in government purchases from the future into the present.
Reduce the amount of tax withheld.
Enact an investment tax credit (called an allowance) to encourage investment in 1992 and 1993 rather than in later years.
Reduce the capital gains tax.
Provide a tax credit to first time home buyers.
Increase the personal tax exemption for children.
Extend unemployment benefits.

Some of the proposals consisted of actions that the president could do unilaterally without Congress. The advantages of these were that the lag would be smaller and there would be less uncertainty that they would take place. Other proposals would require legislation.

The first proposal would speed up government purchases. This meant that laws that had already been passed to build or improve roads or bridges would be implemented more quickly. As a result of this speed-up, government purchases were to rise by $10 billion in the first six months of 1992.

The second proposal was to decrease temporarily the amount of income taxes withheld by the government. For the year 1992 approximately $25 billion was to be refunded to taxpayers in April 1993. If this withholding could be reduced, it might help stimulate the economy in 1992. This meant that people would get more money during the year and less money in their refund the following year. There would be no long-term decrease in taxes, however, because this tax change was temporary and essentially would be reversed in the next year. It would be expected to have a fairly small effect on the economy. The effect would certainly be smaller than a permanent tax cut of this magnitude and probably even smaller than a temporary tax cut that was not completely offset by a higher tax the following year.

The remaining parts of the Bush package required legislation that Congress would have to pass. The investment tax credit meant that firms could reduce their taxes if they invested and purchased new investment goods in 1992. Another part of the proposal requiring legislation was the capital gains tax reduction. The aim was to stimulate investment and purchases of capital assets and to help the economy by adding demand in the short run and by adding productive capacity in the long run. A tax credit for first-time home buyers was also proposed, to give more incentive for residential construction. Yet another part of the proposal was to increase the personal exemption for children on the income tax.

As it turned out, none of the Bush stimulus proposals that required legislation were enacted into law. Congress voted positively on an alternative package with many of the Bush proposals, but the package also included a tax increase, which President Bush said he would veto, and did veto. His veto was sustained, so there was no stimulus package.

Hence, the only stimulus proposals carried out were those that could have been done without legislation—the adjustment of withholding and the speed-up of purchases. These did occur, but the effects were small, trivial in comparison to the automatic stabilizers that were already in place.

After President Clinton was elected in November 1992, he also devel-

TABLE 4

The Clinton Discretionary Fiscal Policy Proposals

An increase in government spending of $16 billion on
items ranging from infrastructure to immunization
programs.
An incremental investment tax credit, temporary, except
for small firms.
A reduction in the capital-gains tax for investments in
certain small companies held for five years or more.
An extension of unemployment benefits.

oped a stimulus program. Many of his economic advisers had recommended a large fiscal stimulus of about $50 billion in magnitude, which
would be in the form of increased grants to state and local governments.
The stimulus package proposed by President Clinton after he was inaugu-
rated did propose a fiscal stimulus program aimed at the short-term problems in the economy, but its total size was much less than $50 billion. The
program is summarized in Table 4.

Note that the investment tax credit, the reduction in the capital gains
tax (though for a limited set of investments), and the extension of unemployment benefits were also on the Bush stimulus list. Unlike the Bush
proposals, however, the Clinton list had an increase in government spending. It did not have any proposals that could have been carried out without
legislation.

Like the Bush proposal, the Clinton proposal was not enacted by Congress. The problem in this case was that the proposal would increase the
budget deficit, and it was clear that the economy was already recovering.
During this period, the main concern had shifted to reducing the structural
deficit rather than taking actions to stimulate the economy. Although the
Democrats had a majority of both houses of Congress, enough Democrats
did not like the president's stimulus package because it would increase the
deficit, so the plan failed. Because it did not have any administrative part to
it, there was no stimulus program at all.

Effects on Long-Term Growth

The fiscal and monetary policy rules in Tables 1 and 2 are specific
quantitative descriptions of a stabilization policy. Together they completely
describe the actions on short-term interest rates and the deficit. They imply
actions for the growth of reserves and for inflation. If the rules are followed
consistently, inflation will average 2 percent per year, barring shifts in the

real interest rate, about the level that corresponds to zero inflation when measurement bias is taken into account. I already reported the evidence on the effect of inflation on productivity growth earlier in this chapter.

But short-term fluctuations in inflation and in real GDP around potential GDP will not be eliminated by the policy rules. The rules take a position on the relative importance of inflation fluctuations and output fluctuations. Should the government push for still smaller fluctuations in inflation, even though it would mean larger fluctuations in output? Or should it push for still smaller fluctuations in output, even if this means larger fluctuations in inflation? Might either of these choices prove better for the long run?

Effects of Recessions (and Booms) on Productivity Growth

More than any other economist, Schumpeter (1939) emphasized the interrelationship between economic growth and economic fluctuations. According to Schumpeter, booms were periods in which inventions spread throughout the economy through innovation. Recessions were periods in which the destruction of firms and jobs overtakes the creation of jobs. This analysis has led to the idea that recessions might be periods in which productivity is enhanced as firms take the opportunity of slack times to make structural adjustments.

Recent evidence by Davis and Haltiwanger (1990) has been interpreted by Caballero and Hammour (1991) to support this view. They find that job creation is much less sensitive to the business cycle than job destruction. Figure 10 indicates this. When real GDP equals potential GDP, job creation is greater than job destruction as the number of jobs in the economy grows. But as real GDP falls below potential GDP, job destruction typically increases and job creation falls. However, the finding that the slope of the job destruction curve is steeper than the slope of the job creation curve does not indicate that recessions are needed to increase productivity growth. Even in normal times, there is a significant amount of job destruction each year. Even with the steeper slope of the job destruction curve in Figure 10, there appears to be little need for recessions to "cleanse" the economy. There is plenty of cleansing going on in normal years.

In addition, the issue is more related to the size of the fluctuations in real GDP, and not to the level which cannot be affected by stabilization policy. Without non-linearities in the job creation and job destruction curves, larger fluctuations in real GDP around potential would not increase the amount of structural adjustment.

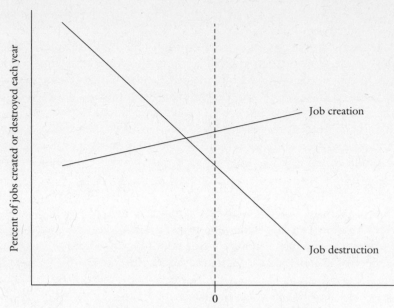

Figure 10. Relationship between job creation and job destruction versus the fluctuations of real GDP from potential GDP.

Effects of the Monetary Policy Rule on Real Output Growth

A frequently expressed concern is that a policy rule such as that in Table 1—which increases interest rates when economic growth rises—could actually lower economic growth. For example, suppose that productivity growth is actually 2 percent rather than 1.1 percent as assumed in the potential GDP growth estimates in Figure 7. Potential GDP would be underestimated. A policy rule that raises interest rates too much or too early would certainly tilt the trade-off toward inflation stability and away from output stability.

However, unless there were a permanent trade-off between the levels of inflation and real GDP deviations, this would not affect long-term growth. In other words, this concern seems to be based on a permanent trade-off between inflation and unemployment, which we showed above is incorrect. Of course, as it became clear that potential GDP growth was higher, the path for potential GDP could be revised and Figure 7 modified accordingly.

An Anti-investment Bias in Stabilization Policy

Another possible effect of stabilization policy on growth could come from an anti-investment bias in the fiscal policy rule. This was the focus of Taylor (1968). Such a bias might come about from the increase in government purchases or consumption due to the fiscal stimulus in the automatic stabilizers.

To be sure, the fiscal policy rule in Table 2 need not be biased in this way. By setting the *average* level of government purchases and taxes at the appropriate level for long-term growth and the provisions of public goods, the fluctuations around the average can be symmetric, biased neither toward nor away from investment.

In practice, however, the anti-investment bias must be taken seriously, as Figure 8 demonstrates. The average, or structural, level of the federal deficit is far from zero in the United States, and many other countries have even higher structural deficits as shares of GDP. On the spending side, the automatic stabilizers are due mainly to entitlement programs. In most countries, the existence of these programs has led to increased structural deficits. As discussed above, the ideal budget reform would reduce the structural deficit while allowing the automatic stabilizers to continue to work. But in practice we are far from that ideal today.

Population Aging and Saving for Retirement

SYLVESTER J. SCHIEBER

AND JOHN B. SHOVEN

In the United States, the group of people born from 1946 through 1964 have come to be known as the baby boom generation. After the end of World War II, birth rates in the United States jumped to a level significantly above the long-term trend and stayed above generally expected levels until the mid-1960s. Because of the high birth rates over this period, the group of people born from 1946 through 1964 constitutes an unusually large segment of the total U.S. population. Due to its size, the baby boom generation has had a more significant effect on various facets of the social structure during its lifetime than other comparably aged segments of the population.

For example, as the baby boomers entered the education system, they placed new demands on it. Between 1951 and 1954, the number of five- and six-year-old children in the primary education system jumped by 70 percent. From 1950 to 1970, as the baby boomers entered school, primary school enrollments jumped from 21 million to 34 million students (U.S. Bureau of the Census, 1976, p. 368). Then, as smaller cohorts of children reached school age, school enrollments began to fall off, dropping to 32 million students by 1975 and then stabilizing at around 28 million by 1980 (U.S. Bureau of the Census, 1991, p. 132). As they came into the primary school system, the baby boomers created a fantastic demand for expanded educational services. As they exited the system, staffing positions were eliminated and schools were closed as student bodies were consolidated.

Counting kindergarten, the typical primary and secondary education program in the United States takes thirteen years. For the baby boomers who did not go beyond a secondary education, the leading edge of the group began to enter the workforce in significant numbers by 1964. The

Vietnam conflict slowed the entrance of the oldest baby boom males, as many of them had a period of military service prior to entering the civilian workforce on a permanent basis. Of course, many of the baby boomers also pursued a college education. Thus, the baby boomers really began to enter the workforce in earnest toward the end of the 1960s and throughout the 1970s. Between 1970 and 1986, the U.S. labor force grew at a compound rate of 2.60 percent per year. By 1985, the youngest of the baby boomers were 21 years of age, and most of those who were going to enter the workforce had done so. In the latter half of the decade of the 1980s, the U.S. workforce grew at an annual rate of 0.45 percent per year (U.S. Bureau of the Census, 1991, p. 384).

Given the predictability of the aging process and the evolving patterns of retirement behavior among workers, it is possible to begin to anticipate the retirement of the baby boom generation. Given its earlier disruptive effects on other aspects of the socio-economic fabric, it is important to consider the implications of the baby boomers' retirements on existing social and economic institutions as far in advance of their retirements as possible. The two largest sources of cash income for retirees today are Social Security and employer-sponsored tax-qualified retirement plans. The extent to which policy makers have focused on the long-term status of the Social Security system and the employer-sponsored pension system varies significantly.

Social Security Funding and the Baby Boom Generation

For some time, policy makers have been aware that the baby boom generation will pose a particular set of challenges for the Social Security program. Traditionally, the Social Security program in the United States had been run largely on a pay-as-you-go basis. The 1983 Social Security amendments included provisions for accumulating a substantial trust fund that would, in effect, pre-fund some of the benefits promised to the baby boomers. In other words, after the 1983 amendments the baby boom generation was expected to pre-fund a larger share of its own benefits than prior generations had pre-funded their own Social Security retirement income. The 1983 amendments also reduced the benefits promised to the baby boom generation by gradually raising the age at which full benefits would be paid to age 67 after the turn of the century.

Shortly after the passage of the 1983 amendments, the Social Security actuaries estimated that the Old-Age, Survivors, and Disability Insurance (OASDI) trust funds would grow from around $27.5 billion in 1983 to about $20.7 trillion in 2045, as shown in Figure 1. The trust funds were expected to have resources available to pay promised benefits until the youngest of the baby boomers reached 100 years of age. In the first projections after the passage of the 1983 amendments, OASDI trust funds were projected to be solvent until at least 2063.

In almost every year since 1983, the estimates of the accumulations in the OASDI trust funds have been revised downward. The most recent projection, also shown in Figure 1, suggests that the trust funds will accumulate only about $3 trillion around 2020, and then decline to a zero balance some time during 2029. At that time the trailing edge of the baby boomers will just be turning age 65 and will be at the front end of their retirement period.

An alternative way to look at the financing of Social Security is to segment it into periods. Table 1 reflects the Social Security actuaries' April 1994 long-term OASDI financing projections, broken into three 25-year periods. For the most part, the first 25-year period from 1994 to 2018 will precede the bulk of the baby boom generation's claim on the program. The baby boomers first will be eligible for early retirement benefits in 2008, and only about half of them will have attained age 62 by 2018. In addition, if the increases in the actuarial reductions for early retirement benefits and the increases in actuarial adjustments for delayed retirement have any ef-

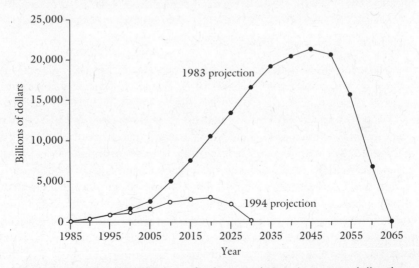

Figure 1. Projected OASDI trust fund accumulations in current dollars by year of estimate. Source: Ballantyne (1983, p. 2), and Board of Trustees (1994, p. 178).

TABLE I

Social Security Income and Cost Rates as Projected Under Current Law

Period	Income rate[a]	Cost rate[b]	Over- or underfunding as percent of income rate
1994–2018	12.70	12.32	2.99
2019–2043	13.10	16.78	−28.09
2044–2068	13.26	18.14	−36.80

SOURCE: Board of Trustees (1994, p. 21).
[a] The income rate is the ratio of OASDI revenues to taxable payroll.
[b] The cost rate is the ratio of OASDI expenditures to taxable payroll.

fect, current trends may reverse and the baby boomers may proceed into retirement somewhat more slowly than prior generations. If they do so, however, it would represent the reversal of a trend toward earlier and earlier retirements that goes back to the 1930s. Even on a purely pay-as-you-go basis, the tax revenues funding OASDI benefits are expected to exceed outgo as late as 2013. Over the 25 years starting in 1994, OASDI has projected revenues that are about 3 percent above projected outlays.

As the baby boomers move fully into retirement, the financial situation for Social Security is now projected to turn decidedly negative. During the second 25 years reflected in Table 1, the period when the majority of the baby boomers expect to get the majority of their lifetime benefits, the projected outlays under OASDI exceed projected revenues by 28 percent. In other words, every bit of evidence available to national policy makers today indicates that Social Security will not be able to provide the benefits currently being promised to the baby boom generation with existing funding legislation. While it is impossible to anticipate exactly how OASDI projections might change over the next five or ten years, assuming no change in legislative mandates, the recent ten-year history of continual deterioration in the projected actuarial balances of the program leads us to conclude that the future may turn out even worse than we now anticipate.

The recent history of major Social Security legislative adjustments, specifically including the 1977 and 1983 amendments, suggests that when benefit promises exceed program revenues, at least part of the rebalancing of the program comes in the form of reduced benefits for retirees. Given the size of the baby boom generation and potential adjustment that may be required in their Social Security benefit expectations, it seems imperative that policy makers begin to address the funding of the baby boomers' benefits as soon as possible so that they will have the maximum amount of time to adjust their other retirement savings relative to more realistic Social Security promises.

Employer-Sponsored Retirement Plan Funding and the Baby Boom Generation

In the general context of retirement policy, it is interesting that there is so much consternation about the long-term prospects of Social Security and the potential underfunding of benefits for the baby boom generation when there is hardly any concern about the long-term prospects of the funded pension system. A review of the effects of recent legislation and contributions to employer-sponsored retirement plans suggests there may be reason for concern on the pension front as well.

Employer-sponsored retirement programs typically operate in a significantly different environment than the federal Social Security program. While the federal government operates its own employer-sponsored retirement programs largely on a pay-as-you-go basis, most state and local governments pre-fund retirement obligations on some basis, and private employers are required to fund their retirement obligations on the basis of rules laid out in the Employee Retirement Income Security Act (ERISA) and the Internal Revenue Code.

ERISA became law in 1974. Its purpose was to provide more secure retirement benefits for all the participants in tax-qualified plans. Among other things, ERISA established rules for including workers in plans, rules for vesting or guaranteeing benefits, and requirements that benefits be funded on a scheduled basis. For a plan to qualify for retirement plan tax preferences, it must meet certain requirements to assure that the benefits being promised are actually provided. For all plans, there are fiduciary requirements seeking to assure that the assets are prudently invested solely for the purpose of providing benefits promised by the plans. In addition, ERISA requires that plan trustees disclose relevant financial and participation data to the government on a periodic basis so that the ongoing viability and operation of the plan can be assured.

For defined contribution plans, the funding requirements are straightforward. On the date that a contribution to the plan is required by the plan rules, the employer makes a contribution to the plan equal to the obligation. In this case, the employer is not obligated to make any additional contributions for prior periods. The ability of the plan to provide an adequate retirement benefit depends heavily on the size of the periodic contributions and the investment returns of the assets in the plan.

For defined benefit plans, the funding requirements are somewhat more complicated because such plans promise future benefits. If a worker enters a firm at age 25, works until age 65, and is retired under the plan for 20 years before dying, his span of life under the plan is 60 years. The purpose of the ERISA funding requirements for defined benefits plans is to assure that the employer gradually contributes enough to the plan so that the promised benefits will be fully funded at the point a worker retires. The annual contribution to the plan is determined on the basis of an actuarial valuation of its obligations and assets, and specific funding minimums and maximums specified in the law. The funding minimums in the law are to assure that employers are laying aside sufficient money to pay promised benefits. The funding maximums are meant to assure that extraordinary contributions are not made simply to avoid paying federal taxes.

It may seem odd to worry about the funding of employer-sponsored pension obligations, at least those of private plan sponsors, when the federal government has seemingly established strong funding and disclosure standards to assure that promised benefits will ultimately be delivered. The problem is that there is an inherent neurosis in federal law governing pensions between the provisions aimed at providing retirement income security on the one hand, and limiting the value of the preferences accorded pensions in the federal tax code on the other. From the passage of ERISA in 1974 until the early 1980s, concerns about benefit security held the upper hand in driving federal policy towards pensions. Since 1982, policies aimed at limiting tax leakages related to employer-sponsored retirement plans have played the dominant role. While a number of tax law changes have had an effect on defined contribution plans since 1982, the effects on defined benefit plans have been somewhat more profound. This was especially true of the Omnibus Budget Reconciliation Act of 1987, which we will refer to as OBRA87. But it was not just tax law that was affecting the funding of retirement benefits.

Defined benefit plans have a special appeal for workers because they ensure a promised level of benefits regardless of the gyrations in financial markets. Over the years, defined benefit plans also have had a special appeal for employers because they have provided the flexibility to fund promised benefits actuarially over the working lives of their employees. Traditionally, employers have sought to use funding methods that allowed them to make relatively level contributions over a worker's career to fund benefits whose value increases steeply at the end of the career. In 1980, the majority of defined benefit plans which had more than 1,000 participants and which based benefits on salaries of covered workers—that is, either final or career-average pay plans—funded the benefits on the basis of the *entry age normal cost method*. Nearly two-thirds of final pay plans used this funding method. Using this method and assuming all actuarial assumptions were met, an employer contributed a steady percentage of a worker's pay over an entire career with the goal of accumulating sufficient resources at retirement to pay expected retirement benefits.

In the early 1980s, the Financial Accounting Standards Board (FASB) began to look at the actuarial methods used for calculating pension obligations and expenses that were reported on plan sponsors' financial statements. They ultimately promulgated accounting rules that required that accruing pension benefits be accounted for using the *projected unit credit actuarial cost method*. The differences in terms of the attribution of costs for a hypothetical worker between the two methods are shown in Figure 2. Changing from the entry age method of calculating costs to the projected unit credit method results in lower costs early in a worker's career and higher costs later in the worker's career.

While the change in accounting rules was significant from the perspective of reporting pension expenses on financial disclosure documents, the actual funding of plans is carried out in accordance with governmental requirements set out in ERISA. The reason that the FASB rules have played an important role in the evolving security of current benefits is that they encouraged many plan sponsors, particularly sponsors of final pay plans—

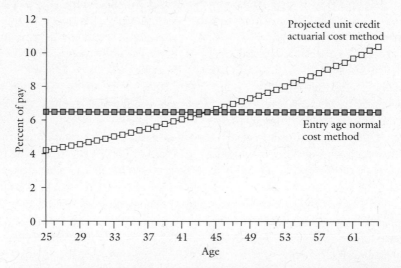

Figure 2. Alternative pension cost perspectives for a 25-year-old worker over a 40-year career under alternative actuarial cost methods. Source: Wyatt Company (1992).

TABLE 2

*Percentage of Large Final Pay Plans Using
Projected Unit Credit Funding Method*

Year	Firms	Year	Firms
1983	10%	1989	49%
1984	19	1990	52
1985	25	1991	54
1986	36	1992	60
1987	44	1993	63
1988	50		

SOURCE: Wyatt Company (unpublished data).

that is, the majority of defined benefit plans—to move to a projected unit credit funding method. The shift in funding methods used by final pay plans since the FASB began to consider its new accounting requirements is shown in Table 2. The baby boom generation ranged in age from 20 to 40 as the FASB rules were discussed and ultimately issued.

Looking back to Figure 2, shifting from an entry age normal cost funding method to a projected unit credit funding method when such a large cohort of workers were so young slowed down the funding of their retirement benefits. The net effect of this shift toward projected unit credit funding of defined benefit plans resulted in the delaying of the funding of the baby boom generation's retirement benefits from the first half of their career to the last half. This is not the end of the story, however. Through 1987, employers were allowed to fund up to 100 percent of the projected benefits that would be paid to a worker at retirement based on his or her current tenure, age, and actuarial probabilities of qualifying for a benefit in the future. OBRA87 dropped the full funding limits for defined benefit plans from 100 percent of ongoing plan liability to 150 percent of benefits accrued to date. The net effect of the new funding limits under OBRA87 was to delay the funding of younger workers' pension benefits relative to prior law.

Figures 3 and 4 help to show the implications of the revised funding standards under OBRA87. For purposes of developing these examples, we assumed that a worker begins a job at a firm at age 25 earning $25,000 per year. We assumed the worker's pay would increase at a rate of 5.5 percent per year throughout his or her career. This individual participates in a defined benefit plan that pays 1 percent of final average salary per year of service at age 65. It also allows for retirement at age 55 with less than a full actuarial reduction in benefits, a fairly common practice with private defined benefit plans. We assumed that accumulated assets in the plan would earn a return of 8 percent per year.

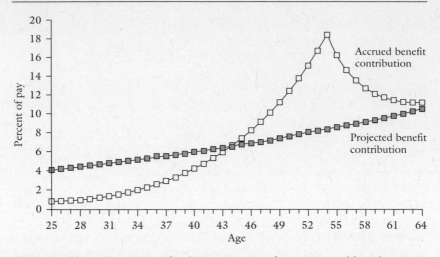

Figure 3. Alternative pension funding perspectives for a 25-year-old worker over a 40-year career under alternative actuarial cost methods. Source: Wyatt Company (1992).

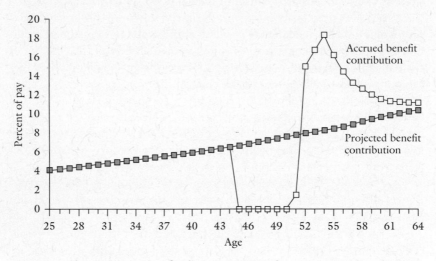

Figure 4. Alternative pension funding perspectives for a 45-year-old worker over a 40-year career under alternative actuarial cost methods with a change from projected to accrued benefit contributions in mid-career. Source: Wyatt Company (1992).

In Figure 3, the relatively flat line labeled "Projected benefit contribution" shows the contribution rate, as a percent of the worker's salary, that would be required to fund this individual's benefit at retirement under the projected unit credit funding method as discussed earlier. The other line in the figure shows the contributions that would be required to fund the benefits for the worker as they accrue during each year of the working career.

For the worker who is covered by OBRA87 throughout an entire career, the full funding limits mean that the plan sponsor's contributions to the plan during the first half of the career, until age 45, will be less than if the plan were being funded on an ongoing basis. Of course, lower contributions in the early part of the career mean that contributions in the latter half of the career would have to be higher to fund the promised benefits under the plan. In this particular example, the contribution rate to the plan during the worker's early to mid-50s would have to be more than twice the contribution rate under the projected unit credit funding method.

For a worker not hit by the contribution limits until he or she was 20 years into the career, the imposition of the contribution limit implies that the employer would have a six- or seven-year contribution holiday when no contributions would be made, as shown in Figure 4. In this case, the accrued benefit would have to catch up with the level of funding accomplished early in the career. Again, the contribution rate in the mid-50s would be more than twice what it was under projected unit credit funding. For the worker hit earlier, the contribution holiday would be longer, but the same general effect of delaying retirement funding would significantly increase late career contribution requirements given the level of promised benefits. Finally, for the worker not hit until age 55 by the new funding limit, the contribution holiday would only be one year, and while contributions during the remaining career would be higher than under projected unit credit funding, the implications are far less significant than in the previous cases.

In 1988, when OBRA87 funding limits took effect, the leading edge of the baby boom generation was 42 years of age. The trailing edge was 24 years of age. The gross effect of the regulatory environment that evolved during the 1980s is that it has significantly delayed the funding of the baby boom generation's defined benefit retirement promises, and creates a significant overall slowdown in pension funding. As this legislation was being considered, The Wyatt Company analyzed its 1986 survey of actuarial assumptions and funding covering 849 plans with more than 1,000 participants to estimate the effects of the new funding limits. They found that 41 percent of the surveyed plans had an accrued benefit security level of 150 percent or greater. All of these plans would have been affected by the new limit and could not have received deductible contributions had the proposed limit been in effect for 1986. For a subset of 664 plans where they could estimate the marginal effects of the new limits, they found that 40 percent would be affected by the new proposal, compared with only 7 percent under prior limits (Wyatt Company, 1987).

In 1987, 48 percent of the defined benefit plans with more than 1,000 participants had an accrued benefit security ratio of 150 percent or more (Wyatt Company, 1987). Because plans at this funding level cannot make deductible plan contributions, the percentage of plans over-funded by this measure should decline over time. In a 1992 survey, only 37 percent of large defined benefit plans had accrued benefit security ratios of 150 percent or greater (Wyatt Company, 1992, p. 4).

While OBRA87 significantly limited the funding of defined benefit plans, it was only one piece of legislation out of several that affected the funding of tax-qualified retirement plans after 1982. In 1982, the Tax Equity and Fiscal Responsibility Act, TEFRA, reduced and froze for a period of time the dollar funding and contribution limits for both defined benefit and defined contribution plans. TEFRA also established new discrimination tests for all plans, which had the practical effect of lowering plan contributions for many of them. The next year, the Deficit Reduction Act extended the freeze in the funding and contribution limits established by TEFRA. The Tax Reform Act of 1986 again reduced and froze funding and contribution limits for tax-qualified plans. Finally, the Omnibus Budget Reconciliation Act of 1993 (OBRA93) includes provisions that reduce the level of an individual employee's compensation that can be considered in funding and contributing to tax-qualified plans. The practical effects of the OBRA93 provisions will be to further limit the funding of employer-sponsored retirement programs.

Figure 5 shows the annual employer contributions to private pension

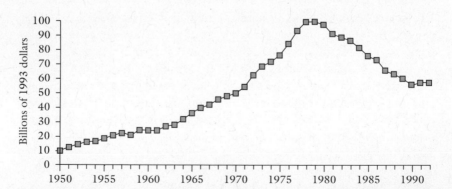

Figure 5. Real employer contributions to private pension and profit sharing plans. Source: Derived by the authors from U.S. Bureau of Economic Analysis (annual).

and profit-sharing plans from 1950 to 1992. There was a gradual increase in contributions up through the early 1970s, and then an escalation in contribution levels as ERISA was passed and implemented. Right around the time that the federal government started passing the various restrictive tax measures affecting employer-sponsored retirement plans, real contributions began to decline. By 1990, inflation-adjusted employer contributions to these plans were about 45 percent below contribution levels in the early 1980s. In fact, real employer contributions were about where they had been in 1972, before the passage of ERISA.

Most of the pension legislation passed in the past decade has evolved within the context of short-term fiscal considerations. The need to raise revenues to reduce the federal government's deficit has delayed the funding of the baby boom generation's pension benefits, with virtually no consideration of the long-term impact that this will have on the cost or viability of those benefits. While the Social Security Act established a Board of Trustees to oversee the financial operations of the OASDI programs and requires that the Board report to Congress on the financial and actuarial status of the programs, there is no similar oversight body to identify pending problems with the funded pension system and to warn policy makers about them. Retirement plan sponsors are individually required to disclose the current funding status of their plans on a periodic basis, but the evolving policy focus pushing plan sponsors to fund for only current obligations hardly encourages planning for longer-term contingencies. In the aggregate, public policy makers have completely ignored the long-term implications of tax policy on pension funding in an attempt to minimize the short-term structural imbalances underlying federal fiscal policy. In the following sections of this chapter, we attempt to lay out a longer-term view of pension funding.

Projections for the Private Pension System

The details of data, methodology, and assumptions in generating our 75-year forecast for the private pension system are described in the Appendix to this chapter. The basic concept can be conveyed here, however. We gathered detailed information about the age, pension participation, and job tenure of the present adult population of the United States. We utilized Social Security intermediate assumptions in terms of demographic and economic projections. We used relatively conservative assumptions regarding asset returns and assumed employer and employee pension contribution rates remain at roughly their levels of the past decade.

TABLE 3

Combined Private Defined Benefit and Defined Contribution Projections for Selected Years, 1992–2065

Year	Assets	Benefits	Contributions	Investment income	Net inflow	Real net inflow	Total payroll	Saving/ payroll
1992	2,870	$86	$105	$181	$201	$86	$2,313	0.037
1993	3,070	93	112	194	214	91	2,465	0.037
1994	3,284	99	120	207	228	97	2,626	0.037
1995	3,512	107	128	221	242	102	2,794	0.036
1996	3,754	116	136	236	257	107	2,971	0.036
1997	4,011	125	145	252	272	112	3,157	0.035
1998	4,283	135	154	269	288	117	3,351	0.035
1999	4,571	145	164	286	305	122	3,555	0.034
2000	4,876	154	174	304	323	128	3,771	0.034
2005	6,664	231	231	413	413	147	5,013	0.029
2010	8,913	347	303	549	505	149	6,580	0.023
2015	11,606	517	392	710	585	121	8,532	0.014
2020	14,662	751	504	891	644	57	10,993	0.005
2025	17,964	1,056	648	1,088	680	(39)	14,121	−0.003
2030	21,399	1,430	838	1,287	694	(162)	18,243	−0.009
2035	24,889	1,876	1,089	1,482	695	(300)	23,683	−0.013
2040	28,287	2,427	1,414	1,660	647	(485)	30,725	−0.016
2045	31,281	3,140	1,824	1,807	491	(760)	39,643	−0.019
2050	33,097	4,088	2,341	1,865	118	(1,206)	50,892	−0.024
2055	32,466	5,345	2,999	1,766	(580)	(1,879)	65,212	−0.029
2060	27,411	6,972	3,847	1,363	(1,762)	(2,858)	83,641	−0.034
2065	15,172	9,038	4,945	462	(3,630)	(4,237)	107,513	−0.039

NOTE: Dollar amounts are in billions. Totals may not sum exactly due to rounding error.

The current dollar figures of our projections for the combined defined benefit (DB) and defined contribution (DC) private pension plans are shown in Table 3, as are the real savings generated by these plans. Under the assumptions of our forecast, the assets of the total private pension system are shown to continue to grow in nominal terms for the next 60 years. However, this growth is almost continuously slowing. For instance, in 1993 the benefits (payouts) of the defined benefit and defined contribution private plans combined are 83 percent of total contributions. This means, of course, that there is a net inflow of funds into the total system, even without taking into account the investment return on the $3 trillion asset pool. However, by the year 2006, benefits are projected to be 102.4 percent of contributions under this scenario, and we expect that aggregate benefits would continue to outstrip contributions for the entire remaining period through 2065. By 2025, benefits are projected to be 163 percent of contributions.

If inflation and asset returns match our assumptions, the value of pension assets will continue to climb, albeit at slowing rates until peaking (in nominal terms) in 2052. In real or relative terms, however, pension assets are projected to peak and begin to fall much earlier. Our model indicates that the ratio of pension assets to total payroll (now at 1.25) will climb modestly until reaching a peak of 1.36 in 2013 and 2014. The ratio is projected to fall after that and drop below 1.0 for the first time in 2038. Real inflation-adjusted pension assets would peak in 2024 with our set of assumptions.

The important story coming from our analysis is that unless contributions increase significantly from current levels, pensions will gradually cease being the major engine of aggregate saving that they have been for the past twenty years or more. This projected occurrence is shown in Figure 6. Here we show the total real saving of the private pension system, projected contributions less benefits plus real inflation-adjusted asset returns, relative to the projected total private payroll in the economy for 1992 to 2065. We use total payroll as the scaling factor simply because it is a readily available by-product of the Social Security projections. Figure 6 shows that (under our assumptions) the pension system continues to generate significant investable funds for the American economy for the next twenty years or so. In fact, the decline is very minor for about the next ten years; then it steepens considerably. By 2024, the pension system is projected to cease being a net source of saving for the economy. In fact, the pension system will then become increasingly a net dissaver. By 2040, the net real dissaving is more than 1.5 percent of payroll, and by 2065, the negative saving is pro-

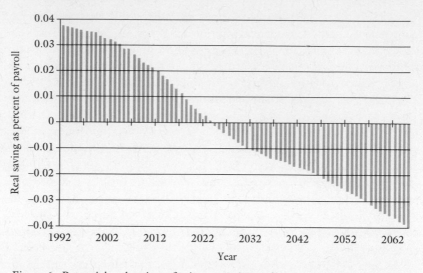

Figure 6. Potential real saving of private pensions relative to total private payroll for 1992 to 2065, assuming current plan characteristics and contribution rates.

jected to reach almost 4.0 percent of payroll. This change of the pension system from a large net producer of saving to a large absorber of saving or loanable funds will likely have profound implications for interest rates, asset prices, and the growth rate of the economy.

It should be emphasized that the timing of the prediction of the change in pensions from a net buyer of assets to a net seller is very sensitive to our assumptions about the rates of return earned on pension investments as well as to the assumed level of pension contributions. However, we feel a decline in the savings generated by pensions is almost inevitable; only the timing could be somewhat different from that pictured. If investment returns exceed our fairly conservative assumptions, then the decline of the savings contribution of pensions will be more modest and delayed in time. Still, the demographic structure is such that it will by necessity occur. It is not even correct to think of this as a negative development. After all, pension assets are accumulated to provide for the resources needed by the elderly in retirement. It is only natural that when we have an extraordinarily large number of retirees, the real saving of the system will shrink and the system may even cease being a source of new investment funds for the economy.

One concern that all of this may raise is the impact on the prices of pension assets, mainly stocks and bonds. We share that concern to some degree, but cannot predict the size or timing of any effect. One thing to note in this regard is that while the pension system will become a less important purchaser of securities, it will not become a net seller for quite a while. As noted earlier, our model predicts that benefits will first exceed contributions in 2006. However, at that point the annual investment income—that is, dividends, interest, and capital gains—on the $7 trillion portfolio should approximate $450 billion in nominal terms and $170 billion in real terms. Needless to say, there would be no reason to be net sellers of assets at that point in time, and in fact, we would suppose that pensions will still be accumulating assets then. The period of time when the pension system begins to be a net seller is more likely in the early part of the third decade of the next century (under our conservative assumptions). This could depress asset prices, particularly since the demographic structure of the United States does not differ that greatly from Japan and Europe, which also will have large elderly populations at that time. In fact, aging populations are common throughout the world (including China), and the resulting financial pressure on pension systems is very widespread ("Death, and Taxes," 1994).

Another comment about the asset price effect is that if it occurs, it would likely affect all long-term assets. What we think may happen is high real interest rates, which could depress the prices of stocks, bonds, land, and real estate. While this might suggest that a good investment for this period would be short-term Treasury bills, the effect if it occurs is likely to be gradual and last for decades. In the twentieth century, the longest stretch of time over which Treasury bills outperformed equities was about fifteen years. We have little else to go on, but we certainly are not advocating that long-term investors invest in short-term instruments to ride out this demographic tidal wave. In fact, it is our opinion that far too many people already invest in short-term instruments for long-term accumulations.

With our assumptions, the private defined benefit plans are the ones that experience net outflows (dissaving) the earliest. These plans already are in a situation where benefits exceed contributions. In fact, benefits are roughly three times contributions. The robust investment returns of the past decade or so have permitted this and in fact forced it to be true. If investment returns drop to our conservative figures and if firms contribute a total of 2.8 percent of payroll to pension plans, then the real assets of the defined benefit (DB) plans begin to fall immediately. DB pension assets, which are now 88 percent of the total payroll in the economy, would fall to 77 percent of total payroll by 2000, 66 percent by 2010, and 42.5 percent by 2025. The net flow of funds into the DB plans (or savings) would be positive, but only in nominal terms. Even nominal DB saving becomes negative by 2025, and the entire stock of DB plan assets would be exhausted by 2043.

It is important to note that this is not a forecast of doom for the defined benefit plans; it is simply a "what if" exercise. If by magic our rate-of-return assumptions proved to be precisely accurate, then employers would be forced to increase their pension contributions above the 2.8 percent of aggregate payroll that we have assumed or to curtail the pension benefits they offer workers. While vested benefits of existing workers cannot be cut, certainly the accrual of new benefits can be reduced by changes in the plan design. This tough choice of higher costs or lower pension benefits would occur far before the 2043 date when the model says that the assets of DB plans would be exhausted. Government regulators and pension actuaries would sound the alarm, perhaps even decades before the forecast could come true. The problem may become apparent and the tough choice may have to be faced very early in the next century.

One concern we have is that employers may have gotten used to the very low contributions that many of them have had to make to defined benefit plans in recent years, thanks to the extraordinary performance of financial markets and the delayed funding related to regulatory policies. When they face the higher long-run funding costs of their pension plans, some employers may choose to curtail the benefits they offer. It is also possible that just about the time this is being resolved, we as a society will have to acknowledge the fact that Social Security is not in long-run equilibrium; once again, the choice will be to either raise taxes or lower benefits. In this sense, both Social Security and the privately funded DB pension system will likely face cost pressure to scale back retirement benefits.

Under our assumptions, the outlook for the defined contribution (DC) plans is decidedly more optimistic. Our model shows DC plan assets growing relative to economy-wide aggregates over the next thirty years or so, and then stabilizing at the relatively larger level. Again using total economy-wide payroll as our scaling factor, DC assets are now about 37 percent of one year's payroll. We project those assets to climb to 52 percent of payroll by 2000, to increase to 70 percent by 2010, and to level out at about 85 percent for 2025 and beyond. The DC system is much less susceptible to "running out of assets," and indeed, we don't project any such occurrence. The private DC system would be a modest net source of saving in the economy even in the period with the maximum number of baby boom retirees.

Other Savings and the Baby Boomers' Retirement Resources

If Social Security and employer-sponsored retirement plans appear to be saving inadequately for the baby boomers' retirement period, it is possible that other forms of saving might be sufficient to make up for these shortfalls. In reality, though, that does not appear to be the case. Figure 7 shows personal, business, and government sector savings rates as a percent of gross domestic product in five-year intervals from 1950 up to 1989 and for the first four years of the 1990s. The net national saving rate in this economy was very stable for the 30 years from 1951 to 1980 at approximately 7 percent of GDP. It has collapsed since 1980 and in the most recent period is less than 1 percent of GDP. Personal saving, which includes pension accumulations, fell over the period, meaning that other personal saving has not increased to offset the decline in employer contributions to retirement programs over the past decade.

While saving rates are lower today than they have been historically,

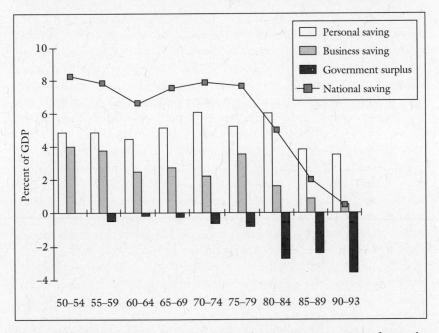

Figure 7. Sectoral saving and U.S. net national saving as a percentage of gross domestic product, 1950–93. Source: Calculated by the authors from U.S. Bureau of Economic Analysis (annual).

there is some evidence that the baby boomers are ahead of their parents' generation in accumulating assets. For example, the Congressional Budget Office (1993) has shown that households in which the head was aged 25 to 34 or 35 to 44 reported greater net worth on the 1989 Survey of Consumer Finances (SCF) than did households at the same ages in the 1962 SCF. For example, in 1962 the median wealth of the households where the head was 25 to 34 years old was $6,100 in 1989 dollars, compared to $9,000 for those in the 1989 survey. The median non-housing wealth for the two groups was $2,400 and $4,200, respectively. For the households where the head was aged 35 to 44 in 1962, median wealth was $29,300, compared to $54,200 in 1989. The median non-housing wealth for these households was $12,200 in 1962 and $17,400 in 1989. The point of this comparison is that the baby boomers appear to be ahead of their parents in accumulating wealth, which might lead one to prognosticate that if the baby boom generation's parents are doing okay in retirement, they themselves are on track to do even better.

There is some concern, however, that this conclusion might not actually come to pass. One reason is that the generations in front of the baby boomers have ended up with higher Social Security benefits than they might have reasonably anticipated in the early 1960s. While Social Security is still holding out to the baby boomers that they will get benefits nearly as generous as their parents are receiving, our analysis suggests that is unlikely. Another aspect of the Congressional Budget Office's analysis is that the largest increases in wealth holdings of the households compared between 1962 and 1989 comes in the form of housing wealth. The baby boomers' parents realized fantastic increases in the values of their homes after the mid-1960s as the baby boomers created significant demand for homes. They also benefited from the erosion of the value of their home mortgages during the high inflationary period of the 1970s. It is unlikely that the boomers themselves will benefit from the appreciation in their housing assets as their parents did. When the boomers get to retirement and begin to liquidate their housing assets, there will be a glut of houses on the market because of the size of the baby boom cohorts and the relatively small size of the cohorts behind them who might be home buyers. In short, we are not very optimistic that other saving behavior will offset the adverse circumstances implied by the operations of Social Security and employer-based pensions. Our position is that the current level of national savings is inadequate for robust economic growth and for the well-being of the baby boom generation in their retirement period.

Conclusion

The major result of this analysis is that the national saving generated by the private pension system can be expected to decline from current levels, gradually for about a decade, and then far more steeply. With our set of conservative assumptions about the rate of return earned by pension assets, the pension system would cease to be a source of saving roughly in 2024. It is our opinion that this scenario is becoming increasingly likely given the track that federal tax policy and public accounting rules have taken us down, although there is considerable uncertainty about the timing of the event.

We also find that the defined benefit portion of the private pension system faces a tough choice. Our model shows that the system would run out of money in 2043 if it was funded according to our assumptions and if rates of return were consistent with those we have projected. The "running out of money" part of our story will not happen. However, what the model is implicitly predicting is that either corporate pension contributions will have to be substantially raised or pension plans will have to be scaled back. It is highly unlikely that the current low contribution rates, caused by the high realized rates of return on financial assets over the past decade, can be sustained.

We briefly speculated about the impact of the reduced saving of the pension system on asset prices. Even though we don't think the change will be as dramatic as our model predicts (due to adjustments in contributions and plan design), we still feel that the demographic structure is such that a major change in pension saving will occur. The timing and magnitude of the effect on asset prices is impossible to determine. Capital markets are worldwide, interest rates are determined by both supply and demand, and forecasts of financial rates of return some 30 or more years into the future are futile. However, the population bulge that we call the baby boom caused considerable strain on the U.S. education system in the 1950s and 1960s. Absorbing those people into the workforce was a challenge in the 1970s and early 1980s and may have been a factor in the slowing of growth in worker productivity. It is probably safe to say that the same numerous cohort will strain the economic system once again during their retirement years, roughly 2010 to 2050.

APPENDIX   *Methods, Assumptions, Inputs*

This appendix gives a brief outline of the underlying methods, assumptions, and inputs that were used to develop the estimates that are presented in this chapter.

Projections of the U.S. pension system require a long-term projection of the population and workforce and their respective characteristics. For purposes of this exercise, we were not interested in developing a long-term demographic and labor force projection model. First of all, to develop such a model would be a Herculean undertaking. Second, we felt the nature of the projection we were making might lead to comparisons with the long-term Social Security projections, and thought that it would make sense to have the same underlying demographic and workforce characteristics as utilized in developing those projections. Thus we began with Social Security's 75-year projections of the U.S. population, which gave us estimated numbers of people by single-year attained ages between the ages of 0 and 99 for each of the projection years. We also started with their projections of the workforce in each year, distributed in five-year age cohorts.

We utilized published data and our own computations developed from the U.S. Department of Labor's Form 5500 pension reporting forms plus computations from the March 1992 Current Population Survey (CPS) and the 1991 Survey of Income and Program Participation (SIPP) to develop age- and sex-specific participation and vesting in and receipt of benefits from defined benefit and defined contribution plans. We developed age- and sex-specific distributions of tenure in current jobs, which is important for projecting the vesting rates of participants in pension plans. We developed estimates of total wages for the private, state and local, and federal sectors of the economy from data published by the U.S. Bureau of Economic Analysis in the *National Income and Product Accounts*. Estimates of age- and sex-specific pay levels were developed.

We used the DOL Form 5500 files in conjunction with data from the Employee Benefit Research Institute's *Quarterly Pension Investment Report* (QPIR) to estimate the starting total distribution of assets and contributions between defined benefit and defined contribution plans. We also used the QPIR data to estimate the distribution of financial assets held by plans across various forms of investments. The resulting distribution of assets by plan type is shown in Table A1. We are focusing on the private defined benefit and defined contribution plans in this chapter. We note with interest the relatively large amount of cash and other short-term investments held by these pension funds, despite the long-run nature of the funds themselves. Equities, which have a superb track record over long holding periods, amount to only 36 or 41 percent of the total portfolio. Given historic returns, the pension funds would be better off with a larger stake in stocks. Our assumed real rates of return for the different asset categories are also shown in Table A1. The numbers are loosely based on the information in Ibbotson Associates (1993), although we are admittedly conservative. Ibbotson reports that the geometric average real rate of return for the Standard and Poor's 500 stock portfolio over the years 1926–92 was 7.0 percent. The corresponding average real rate of return on long-term corporate bonds was 2.3 percent, while it was 0.5 percent for short-term Trea-

TABLE A1

Asset Allocation of Pension Plans as of July 1992

(*percentage points*)

Type of plan	Equities	Bonds	GICs	Real estate	Cash
Private DB	36	33	0	15	16
Private DC	41	14	13	6	26
Federal DB	44	44	1	6	5
Federal DC	30	70	0	0	0
State and local DB	44	44	1	6	5
State and local DC	33	49	5	8	5
Real return rate[a]	5.0	2.0	1.2	2.0	0.0

SOURCES: Asset allocation: EBRI (various years). Rates of return: Authors' assumptions.

[a] Blended real rate for private DB plans: 2.76. Blended real rate for private DC plans: 2.646.

sury bills. We don't have any corresponding data for Guaranteed Interest Contracts (GICs), which are fixed-income contracts typically issued by insurance companies and featuring a somewhat shorter maturity than long-term bonds. As the reader can see, we have consistently assumed rates of return somewhat below the long-run averages calculated by Ibbotson.

The Social Security population projection was distributed by age, sex, and workforce participation for each year of the projection. Our analysis distributed the workforce into three separate sectors: the private employment sector, the state employment sector, and the federal employment sector. The working population was further distributed by tenure and pension participation status. In each year of the projection, the population and workforce were rolled forward one year with appropriate mortality decrements and workforce adjustments to account for job leavers, entrants, and changers. We had an underlying assumption that there was 14 percent turnover of workers between jobs each year.

The projections were developed separately for private employer plans, state and local defined benefit plans, and the federal employee thrift plan. In each case, separate projections were developed for defined benefit and defined contribution plans and then aggregated. For example, in the case of the projection for the private sector, we estimated that total employer contributions to private plans were 2.8 percent of payroll, approximately 30 percent of which has been going into defined benefit plans in recent years. Employee contributions to private plans were estimated to be 1.75 percent of payroll, with slightly less than 2 percent going to defined benefit plans. Based on estimates from the Form 5500 files of plans with 100 or more participants, we estimated that employer contributions to defined contribution plans were 1.13 times employee contributions to those plans.

In the initial year, benefits were estimated from the Form 5500 files and the QPIR data. Going forward, benefits were estimated on the basis of workers being covered by a pension and passing into immediate retirement starting at age 54. At that age, we assumed 3.7 percent of existing workers would retire. By age 80, we assumed all remaining workers would retire. For workers who terminated their employment under a defined benefit plan, if they were vested, we assumed they would be paid a deferred benefit at age 65. The accrual rate of the benefit formula for people working up until retirement calculated out to be 1.25 percent of final salary per year of service on average. For people receiving a deferred benefit, it was 1.00 percent of final salary per year of service. For people participating in a defined contribution plan, we assumed that 40 percent of the workers who terminated prior to retirement would take a lump-sum benefit and use it for some purpose other than meeting their retirement needs. For defined contribution plans generally, benefits commence at retirement and are paid out as an annuity over a maximum of 30 years.

Future contributions and trust fund accumulations are driven in large part by economic assumptions. Our assumptions on inflation, 4.0 percent per year, and wage growth, 5.1 percent per year, correspond with those used in the Alternative II Social Security projections.

Science and Technology Investment and Policy in the Global Economy

A. MICHAEL SPENCE

In this short chapter, I want to try to set out some of the characteristics of the American system for developing and deploying technology and some of the evolving features of the economic environment, principally in its international dimensions, that should influence how the current system performs and how it should be adapted in the future.

Part of the system of developing and deploying technology is in the public and non-profit sectors. But a very important part resides firmly in the private sector, both in the United States and increasingly around the world. In Figure 1, I have tried to put the elements of the U.S. science and technology system on a single piece of paper. I will be speaking about the relative size of these elements, their internal characteristics, and the ways in which they relate to each other. This sounds more formal than it will turn out to be. But I have found it useful in discussions about these general subjects to try to avoid situations in which conversations (sometimes quite heated) apparently about the same subject turn out to be about two or more different aspects of the system.

Now let me state in the most general terms where I am going, and then turn to the details. I will assume that most of the readers are familiar with the U.S. system for developing and deploying technology. I want to argue that the U.S. system currently in place was built immediately after World War II, at a time when the United States was the only substantial economy intact and capable of both developing and deploying technology.

I want to thank my colleagues at the Graduate School of Business at Stanford University and those who served with me on the National Research Council's Board on Science, Technology, and Economic Policy for their useful critical comments. Also, thanks to Ralph Landau for his numerous comments and insights.

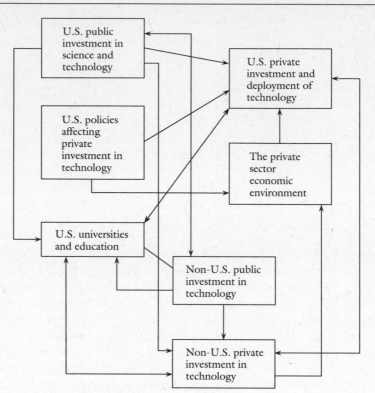

Figure 1. Elements of a global science and technology system.

I will then argue that this is no longer true, in fact that it has been getting steadily less true for 30 years. I will try to identify two or three broad options for adapting to the new circumstances. On the way by, so to speak, I want to rely on a recent report from the Board on Science, Technology and Economic Policy of the National Research Council (1994), to suggest that there are some problems in the U.S. private sector and in policies that surround it, principally in the areas of saving, investment, and the cost of capital, that bear on these issues and that affect the U.S. economy's ability to take advantage of technology to improve productivity, competitiveness, growth, and per capita income.[1]

Finally, let me give away the answer, or the option I think we should

1. The two main papers from the conference on which the report was based are Hatsopoulos and Poterba (1994) and Porter (1994). Note that the report of the NRC and the conference volume have the same name. The conference volume will eventually include the NRC report as well as the supporting papers. However, as of this writing, the NRC summary is available on its own from National Academy Press in Washington, D.C.

prefer. It is that we should try to maintain most of the features of our current system for developing civilian technology, augment it a little to compensate for the vacuum that the withdrawal from defense will leave, and attempt to persuade our principal industrialized partners to do approximately the same thing. In a nutshell, this system would involve all developed nations investing proportionate amounts in science and technology, in a system which is open, so that the results are available to research personnel in governments, universities, and companies on a global basis.

The alternatives are to continue on the present course and hence continue to be a very large net supplier of technology and human capital to the rest of the industrialized world, or to undertake an elaborate sequence of steps, the intent of which would be to partially close the U.S. system in the global sense so that the benefits of U.S. investment become more proprietary from a national point of view. The problem with the first of these is that it will continue to come under increasing adverse political pressure. The underlying issue will be: "Why should a large asymmetry continue to exist at taxpayer expense when there is a much more even distribution of wealth than there was 30 or 40 years ago?"[2] This kind of pressure will lead to a tendency to adopt the second alternative: closing the system. The problem with it, I will argue, is that to close the U.S. system even partially, one will have to take measures that affect all the players (government labs, universities, companies, and investors) and that reduce dramatically the efficiency of the national investment in technology.[3]

Some Observations About the Global Economy and Related Matters

The U.S. approach to science and technology was put in place after the Second World War, using the model of the war effort to generate science and technology and to respond to the technological demands of the cold

---

2. It might be objected here that the data show that Germany and Japan have national investment rates in R&D that are as high or higher than the United States. This is true if you add together public and private R&D investment and particularly if you remove the defense R&D in the United States. However, though the data are less good, I would argue that there remains an imbalance in the upstream, non-proprietary, open segment of the R&D portfolio, where the free-rider problem is potentially greatest and our system most vulnerable to the criticism implied by this question.

3. Cohen and Noll (in this volume) argue that we are well on the way down the competitive path with respect to technology. This is the path I am referring to as "closing the system." Cohen and Noll are certainly right about the directional shift and the consequences in terms of efficiency. I guess my view would be that there is still the opportunity to adopt the other option, what I call the multilateral approach at the end of this chapter.

war. Whatever the U.S. fraction of industrial country GDP was at the time (a conservative estimate would be 65 to 70 percent), it has now declined to 30 to 35 percent. The amount of technology generated by public sector investment and private investment outside the United States has therefore increased tremendously, as has ability of economic actors in other nations to absorb the technology generated here.

These trends will continue. It is almost certainly true—indeed, it is becoming commonplace to predict—that a large fraction of world growth will be in Asia and Latin America in the next two decades.[4] Eastern Europe may also be a center of growth. (The reader will find in the chapter by Rowen in this volume a very interesting forecast of global economic growth in the next few decades.)

In addition, these regions—especially parts of Asia and eastern Europe—have quite highly developed human resources but do not yet have the incomes and prices of the most advanced industrial countries of Europe, North America, and Japan. These emerging economies thus have large advantages as places to locate high-quality, low-cost manufacturing facilities; one large global company that has moved aggressively into eastern Europe estimates that it has at least a 30 percent cost advantage in manufacturing there relative to comparable facilities in western Europe. As long as the world economy remains relatively open, these cost differentials will cause, in fact force, a fairly rapid evolution in the advanced industrial countries. One can see some of the effects both in countries like Korea and in the United States and Japan.

The direction of this evolution is not easy to predict or characterize accurately. The notion that all U.S. workers will end up in non-tradable, low value-added per worker services is surely wrong, because of exchange rates adjustments and the infeasibility of running permanent large trade deficits. A trend in the advanced industrial countries, however, toward exportable services industries based on expertise and human capital is entirely feasible and even likely. It is also likely that these activities will include using information technology to direct global manufacturing and distribution systems. I sometimes ask the Stanford business school students what the Gap, Nike, and (almost) Sun Microsystems have in common. The answer

---

4. I recently had the opportunity to look at the figures on per capita consumption of electricity in China, the same figures the principal suppliers of power generation capacity are looking at. To move China to even low-to-moderate per capita consumption levels by industrial country standards will require the opening of power plants in the 1000 to 2000 megawatt range every month for the better part of twenty years. Similar statements could be made about roads, information systems, and a host of other parts of what we normally think of as infrastructure.

is that in a certain sense they are quite completely vertically integrated from product development through to the final consumer. The only step they do not undertake in-house is manufacturing.[5]

The pattern is far from clear, however. In the 1980s, the computer industry changed its basic structure from vertically integrated (like IBM) to a series of horizontal market bands in each of which there is intense competition. I think it is fair to say that economists do not yet have a comprehensive framework for understanding the forces that cause the shifting pattern of vertical integration, disintegration, alliances, and changes in economic relationships among companies in the value-added chain in various industries and sectors.

But whatever emerges from this process, it is a reasonably good guess that technology, particularly information and communication technology, will play a central enabling role. And the transitions will be accompanied by substantial investments in technology and in capital that is complementary to the new technology.

The U.S. Economic Environment

I would like to step back now for a short period and look at the U.S. economy in terms of adaptability, investment, and savings.

The good news first: U.S. companies were confronted in the late 1970s and early 1980s with the effects of substantial innovation in manufacturing in Japan, including an orientation to quality, effective supply-chain management, and continuous incremental process improvement. After a lag, U.S. companies (and I might add schools of management) have responded. There is clearly an improved situation with respect to relative productivity as a result of taking the international challenge seriously. U.S. firms have made major efforts to increase efficiency, speed, and quality; the automobile and semiconductor industries serve as vivid examples. Further, in the deployment of information technology to improve on best practice in both internal processes and supply-chain management, it appears to this observer that U.S. companies and U.S. technology are (on average) in the lead.

The less good news comes from the more macroeconomic long-term view of the economy. I will not dwell on this, but I need to mention it because it bears directly on the development and use of technology in the

---

5. Benetton is often cited as the extreme example of the corporation as architect of the system as it contracts out virtually every step of the value-added chain.

private sector, which we have already seen is potentially important to the future.[6]

Savings and Investment

The U.S. savings rate has been well below industrial country norms for all of the 1980s and thus far in the 1990s. The savings rate net of the federal deficit is under 3 percent of GDP and at times recently has fallen close to zero. Even leaving aside the federal deficit, the national savings rate is low, on the order of 7 to 8 percent of GDP. It is also below the national levels of net investment, so for several years the United States has been a net importer of capital.[7]

There are two consequences of having low savings rates relative to other countries and relative to domestic investment. To the extent that capital markets are integrated on a global basis, the shortfall of capital in the United States raises global interest rates and the cost of capital. In itself, this is not a disaster. But at a time when the demand for capital in Asia, Latin America, and eastern Europe is huge, it is certainly not helpful that the world's richest country is a net absorber of capital. A second consequence involves the partial integration of global capital markets. It is generally agreed that integration in fixed income securities is quite far along and more advanced than integration with respect to equity.[8] To the extent that equity markets are not fully integrated globally, a savings shortfall in the United States has the effect of differentially raising the cost of equity capital in the United States.

There are other causes of an elevated cost of capital in the United States, such as the tax system, so I do not wish to appear to be basing the entire case on savings behavior and the amount of integration in global financial markets. Below, I will discuss some of the direct evidence that the U.S. cost of capital is higher than in other industrial countries.

U.S. investment rates as a percentage of GDP have been below the average for other industrial countries for at least fifteen years. The rates of productivity growth have been similarly below average for longer than that. Meanwhile, the measured return on corporate investment in the United

---

6. The discussion that follows relies heavily on National Research Council (1994).

7. As economists recognize, but much public discussion does not, this excess of domestic investment over domestic savings, plus some accounting identities, explains the trade deficit.

8. There are reasons for this. The information flows required to support full integration of equity markets are very substantial. There is, of course, partial integration of equity markets through the dependence of asset prices, including equity, on interest rates, which increasingly are set in global markets.

States has been *above* that of Japan and Germany. This suggests that the costs of capital faced by U.S. companies have been and continue to be above those used by companies in other countries. In addition, there is quite a bit of qualitative evidence that U.S. publicly traded corporations interact with many financial investors who have relatively short time horizons, which is what one expects of investors who face a higher cost of capital.[9]

In terms of the focus of this chapter, the key connection is that long-term investments in private sector technology are most appropriately financed by equity. With technology investments, there is often little in the way of measurable collateral or tangible assets that normally accompany the use of debt financing. A higher cost of equity is therefore a problem for private technology investment, and in turn, a problem for an economy like ours, which will evolve in the shifting patterns of global competition in part based on its capacity to invest in and deploy new technology.

It would take me too far afield here to document the evidence, the arguments, and the counterarguments for these propositions. The point I want to make is just that if we are entering a period of relatively rapid evolution in most advanced industrial countries, as I and many others expect, then impediments to long-term investments in critical intangible assets like technology, human capital, and training and the development of new products and markets are a worrying handicap. And having a high relative cost of equity capital is precisely such an impediment.

Improving the Macroeconomic Environment

A report of the Board on Science, Technology and Economic Policy (STEP) of the National Research Council (NRC) (1994) recommended a number of changes in policy that are intended to improve the U.S. macroeconomic environment for saving and investment. I recap the substance of those recommendations here. I believe that without changes of this type, more microeconomic technology policies will not translate into the desired effect on overall economic productivity.

Any democratic political system creates substantial pressures to deal with immediate short-run problems. These need to be counterbalanced with a longer-term view. It would be desirable for the administration and Congress to set specific longer-term goals with respect to private investment, net saving, and productivity growth. I believe that the American public would and should support such efforts, if they were publicly explained and justified.

---

9. These comments are summaries of the work of Hatsopoulos and Poterba (1994), Porter (1994), and Landau (1994).

The STEP board of the NRC argued that having net saving and investment rates of 8 to 10 percent of GDP over a five- to ten-year period would contribute measurably to enhancing productivity and wage growth in the United States. Such rates would also not hurt and would probably help the global economy. It would make the U.S. neither a net importer nor a net exporter of capital, and it would put U.S. domestic investment in the range of other advanced industrial countries. To advance these objectives, the tax system would have to be changed over the next decade in accordance with several key principles:

1. Steady movement toward a progressive consumption-based tax system, in which saving and investment income are taxed less or not at all and consumption is taxed more.[10]

2. Eliminating the double taxation of that part of corporate income paid as dividends to holders of equity, to close the gap between the return on the corporate investment and the return to the financial investor.

3. Reducing the investment subsidy for residential real estate, and using these revenues to reduce taxes on corporate investments.

4. As an interim measure, extending the favorable tax treatment of long-term gains on corporate stock to equity investments in companies *regardless of size*. This would have the dual effects of partially reducing the double taxation of corporate income and encouraging longer-term investments and time horizons among financial investors.

5. Over time, government dissaving (that is, the budget deficit) needs to be eliminated to restore the rate of saving to an appropriate level and to stem the growth of interest payments as a fraction of the federal budget. Interest payments now represent about 14 percent of the federal budget. Even after taking into account the planned effects of the 1993 deficit reduction measures, interest costs are expected to consume the same share of federal spending by the end of the century.

6. Private saving needs to be increased. The tax measures mentioned above should help. But since economists do not now have a systematic understanding of the large differences in savings rates across countries, it is therefore difficult to know what other measures might be effective in encouraging private savings.

7. Expand the cadre of long-term investors, by giving management and directors restricted stock and options, and by removing various impediments to institutional investors holding large equity positions of particular companies.

Over an extended period of time, these steps will improve the environ-

---

10. The Nunn-Domenici proposal is a recent example of such an approach.

ment for corporate investment, and particularly for longer-term investments in technology. Without such measures, the availability of funds and the high required after-tax returns on investment threaten to diminish U.S. economic performance in the critical areas of productivity growth and new market development.

The U.S. Science and Technology System

The U.S. system for generating science and technology and deploying it has been in place for 40 years. It has had and retains many attractive features. Among them are the following.

1. There has been a broad portfolio of basic science and civilian technology invested in by the federal government.

2. As a result of the peer review system, that investment has been quite efficient as measured by results per dollar invested.

3. Overhead, being tied to direct funding, has in effect also been subject to the peer review system, and hence based upon a measure of merit.

4. By conducting a substantial fraction of the research in universities, the country has obtained as a joint product a highly educated scientific and engineering workforce.

5. The system has been open, so results once produced are relatively freely available. This by itself dramatically increases the efficiency of the whole system. The system is open not just domestically but internationally.

6. Defense, a substantial fraction of the total national R&D investment, has been mission-oriented, more proprietary from a national point of view than either basic science or civilian technology investment, and characterized by variable (over time) spillovers into the civilian R&D sector. The majority view appears to be that defense R&D spillovers into the civilian sector have declined substantially and steadily over time.

7. The National Academies have assembled the ablest scientific and engineering talent in the country and made it available at marginal cost to the government in the form of advice on matters of science and technology.

8. In the private sector, the availability of knowledgeable venture capital and substantial research capacity in large corporations helped ensure that technology was rapidly developed and used commercially.

9. The private sector's culture and legal environment have been tolerant of spin-offs, which have been the source of much innovation and growth in many high-technology sectors. Schools of engineering and medicine have also been sources of spin-offs with similar effects.

10. Intellectual property, while a complex area of the law, has been reasonably effective in ensuring adequate returns to the investor in technology, without stifling new product development or the creation of new enterprises.

11. There has been some evolution in policy surrounding the system in the area of joint technology ventures, whether among private firms or with government as a partner. Initially, antitrust was hostile to this kind of collaboration, since it looked as if it might be a concealed form of price collusion. More recently, the prevailing view is that in many contexts, international competition is a sufficient regulatory device to protect consumers. The Advanced Technology Program of the National Institute of Standards and Technology (part of the Department of Commerce) is now conceived of as a collaboration between government and groups of companies. It is projected to grow substantially in the federal budget. There remain issues in this area to be resolved, such as who has access to the technology funded in part with public funds. In general there remains a wide range of opinion about whether there is some middle ground between public investment in technology (mostly upstream) and individual corporate private investment in which there is underinvestment. I suspect that the prevailing view in Washington is that the public sector science and technology investment is somewhat overbalanced toward upstream, basic research, and thus that the government science and technology portfolio should shift somewhat (though not dramatically) toward the downstream, applied, commercial applications.

What, Then, Is New?

The international environment for the creation and dissemination of science and technology is changing, which raises questions of what modifications, if any, would be appropriate technology practices and policies. Let me list some of these changes, in no particular order.

As the industrial and industrializing countries grew over the last 40 years, their capacity to produce and to absorb technology increased, too. Although the U.S. science and technology system was formally open in the 1950s, it was de facto mostly of benefit domestically. But now, the openness of the U.S. system produces major benefits on a worldwide basis.

There is now substantial production and absorption of technology outside the United States. It is undertaken by both government investment and private corporations. As a result, the complexity of the international flows of technology, and the activities required by companies to ensure that they have access to the most advanced technology, have increased substantially. One gets an impression of this complexity from Figure 1, presented earlier.

The investment in defense-related technology will likely decline in the United States as a result of the end of the cold war. From a national perspective, this component of the R&D portfolio tended to be more proprietary, in the sense that the fruits of this spending redounded to U.S. companies. To the extent that the defense R&D is replaced by civilian R&D under the current system, the effect will be even more openness from a global perspective. Of course, if the federal government reduces R&D without a corresponding increase in the civilian sector, the total commitment of resources to science and technology will decline.[11]

In the past, there have been major basic science research programs in corporations. IBM and AT&T are perhaps the leading examples. Under global competitive pressure, this corporate support for basic research has declined and is unlikely to return.

The United States (and to some extent the United Kingdom) have become the global training centers for high-level scientific and engineering personnel. There is an asymmetry here. It is not that other advanced countries are incapable of providing advanced scientific education, or completely avoid doing so. Rather, the flows tend to be one-way because of the relative universality of the English language in scientific communication. There are tens of thousands of foreign citizens of great ability in U.S. postgraduate degree programs. Upon graduation, many of these stay in the United States and expand the scientific base here. Others return to their countries. There is then an implicit transfer of technology in the process.[12]

Before considering possible ways of thinking about the consequences of these changes in the international environment, it is important to dispose of one notion. It is commonly thought that the substantial U.S. public sector investment in science and technology is a source of competitive advantage. There are undoubtedly what might be called local or neighborhood effects in the transfer of technology from the public domain to the private sector. It would be hard to live for long in Silicon Valley and argue that these do not exist. On the other hand, except for defense, public investment in technology occurs in a largely open global system. In such an

---

11. Even if one thinks that the spillovers from defense R&D have been low, the reduction in defense R&D will still reduce the resources devoted to training scientific and engineering manpower. The latter do move between the defense and civilian sectors.

12. This asymmetry created in part by language need not be permanent. It is quite possible that in two or three decades, the volume of science and technology investment and training in Asia will be such that Chinese will become an important second international language for scientific education.

environment, public investment in technology could not be a long-run source of advantage, because the technology generated by public investment has been, by choice, very accessible. It is more like an international public good.

Directions for Technology Policy and Investment

If one accepts the general direction of the preceding analysis, there are some issues to be considered and some conclusions to be drawn. In general terms, it is important that government policies (including those not normally thought of as strictly technology policies) be conducive to vigorous private sector investment in technology and in complementary assets.

To maintain a healthy level of private sector investment in technology, it is necessary to ensure that the availability and cost of capital is competitive. That probably means moving over time toward a system in which investment and saving is taxed less and consumption is taxed more. This is not a new idea. But it may be gaining ground. The most recent proposal is the Nunn-Domenici proposal for a progressive consumption-based tax system using the apparatus of the current income tax system. There have been several proposals for tax integration, the elimination of double taxation of income flows from equity investment (for example, see U.S. Department of the Treasury, 1992). There are other ways of lowering the taxation of income from investment, and hence the cost of capital, for investment in productive intangible assets like technology. For example, the STEP board has proposed that the non-taxation of mortgage interest on residential real estate for principal amounts in the higher ranges be phased out and replaced with reduced taxes on capital gains from longer-term holdings of equity (National Research Council, 1994).

In the longer term, increasing the savings rate will be necessary. That means reducing the federal deficit and finding a way to increase the private savings rate. To the extent possible in our political system, it is also desirable to avoid policies that create rather than reduce risk in the private sector investment process. Unpredictable variations in policy will tend to create risk and deter investment. This is important in regulated areas like the environment and health and safety.[13]

---

13. Many believe that our tax system creates perverse incentives for U.S. multinationals to put their R&D activity abroad, and that the tax system does not put the United States on a level playing field with international competitors. Since much of the tax system evolved during the period when U.S. technology was the dominant force, it is probably a good time to undertake a thorough reexamination of its provisions and their consequences with respect to R&D.

On the issue of direct government investment in science and technology, the central issue is whether there are adaptations of the current system that are wise in view of the changed international environment. Let me start by clarifying what the objectives are. For this purpose, I will take the objective of public investment in science and technology to be to contribute materially to the steady improvement in the standard of living and quality of life of U.S. citizens. Notice that this objective is different from "winning" in some global competitive battle. Also, the adoption of this objective does not preclude that those in other countries also benefit from U.S. science and technology investment—my proposed objective is neutral on that point. I emphasize these points simply because I have found in discussions of these issues that proponents of alternative approaches often have quite different underlying objectives.

Given the characteristics of the current science and technology system, its continuation with little modification is one option. Other countries will then continue adapting to the U.S. system. They will take the upstream part of the U.S. research system as an international public good and then invest in ways that are complementary and that further their goals. In most countries, there is not much point in trying to match or duplicate the massive U.S. investment in biomedical science. The smart thing to do, and what is in fact being done, is for other countries to rely on the United States for much of the basic science and advanced scientific research and training, and then to devote relatively more of their own resources to supporting the downstream, private sector, and relatively more proprietary parts of the science and technology value-added chain. Historically, in most countries, this has meant that the relative size of the private R&D sector (relative, that is, to the public investment) is larger than it is in the United States, not because the U.S. private sector investment in technology is small, but rather because the public investment is large.

Over time, if this scenario were to be played out, it would lead to increasing skepticism from U.S. policy makers and legislators. We have seen this pattern before.

For example, prior to the end of the cold war, there began to be concern in the area of defense that the United States was providing a disproportionate share of what amounted to a public good for the democratic part of the world. What seemed quite natural 25 years ago—given the large differences in size and wealth—will increasingly seem less natural and equitable. We also see a similar pattern in international trade negotiations in the postwar period. For a couple of decades, the United States was prepared to play a leading role in promoting free trade, provided that the general evolution proceeded under the auspices of the multilateral GATT, implicit in which was the notion that while there might need to be a period of asymmetrical behavior as the industrializing countries grew and recovered, the goal was a symmetric multilateral system supported by all the industrialized countries. By and large, the direction of movement has been consistent with the intent. But when other countries do not evolve quickly enough toward the prescribed multinational behavior as they become richer, friction results.

In the area of science and technology, these concerns could take two broad directions. One direction would be a series of actions which attempted to confine the benefits of U.S. science and technology investment as much as possible to the domestic economy; in a phrase, to close the system at least partially. The second direction is to maintain the openness, but seek through international negotiation to reach an agreement that all advanced countries will adopt a broadly similar approach and contribute proportionately (in very gross terms) to a global public good of a science and technology base. This seems to me similar in broad terms to the pattern in trade and the still-evolving pattern in defense. Let me refer to the latter as the multilateral approach and to the former (that is, partially closing the domestic system) as the competitive approach.

My view is that the multilateral course is vastly preferable, for a number of reasons.

The first point I want to make is that the incentive structure of this situation is not zero-sum. Certainly, the multilateral approach is designed to cause mutual benefits to accrue to all the parties. There is a free-rider problem with which the multilateral approach is designed to deal. If all nations adopted the competitive approach and tried to close off their science and technology to the extent possible, the world would be a poorer place.

The second point is that the multilateral approach is consistent with specialization by country. Specialization will require some sophistication in the system of accounting. But there is no reason in principle why one or a few nations could not become the leading suppliers of advanced environmental technology while others do biomedical science and still others invest more heavily in materials.[14] Because of its size, the United States is likely to have the broadest portfolio for the foreseeable future. The multilateral approach is also consistent with having certain countries specialize

---

14. Timothy Taylor pointed out that in the interests of promoting goodwill in the multilateral approach, it would be useful if each of the advanced countries did not invest in one or two technologies, so that the mutual dependence and reciprocity would be more visible.

in science and technology. That is to say, the country-level investments need not coincide exactly with the location of the activity. If the United States has a comparative advantage in science and technology investment, then the public and private sectors in other countries can put investment resources into these activities in the United States. The multilateral approach refers mainly to the origins of the resources to be invested in the international public good, and not to the balance of the locations in which the investments are carried out.[15]

But the main point I want to make is that the competitive approach, despite its likely political appeal, has problems. To close the U.S. system even partially, one would need to take a series of policy actions the effect of which would be not only to reduce the outflow of technology internationally, but also to substantially reduce the internal openness of the system.[16] Consider Silicon Valley, or any one of many advanced centers of biomedical science in the United States. Upon close inspection you will find companies and university sciences interacting daily. You will find investors, venture capitalists, and entrepreneurs in constant contact. New companies are started and then taken public or purchased by larger companies. In biotechnology, many companies make marketing contracts with multinational pharmaceutical companies. Large companies increasingly enter into alliances with multinationals based outside the United States to develop new and expensive technologies: the IBM-Siemans-Toshiba joint venture for the 256-megabyte memory chip would be an example.

Even trying to close this system is difficult to imagine. If a serious attempt were made to do so, the required steps would substantially interdict the flow of scientific and technical information in the U.S. economy, within the scientific community, and between that group and the private sector. The openness of that complex system has been one of the most important contributors to the efficiency of the science and technology investment process.

15. I am indebted to Robert Hall for making this useful distinction and a related point, that requiring balance in the location of the activity could lead to large inefficiencies. There are potential problems. Foreign investment in U.S. institutions that develop technology can be (and has been) seen as buying American technology cheaply, rather than as sharing in the investment in international public goods. It will therefore be important to underscore in policy discussions that such investments are reciprocal and part of an overall system that is fair.

16. The efficiency cost of doing this can be enormous. The chapter by Nathan Rosenberg in this volume points out that there is a large unpredictable element in the process of advancing technology. An advance in one area can unlock an impasse in another seemingly unrelated area. The openness promotes the finding of these linkages promptly and also reduces redundant and wasted effort.

Let me put this point differently and slightly more technically. The wisdom of the U.S. science and technology system has been the combination of substantial public investment combined with low-to-negligible appropriability of technology, at least until one gets well down in the value-added chain toward product development. The low appropriability increases efficiency by reducing redundancy. But it also reduces private sector incentives for investment in basic research by lowering the returns for such investment. The substantial public investment restores those returns sufficiently to induce private investment at the appropriate downstream points.

I do not detect a strong inclination to move in the direction of the competitive approach. Hence I do not want to leave the impression that there is an imminent threat of such a move. Rather, I suspect that the problem will be one of continuing and escalating tension and public criticism surrounding the commitment of public funds to science and technology in an environment in which it is relatively easy to demonstrate that the benefits are dispersed globally at a rapid rate. Ultimately, that could lead directly to reduced investment in technology. The best defense against this line of argument seems to me the multilateral approach, which would make it possible to argue that the direction of movement is one in which advanced countries contribute to the base of knowledge in science and technology in such a way as to benefit everyone. Although I have not made the point here, it is perhaps obvious that if our science and technology system is open to advanced countries, it will necessarily be open to developing ones, as well.

This general stance is responsible and consistent with America's general approach in international economic relations. I would hope that the administration, Congress, and the influential National Academies would take up the issue of U.S. science and technology policy in a global economy and that after due consideration and debate they would push us in the multilateral direction.

PART III

International Exchange
and Economic Growth

Threats to 21st-Century Growth: The Challenge of the International Trading System

ANNE O. KRUEGER

Whether one takes a long view over several centuries, or a shorter view of the post–Second World War period, the increased integration of the world economy has been a striking trend. Throughout almost all of the two centuries for which estimates are available, world trade has grown more rapidly than world real output. Periods of slow growth of trade have been those with slow growth of output, and conversely.

There is little question about the association of expanding trade in goods and services and economic growth, nor is there much question about causation. There is something of a question as to the precise mechanisms through which trade and growth are interlinked. Nonetheless, there is little doubt that the future growth prospects for the world as a whole are interlinked with prospects for the international trading system.

Despite the recent signing of the Uruguay Round trade agreement, there is considerable basis for concern as to the future evolution of the system, and therefore of world trade. The world appears to be near a crossroads. Either the multilateral trading system that has served the world so well over the past four decades will be strengthened to cope with the new issues that have arisen as integration has proceeded, or the trading system will gradually degenerate. The outcome would then be regional trading blocs and/or much higher levels of protection and less integration. Should the system degenerate, it would constitute a grave challenge to global economic growth in the 21st century.

It is the purpose of this chapter to review the role of trade in contributing to economic growth, and then to examine the evolution of the world

I am indebted to Roderick Duncan for valuable research assistance in the preparation of this manuscript.

trading system to the 1990s. It will be seen that U.S. leadership of the open multilateral system was important not only in the initiation of the GATT system, but in the unprecedented reciprocal reductions in trade barriers that took place in the three decades after the Second World War. The chapter then discusses how U.S. policy exhibits schizophrenia between support of the multilateral trading system through the World Trade Organization (WTO), on the one hand, and reliance on bilateral negotiations with individual trading partners, on the other. Finally, the discussion examines the reasons why this weakened U.S. commitment constitutes a threat to the multilateral trading system and draws conclusions.

Historical Trends in the Growth of Trade and Real Output

The increasing integration of the world economy has been a long-term trend at least since the spice trade began between Europe and Asia. That integration has come about both among regions and among nations. As linkages have increased, producers have been enabled to specialize and take advantage of economies of scale in production and marketing, and to locate inputs more ideally suited for their production processes. Integration has also permitted more competition in local markets, with a spur to greater productivity growth and lower costs of production. Distant regions have been enabled to acquire goods and services from lower-cost distant sources rather than less competent local producers, and to sell goods and services of their more talented entrepreneurs in larger volumes than was earlier the case. Improved communications, speedier transportation, and the increased flow of goods and services have all enabled more rapid transmission of new technology and know-how.

There have been a number of reasons for this integration, but unquestionably a major one has been the fall in barriers to interregional and international trade. These barriers were, historically, of several kinds. Costs of transport and communications were high until new technologies (such as steam) were developed. They were high also because of dangers posed by an inability of nations to maintain law and order on transport routes.[1] Trade barriers erected by feudal lords constituted yet another obstacle to trade, and have declined substantially.

An important characteristic of the evolution of modern economies has

---

1. North (1958) has estimated that the elimination of piracy on the high seas in the nineteenth century enabled a virtual halving of shipping costs, as the weight and space earlier allotted to cannon and defense could instead be used to additional cargo. North estimates that ocean freight rates for U.S. exports fell from 363 (on an 1830 = 100 base) in 1815 to an average of 75 for the years 1855–59 (North, 1966, p. 245).

been the rapid decline in the real costs of transportation and communications (for example, North, 1958). As these fell, the price/cost differentials that had to exist before exchange was profitable for more distant places decreased, enabling trade in more goods and services as well as increasing volumes of goods already traded. In addition, there were numerous man-made obstacles to trade. Hecksher (1955) has pointed out that a ship sailing up the Rhine had to stop and pay tolls to each feudal lord en route—often entailing more than 100 stops. In mercantilist times, feudal lords were attempting to prevent imports to their countries, while simultaneously trying to encourage exports—not an achievable goal for the world as a whole. As nation-states lowered their barriers to trade (and as England led the world economy with virtual free trade in the nineteenth century) and as transport and communications costs fell dramatically, economic growth was spurred by integration nationally and internationally. Estimates for the growth of world trade and output for the period from 1800 to 1937, and for 1948 to 1963, are given in Table 1. As can be seen, over the 113 years after 1800, it is estimated that the volume of world trade grew more than 4 times as rapidly as did world output. World output is estimated to have grown at 7.3 percent *per decade*, while the per decade growth rate of trade is estimated at 33 percent.

Estimates of the *annual* rates of growth of trade and output from 1948 to 1963 are presented in the last row of Table 1. As can be seen, annual rates of growth of output were almost as high in the postwar years as decadal rates had been in 1913–37. An average annual rate of growth of 6 percent in trade volumes results in a rate of growth of 70 percent for the decade, contrasted with 33 percent during the rapid growth period of the nineteenth century!

TABLE I

Long-Term Estimates of Rates of Growth
of World Output and Trade, 1800–1963

	Output growth	Trade growth
Per decade		
1800–13	7.3%	33.0%
1913–37	5.0[a]	3.0
Per year		
1948–63	4.1	6.0

SOURCE: Kenwood and Lougheed (1983, pp. 90, 222, 313).

[a] Based on rates of growth of output in thirteen developed countries.

TABLE 2

Growth Rates of World Trade and Output, 1965–92

(*percent per year*)

	1965–73	1973–80	1980–90	1990–92
World trade volume	11.8	5.7	4.3	3.1
GNP per capita				
High-income countries	3.7	2.1	2.3	0.9
Developing countries	4.3	2.7	1.2	−1.1

SOURCES: For trade, International Monetary Fund (*International Financial Statistics*, various years). For per capita income estimates, World Bank (1993).

With trade volumes growing at more than four times the rate of growth of output, the shares of exports and imports in real GDP increased significantly in the nineteenth century, especially in Europe.[2] It should also be noted that the rate of growth of trade volumes fell below that of output in the 1913–37 period. Indeed, during the 1930s, it is estimated that trade volumes actually shrank, and of course, during the Great Depression, so, too, did world output. Indeed, throughout the entire period, decades with more rapid growth of world trade were also decades with more rapid growth of world output.

This trend was, if anything, intensified after the Second World War. The quarter-century from 1948 to 1973 will surely long be remembered as a period of sustained growth at an unprecedented rate, combined with, if anything, accelerated integration of the world economy. Transport costs (in time as well as money) were continuing to fall,[3] and increasingly cheap and effective communications lowered transactions costs between distant buyers and sellers. Likewise, as will be discussed in the next section, trade barriers between nations were being greatly reduced, at least until the 1980s.

Growth rates of trade volumes and real output for the period 1965–92 are given in Table 2.[4] Many had viewed the rapid economic growth, especially of the industrialized countries, in the 1950s as transitory and resulting from postwar reconstruction. But, if anything, growth in output

2. Kenwood and Lougheed (1983) divide growth prior to 1913 into two periods. In their analysis (p. 103), prior to 1860 most trade was "disconnected trading arrangements mainly centred on Britain," which was replaced by "a new multilateral trading system based on a worldwide pattern of economic specialization."

3. The ratio of world imports at c.i.f. (cost, insurance, freight) prices, which include all transport costs, to world exports f.o.b. (free on board), which exclude transport costs, stood at 1.20 in 1948, had fallen to 1.09 in 1960, and stood at 1.058 in 1990 (International Monetary Fund, 1991, pp. 128–29).

4. These data are based on International Monetary Fund and World Bank estimates, and are not strictly comparable with the data from Table 1.

and in the volume of trade actually accelerated in the 1960s and until 1973. These were, indeed, golden years for the world economy.

Interestingly, developing countries also grew very rapidly after the Second World War, although their share of world trade diminished as they followed protectionist policies in order to encourage domestic industrialization through import substitution.[5] In effect, their exports grew fairly rapidly because of buoyant demand in the world market, although the supply of exports from developing countries was not increasing rapidly, as resources were diverted to new, import-competing, activities.[6]

The year 1973 marked a watershed in the international economy. That was the year in which the oil price tripled. The short-term response was a severe recession in most industrialized countries. As can be seen from Table 2, the growth rate of developed countries' per capita income fell by almost half—from 3.7 to 2.1 percent—in the remainder of the decade. Developing countries also experienced a drop in growth rates, although it was proportionately less severe.

The developed countries' response to the oil price increase included measures that resulted in inflationary pressures. Unit values, which approximate the prices of goods traded on world markets, had risen at an average annual rate of 5.4 percent from 1965–73 (in contrast to virtual stability from 1955 to 1965). The rate of increase of world prices of tradables tripled after the oil price increase—reaching a 16.6 percent annual average in the late 1970s.

The 1980s witnessed a slightly higher rate of economic growth for the industrial countries (2.3 percent, contrasted with 2.1 percent for 1973–80), although there was a sharp recession in the early 1980s as disinflationary policies were followed in the wake of the second oil price increase in 1979. Disinflationary policies resulted in high real interest rates, which, combined with the recession and an inability of old policies to deliver more growth, resulted in a marked slowdown in growth for the developing countries. Their accumulated debt and debt-servicing difficulties, combined with a recognition of the need for altered policies (especially toward the

5. Developing countries' share of world agricultural exports fell from 44 percent in 1955 to 27 percent by the mid-1980s. Their share of manufactured exports fell from 6.5 percent in 1955 to 3.5 percent in 1970, and began rising thereafter, reaching 13.6 percent by 1986 (Krueger, 1992).

6. See below for a discussion of developing countries' reentry into the world economy in the 1970s and 1980s. With hindsight, it is clear that some of the growth achieved in the 1950s and 1960s was attributable to increased investment in health, education, and infrastructure, but that some of the import-substitution growth was unsustainable. Over time, it became increasingly difficult to sustain growth as the inefficiency costs of closed economies increased.

international economy), resulted in a drastic reduction in the growth of per capita incomes to an average of 1.2 percent annually.[7] Those negative trends, along with much slower growth of industrialized countries, persisted into the early 1990s.

For present purposes, several other phenomena should be noted from the data in Table 2. The first is the tendency toward slower global growth of *both* trade and per capita incomes after 1973. To be sure, growth rates were still above their level of the nineteenth century, but they had clearly decelerated.[8] In part, that may reflect the global disinflation of the early 1980s and the recession of the early 1990s: an optimist could predict that growth rates for the rest of the 1990s will rebound as disinflation has run its course and the recession of 1990–92 has ended.

The second phenomenon is the fact that for each period since the Second World War (as well as for most of the earlier century and a half except for years surrounding the Great Depression), growth rates of world trade exceeded the growth rates of world output. Whether it is underlying changes in the technology of communications and transport that drives both GDP growth and the growth of world trade, or whether there are other linkages is an important question, but one that is not central to assessing the threat to the global trading system. Regardless of the mechanisms by which growth of trade and output are linked, it is clear that restrictions on the growth of trade will reduce the benefits of technical change and reduced transport and communications costs in ways that will be detrimental to further growth.

What is true for the world is true for individual countries: those with more rapid growth of trade also tend to have more rapid growth rates of GDP. Table 3 presents data on growth rates for a number of individual countries for various time periods since 1950.

Leaders in many developing countries have now recognized that their earlier rejection of the international market seriously jeopardized their growth prospects.[9] Policy reforms have been undertaken in many developing countries. Those which have succeeded in changing their trade

---

7. These averages conceal sharp differences among groups of developing countries. See below, and especially the discussion surrounding Table 4.

8. Recall that the growth rates listed in Table 1 are for decades, whereas Table 2 records average annual rates of growth.

9. The "debt crisis" of the 1980s was in part a symptom of underlying difficulties in the policy stance of the developing countries. Many had encountered increasing economic inefficiencies as they maintained their inward-oriented statist policies. With hindsight, it is clear that borrowing from abroad to finance rising investment ratios (to offset falling output per unit of input) was a major factor in maintaining growth rates in the 1970s. When that was no longer possible, growth rates fell in the 1980s.

TABLE 3

Growth Rates of GDP per Capita and Exports for Selected Countries

(*annual rates at constant market prices*)

	1950–60	1960–65	1965–73	1973–80	1980–90
United States					
GDP	1.5	3.2	2.5	1.0	2.0
Exports	5.3	6.2	7.5	5.7	6.0
Germany, F.R.					
GDP	7.7	3.5	3.6	2.2	1.9
Exports	15.1	5.9	8.6	4.3	4.9
Japan					
GDP	5.3	8.6	8.2	2.4	3.5
Exports	10.6	13.7	12.7	9.4	5.7
Korea					
GDP	3.0	3.8	7.8	5.9	7.7
Exports	7.1	21.1	30.0	13.2	10.4
Thailand					
GDP	2.9	4.2	4.9	4.2	5.7
Exports	5.4	10.5	8.5	9.1	13.0
India					
GDP	2.0	1.7	1.2	1.3	3.3
Exports	0.2	2.7	4.3	6.3	5.6
Egypt					
GDP	1.5	5.0	0.5	7.0	2.4
Exports	—	5.2	−0.1	10.1	3.3
Morocco					
GDP	−0.7	1.6	2.2	3.8	0.9
Exports	—	−0.7	6.0	0.4	5.4
Ghana					
GDP	−0.4	0.6	0.0	−2.0	−1.1
Exports	3.2	7.0	−0.7	−10.1	3.8
Sudan					
GDP	3.4	−0.3	−2.7	3.0	−1.6
Exports	—	3.3	5.1	1.1	−4.1
Brazil					
GDP	3.6	1.0	6.6	4.3	−0.6
Exports	1.7	2.2	12.3	7.8	6.8
Bolivia					
GDP	—	2.7	2.4	0.8	−2.4
Exports	—	4.3	4.9	−3.6	4.0
Argentina					
GDP	0.9	2.8	2.4	0.8	−2.5
Exports	—	5.2	3.8	6.0	5.9
Chile					
GDP	1.8	1.6	1.3	1.8	1.1
Exports	2.3	4.1	0.2	15.8	5.5
Mexico					
GDP	2.5	4.0	4.3	3.5	−0.4
Exports	4.5	6.3	6.5	6.9	7.3

SOURCES: World Bank (1983, 1992).

TABLE 4

Trade Orientation and Growth

(*percent per year*)

	GDP growth rate	Contribution to growth of:		
		Capital	Labor	Total factor productivity
Strongly outward-oriented countries				
1975–82	8.4	4.6	1.1	2.7
1983–89	7.7	3.3	0.7	3.7
Moderately outward-oriented countries				
1975–82	4.6	2.8	1.3	0.5
1983–89	4.1	1.7	1.2	1.2
Moderately inward-oriented countries				
1975–82	4.0	2.6	1.5	−0.2
1983–89	2.7	1.4	1.5	−0.2
Strongly inward-oriented countries				
1975–82	2.3	1.6	1.6	−0.9
1983–89	2.2	0.7	1.6	−0.1

SOURCE: International Monetary Fund (1990, p. 69).
NOTE: All figures are unweighted averages. The classification of countries by trade orientation is in World Bank (1987).

strategies have shown much improved growth performance. Table 4 provides estimates from the International Monetary Fund as to the systematic differences in growth performance associated with trade performance. While there are a large number of factors accounting for these differences (and good reasons for believing that growth rates will be higher for countries that eschew protectionist policies independently of global conditions), the growth prospects of those developing countries that have recently reformed their trade policies are integrally connected to the health and growth of the international economy.

Attention must, therefore, turn to the international trading system—the underpinning for the rapid expansion of trade and other economic linkages which characterized the 1948–90 period—and the prospects for its role in the 21st century.

Evolution of the International Trading System

It will be recalled that the Great Depression, which preceded the Second World War, was traumatic. Among other events, the Smoot-Hawley tariff, passed by Congress in 1930, had raised tariffs to extremely high levels.[10] Other countries had retaliated, and the "beggar-thy-neighbor" policies which followed in an effort to boost employment in recession-ridden countries were widely blamed for the collapse of international trade and the Great Depression itself.[11]

When thought about the structure of the postwar economic system began, much concern was devoted to avoiding a repetition of the 1930s. As the dominant country emerging from the war, the United States exercised leadership. The initial design of the international trading system, like that of other international economic institutions, was left largely to economists. They viewed the challenge as the development of an international system which would largely function as a policeman, preventing individual countries from taking unilateral actions, such as devaluation or increasing barriers against imports, that would be countered by their trading partners and result in a mutual worsening of well-being. To that end, an International Trade Organization (ITO) was proposed, along with an International Monetary Fund (IMF) and International Bank for Reconstruction and Development (IBRD, subsequently known as the World Bank).

It was intended that the ITO would oversee conduct with respect to tariffs and countries' other policies with respect to trade. Since virtually all trade was in commodities, the proposed ITO charter related largely to trade in commodities.[12] The basic principles were to be: (1) that the system should be multilateral, with countries treating all of their trading partners alike (the most favored nation, or MFN, principle); (2) that barriers to trade would be transparent and consist only of tariffs except in certain well-defined circumstances;[13] (3) and that the principle of "national treatment"

---

10. This section draws on chapter 2 of Krueger (1994).

11. The collapse of the international capital market in the 1930s also had long-lasting repercussions and impact on thought. Capital flows are ignored in this chapter, largely on the grounds that a well-functioning capital market, while essential to the trading system, is also a concomitant of it. Should flows of goods and services be seriously threatened, international capital flows would certainly shrink drastically.

12. At the insistence of the United States, countries' existing policies, especially with respect to agriculture, were "grandfathered" in such a way that they did not come under the general principles.

13. These circumstances were: balance of payments difficulties and developing countries' infant industry considerations. In practice, the developing countries found it simpler to justify their protection as existing for balance of payments reasons than to resort to the infant industry defense. After the Second World War, the United States incurred a huge current-account surplus, and almost the entire rest of the world was in current-account deficit. Most trading nations relied on quantitative restrictions of trade in the early postwar years, invoking the balance of payments provisions of the articles.

was to apply in most circumstances.[14] Countries have always, by virtue of their sovereignty, regulated various aspects of domestic economic activity if they so chose for such reasons as setting health and safety standards, raising revenue, and providing consumers with information. Under GATT rules (and for economic efficiency), foreign products entering a country's national market may be subject to the same regulations as domestic industries. In addition to these principles, provisions existed for countries to negotiate reciprocally for reductions of trade barriers and, once negotiations were complete, to "bind" tariffs to their new lower negotiated levels. There was an "escape provision," so that if a negotiated tariff reduction caused "serious injury" to an import-competing industry, the importing country could restore previous tariff barriers, although it would have to "compensate" the other country with reductions of other tariffs to offset the "snapback" of the tariff in question.[15] There were provisions for the establishment of "dispute settlement panels" under GATT, in the event that two or more countries disagreed about trading arrangements.

While the ITO charter was under consideration in national capitals, a framework for international trading relations, GATT, was established by executive agreement in 1947. It was intended that GATT would provisionally govern international trading relations until such time as the ITO came into being.[16] The GATT articles contained the key provisions pertaining to trading arrangements (just outlined) that were intended to be embodied in the ITO. However, the ITO was never approved by the U.S. Congress, and GATT has continued as the international organization governing trad-

---

14. This provision is intended to permit countries to adopt health and safety standards and other standards which apply to domestic and foreign products in like manner. When auto emissions standards are considered by the U.S. Congress, for example, they are intended to cover all autos sold in the United States, not just those manufactured in the country. While such a provision seems eminently reasonable, many producers in the United States and elsewhere lobby vigorously for standards that they believe will be disadvantageous to their foreign competitors.

15. GATT articles also permit members to take action to offset "dumping" or governmental "subsidies."

16. The ITO charter was never ratified by the U.S. Senate. In the fall of 1950, a press release from the White House indicated that the president did not plan to submit the ITO charter to Congress for its approval, which was tantamount to announcing its demise. The reasons for the failure of the ITO to emerge were several. On one hand, a number of supporters of free trade opposed it, on the grounds that there were too many exceptions to free trade principles in the charter. On the other hand, protectionists opposed it, believing that it "gave away" too much sovereignty over major issues pertaining to full employment. In addition, with GATT a functioning institution, the need for the ITO was greatly reduced, and the U.S. Executive had other, more pressing, items on which it needed Congressional action. See Diebold (1952) for an account.

ing relations among nations.[17] The GATT secretariat was established as a relatively small staff, with headquarters in Geneva, dependent on funding from national capitals.

A system embodying the GATT principles can best be described as an open multilateral system. "Openness" refers to the fact that reliance only upon tariffs implies that all goods may be imported freely, subject only to paying whatever rate of duty is in force. "Multilateral" embodies the notion that there will be no discrimination among trading partners.

That system has served the world very well. At the end of the Second World War, most industrialized countries still relied upon quantitative restrictions and bilateral trading arrangements. The United States emerged with its productive capacity largely intact, and was a highly open economy contrasted with most European countries, Japan, Australia, New Zealand, and the developing countries.

Reliance on exchange control and even bilateral trading arrangements on the part of these countries was in part a residual from the traumatic 1930s and in part a consequence of the large demand for foreign exchange (which, at that time, meant almost exclusively U.S. dollars) needed to obtain supplies and equipment for reconstruction. Domestic productive capacities to produce and hence earn foreign exchange were dislocated by the war, and the United States was virtually the only country with adequate productive capacity. In consequence, the U.S. current account was large and positive, both because countries were running down their assets to purchase needed goods and because the United States was helping to finance reconstruction through the Marshall Plan and other measures.

Tariffs were also high in many countries, as a legacy of the Smoot-Hawley tariff and the beggar-thy-neighbor policies of the 1930s. In return for Marshall Plan assistance, the United States exerted pressure for moves away from quantitative restrictions, bilateral trade, and barter trade, and for reductions of tariffs. Bilateral trade and payments arrangements were superseded by multilateral trade and payments arrangements, moving toward currency convertibility and removal of quantitative restrictions (combined with MFN treatment of all parties under GATT). As recovery proceeded, quantitative restrictions were also gradually lifted.

Successive rounds of multilateral trade negotiations (MTNs) have

---

17. Under the Uruguay Round agreement, GATT is to be superseded in 1995 by an International Trade Organization (distinct from that envisaged under the Havana Charter) which will be responsible for trading arrangements in services as well as goods and will have considerably enhanced oversight responsibilities. See Krueger (1994, chap. 6) for a further discussion.

taken place since the late 1940s. In the first round in Geneva, tariffs were cut by an average of 21 percent, leaving the remaining duties at an average about half of their level in 1930—the year of the infamous Smoot-Hawley tariff. Bargaining took place between pairs of countries, with each participant identifying tariffs they would like the other to reduce, and the other responding with suggestions as to tariffs that might be reduced in return. Once bargains were struck, tariffs were reduced on an MFN basis for all participants, including even the developing countries that did not themselves participate significantly in multilateral tariff negotiations.

As early as the early 1970s, it could be argued that GATT negotiations had had such "remarkable success" that non-tariff barriers should be the chief concern of negotiators (Baldwin, 1970).[18] By the end of the 1970s, the average tariff level among the negotiating countries was about 20 percent of its 1930 level (Baldwin, 1988, Table 2.1).

As already discussed, the first quarter-century following the establishment of GATT was the most prosperous in history. The trend toward multilateralism was strong: even the British Commonwealth, which had provided preferential tariff treatment for member countries, was disbanded. Only the emergence of the common market of the European Community (EC) represented a divergence from this trend. Even there, EC tariffs were lowered greatly under successive rounds of GATT trade negotiations so that Europe's trade with the rest of the world expanded strongly. It was only when European trade barriers on manufactured goods had been all but eliminated, and when the protectionism inherent in the European Common Agricultural Policy began increasing, that questions could be raised as to whether the EC was liberalizing or becoming more a "fortress Europe."

With U.S. leadership in negotiations for tariff reduction and a rapidly expanding world economy, the open multilateral system under GATT served the world economy well. By any measure, trade among the industrial countries was increasingly liberalized from the 1950s at least until the 1980s. While part of the rapid expansion in trade and world output would have occurred without liberalization of trade barriers, the removal of those barriers also served as a spur to growth. The world was caught up in a virtuous circle.

---

18. P. I. Baldwin reported that after Kennedy Round tariff cuts were completed, tariffs on non-agricultural imports subject to any duty at all would average 9.9 percent in the United States, 8.6 percent in the European Community, 10.8 percent in the United Kingdom, and 10.7 percent in Japan. Tariffs were further reduced by almost another 50 percent under the Kennedy Round.

However, as that happened and natural barriers in the form of transport and communications costs continued to fall, forms of trade not traditionally covered under GATT became increasingly important. Simultaneously, increased interdependence meant that the competition became more and more global.

American leadership was vital in the push for trade liberalization. The United States was itself a highly open economy at the end of the Second World War. The United States signed, and urged leaders of other countries to sign, the GATT articles. The United States promoted trade liberalization of the European countries under the Marshall Plan and through its leadership in proposing and supporting successive rounds of tariff negotiations under GATT.

Not only did the United States assume leadership in urging the reduction of trade barriers in other countries, but until at least the 1970s, U.S. policy was unequivocally supportive of free trade and the United States was one of the most open economies in the world. Even the AFL-CIO, now an outspoken supporter of increased protection, supported free trade until the late 1960s.[19] In part, this support derived from foreign policy concerns. But in addition, memories of Smoot-Hawley contributed to general acceptance of a liberalized, open trading regime. Although there were some departures from free trade, they were defended as "exceptions" to the general policy by politicians, and the burden of proof lay squarely with those who advocated protection.[20]

Since the 1970s, however, U.S. policy has become increasingly schizophrenic. On one hand, there has been support for successive GATT rounds and other trade-liberalizing measures. At the same time, however, the United States has increasingly resorted to restrictive trade measures both in practice and in rhetoric, and is no longer unswerving in its support for multilateralism. In rhetoric, much of the discussion has used catch-words

19. In recent years, the American labor movement has been highly critical of open trading policies. Until late in the 1960s, however, U.S. labor unions supported trade liberalization. See Baldwin (1988, pp. 26–27) for an account.

20. Two such departures deserve mention. First, the first agreement restraining imports into the United States of textiles and apparel was signed in 1957 with Japan. Subsequent regulation of textile and apparel imports extended country and commodity coverage. Until the 1980s, however, imports of textiles and apparel rose rapidly, and it could be argued that the Multifiber Arrangement had not been highly restrictive. By the mid-1980s, there was considerably more evidence of its "bite" with respect to imports. The second departure pertained to agriculture. In the 1930s, the Roosevelt Administration had instituted a farm program which entailed price supports and production controls. That system was still in effect in the 1940s, a time when many expected that depression conditions would rapidly return. The United States therefore insisted that its agricultural policies be "grandfathered" out of GATT.

TABLE 5

World Trade and Trade in Manufactures, 1950–90

Year	World exports			
	Total (billions of U.S. dollars)	Manufactures (billions of U.S. dollars)	Manufactures (percent of total)	U.S. (percent of total)
1950	61	23	37.7	16.7
1960	129	64	49.6	17.9
1970	312	190	60.9	14.7
1980	1,989	1,097	55.2	11.8
1990	3,485	2,445	70.2	11.9

SOURCE: GATT (*International Trade*, various years).

such as "free trade but fair trade" to imply that intervention is warranted if other countries are "unfair" traders. And in the 1980s, U.S. official policy shifted away from unequivocal support for the open multilateral trading system to a "two-track" approach under which support for GATT would be coupled with measures to enter into free trade agreements with particular countries.

Restrictive measures have included bilateral bargaining on sector-specific and country-specific issues in response to domestic protectionist pressures from individual industries. They have also included increasingly frequent resort to "administered protection" as a means of protecting domestic producers.

At least two major factors contributing to the shift in American policy can be identified.[21] The first relates to the declining relative position of the United States in the world economy. The second concerns U.S. macroeconomic conditions since the early 1980s.

The gradual shift in trade policy roughly coincides with the reduced relative economic importance of the United States. Table 5 provides data on overall trade. As can be seen, trade grew phenomenally. World trade

---

21. It is evident that the shift in policy corresponds to a reduced concern for "global," or systemic, issues and an increased concern for narrower domestic interests. This has been described by Baldwin (1988) as a shift from circumstances in which foreign policy considerations were predominant to those in which domestic political interests held sway. While that has certainly happened, it does not explain why the shift began in the 1970s, when national security concerns were still regarded as crucial. The "end of the cold war" could, perhaps, explain an acceleration of the shift to domestic considerations in the 1990s. It is too early to ascertain whether there has been any such acceleration, and, indeed, it can be argued that domestic considerations of "overall" economic welfare and the public interest argue for a return to unequivocal support for the open multilateral system, and that the drift away from multilateralism and free trade represents a shift toward support of special interests.

doubled in value terms between 1950 and 1960, and then more than doubled between 1960 and 1970; it increased even more rapidly in each of the subsequent two decades (despite a much lower rate of inflation in the 1980s than in the 1970s). The rate of growth of trade in manufactures is estimated to have been more than twice the rate of growth of real world GDP.

The fourth column of Table 5 gives total U.S. exports as a share of world trade. At the end of the Second World War, the United States emerged as the single most economically powerful country; the war-destroyed economies of Europe and Japan had limited productive capacity and large demands for all sorts of commodities which were available only from the United States; the only limits on U.S. exports were American capacity and the financial resources of U.S. trading partners. After that, U.S. exports grew rapidly, but the U.S. share of world trade dropped as Europe and Japan completed reconstruction and began growing rapidly. Especially between 1960 and 1980, the U.S. share was falling; the United States still remained a very large and important trading nation but no longer was *the* dominant country.[22] Ironically, as the U.S. share of world trade fell, the importance of trade to the United States was rising. In 1950, exports had constituted only 5.0 percent of U.S. GNP; by 1960, exports were 5.8 percent. They rose to 12.8 percent in 1980, before falling back to 9.9 percent in 1990 (Council of Economic Advisers, 1992).

Interestingly, U.S. support for the open multilateral trading system was greatest when the United States held unrivaled economic power in the world economy, and yet exhibited considerably less interdependence with the rest of the world than it does today. As the U.S. pre-eminence has diminished and American dependence on the international economy has increased, it could be argued that U.S. interest in an orderly international *system* should have increased. Instead, attention has focused much more on parochial interests in particular industries. It is precisely this shift in interest which is cause for great concern, and the subject of the next section.

Protectionist and Bilateral Tendencies in U.S. Trade Policy

The United States took leadership in the formation of GATT and in the first seven rounds of multilateral tariff negotiations. As the most im-

22. The small increase in the U.S. share between 1980 and 1990 obscures a large intra-decade shift. In the early 1980s, the U.S. dollar appreciated relative to the currencies of the major U.S. trading partners, and the U.S. share of world exports fell; in the second half of the decade, the dollar depreciated, and the U.S. share of world exports grew rapidly.

portant trading country in the world, little can be done without U.S. leadership, and U.S. support for the open multilateral system has been a key factor in its success.

Official U.S. trade policy is still supportive of the open multilateral system, although support is for "fair" trade instead of the earlier "free trade." U.S. policies, however, have been highly schizophrenic in three significant regards. First, the United States has acted as if its own trade policies were "free." Second, the United States has acted unilaterally and bilaterally to deal with practices of individual trading partners. Third, the United States has itself entered into preferential trading arrangements.

Despite official statements of support for the open multilateral system, U.S. trade policy in practice has therefore to a considerable degree diverged from the GATT ideals. It is the purpose of this section to attempt to sketch the magnitude and extent of U.S. protectionism and divergences from multilateralism. A final section then outlines why these practices represent such a threat to 21st-century growth.

It was already seen that the United States was a highly open economy right after the Second World War. In the ensuing 25 years, the United States, like other countries, reduced tariffs and other trade barriers under GATT, although protection of textiles and apparel began in 1961 when Japan was persuaded to enter into the Short-Term Cotton Textile Arrangement, which has since become the Multifiber Arrangement (MFA).[23]

Several sets of practices have combined to increase U.S. protectionism. For agriculture, U.S. agricultural laws provide for the imposition of restraint on imports whenever domestic agricultural programs are "threatened" by imports. In addition, there is "administered protection." Finally, "voluntary export restraints" (VERs) are negotiated with trading partners individually.

Average tariff rates by sector for 1989 are given at the top of Table 6. Although these averages obscure a few individual high rates, GATT-bound tariffs are not the major form of protection. The second part of Table 6 provides estimates of the "producer subsidy equivalent" of import restric-

---

23. The MFA is an arrangement under which importing countries agree with exporting countries on the levels to which imports are to be restrained and then, under an umbrella agreement, negotiate "voluntary export restraint" (VER) agreements for over 60 different categories of textiles and clothing with upwards of 100 countries. It is arguably the largest single impediment to imports from developing countries. For the United States in recent years, it is estimated that the tariff-equivalent of VERs on textile and clothing imports is between 30 and 50 percent, depending on the item in question. See Keesing and Wolf (1980) for an account of the MFA arrangement, and Hufbauer and Elliott (1994) for estimates of the height of protection.

TABLE 6

Estimates of Height of U.S. Protection, 1989

(percentage tariffs and tariff equivalents)

Average sectoral tariffs			
Animal and vegetable products	8.0	Non-metallic mineral products	4.8
Textile fibers and products	17.2	Chemicals and related products	2.8
Wood and paper products	2.0	Miscellaneous products	6.3
Metals and metal products	3.8	Weighted average	4.9
Producer subsidy equivalents in agriculture			
Crops (1988)	34.0	Livestock (1988)	33.0
Dairy products	50.0	Peanuts	50.0
Sugar	66.0		
Protection through import quotas or restraints			
Maritime shipping	85.0		
Tariff equivalents of voluntary export restraints, 1990			
Apparel	48.0	Machine tools	35.2
Textiles	23.4		

SOURCES: For sectoral tariffs and producer subsidy equivalents, GATT (1990, pp. 224, 228); for import quotas and voluntary export restraints, Hufbauer and Elliott (1994, p. 9).

tions in agriculture.[24] As can be seen, these protection rates are substantially higher than those conferred through tariffs. U.S. protection for individual agricultural commodities such as sugar, peanuts, and rice is fairly high by world standards.

"Administered protection" is one of the practices which flourished in the United States in the 1980s. As in other countries, there were for many years American trade laws which provided for procedures under which domestic producers could file complaints about foreign "dumping" in the U.S. market or foreign competitors' receipt of subsidies (asking for countervailing duty relief) from their governments. These "administered" trade remedies were regarded as applying when trade practices were "unfair" and were GATT-legal. There was also provision, again GATT-consistent, for relief if imports were found to be doing "serious damage to U.S. producers" (the so-called "escape clause"). However, until the mid-1970s, few complaints were filed under these laws. Then, as protectionist pressures mounted, the laws were relaxed so that the "injury test" under the escape clause was relaxed and administrative procedures were changed so that the test for positive findings of dumping or of subsidies became easier to pass. Indeed, a number of biases were built into the Department of Commerce tests, meaning that a foreign firm might be pricing

---

24. The "producer subsidy equivalent" concept is the one used internationally to compare levels of agricultural protection across countries.

at home and abroad in the same way and nonetheless be found guilty of dumping.[25]

By the 1980s, the United States was the leading user of anti-dumping and countervailing duty measures in the world, and it is estimated that about 20 percent of U.S. imports were covered by these duties by the end of the 1980s. It is difficult to estimate the extent to which the "unfair" use of "unfair" trade laws conveys protection to U.S. producers, but there is considerable reason to believe it is substantial and may serve as a significant deterrent to would-be exporters to the United States.

Perhaps the most telling indicator of the extent to which administered trade laws in fact confer protection is indicated by the lengths to which foreign governments will go to avoid the administered protection processes.[26] Several U.S. industries have filed a variety of anti-dumping or countervailing duty suits against foreign producers, and then withdrawn them once a "voluntary export restraint" was placed, by the exporting country, on exports of the offending product to the United States. The steel industry is probably the champion filer of such cases: in 1982 alone it filed more than 200 cases in order to force the U.S. administration to act (Moore, 1994). Other industries that have filed such suits include machine tools, automobiles,[27] and stainless steel products, as well as textiles and clothing under the MFA. It is also significant that the Canadians are reported to have seen avoidance of U.S.-administered protection as a major

---

25. This could happen in a number of ways, but two will illustrate. If a foreign firm is unable to provide all the data requested by the Department of Commerce in the format indicated (on tape, consistent with U.S. accounting standards), the Department of Commerce is instructed by law to use the "best available evidence." This is normally taken to be the data provided by the domestic producer filing the complaint. When the Department of Commerce does have data on pricing from the foreign firm, it calculates the average price at which the firm sold in its own, and other, markets and the price at which it sold its product in the U.S. market. In ascertaining whether the foreign firm "dumped" in the U.S. market, the Department of Commerce calculates an "average price" in each market. To do so, it rejects "unusually high" prices in the U.S. on the grounds that a profitable sale cannot be used to offset an unprofitable one, and it rejects "low" prices of sales abroad. Hence, a firm might follow identical pricing in the U.S. and abroad, and nonetheless be found guilty of dumping. Boltuck and Litan (1991) offer more particulars.

26. To be sure, when there is a voluntary export restraint, the foreign producer gets the benefit of the higher price in the U.S. market, whereas if the United States imposes a tariff, the additional revenue associated with the highest domestic price of the product goes to the U.S. government.

27. In the case of automobiles, the International Trade Commission found that increased imports had not been a sufficiently major cause of "injury" to the U.S. auto industry to provide relief.

objective when they negotiated the Canada-U.S. Free Trade Agreement (Rugman and Anderson, 1987).

Voluntary export restraints have not always achieved their desired results.[28] In the case of automobiles, Japanese VERs in the mid-1980s clearly increased the price at which Japanese cars sold in the American market by an estimated $1800. According to some analysts, the increased profits in the Japanese auto industry enabled the industry to increase investment and raise productivity more rapidly than would otherwise have been possible. Likewise, the United States negotiated a "semiconductor" agreement with Japan in 1986 under which the Japanese were, among other things, to raise the prices at which they sold in the U.S. market.[29] The results were a sharp run-up in the price and shortages of semiconductors in the United States, with consequent protests from those industries which were semiconductor users.

Estimates of the tariff equivalents of some of the major voluntary export restraints in effect in 1990 are given in the bottom part of Table 6. As can be seen, they, too, confer considerable protection.

Examination of Table 6 provides an indication of the extent to which tariff and non-tariff barriers were restricting imports early in the 1990s.[30] Maritime shipping, the highest tariff listed, has long been a highly protected U.S. industry. In the Uruguay Round and other tariff negotiations (including NAFTA), trading partners have sought a reduction in protection. To date, however, the United States has been unwilling to negotiate at all with respect to maritime shipping.

Considering only the data in Table 6, one might conclude that the United States practiced a fair amount of protection, perhaps no more but probably not less than many of its trading partners. However, U.S. trade policy has gone well beyond protection through administered trade remedies, tariffs, and voluntary export restraints. In recent years, the U.S. Trade

---

28. Despite the continuous presence of protection for textiles and apparel through voluntary export restraints since the mid-1950s, the industries have continuously complained about the ineffectiveness of such restraints. However, instead of recognizing the limitations of VERs and the fact that the industry difficulties stemmed from a multitude of sources of which imports were only one, the industries always sought more restrictive VERs.

29. The Japanese also agreed, under U.S. pressure, to increase the prices at which they sold semiconductors in third-country markets. But several importing countries objected to that practice and took their complaint to GATT; Japan stopped the practice after it was found to be GATT-inconsistent.

30. It should be recalled that these numbers do not include the anti-dumping and countervailing duty tariffs imposed under administered trade law.

Representative (USTR, the equivalent of the Minister for Foreign Trade in many other countries) has undertaken annual "consultations" with individual trading partners.[31]

In these consultations, which are inherently bilateral, the practice is to raise issues regarding the trading partner's trading policies and to "demand" action. These issues are wide-ranging. They have included tariff levels, customs valuation practices, health and safety regulations, standards, intellectual property rights laws, laws governing foreign investment, laws and regulations governing the entry of foreign banks, and many other items. Trade "demands" with Japan have become virtually institutionalized, beginning with the Market Oriented Sector Selective (starting in 1986) and Structural Impediments Initiative (starting in 1989) talks, and continuing under the Clinton administration with "framework" talks scheduled to take place every six months. Although care has been taken to place the negotiations in a GATT framework, many aspects are clearly bilateral. U.S. "demands" that Japan open up its rice market to U.S. exports, for example, are subject to question in light of U.S. subsidies to American rice farmers and the unquestioned comparative advantage of countries such as Thailand.

These negotiations have often been acrimonious, but broke down completely in the winter of 1994 when the Japanese refused to agree to the U.S. demand that quantitative targets be set. Aside from the fact that a bilateral trade balance is not a function primarily of trade policy, to have accepted quantitative targets would have implied an enhanced role for the Japanese bureaucracy: yet the complaint often registered about Japan is the power of the bureaucracy! In response, President Clinton by administrative decree reinstated "Super-301," under which the USTR is instructed to identify "unfair trading practices" and seek remedies from the offending trading partner. Failing to achieve satisfactory remedies requires USTR to label the country an "unfair trader" and to propose punitive actions in the form of high tariffs (100 percent is the number usually mentioned) on imports from the offending country.

The GATT-inconsistency of Super-301 has been much discussed. Super-301 was first enacted in 1988 during Uruguay Round negotiations and was widely criticized,[32] even by the director-general of GATT, as being a

---

31. An account of the major items negotiated with major trading partners is included each year in the International Trade Commission's annual *Operation of the Trade Agreements Program*.

32. Japan, India, and Brazil were named "unfair traders" under Super-301 in 1989, its first year of existence. The USTR was reluctant to use the designation, precisely be-

major contributor to the delay in that round (Krueger, 1994). It is inherently bilateral, and can be used to raise tariffs previously bound under GATT even when the trading partner's offense is not GATT-inconsistent.

It should be noted that there are many issues, including semiconductors, steel, autos, intellectual property rights, and especially agriculture, where solutions are inherently multilateral. Attempts at bilateral resolution cause misunderstandings with other trading partners, and are also destined to raise problems for other trading nations. To desert the forums of GATT (or WTO) for bilateral bargaining undermines the open multilateral system, and over the longer term creates more problems than those being addressed in these negotiations.

As bilateral negotiations have continued over the years, especially with Japan, the acrimony surrounding the talks has intensified. *The New York Times* described the tension this way on May 2, 1994 (p. C6): "However the validity of the . . . reports is assessed, they leave no doubt that the well of distrust between the world's two economic superpowers is deepening. . . . In some respects, the arguments sound a lot like those that took place between the United States and the Soviet Union a decade ago, except that instead of debating the arcana of warheads and missiles the two sides are arguing over the arcana of market-sharing measures."

There have been similar acrimonious disputes with the European Union (EU), including bitter wrangling over agricultural policies in the final phases of the GATT negotiations.[33] However, the United States has not thus far used the Super-301 designation against the EU. In individual trade disputes, punitive tariffs have been threatened, but to date, the issues have been resolved before the threats have been carried out.

While bilateral trading relations have become increasingly acrimonious with many U.S. trading partners, the U.S. has simultaneously entered into NAFTA, and indicated its willingness, if not desire, that other Western Hemisphere countries may join at a later date.

---

cause it was so resented by U.S. trading partners. The Super-301 provision was allowed to lapse in 1990. The concern of Congress for intellectual property rights prompted Congress to instruct the USTR to name countries that were unfair with regard to their intellectual property rights laws. The USTR, however, reported that almost no countries had satisfactory laws, and it instead created a "watch" list and a "priority" watch list. Changes in intellectual property rights laws have been undertaken in many countries in response to this pressure.

33. In March 1994, a dispute was heating up with the European Union because the United States had tried to obtain a separate undertaking from the Germans with respect to public procurement. The U.S. effort to "woo Germany" away from other EU members was seen as a deliberate attempt to undermine common EU trade policies. For a description of the events, see the March 14, 1994, issue of the *Financial Times*, p. 2.

While NAFTA is generally regarded as being consistent with GATT, which as already seen permits preferential trading arrangements, there are two perceived dangers. On one hand, many U.S. trading partners are concerned that protectionist pressures in the United States, as reflected in administered protection and in the NAFTA debate, may result in higher trade barriers to the rest of the world as trade barriers are reduced among Western Hemisphere countries.[34] In addition, concerns have been expressed that increased imports resulting from reduced trade barriers with Latin American countries might result in the use of administered protection against third countries, especially in East Asia, in consequence (Bhagwati, 1991).

The Threat to the Multilateral Trading System

Were the United States a smaller trading nation, one would still be concerned about U.S. tendencies toward unilateral and bilateral trading actions and protectionism because of the costs to American consumers and producers. However, were the United States a smaller trading nation, it would not be able to place "demands" on its trading partners in the manner in which it does. It is the very fact of America's size and importance in the world economy which simultaneously makes the use of bilateral negotiations possible but also makes them dangerous for the entire world trading system.

If the U.S. position were overtly protectionist and bilateral/unilateral, that would already undermine the multilateral system. In fact, the U.S. stated position is more supportive of the multilateral system than U.S. actions. Much of U.S. rhetoric, and even some of U.S. bilateral pressure, is expressed in terms implying that the U.S. itself is "clean," while other countries are "unfairly" trading. The incongruity of the highly publicized American demands for removal of all European agricultural protection in light of America's own agricultural policies could not help but strike many as hypocritical.[35]

---

34. Credence is lent to this concern by the rules of origin negotiated under NAFTA, which confer protection on several key industries.

35. The official U.S. position was that all American agricultural protection would be removed if the European Community did the same. There was reason for foreigners to question, however, whether the U.S. Senate would approve a measure removing all supports for peanuts, cotton, tobacco, sugar, livestock, dairy farming, wheat, and other major agricultural commodities. Ironically, it is nonetheless the case that American agriculture would benefit were the United States, Japan, and the EC simultaneously to remove their protections of agriculture. The argument for all three trading partners (and hope-

Over the past decade and a half, trading relations between the United States and many of its major trading partners have clearly become more acrimonious. The threat of a split of the world into regional trading blocs is still only that, but it is a more plausible danger in the mid-1990s than it was a decade ago. Increasingly bitter negotiations have reduced the goodwill that previously characterized U.S. trade relations. The presence of the strengthened EU and of NAFTA raises the possibility of the emergence of regional trading blocs.

Regional trading arrangements are clearly compatible with a strengthened open multilateral trading system if they are of the "GATT-plus" nature originally envisioned by the USTR in 1982. To be GATT-plus, they must have low external barriers to third countries, and the arrangements must focus on going beyond the multilateral rules in harmonizing standards and integrating economies.

If, instead, regional trading blocs emerge and become protectionist, that would constitute a major threat to 21st-century growth, especially if increased protection and retaliation characterized the relations between trading blocs. Just as world growth in the 1948–73 period was enhanced by the "virtuous circle" of trade liberalization–rapid growth–trade liberalization, a "vicious circle" of heightened protection–reduced growth–increased pressures for more protection could well emerge.

The completion of the Uruguay Round offers the world an opportunity for continuing the long-term trends toward increasing the integration of the world economy. In that agreement, not only were a number of substantive arrangements agreed upon which will augment world welfare,[36] but in addition it was agreed to strengthen GATT significantly, renaming it the World Trade Organization (WTO) to underscore the notion that the multilateral system would cover tariff and non-tariff barriers to trade in goods and services, and strengthening its dispute settlement procedures.

GATT is an imperfect instrument for supporting the increasingly complicated trading relations between countries. It needs strengthening, both in including items such as intellectual property rights in its domain, and in increasing the effectiveness of procedures within GATT for resolving trade disputes. Likewise, there are a number of aspects of partner countries' trading practices which should be of legitimate concern to the United States.

---

fully also Korea and some major importing countries) moving simultaneously is strong, since the adjustment costs would be smaller than if any acted alone. The need for multilateralism in agriculture is all too evident.

36. These included an agreement to limit agricultural subsidies, to bring many services under GATT for the first time (at the insistence of the United States), and to phase out the MFA, as well as a strengthened government procurement code.

The question is not whether the United States should raise these issues. Instead, it is whether the country should use its size and consequent bargaining power in bilateral forums and through unilateral measures, or whether instead the United States should use its size and bargaining power to strengthen GATT/WTO processes and procedures.

The WTO came into existence in January 1995. Since the Uruguay Round agreement in December 1993, U.S. attentions have focused on a large number of trade issues: wheat from Canada, quantitative indicators with Japan, workers' rights as a side issue to the Uruguay Round accord (an issue which was raised only after the Uruguay Round was agreed upon), and human rights with China, to name just some of the more visible ones.

Simultaneously, there has been no public focus on the new WTO. There is a significant risk that the funding, staffing, and arrangements that would be necessary to strengthen it effectively will not be forthcoming. As the largest trading nation, the United States has a great deal to gain from a well-functioning multilateral trading system. Failure to exert leadership with respect to the WTO could be an important contributor to its inability to carry out its enlarged mandate.

When the United States is seen to be resurrecting Super-301, reconsidering its adherence to the Uruguay Round by raising additional issues after the agreement was completed, and undertaking aggressive bilateralism that is at least partly GATT-inconsistent (bilateral targets with Japan and Super-301 revival), the rest of the world questions U.S. commitment to the open multilateral system. Yet, without a strong U.S. commitment, the WTO cannot effectively carry out its necessary tasks.

The threat to the world trading system is partly one of American omission and failure to provide sufficient support and leadership for the multilateral system through the new WTO, and partly one of commission in the ready resort to bilateral bargaining and unilateral actions.

The gains from world economic interdependence are obviously huge. It is to be hoped that the gains from an open multilateral trading system will become recognized before the dangers of regression into protectionism and regional trading blocs become a reality. Should that situation occur, the growth of world trade would be retarded, if, indeed, trade in goods and services did not shrink. At a minimum, such a reduced growth rate would serve to diminish world growth prospects. But if historical experience is any guide, periods of slow growth or contraction of world trade are also periods of slow growth or contraction of the world economy. That is the risk at the present crossroads of the international trading system.

Dollar and Yen: The Problem of Financial Adjustment Between the United States and Japan

RONALD I. MCKINNON

How does the arcane subject of the yen/dollar exchange rate affect growth and development into the 21st century? At first glance, the balance of payments problem between Japan and the United States seems one of securing proper short-term financial adjustment between the two countries, rather than an issue involving longer-term productivity growth, saving, and capital accumulation.

However, getting the yen/dollar exchange rate right by harmonizing American and Japanese monetary policies has two important long-term consequences. First is whether mutual adjustment to ongoing, but differential, productivity growth in the two countries can proceed with minimum friction—that is, without unnecessary losses in output through protectionism or cyclical downturns. The second issue, given the savings shortage in the United States and Japan's emergence as the dominant creditor country in the world economy, is whether saving is efficiently transferred from one country to the other. Unfortunately, the current regime, where the yen has been appreciating erratically for well over two decades, satisfies neither criterion.

In this chapter, I argue against using the exchange rate as an instrumental variable to "correct" current-account imbalances or to equalize international competitiveness. Beginning in 1971, when a dollar was worth 360 yen, until July 1994, when it dipped to 98 yen, the efforts of the American government to "talk" or otherwise force the yen up and the dollar down has harmed both countries. While failing to correct trade imbal-

I would like to thank Kenichi Ohno of Tsukuba University in Japan for his invaluable help in preparing this paper. Thanks also to Ralph Landau and Hiroshi Nakamura of Stanford University, and Timothy Taylor of the *Journal of Economic Perspectives*.

ances for reasons I will explain, continual yen appreciation has induced episodes of severe wage-price misalignments between the two countries, leading to unnecessary cyclical instability and losses in real output in the short run.

In the longer run, the ever-higher yen has undermined the natural wage adjustment process for balancing international competitiveness. In the 1950s and 1960s, when the exchange rate was fixed at 360 yen to the dollar, each country's money wages grew in conformity with its (differential) growth in manufacturing productivity—much faster in Japan than in the United States. Subsequently, the ever-higher yen has imposed relative deflation on Japan. Growth in money wages in Japan has slowed dramatically, and is now slower than money wage growth in the United States—despite the fact that long-term productivity growth in Japanese manufacturing remains relatively high.

A related problem for the 1990s is the capital shortage in the United States. Large fiscal deficits and low private saving virtually require the United States to run a current-account deficit in trade in goods and services of the same order of magnitude. Without net inflows of foreign capital, as measured by its current-account deficit, the American economy would suffer from a credit crunch and an economic slowdown such as that experienced in 1990–92, when the American current-account deficit was suddenly reduced. Correspondingly, American pressure on the Japanese to engage in a Keynesian-style fiscal "expansion"—that is, reduced saving through larger fiscal deficits—is also inappropriate. Unlike yen appreciation, lower Japanese saving would indeed reduce Japan's trade surplus. But it would also harm the United States and other (potential) debtor countries in the world economy.

The near-term adjustment problem—the overvalued yen, the 1992–94 slump in the Japanese economy, the current-account deficit, and incipient capital shortage in the United States—will be tackled later in the chapter. First, however, consider a longer-term view of financial adjustment between Japan and the United States. How has the yen-dollar exchange rate been linked to the past evolution of prices and wages in each country, and how should they be linked in the future?

Wage and Price Adjustment Under the Fixed-Rate Dollar Standard, 1950–70

In retrospect, the years from 1950 to 1970 were the most harmonious in Japanese-American financial history. Under the fixed-rate dollar stan-

TABLE I

Prices, Money Wages, and Exchange Rates: Japan and the United States, 1951–93

(*annual averages; 1985 = 100*)

Year	Wholesale prices		Money wages[a]		Consumer prices		Yen/dollar exchange rate
	U.S.	Japan	U.S.	Japan	U.S.	Japan	
1951	29.5	41.6	16.4	6.4	24.1	16.6	360
1961	30.6	43.2	24.4	10.3	27.8	22.3	360
1970	35.7	48.6	35.2	24.0	36.1	36.9	360
1971	36.9	48.2	37.4	27.6	37.6	39.3	349
Total change, 1951–71	25.1%	15.9%	128%	331%	56%	137%	−3%
Annual change, 1951–71	1.1%	0.7%	4.2%	7.6%	2.2%	4.4%	−
1972	38.6	48.6	39.9	31.9	38.9	41.2	303
1982	96.9	103.7	89.1	90.8	89.7	94.1	249
1983	98.1	101.4	92.6	93.7	92.6	95.8	238
1984	100.5	101.1	96.3	96.9	96.6	98.0	238
1985	100.0	100.0	100.0	100.0	100.0	100.0	239
1986	97.1	90.0	102.1	102.9	101.9	100.6	169
1987	99.7	87.5	103.9	105.0	105.7	100.7	145
1988	103.7	86.6	106.7	108.6	109.9	101.4	128
1989	108.8	88.8	109.8	112.1	115.2	103.7	138
1990	112.7	90.6	113.6	116.3	121.4	106.9	145
1991	112.9	90.8	117.3	120.3	126.6	110.4	135
1992	113.6	89.5	120.4	122.9	130.4	112.3	127
1993	115.3	86.1	123.2	125.4	134.3	113.7	111
Total change, 1972–92	194%	84.2%	202%	285%	235%	173%	−58.1%
Annual change, 1972–92	5.5%	3.1%	5.7%	7.0%	6.2%	5.1%	−4.3%
Total change, 1982–92	17.2%	−13.7%	35.1%	35.4%	45.4%	19.3%	−49.0%
Annual change, 1982–92	1.6%	−1.4%	3.1%	3.1%	3.8%	1.8%	−6.5%
Change, 1992–93	1.5%	−3.8%	2.3%	2.0%	3.0%	1.2%	−12.6%

SOURCE: IMF (1994).

[a] Monthly earnings in Japan and hourly earnings in manufacturing in the United States.

dard, the Bank of Japan geared its domestic monetary policy to keeping the exchange rate at 360 yen per dollar, while the U.S. Federal Reserve anchored the common price level for tradable goods. Until the end of the period, inflation in both countries' wholesale price indices was confined to about 1 percent per year, as documented in Table 1. However, this remarkable record of stability subsequently gave way to floating exchange rates and the great inflations of the 1970s, shown in Figure 1. In the 1950s and 1960s, however, protectionist barriers came down, and trade between the

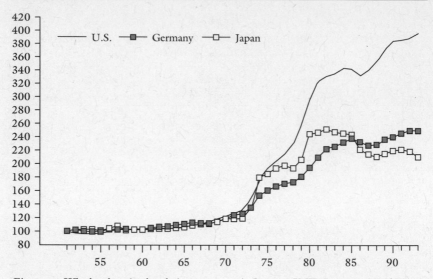

Figure 1. Wholesale price levels (1951 = 100). Source: IMF, *International Financial Statistics* (various years).

two countries grew rapidly. Fiscal and current-account imbalances remained comparatively modest. From financial stability came the postwar era of rapid economic growth. From 1951 to 1971, Japan's real GNP grew at an amazing 8.5 percent per year; and, starting from a much higher absolute level, U.S. real GDP grew at a robust 3.2 percent per year (see Table 2). From the 1950s to the early 1970s, economic growth in the United States, Japan, and other industrial countries was generally higher—with minimal inflation—than that seen before or since (Maddison, 1989).

Then, more than now, the pace of growth varied across countries and industries (Ohno, 1993). Starting from much lower absolute levels in 1951, Japanese industrial output grew more than three times faster than American until the early 1970s (Table 2). With the exchange rate fixed and Japan retaining exchange controls on capital flows,[1] how did the balance of payments adjust?

First, in tradable goods sectors, secular adjustments in average money wages more or less accurately offset this differential growth in average productivity. From 1951 to 1971, money wages in Japan grew by 331 percent, compared to just 128 percent in the United States (as shown in Table 1).

---

1. Under the old fixed-rate dollar standard of the 1950s and 1960s, most industrial countries other than the United States maintained exchange controls on capital accounts.

On an annual basis, the IMF data in Table 1 show that monthly earnings in Japanese manufacturing grew about 3.4 percentage points faster than hourly wages in U.S manufacturing—7.6 percent versus 4.2 percent. But Table 1 also shows that inflation in tradable goods prices was virtually the same in both countries: the U.S. wholesale price index (WPI) increased annually by 1.1 percent and the Japanese WPI by 0.7 percent in the same

TABLE 2

Real Output: Japan and the United States, 1951–93

(*annual averages;* 1990 = 100)

| Year | Industrial production | | GDP, | GNP, |
	U.S.	Japan	U.S.[a]	Japan[b]
1951	25.3	3.9	1,764.4	372.8[c]
1961	34.6	15.2	2,293.3	771.5
1970	55.4	45.3	3,256.0	1,822.3
1971	56.1	46.5	3,357.0	1,901.5
Total change, 1951–71	122%	1,092%	90.3%	453%
Annual change, 1951–71	4.0%	12.4%	3.2%	8.5%
1972	61.6	49.8	3,517.8	2,060.8
1982	72.7	68.7	4,257.3	3,032.7
1983	77.0	70.7	4,423.0	3,117.3
1984	85.7	77.4	4,698.8	3,252.2
1985	87.4	80.3	4,845.5	3,420.6
1986	88.3	80.1	4,986.7	3,510.9
1987	91.6	82.8	5,140.1	3,663.2
1988	96.5	90.8	5,342.3	3,891.8
1989	99.0	96.1	5,477.6	4,079.3
1990	100.0	100.0	5,522.2	4,274.7
1991	98.1	101.8	5,458.3	4,457.4
1992	99.6	95.6	5,645.4	4,518.0
1993	101.7	91.2	5,811.1	4,523.1
Total change, 1972–92	61.7%	92.0%	60.5%	119%
Annual change, 1972–92	2.4%	3.3%	2.4%	3.9%
Total change, 1982–92	37.0%	39.2%	32.6%	49.0%
Annual change, 1982–92	3.1%	3.3%	2.8%	4.0%
Change, 1992–93	2.1%	−4.6%	2.9%	0.1%

SOURCE: IMF (1994).

[a] Billions of U.S. dollars with 1990 as the base year.

[b] 100 billions of yen with 1990 as the base year.

[c] 1952 data earliest available; (percentage change was calculated from 1952 to 1972).

twenty-year period of unmatched worldwide growth. Because Japanese money wages grew much faster than their American counterparts, balanced international competitiveness, in the sense of maintaining the alignment of national price levels at the "factory gate," was pretty well preserved in the 1950s and 1960s. After 1968, however, excessive upward drift in U.S. money wages nudged U.S. wholesale price inflation above that in Japan and other industrial countries.

Alternatively, more direct measures of labor productivity growth in the 1950s and 1960s might be compared to growth in money wages to determine whether relative wage adjustment was "sufficient" between the two countries. In a large-scale empirical study of fourteen Japanese manufacturing industries at the SITC (Standard Industrial Trade Classification) two-digit level, Kenichi Ohno (1993) estimates that Japanese labor productivity in manufacturing from 1952 to 1971 grew about 7.6 percent per year—with enormous differences from this average for individual industries, as will be discussed in more detail later in this chapter.

Ohno (1993) also estimated that hourly wages in manufacturing increased at 9.2 percent per year—thus apparently overadjusting to absolute productivity growth. Because of a shortening work week in Japan in this period, hourly wages apparently grew somewhat faster than the 7.6 percent growth in monthly earnings recorded in Table 1. But with the Japanese WPI rising only slightly from 1951 to 1971, overadjustment in Japanese wages at most would be slight. (Because of the particularly rapid introduction of new products in the 1950s and 1960s, output and productivity indices are inherently ambiguous.)

Starting from a much higher absolute level in 1951, American labor productivity in manufacturing grew about 2.4 percent annually from 1952 to 1971—about 5 percentage points less than shown in Ohno's data for Japan.[2] However, the U.S. Bureau of Labor Statistics also shows that American hourly wages grew more slowly—about 4.8 percent compared to Ohno's estimates of 9.2 percent for Japan, a difference of about 4.4 percentage points that almost offset the gap in productivity growth when the exchange rate was fixed at 360 yen/dollar. *Within the bounds of measurement error, differential adjustment in average money wages between Japan and the United States in the 1950s and 1960s was sufficient to balance international competitiveness between the two countries.*

2. More detailed data on labor productivity and wages in both Japan and the United States, which support some of the statements in this paragraph and the previous one, are presented in Table 5, which is discussed in more detail later in the chapter.

In addition to adjustment in relative money wages across countries, the absence of substantial saving-investment gaps within the Japanese or American economies further helped balance international payments in the 1950s and 1960s. Unlike in the period to come, the U.S. federal government did not run significant fiscal deficits: it behaved as if it had a hard budget constraint.[3] The right-hand column in Table 3 shows that the dollar values of U.S. fiscal deficits were modest—and were even punctuated by the occasional surplus. For the 1950s and 1960s, Table 3 also shows that the United States always ran trade surpluses and usually ran current-account surpluses: there was no heavy net borrowing from the rest of the world. The United States was a major creditor in world capital markets.

Even when its per capita income was low, Japan was not a major borrower. In the 1950s and 1960s, Japan alternated between small current-account surpluses or deficits. Any substantial change in the balance between private saving and private investment was offset by an opposite change in the government's net financial saving position (Bayoumi, 1990). Because exchange controls on capital flows made the private financing of any large current-account imbalances next to impossible, governments in the industrial countries oriented their fiscal policies more toward balancing their current accounts.

For relative wages to adjust so well, Japanese monetary policy had to be expansionary. Although Japan's tradable goods prices—as measured by the WPI—were well anchored by the fixed exchange rate (Figure 1), consumer prices increased relatively fast. Because Japanese productivity growth in services was much less than in manufacturing even as wages in both sectors rose equally fast (Ohno, 1993), the cost of non-tradable services rose sharply.[4] Table 1 shows that from 1951 to 1971, Japan's CPI increased by 137 percent whereas the American CPI increased by only 56 percent. If the Japanese monetary authorities had focused on stabilizing

---

3. Under the Bretton Woods agreement of 1945, the American commitment to convert official foreign holdings of dollar assets (largely Treasury bills and bonds) into gold at $35 per ounce may have restrained the U.S. government from running fiscal deficits. This agreement was formally terminated in August 1971, when President Nixon slammed the gold window shut.

4. Measured productivity growth typically tends to be higher in goods production than in services: the well-known "Balassa effect" (Balassa, 1964). Because wages in both goods and services moved together and tracked the higher productivity growth in Japanese manufacturing, the price of services in Japan rose fairly fast. And services are a significant component of the CPI but don't enter the WPI. Thus the Japanese CPI rose between 3 and 4 percentage points per year faster than the Japanese WPI (as shown in Table 1).

TABLE 3

*Japanese-American Trade and Current-Account Balances,
and the U.S. Federal Fiscal Deficit, 1956–93*

(*billions of U.S. dollars*)

Year	Trade balance		Current account		U.S. federal fiscal surplus
	U.S.	Japan	U.S.	Japan	
1956	4.57	−0.12	1.57	−0.03	4.5
1957	6.10	−0.39	3.41	−0.61	1.2
1958	3.31	0.38	−0.13	0.28	−7.2
1959	0.99	0.36	−2.28	0.35	−7.9
1960	4.89	0.27	2.82	0.14	0.3
1961	5.57	−0.56	3.82	−0.98	−3.5
1962	4.52	−0.40	3.38	−0.04	−7.2
1963	5.22	−0.16	4.40	−0.77	−4.8
1964	6.80	−0.37	6.82	−0.48	−5.9
1965	4.95	1.90	5.41	0.92	−1.6
1966	3.82	2.27	3.03	1.25	−3.8
1967	3.80	1.16	2.59	−0.18	−8.7
1968	0.64	2.53	0.59	1.03	−15.2
1969	0.60	3.69	0.42	2.12	5.4
1970	2.59	3.96	2.33	1.99	−11.4
1971	−2.27	7.76	−1.45	5.80	−24.8
1972	−6.42	8.94	−5.78	6.64	−18.7
1973	0.91	3.64	7.07	−0.13	−16.2
1974	−5.51	1.35	1.94	−4.72	−4.5
1975	8.90	4.94	18.06	−0.68	−53.9
1976	−9.47	9.80	4.18	3.71	−74.9
1977	−31.11	17.16	−14.49	10.91	−52.2
1978	−33.94	24.30	−15.40	16.54	−58.9
1979	−27.54	1.74	0.20	−8.74	−36.0
1980	−25.51	2.13	2.25	−10.75	−76.2
1981	−28.02	19.96	5.05	4.77	−78.7
1982	−36.48	18.08	−11.42	6.85	−125.7
1983	−67.09	31.46	−43.65	20.80	−202.5
1984	−112.48	44.26	−98.78	35.00	−178.3
1985	−122.18	55.99	−121.79	49.17	−212.1
1986	−145.06	92.82	−147.54	85.83	−212.6
1987	−159.56	96.42	−163.45	87.02	−147.5
1988	−126.96	95.00	−126.67	79.61	−155.5
1989	−115.68	76.89	−101.19	56.99	−143.8
1990	−108.84	63.58	−90.46	35.87	−218.1
1991	−73.44	103.09	−3.69	72.91	−272.5
1992	−96.28	132.40	−62.47	117.64	−289.3
1993	−132.5	141.40	−109.24	131.35	−281.1

SOURCE: IMF (1994).

TABLE 4

Growth in Narrow Money and Nominal GNP:
Japan and the United States, 1955–93

(*annual percentage changes*)

	United States		Japan	
	Money	GNP	Money	GNP
1955–71	3.46%	6.24%	15.47%	14.13%
1972–82	6.33	9.62	8.85	7.48
1983–93	7.20	6.19	5.88	5.17

SOURCE: IMF (1994). Narrow money is defined by line 34 of IMF (1994).

the CPI rather than on the dollar exchange rate and the WPI, Japan's money wage growth would have had to be much slower with the yen continually appreciating against the dollar in order to keep tradable goods prices—that is, WPIs—approximately aligned between the two countries.

To assess further how relatively expansionary monetary policy in Japan actually was, Table 4 compares rates of growth in "narrow" money in each country to growth in their nominal GNPs from 1955 to 1993.[5] Changes in the velocity of money are notoriously difficult to interpret, although perhaps less so in the 1950s and 1960s when inflationary expectations (in goods prices) were minimal. Nevertheless, from 1955 to 1971 the stock of narrow money in yen grew significantly faster than even the rapid growth in Japanese nominal GNP—15.47 percent versus 14.13 percent, respectively, on an annual basis. In the more financially mature American economy, where the U.S. Federal Reserve system effectively anchored the common price level in both countries, the opposite was true. From 1955 to 1971, American narrow money grew more slowly than American nominal GNP, 3.46 percent versus 6.24 percent, and much more slowly than money growth in Japan.

From both perspectives—higher internal CPI inflation as well as higher money growth—Japanese monetary policy was indeed relatively expansionary compared to that pursued by the United States during the era of fixed exchange rates and very high real growth.

Japan's relatively expansionary monetary policy arose naturally out of its obligation to fix the exchange rate within a narrow 2 percent band. The Japanese authorities did not base their monetary policy on immediate do-

5. "Narrow money" is measured in Line 34 of the IMF's *International Financial Statistics*, which corresponds roughly to M1: coin and currency plus checking accounts in commercial banks.

mestic considerations. If a balance of payments surplus appeared, the Bank of Japan tended to expand domestic credit—and vice versa for a balance of payments deficit. Rather than using foreign exchange interventions themselves as the principal technique for altering the domestic monetary base, however, the Bank of Japan preferred to keep foreign exchange reserves fairly small and constant by varying domestic credit availability to offset (incipient) changes in the balance of payments, at least up to 1968.

In summary, the 1950s and 1960s did have adjustment problems, but they were more micro than macro in nature. Because the pace of productivity growth across individual Japanese industries was uneven (Ohno, 1993; and see Table 5), some U.S. industries lost worldwide market share to Japanese competitors uncomfortably fast. But overall macroeconomic adjustment, where differential growth in average productivity between the

TABLE 5

Labor Productivity and Wages in Manufacturing,
Japan and the United States

(*average annual percentage increase*)

	1952–71		1972–90	
	Labor productivity	Wages	Labor productivity	Wages
Japan (all manufacturing)	7.6%	9.4%	4.3%	7.4%
Food	3.4	9.2	1.6	6.3
Textiles	8.4	10.2	4.2	7.1
Wood	0.3	10.6	1.7	7.5
Paper	8.1	7.8	2.6	7.1
Chemicals	11.1	9.8	4.8	7.8
Oil and coal	11.0	9.9	1.5	8.3
Ceramics and stone	6.6	9.1	2.1	7.5
Iron and steel	9.2	9.3	4.0	7.4
Non-ferrous metals	6.5	n.a.[a]	1.9	7.3
Metal products	6.3	9.6	3.5	7.4
General machinery	8.3	9.7	5.8	7.5
Electrical machinery	10.1	8.1	9.0	7.5
Transport machinery	12.4	8.9	7.2	7.5
Precision machinery	9.6	8.7	6.9	7.5
Standard deviation	3.1	0.8[b]	2.3	0.4
United States (all manufacturing)	2.4	4.8[c]	2.3	6.7[c]

SOURCES: For Japan, Japanese Ministries of Labor (employment and wages) and International Trade and Industry (production in current prices), and Bank of Japan (prices). Labor productivity is derived from employment, production, and price data. Compiled by Kenichi Ohno. For United States, U.S. Bureau of Labor Statistics (1989; *Employment and Earnings,* various years).

[a] Not available.
[b] Excluding non-ferrous metals.
[c] Hourly compensation, including wages plus other employer contributions.

United States and Japan was offset by higher money wage growth in Japan, worked smoothly. Payments imbalances and producer price-level misalignments, which loomed so large in the years after the par value system for exchange rates broke down, were comparatively minor.

Dollar Devaluations and Forced Relative Deflation in Japan: The Breakdown of Wage Adjustment, 1972–93

Beginning in 1968, U.S. wages began to increase a bit too fast for keeping the American WPI stable, and for offsetting the gap in productivity growth with Japan. In contrast to the 1 percent annual growth observed from 1951 to 1967, American wholesale prices began rising about 3.5 percent per year from 1968 to 1971. The American nominal anchor, and the economic rationale, for the fixed-rate dollar standard began to slip. Economists in Europe, Japan, and the United States began to advocate more flexibility in exchange rates (McKinnon, 1993). On the American side, exchange rate flexibility meant dollar devaluation.

When President Nixon shut the gold window in August 1971 and imposed a temporary import surcharge to enforce his demand that the dollar be officially devalued against the yen and other important currencies (as it was by the following December), he was following conventional economic wisdom. Most of his economic advisers, whether monetarist or Keynesian, applauded transforming the heretofore rigid exchange rate into an "adjusting" variable. Subsequently, U.S. secretaries of the Treasury have not hesitated to attempt to talk the dollar down publicly: Blumenthal in 1977, Baker 1985–87, and Bentsen in early 1993, to take some of the better-known examples. Except for the brief period of the overly strong dollar in the early 1980s, this process continued in economic "summits" and other less formal channels.

And the dollar has indeed fallen, albeit on an extremely erratic path sketched in Figure 2. Over the past 23 years, the dollar fell from 360 yen and 3.7 marks in 1970 to about 98 yen and 1.53 marks in July 1994. Has this exchange rate flexibility—that is, continual dollar devaluation—made the international adjustment mechanism more efficient?

I shall argue that American pressure on trading partners to depreciate the dollar has undermined the wage adjustment mechanism that had prevailed in the 1950s and 1960s. Because greater price and wage inflation was induced in the United States itself with corresponding deflationary pressure in Japan, relative growth in money wages after 1971 no longer reflected differences in productivity growth across the two countries. In

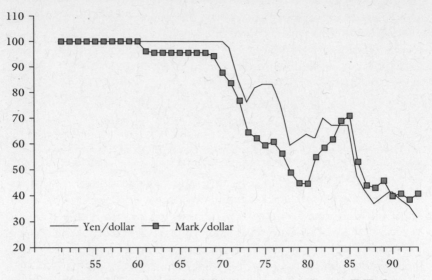

Figure 2. Exchange rates against the dollar (1951 = 100). Source: IMF, *International Financial Statistics* (various years).

addition, a flexible exchange rate is also naturally an untethered exchange rate: a new source of net financial volatility in the world economy—as with the yen's current sharp overvaluation.

Before considering the current overvaluation of the yen, however, Table 1 shows the price/wage/exchange rate experience for both countries from 1972 to 1993. Two facts stand out. First, without a stable U.S. anchor for the world price level, average wholesale price inflation was higher in this twenty-year period, particularly in the 1970s, than from 1951 to 1971. Second, from 1972 to 1993, Japan experienced price deflation *relative* to the United States measured by either the WPI or the CPI. In addition, Table 4 shows the even sharper slowdown in Japanese money growth relative to American in more recent periods.

Comparing the data on the United States and Japan in Table 5, the gap by which wage growth in Japan exceeded that in the United States shrank from 4.6 percentage points over 1952–71 to 0.7 percentage points from 1972 to 1990. More recently, from 1982 to 1992, Table 1 shows that the pace of money wage growth was about the same, averaging 3.1 percent per year in each country. Finally, taking the very last year, from 1992 to 1993, Japanese money wage growth was less than that in the United States—2 percent versus 2.6 percent (Table 1). Into 1994, this trend toward absolutely lower growth in money wages in Japan vis-à-vis the

United States continues (*The Economist*, August 6, 1994, p. 93). The old wage adjustment mechanism of the 1950s and 1960s has been turned on its head!

The statistical story on the price side also shows rising relative inflation in the United States, as a glance at Table 1 and, more spectacularly, Figure 1 indicates. From 1951 to 1971, WPIs in both countries stayed close together, increasing about 1 percent per year. From 1972 to 1992, the gap widened with 5.5 percent inflation in the U.S. WPI compared to 3.1 percent in Japan's. In the more recent decade from 1982 to 1992, the gap widened further: Table 1 shows the American WPI rising by 1.6 percent per year and the Japanese WPI *falling* 1.4 percent per year. Finally, from 1992 to 1993, U.S. producer prices rose by 1.5 percent per year while Japan's fell by 3.8 percent.[6] (Table 1 also shows that the one-year decline in the Japanese WPI in 1986 was actually greater during this earlier period of massive yen overvaluation.)

What caused this remarkable fall in the relative (and absolute) growth in Japanese money wages and prices? After all, long-term productivity growth in Japanese manufacturing remains substantially higher than in the United States, as shown in Table 5. I shall distinguish two competing hypotheses for explaining the same data. Both revolve around the appropriate interpretation of the fall in the yen/dollar exchange rate from 1971 to now.

The first and more conventional hypothesis treats the exchange rate as a *passively adjusting variable*. Monetary policies in each country are determined independently, and the exchange rate then adjusts. The second hypothesis treats the exchange rate as a *forcing variable*, which itself has a first-order impact on relative monetary policies in the two countries. Let us consider each in turn.

Hypothesis I: The Exchange Rate as a Passively Adjusting Variable

The relative deflationary pressure on Japanese prices since the early 1970s, as so vividly shown in Figure 1, is often explained in conventional monetarist terms. After the breakdown of the Bretton Woods system of par values in 1971, and more particularly the further collapse of the short-lived Smithsonian par-value system in February 1973, Japan seemed finally free to choose its own monetary policy. No longer did Japan have to defend a

---

6. Although not identical, movements in domestic producer price indices track those in the WPI very closely. For purposes of this analysis, producer prices might be slightly preferred. But only WPIs are available in a very long historical time series going back to the early 1950s—as in Table 1 and Figure 1.

dollar-based par-value system which had become very inflationary.[7] Under Hypothesis I, the Bank of Japan chose independently to follow a less inflationary policy than the U.S. Federal Reserve system. Table 4 shows the marked slowdown in Japanese money growth relative to the United States. Over 1955–71, annual narrow money growth in Japan was 15.47 percent versus only 3.46 percent in the United States; over 1972–82, Japanese money growth slowed to 8.85 percent while American speeded up to 6.33 percent; for the decade 1983–93, Japanese money growth became even *lower* than American—5.88 percent versus 7.2 percent.

Initially, the ostensible monetary independence of Japan under Hypothesis I looked good. In the late 1970s and early 1980s, the appreciated yen (shown in Figure 2) succeeded in insulating Japan from the second great worldwide inflation (shown in Figure 1). This apparently independent choice of a relatively deflationary monetary cum exchange rate policy kept Japan's price level much more stable than its American counterpart. Then, by letting its currency depreciate slightly, Japan could avoid following the sharp American disinflation of 1981–84. (The Reagan years from 1981–84 were the only period where Americans were not continually pressuring the Japanese to appreciate.)

The objection to accepting Hypothesis I, however, arises from its apparent inconsistency with the unduly sharp deflations in the Japanese WPI in 1986–87 and again in 1992–94. If the Bank of Japan's monetary policies were (are) truly independent, why would it choose to suddenly deflate in two situations when Japanese tradables prices (and world prices measured in dollars) were quite stable? Both deflationary episodes have been accompanied by severe industrial distress.

The aftermath of a sharp deflation can also cause difficulties. To get out of the 1986–87 deflation, the Bank of Japan reduced nominal interest rates so sharply that it set in motion the so-called bubble economy: the unsustainable bidding up of longer-term asset values. Anxious to stimulate domestic spending, the Japanese Ministry of Finance took further measures to encourage the bidding up of property and stock market values from 1987 to 1990 (Taniguchi, 1993)—thus setting the stage for the financial crash of 1991–92.

Contrary to Hypothesis I, the short-run business cycle costs of sharp yen appreciations in the mid 1980s and early 1990s have been so high that the Bank of Japan seems not to be following an independent monetary

---

7. Because of last-ditch efforts by countries like Japan to defend their dollar parities and prevent their currencies from appreciating, their domestic money supplies exploded in the early 1970s (McKinnon, 1982).

policy with a passively adjusting exchange rate. Is there an alternative way of explaining relative Japanese and American monetary experiences over the past twenty years?

Hypothesis II: The Exchange Rate as a Forcing Variable

Modern theory tells us that in the absence of exchange controls on capital movements, the exchange rate is a forward-looking asset price (Frenkel and Mussa, 1990). Instead of adjusting passively to current or past price-level misalignments or trade imbalances, the spot exchange rate is determined by the portfolio preferences of holders of yen and dollar assets at all terms to maturity. These preferences continually change in response to "news" about how the future exchange rate is likely to evolve. And the yen-dollar rate will evolve according to how expansionary the Bank of Japan becomes relative to the Federal Reserve system. Thus, how international investors judge *prospective* monetary policies in Japan vis-à-vis the United States determines today's yen-dollar rate.

The converse of this asset market approach to the exchange rate underlies Hypothesis II. If either or both governments succeed in changing today's equilibrium exchange rate, they are credibly telegraphing to the market that relative monetary policies in the future will be different from what international investors had previously presumed. To preserve this credibility, the governments involved must lean (at least implicitly) on national monetary authorities to begin altering their monetary policies toward each other in order to sustain today's exchange rate. In this sense, today's exchange rate target "forces" the evolution of relative monetary policies in the longer term. For example, the continual American pressure to appreciate the yen, even if only by "talking it up," has forced Japanese monetary policy to be relatively contractionary compared to American. Since the early 1970s, the result has been the slowdown in Japanese monetary expansion and the relative deflation shown in Tables 1 and 4.

Not all the monetary adjustment need be on the Japanese side. Under Hypothesis II, the exchange rate can only force *relative* monetary adjustment on the two countries. In the 1970s, American monetary policy was too expansionary and inflationary, in part because the American government was determined to keep the dollar too low in the foreign exchange market against hard-currency trading partners (McKinnon, 1982, 1984). At that time, the relatively deflationary monetary policy forced on Japan by the high-yen strategy turned out to be a lucky accident for Japan—unlike Hypothesis I above would have it. Once the American price level became more stable over the last decade or so, however, recurrent bouts of yen appreciation and deflation have been more damaging to Japan, and to the cause of smoother international adjustment in prices and wages.

A Liquidity Trap for Japanese Interest Rates?

Japan's industrial slump in 1993 nicely illustrates how an inappropriate exchange rate can trap the central bank into following an overly deflationary monetary policy. In response to a rising American trade deficit in 1992 into 1993, which was the counterpart of a rising Japanese trade surplus (Table 3), officials in the new Clinton government intimated in early 1993 that the yen should increase against the dollar. In the first half of 1993, the yen rose from 125 to the dollar in early January to just 105 to the dollar by late July. For mid-1993, Table 6 shows the exchange rate that would have

TABLE 6

Purchasing Power Parity Estimates for 1993: Q2 [a]

(*for a broad basket of tradable goods unless otherwise noted*)

	Yen/ dollar	Mark/ dollar
Long-run averaging method (12-year moving average)	146	2.01
Price pressure method[b]	151	2.00
Economic Planning Agency price survey for consumer durables only[c]	141	2.04
RIIPM price survey on manufactured goods[d]	143	1.85
OECD price survey for machinery and equipment only[e]	134	1.98
OECD price survey adjusted for tradability[f]	181	2.26
Economist Big Mac index[g]	174	2.05

SOURCE: Ohno (personal communication, 1993).

NOTE: Actual exchange rates in 1993: Q2 were 110 yen/dollar and 1.62 mark/dollar.

[a] Original estimates for periods other than 1993: Q2 are updated using the Cassel-Keynes method with wholesale price indices.

[b] Ohno (1991).

[c] Economic Planning Agency (1992).

[d] Research Institute for International Price Mechanism, Tokyo. Survey results to be published shortly.

[e] Organization for Economic Cooperation and Development (1992).

[f] Subject to upward biases as the original data include net indirect taxes.

[g] *Economist*, Apr. 17, 1993. The magazine surveys the price of the popular McDonald's hamburger annually. Since the product contains both local labor and ingredients and imported materials, the results could be seen as a very limited and mixed PPP index.

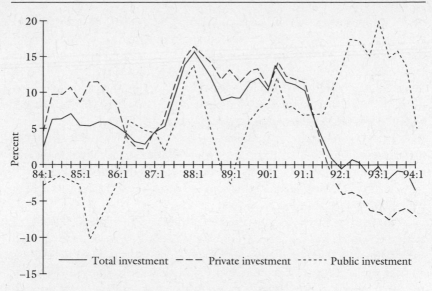

Figure 3. Japan: Investment growth rate (quarterly data).

more or less equalized producer prices in Japan and the United States: by alternative measures, this purchasing power parity (PPP) was about 140 to 150 yen per dollar. Because of the yen's further appreciation above its PPP in 1993, the decline in Japan's WPI accelerated from about 1 percent in 1991–92 to about 4 percent in 1993 (Table 1). Without driving the yen back down, the Bank of Japan could not stop the fall in domestic prices.

Although normally exhibiting high positive growth, Japanese aggregate investment slumped in 1992–93 and showed negative growth, as shown in Figure 3. Public sector investment increased sharply in 1992–93, in part because of American pressure on Japan to be more "Keynesian." But this was dwarfed by the huge decline in private investment, which is highly sensitive to interest rate and exchange rate effects.

Interest rate policy itself was not, and could not have been, sufficient to alleviate the deflation and economic slump in Japan as long as the yen remained overvalued. In September 1993, the Bank of Japan reduced its discount rate to an all-time low of 1.75 percent and interbank lending rates were a little over 2 percent. Even if nominal interest rates had approached zero, "real" interest rates[8] would still remain high if domestic producer

8. In deflating nominal interest rates to construct real ones, which price index one selects makes a big difference. In 1993, the Japanese consumer price index actually rose

prices were expected to fall, perhaps by more than the 4 percent fall that actually ended up occurring. Certainly, domestic firms, which were potential investors in fixed assets or inventories, saw increased risk from price-level uncertainty. In addition, the overvalued yen itself made investing in Japan look prohibitively expensive. Instead, many multinational corporations had the option of investing in neighboring countries whose price levels, at prevailing exchange rates, were lower. In effect, Japan was in a Keynesian liquidity trap: the nominal interest rate couldn't be reduced below zero to get the real interest rate low enough to restore investment and employment to "normal" levels. And because of high national saving, but depressed investment, Japan's trade surplus in 1993 rose to an all-time high of over $140 billion (Table 3).

Nor in 1993 was it possible, even if desirable, to reinflate the "bubble" economy, which was the way out of the 1986–87 deflation. Badly burned speculators were too close in time to bid up Japanese long-term asset values all over again. Instead, monetary expansion that drove the yen down toward purchasing power parity—by selling yen for dollars in the foreign exchange market if need be—was the most efficient way out. But that avenue was blocked by America's protectionist threats if the Japanese monetary authorities deliberately engineered a fall in the yen!

The Trade Balance, Current Account, and Exchange Rate

Suppose, therefore, we tentatively accept Hypothesis II. Rather than passively adjusting, the forward-looking yen-dollar exchange rate has forced changes in relative monetary policies. If so, why since 1970 has the American government pursued, and Japan acquiesced to, the apparently quixotic policy of continual yen appreciation that imposes relative deflation on Japan with no predictable effect on Japan's surplus or America's deficit on current account?

The problem lies more with academic economists and economic theory than with politicians or government officials. The views of policy makers, perhaps formed earlier when they were students, are influenced by theories propounded by academics. The basic theoretical issue is whether or not the exchange rate should be used as an instrumental variable for "correcting" trade or current-account imbalances.

slightly—1.2 percent, as shown in Table 1. In McKinnon (1979, chap. 10), I make the argument that the producer price index is the more appropriate deflator for measuring the real interest rate that enters business decision making on new investment.

The Elasticities Model of the Balance of Trade and the Syndrome of the Ever-Higher Yen

The prevailing textbook view derives from the elasticities model of the balance of trade (Robinson, 1937; Meade, 1951). Suppose a country has a trade deficit[9] and the exchange rate is a variable that the government directly controls by pegging it in the foreign exchange market while sterilizing the domestic monetary consequences. Then, under not very exacting conditions within the context of the model (if the sum of price elasticities of exports and imports is greater than unity), devaluing that country's currency will reduce the trade deficit in monetary terms. Without going through the painful process of reducing domestic money wages, devaluation is seen as a relatively painless way of reducing all domestic prices and wages relative to their foreign counterparts uniformly.[10] Export expansion and import contraction then follow naturally.

If policy makers embrace the venerable elasticities model uncritically, they see the exchange rate as an instrumental variable for eliminating trade deficits or surpluses. Under the model's thrall, American economic advisers have pressured successive presidents, starting with President Nixon in 1971, to devalue the dollar whenever trade or current-account deficits appeared. In addition, because Japan and other industrial countries continued to gain market share in manufacturing, dollar devaluation—by making American manufacturing industries more competitive in the short run—seemed to forestall protectionist pressure. Similarly, academic economists in Japan have viewed yen appreciation as a natural or "textbook" response for reducing the burgeoning Japanese trade and current-account surpluses. The upshot has been to aggravate the syndrome of the ever-higher yen.

But the elasticities model applies only in fairly special circumstances (McKinnon, 1981; McKinnon and Ohno, 1988). Suppose exchange controls limit capital movements and trade itself is a fringe activity. Then the economy is defined to be "insular," and the government of an insular economy can peg its exchange rate directly without having to adjust its national monetary policy simultaneously. Because of the exchange controls, the central bank can effectively sterilize the domestic monetary con-

---

9. Within the confines of the elasticities model, the trade deficit is usually not distinguished from the deficit on current account.

10. Ohno (1993) provides convincing evidence to the contrary. Rather than smooth and uniform adjustment, sharp exchange rate changes heavily distort relative prices in the economies in question.

sequences of intervening in the foreign exchanges. With the domestic macroeconomy thus insulated, a devaluation will improve the trade balance if the standard conditions on the price elasticities governing imports and exports are satisfied.

At Bretton Woods in 1945 and for some years afterward, when controls on trade and capital flows were almost universal, economies were insular and the elasticities doctine was empirically valid for economies that had some slack in resource use. Therefore, to limit trade imbalances among what were then insular economies, the Bretton Woods negotiators wanted pegged but adjustable exchange rates. Because capital flows were restricted, the negotiators imagined that national governments should be fairly free to change the pegs so as to correct trade imbalances.

Today, by contrast, economies are open rather than insular. Capital and trade flows among the industrial economies are huge and virtually unrestricted. Rather than being directly controllable by Treasury authorities, any exchange rate is endogenously determined by the current and prospective monetary policies of the countries in question. Among open economies, the exchange rate behaves as a forward-looking asset price as per Hypothesis II above. Because the government cannot directly peg the exchange rate independently of its (future) choice of monetary policy, the endogenously determined exchange rate cannot be predictably related to the net trade balance—nor to the current account.

For example, consider the financially open Japanese and American economies in 1993. Having policy makers successfully "talk the yen up" against the dollar early in the year was equivalent to promising market participants either that Japanese monetary policy was going to be tighter, or that American was going to be easier, or some combination of the two. In anticipation, aggregate expenditures for (absorption of) all goods and services tended to fall in Japan and to increase in the United States. In the short and intermediate runs, these expenditure effects increased Japan's current surplus—thus offsetting the relative price effect from Japanese goods becoming more expensive compared to American goods.

To summarize, a higher yen, relative to its current purchasing power parity, promises the market that Japanese monetary policy will be relatively tighter compared to American—as per Hypothesis II. In the short and intermediate runs, actual and prospectively tighter money policy reduces aggregate expenditures and is unlikely to reduce a Japanese trade surplus. In the very long run, the real exchange rate and expenditures are unaffected: relative deflation in prices and wages in Japan (Table 1, Figure 1) offsets yen appreciation so as to restore purchasing power parity. Between financially open economies, there is no time horizon over which an exchange rate change influences the current-account balance between them in a predictable fashion.

The Savings Shortage in the United States, and Japan as International Creditor

The elasticities approach would hold that burgeoning U.S. trade and current-account deficits are an exchange rate issue. But there is a familiar alternative explanation for burgeoning U.S. trade and current-account deficits: a shortage of domestic saving for financing "normal" levels of investment. Courtesy of the National Research Council (1994b), Table 7 shows U.S. savings and investment data—both net and gross—from 1960 through 1993. From 1960 through 1989, gross domestic investment averaged about 16 to 17 percent of GNP; then it dipped erratically in the early 1990s to about 13.6 percent of GNP (more on this below). Although its components varied, U.S. private gross saving has remained fairly steady at about 16 percent of GNP for over three decades, which was, and is, low by international standards. Since 1981, however, government dissaving has risen sharply. In the 1980s and 1990s, the driving force behind the overall American savings shortage has been higher U.S. fiscal deficits varying between 2.5 and 4.7 percent of GNP.

In the past decade, much of this potential savings "gap" has been covered by foreign borrowing from a variety of Asian and European sources. From 1985 through 1989, Tables 3 and 7 indicate that the U.S current-account deficit was of the same order of magnitude as the U.S. fiscal deficit—about 2.5 percent of American GDP—thus financing American investment at "normal" levels so that the Reagan boom could continue.[11] But this left (and still leaves) the American economy vulnerable to any exogenous disturbance in foreign capital inflows that forces a reduction in the current-account deficit—that is, in the economy's access to foreign saving.

The U.S. Credit Crunch of 1991

When the U.S. current-account deficit narrowed substantially in 1990–92 but the fiscal deficit stayed high (Table 3), a domestic "credit

---

11. Earlier in 1982–83, the ballooning U.S. fiscal deficit was not offset by similarly sized current-account deficits, as shown in Table 3. And investment did fall below normal. The Volcker disinflationary shock then was the prime determinant of the output slump in the American economy and the partly endogenous rise in the fiscal deficit.

TABLE 7

U.S. Savings and Investment

(percent of GDP)

	Net personal savings	Plus corporate savings	Plus government savings	Equals net national savings	Plus foreign savings	Plus statistical discrepancy	Equals net domestic investment	Plus depreciation	Equals gross domestic investment[a]	Percent of GDP consisting of plant and equipment[a]
1960–64	4.4	3.4	(0.1)	7.8	(0.8)	(0.3)	6.6	8.6	15.2	9.3
1965–69	4.9	3.6	(0.2)	8.3	(0.4)	0.0	7.9	8.2	16.1	10.5
1970–74	5.9	2.3	(0.5)	7.7	(0.3)	0.1	7.5	9.0	16.5	10.7
1975–79	5.0	2.8	(1.1)	6.8	(0.1)	0.5	7.1	10.4	17.6	11.6
1980–84	5.8	1.4	(2.6)	4.6	0.7	0.1	5.3	11.9	17.2	12.6
1985–89	3.6	1.9	(2.4)	3.0	2.7	(0.3)	5.5	11.1	16.5	11.3
1990	3.2	1.4	(2.5)	2.1	1.4	0.1	3.6	10.9	14.5	10.5
1991	3.5	1.3	(3.4)	1.4	(0.2)	0.4	1.7	11.0	12.7	9.5
1992	3.6	1.8	(4.7)	0.7	0.8	0.6	2.1	11.0	13.1	9.2
1993	3.0	1.9	(3.5)	1.4	1.5	0.2	3.1	10.9	14.0	9.8

SOURCE: National Research Council (1994).
NOTE: Due to rounding, rows may not sum exactly.

[a] Gross domestic investment includes investment in residential structures, changes in inventories, and plant and equipment investment.

crunch" ensued with a slump in U.S. investment, which bottomed out at 12.7 percent of GDP in 1991 (Table 7). The resulting fall in real U.S. GDP in 1991 (Table 2) was sufficient to dis-elect a surprised George Bush! But what was cause and what was effect? Did investment and output fall first, which then reduced imports, the current-account deficit, and capital inflows—or the reverse?

Associating the credit crunch of 1990–92 with a sharp slowdown in net capital inflows into the United States is not conventional wisdom. The usual explanation is that over-zealous regulators placed excessive restraint on lending by commercial banks. Because of the newly signed Basle Accord raising bank capital requirements, and because the regulators themselves had been burned by the failure of so many commercial banks and savings institutions in the 1980s, it was alleged that bank regulation became overly restrictive in the early 1990s. This explanation was sufficiently potent politically to cause the Bush administration to lean heavily on bank regulators to ease up.

But this domestic regulatory explanation seems out of keeping with the sharpness and magnitude of the 1991 downturn on the one hand, and conflicts with the strange behavior of the term structure of interest rates on the other. Suppose that the domestic regulatory "disturbance" had indeed predominated. Then the sudden preference of American banks for longer-term securities—requiring less bank capital (zero in the case of government bonds) under the Basle Accord—over normal shorter-term commercial lending with high capital requirements should have driven long-term interest rates *down* relative to short-term rates. But, as analyzed below, just the opposite happened: U.S. long-term rates rose sharply.

Without the space or inclination to construct an econometric model to differentiate one hypothesis from another, I identify the initial "cause" to be sudden external restraint in 1990–91 on the U.S. economy's access to foreign capital. In making this identification, we see two factors exogenous to the American economy suddenly reducing capital inflows.

First, the fiscal costs of reunification changed Germany almost overnight from being a big net international lender in 1989 to being a net borrower in 1991. The upper panel of Figure 4 shows the remarkably sharp fall in Germany's current-account surplus from about $50 billion per year before 1991 to a deficit of about $20 to $25 billion in 1992–93. The shock took the international financial mechanism—including American borrowers—by surprise and contributed to America's short-term credit crunch in 1991.

But what is the longer-term prognosis once the reunification shock

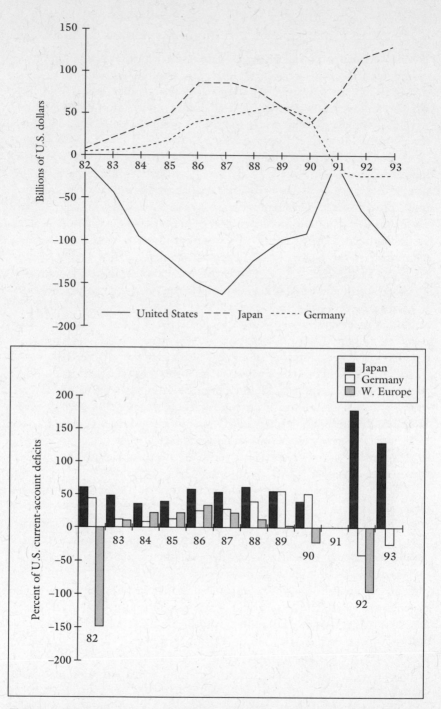

Figure 4. Current account, 1982–93, and foreign saving sources for the United States, 1982–93 (both yearly data). Sources: OECD *Economic Outlook* (June 1994); OECD *Monthly Statistics* (various years).

wears off? Because the German government's continuing huge fiscal expenditures in the eastern part of the country could last a decade or more, and because the German economy was "unnaturally" depressed in 1992–93 by the Bundesbank's tight-money high-mark policy, Germany seems unlikely to return to current-account surplus and again become a substantial savings sink for the United States. Indeed, an economic recovery in Germany may well increase imports, causing further deterioration in its current account.

Second, the bursting of the Japanese bubble economy in 1990–91 suddenly reduced long-term capital outflows[12] from Japan, including those to the United States. The crash in the Japanese stock and property markets in 1990 and 1991 so impaired the capital positions of important Japanese financial institutions—banks, insurance companies, trust funds, and so on—that they shifted out of long-term international lending. Consequently, foreign financial capability of buying Japanese goods was reduced so as to narrow Japan's current-account surplus in these two years, as also shown in the upper panel of Figure 4.

This remarkable shift in the pattern of Japanese long-term lending is shown in Table 8. Before 1990, long-term capital outflows (column 2) actually overfinanced the Japanese current-account surplus (column 1). The Japanese financial system covered this gap by borrowing short in international markets (column 5), largely by having Japanese banks accept Euro-dollar deposits (Tavlas and Ozeki, 1992). In effect, Japan behaved as a giant financial intermediary borrowing short in order to augment its long-term lending—much like the earlier behavior of the United States in the 1950s and 1960s.[13] With the bursting of the asset bubble, however, long-term capital was actually repatriated back to Japan in 1991! Table 8 shows this swing in long-term capital: from an outflow in the mid-1980s to an inflow in 1991 was a change of about $160 billion annually. To complete our picture of this radical change in the external balance sheet of the Japanese financial system, about $117 billion of short-term capital flowed out of Japan in 1991 (column 5)—largely by the Japanese banks running off much of their Euro-dollar liabilities—as the counterpart of the inflow of long-term capital coupled with a current-account surplus.

The direct effects of these two shocks on the German and Japanese

---

12. This included direct and portfolio investments, including bank lending, in instruments greater than one-year duration.

13. One significant difference, however, is that in the 1980s most of Japan's external assets and liabilities were denominated not in its own currency but in U.S. dollars (Tavlas and Ozeki, 1992), whereas in the 1950s and 1960s the U.S. dollar was the numéraire currency for America's external assets and liabilities.

TABLE 8

Japan: Summary Balance of Payments, 1980–93

(*billions of U.S. dollars*)

Year	Current-account balance	Long-term capital account, net	Basic balance	Overall balance[a]	Short-term capital flows plus errors and omissions
1980	−10.746	2.324	−8.422	5.03	13.452
1981	4.77	−9.672	−4.902	3.64	8.542
1982	6.85	−14.969	−8.119	−4.7	3.419
1983	20.799	−17.7	3.099	1.55	−1.549
1984	35.003	−49.651	−14.648	2.12	16.768
1985	49.169	−64.542	−15.373	−0.58	14.793
1986	85.845	−131.461	−45.616	14.84	60.453
1987	87.015	−136.532	−49.517	37.94	87.457
1988	79.631	−130.930	−51.299	16.52	67.819
1989	57.157	−89.246	−32.089	−12.76	19.329
1990	35.761	−43.586	−7.825	−6.59	1.235
1991	72.901	37.057	109.958	−6.63	−116.588
1992	117.551	−28.459	89.092	0.63	−88.462
1993	131.35	−78.091	53.259	35.95p[b]	−17.309p

SOURCES: International Monetary Fund, International Statistics Bank of Japan, Balance of Payment Monthly.
[a] Changes in official reserves.
[b] p = preliminary.

economies and the world at large were complex. By 1991–92, the collapse in domestic asset values had significantly depressed the Japanese economy, causing declines in industrial output and sluggish growth in real GNP (Table 2). However, my main concern here is the echo effect of these two more or less simultaneous shocks on the American economy over 1990–92—with their impact most sharply focused in 1991. Not only was the total amount of foreign capital available to the American economy suddenly reduced, but because of the Japanese financial crash, the form of finance shifted dramatically from long-term to short-term.

Nevertheless, the undiminished U.S. fiscal deficit—resulting in bond issues of about $270 billion per year in 1991 (Table 3)—somehow had to be financed. In 1991, the U.S. yield curve began to steepen sharply. Long-term interest rates rose from being 1 or 2 percentage points higher than short-term rates at the beginning of the year to being over 4 percentage points higher at the end. In the absence of foreign buying of U.S. Treasury bonds and other long-term securities, the bond market yield curve had to steepen sufficiently to make bonds attractive to domestic financial institutions and individuals. By mid-1991, normal lending by commercial banks began to fall sharply. Instead of meeting the normal working capital needs of American business, commercial banks bought Treasury bonds and other securities; they played the yield curve to increase their profitability. In addition, there was disintermediation: people who normally held short-term bank deposits (M2) switched to longer-term higher-yield bonds. The resulting sharp fall in normal bank lending in 1991 created what was then called "the credit crunch."[14] It induced the American cyclical downturn in 1991, and sluggish growth in 1992.

A fuller statistical analysis of this episode is beyond the scope of this chapter. Here, I just illustrate how dependent the American economy has become on foreign capital. Future disruptions in its availability could work themselves out financially somewhat differently.

Japan as Dominant International Creditor in the 1990s?

In 1993, Japan's deepened slump in domestic investment from the overvalued yen released a huge amount of savings onto the world market: her current-account surplus ballooned to over $130 billion. Recovering from the financial calamities of 1990–91, Japanese investors once more began to invest long-term overseas: outflows rose to $78 billion in 1993 (Table 8). But this long-term financial outflow remained substantially less than the huge current-account surplus. Unlike the 1980s, long-term capital outflows are (1993–94) not yet fully financing, let alone "overfinancing," Japan's savings transfer to the rest of the world.

Nevertheless, complaints of a credit crunch disappeared from the American financial press. Although still below normal, U.S. gross investment did recover to about 14 percent of GDP in 1993 (Table 7). As in the 1980s, this was made possible by the sharp increase in foreign capital inflows. Table 3 shows that the U.S. current-account deficit reached about $109 billion in 1993, and U.S. long-term interest rates fell by about two percentage points compared to 1991, although they still remained about 2.5 percentage points above short-term rates. With this relaxation of the capital constraint, we had the "Clinton boom" in 1993 into 1994.

In contrast to the 1980s, however, Japan emerges as the overwhelmingly dominant creditor country in the world economy of the 1990s. Her current-account surpluses now exceed America's deficits (Table 3). Other savings sinks on which the United States had relied in the 1980s, western Europe in general and Germany in particular, have disappeared and are

---

14. If one accepts the hypothesis that domestic banks are special in serving smaller industrial enterprises where customer relationships and specific knowledge are important (Gertler and Gilchrist, 1992), then any sudden diminution of normal lending could not immediately (in 1991) be offset by borrowing from other sources—for example, by issuing commercial bills—at home or abroad. But in the longer run, many enterprises could escape from the banking crunch by turning to other sources of finance.

now net borrowers in the world economy—as shown in the lower panel of Figure 4. By 1993, other prospering Asian economies—China, Singapore, Taiwan, and South Korea—had reduced their collective saving (current-account) surpluses to negligible levels. In the remainder of the 1990s, how secure is this sole source of net finance for the world economy?

In the short run, any "normal" recovery of Japanese domestic investment (Figure 3) will substantially reduce the size of Japan's saving surplus from that seen in 1993–94. Even so, if we project Japan's domestic investment that prevailed in the 1980s into the later 1990s, her high private saving should still generate substantial, if smaller, current-account surpluses.

In the longer run, any projections are very speculative. On the pessimistic side, if Japan embarks on Keynesian-style fiscal "expansion" to alleviate its economic slump while incidentally eliminating its current-account surplus, the result would be a worldwide credit crunch. Figure 3 shows the already-high percentage increase in Japanese public sector investments in 1992–93. Higher government expenditure and lower taxes in Japan would reduce the vital source of saving on which the rest of the world—most particularly the United States—depends so heavily.

More optimistically, suppose that Japan recovers from its high-yen slump by a properly managed monetary expansion with some real exchange depreciation but no significant impairment of the economy's high-saving capacity. Then the ongoing financial problem between Japan and the United States is one of managing the savings transfer between the two economies more efficiently without provoking similar macroeconomic disruptions in the future. In effect, any new exchange rate regime should seek to restore stability in "real" exchange rates, as measured by broad baskets of tradable goods, much as it existed in the 1950s and 1960s.

To further limit interest volatility, including asset "bubbles" and credit "crunches" in the future, the incredible ebb and flow of long-term capital from Japan should also be smoothed. But between financially open economies, this smoothing is largely a question of harmonizing national monetary policies to assure the capital markets that *nominal* exchange rates will remain stable in the long run. Otherwise, as they try to guess the future evolution of the yen/dollar and other exchange rates, international investors will continue to churn their portfolios of yen versus dollar, or short-versus long-term, financial instruments.

Purchasing Power Parity and Monetary Cooperation

For monetary cooperation to be successful between any pair of economies like Japan and the United States, or within a broader group of industrial economies, the focal point must be a common price-level objective—before moving on to exchange rate stabilization per se. Such a pact would only be satisfactory if the common price level was truly anchored, and each national monetary authority could report to its government that it was stabilizing "the" domestic price level as well as the exchange rate.

The choice of a suitable price index is then critically important in ensuring that if each participating government actually hit its price-level target, the result would be fully consistent with maintaining fixed nominal exchange rates (within narrow bands) into the indefinite future because the purchasing powers of national monies are more or less equalized. Elsewhere, I have argued (McKinnon, 1988, 1993, 1994) that broad price indices for tradable goods which are already in common use—the wholesale price index (WPI) or the closely related producer price index (PPI)—have this desirable characteristic. And this conclusion is fully born out by the earlier Japan-U.S. experience when the yen/dollar rate was fixed for over 20 years.

Many, but not all, of the desirable features of ongoing cooperation between the Bank of Japan and the Federal Reserve were realized during the 1950s and 1960s. A relatively expansionary monetary policy by the Bank of Japan was consistent with pegging the exchange rate at 360 yen/dollar on the one hand, and stability in the common price level for tradable goods (the American and Japanese WPIs) on the other (Figures 1 and 2). At this stable price level, workers could bargain so that, on average, money wage growth more or less matched the growth in manufacturing productivity in each country. In effect, the two monetary authorities behaved as if "price" stability meant stability in tradable goods prices rather than in their domestic CPIs—where Japanese CPI growth was naturally much higher than American because of higher equilibrium growth in money wages. To be consistent with exchange rate stability, any future monetary pact should also target the common price level measured in tradable goods, while tolerating (slightly) different growth rates in member countries' CPIs if necessary.

Although this price-level objective would remain the same in any future monetary pact, the operating procedures followed by the Bank of Japan and the Federal Reserve for getting there would necessarily be somewhat different. The marked asymmetry characterizing the fixed-rate dollar standard of the 1950s and 1960s—where the Federal Reserve independently targeted the common price level and the Bank of Japan pegged the exchange rate—would be both politically unacceptable and economically inefficient in any new, more symmetrical regime.

The political unacceptability of reintroducing the fixed-rate dollar standard of the 1950s and 1960s, where the U.S. could successfully focus on stabilizing its own price level and pretty well ignore the economic circumstances in other countries as long as they maintained their dollar exchange parities, is obvious. This international monetary asymmetry arose naturally out of the aftermath of World War II—particularly the success of postwar reconstruction under the Marshall Plan in Europe and the Dodge Plan in Japan (McKinnon, 1993).

But any new pact between Japan and the United States should be a more symmetrical partnership. The weight of the huge Japanese economy in both the financial and commodity markets is now such that the United States can no longer easily provide the nominal anchor for both countries. The state of Japan's macroeconomy now makes a difference to the cyclical stability of the American economy itself.

Elsewhere, I have gone into more details on how such ongoing cooperation might be structured (McKinnon 1988, 1994). Here, it suffices to note that both central banks should gear their domestic credit expansion to stabilizing their internal WPIs (tradable goods prices). This would be consistent with a nominal exchange rate target based on the principle of purchasing power parity (PPP), which aligned these two (stationary) WPIs in the 1950s and 1960s. If the market value of the yen/dollar rate tended to stray from this initial PPP rate, fairly minor symmetrical monetary adjustments—say through lowering short-term interest rates in one country and raising them in the other—would likely be sufficent to bring it back. Failing that, concerted official intervention in the foreign exchanges would be relied on to keep the rate within a pre-announced narrow band.[15]

In the early years of this cooperative agreement, the exchange rate band might be kept fairly broad, say 6 or 8 percent wide. If and when the pact was seen to be successful for some years, the band could be progressively narrowed toward 2 percent. But Japan and the United States would have a nominal anchor in common: their commitment to stabilize their domestic WPIs.[16] To minimize stress, each monetary authority could give some weight to the other country's WPI in its own decision making. Such symmetry is all important to avoid a European-style debacle, such as when

---

15. Since the Plaza and Louvre Accords of 1985–87, the evidence is now pretty strong that sterilized official intervention can work—as long as it is concerted and open (Dominguez and Frankel, 1993).

16. Producer price indices, which track WPIs rather closely, might provide a slightly better nominal anchor for the two countries. Price movements originating in third countries are more likely to be excluded. In addition, the authorities must track price levels, rather than inflation rates, for the fixed exchange rate regime to hold together (McKinnon, 1994).

Germany's Bundesbank in 1992–93 determined its monetary policy uni-laterally, irrespective of the needs of the rest of the community.

It is far easier to sketch the nature of Japanese-American monetary co-operation in a steady state—drawing on the experience of the 1950s and 1960s—than to sketch possible transitions to this desired equilibrium. In the third quarter of 1994, the yen remained extremely overvalued by any measure of purchasing power parity based on the alignment of national WPIs. Using several direct and indirect measurement techniques shown in Table 6, Kenichi Ohno estimated that in the second quarter of 1993 the PPP yen/dollar rate would have been between 140 and 150. By compari-son, the highly volatile market rate averaged about 110. In the third quar-ter of 1994, with the market rate at about 100, the drift in the PPP rate (Figure 4) probably would have placed it in the neighborhood of 135.

The overvaluation of the yen is only one aspect of the current disequi-librium. Unfortunately, the last twenty years of forced deflation in Japan vis-à-vis the United States have set in motion a declining price level (mea-sured by the Japanese WPI) and, less tractably, unduly low growth in Japanese money wages in 1993 into 1994. Because the lags behind the exchange rate in this wage-price deflation are substantial (Ohno, 1990), one would expect the PPP yen/dollar rate to continue to drift downwards (as shown in Figure 4) even if there was a major monetary correction. If the Bank of Japan expanded Japanese monetary policy to drive the yen/dollar rate upwards and pull Japan out of its current deflationary slump, increased growth in money wages would come only with a lag.

How does one achieve monetary expansion in Japan's circumstances? The scope for further interest rate cuts in Japanese money markets is lim-ited because nominal interest rates are bounded from below by zero, in the Keynesian liquidity trap discussed above. An effective easing of Japanese monetary policy might well require the Bank of Japan to buy dollars with yen directly: that is, to use unsterilized intervention in the foreign ex-changes to bring the yen down and stop Japanese producer prices from falling.

Laying out the most efficient transition to the blissful steady-state equilibrium sketched above, taking into account all the lags involved, is complicated and would require a separate paper. However, we can safely say that short-run monetary expansion in Japan should aim to drive the current yen/dollar rate up sharply, but not all the way to 135 yen. Because of PPP drift, that would cause some overshooting in the yen/dollar rate in the sense that it might have to come down again at some future time if PPP is to be maintained. Rather, with American cooperation, current monetary expansion in Japan should aim for some intermediate rate, perhaps 125 yen/dollar. If the calculations were done right, such an exchange rate could be sustainable into the indefinite future, and the PPP rate with ever-slowing drift would eventually converge to this "market" rate. Japan's (and America's) WPI would stabilize, Japanese money wages would start growing faster, and the machinery sketched above for our blissful, if hypothetical, steady state could kick in. But the official exchange rate band could not be narrowed and hardened until national interest rates became fairly well aligned (McKinnon, 1994).

The faint of heart don't have to buy my ideas for long-term monetary cooperation between Japan and the United States to agree with the conclusion that, in the short run, there should be a strong monetary expansion in Japan that can only happen if the yen depreciates. Besides buoying the American economy, the consequent revival of the Japanese economy will reduce (but not eliminate) the trade and current-account imbalances between them. There is no conflict between the short- and long-run directions of desirable change in current Japanese monetary policy.

But fiscal policy is a different story. If the Japanese undertake a fiscal "expansion," as some Americans have (perversely) urged them to do, this will destroy a savings resource on which the American economy is highly dependent. To minimize the frictions involved, the American government should agree that Japanese monetary expansion, accompanied by the inevitable yen depreciation against the dollar, is also in the best interests of the United States.

An Evolutionary Parable of the Gains from International Organizational Diversity

MASAHIKO AOKI

In both classical and neoclassical trade theories, a nation's relative factor endowment is recognized as the only source of comparative advantage of its economy, and differences in factor endowments give rise to welfare gains from free trade. In these theories, the technology of production is generally assumed to exhibit constant returns to scale and be identical among nations. However, these theories face a difficulty of explaining the emergent phenomena of intra-industry trades between developed economies. For example, the trade of semiconductors flows both directions between Japan and the United States. How can such bilateral flows of the same industrial goods be explained by a difference in relative endowments of factors, such as land, capital, and labor, between the two economies?

To provide an explanation for such phenomena, the "new" trade theory introduced the possibility of increasing returns to scale for differentiated products, and thus that firms may have monopolistically competitive power (Helpman and Krugman, 1985). According to this theory, Japanese autos exported to the United States and American autos exported to Japan are differentiated by various product attributes, which can be efficiently produced only in large quantities. At least at this stage, however, the new trade theory has not primarily focused on what underlies these increasing returns to scale; the technology of the firm remains largely as a black box, as in the neoclassical theory. From a dynamic perspective, one possible cause for these increasing returns to scale may be sought in the

In writing this article, I benefited from discussions and comments by Clive Crook, Michihiro Kandori, Andreu Mas-Collell, Sedar Dinc, Kiminori Matsuyama, Aki Matsui, John Roemer, Andrea Prat, and Fernando Vega. Also, Timothy Taylor helped me greatly in editorial and substantial comments. This chapter is based on Aoki (1993), a more technical paper.

accumulation of learning within the firm, which translates into product innovation, firm-specific formation of worker skills, and so on.

This chapter focuses on ways that firms are organized and explores the possibility that different organizational conventions may constitute a source of comparative advantage of different economies. For example, one reason why American firms have a competitive advantage in the innovation and manufacturing of logic chips, while the Japanese enterprises have comparative advantage in memory chips, may be found in differences in the organization of R&D, manufacturing, and marketing as well as feedback mechanisms operating among those functions. One can cite many other examples to argue that the costs of production are not the same across economies, due to organizational factors.

Of course, one may ask why each firm doesn't simply adopt the most efficient organizational mode for the industry in which it is embedded, independently of its national origin. If firms did behave in that way, we ought to observe that firms within particular industries would tend to be organized in similar ways, even across national economies. However, contrary to this prediction, each advanced national economy tends to develop a more or less uniform organizational convention regardless of industries. Differences in enterprise organization between the American semiconductor industry and the American automobile industry may not be as large in many important respects as those between the American semiconductor (or automobile) industry and the Japanese semiconductor (or automobile) industry. From this perspective, the cost function should not be treated as "technologically" determined and thus exogenous to economics. Instead, the organization of firms and the cost function are tied together.

Why is this so? Is it merely because of the lack of perfect competition across economies? Will global competition eventually eliminate international differences in organizational conventions? If so, will the result be a certain uniform organizational convention across economies? Or the emergence of greater organizational diversity across industries within each economy? If these alternatives can be an object of international public policy choice, which option is welfare-enhancing? In this chapter, I plan to tell an economic parable which may provide some insight into these novel questions.

I will begin in the first section by breaking open the black box of the firm and explicitly recognizing the firm as a system of information for solving the coordination problem among many internal units. My discussion will recognize three prototype modes of coordination. The relative efficiency of these modes will depend on the technological and market environments of industry, as well as the existing distribution of different information processing capacities among the population.

The second section asks why different organizational conventions tend to arise in different economies independently of industrial characteristics. Moreover, it will argue that a closed economy is not especially likely to generate the optimal mix of organizational modes. Some key issues in considering these questions will include the bounded rationality of economic agents in investing in information processing capacity, the path-dependent nature of organizational selection, and the complementarity relationships among supporting institutions.

The final section then asks what is the best way to realize gains from organizational diversity, once different conventions are established in different economies. It discusses how the gains of organizational diversity may be recognized through free trade of products, through the sort of economic integration that facilitates factor mobility, and through foreign direct investment. The relative size of the interacting economies is also important.

Why Is Organizational Diversity Desirable?

A firm can be viewed as an organization of the management and multiple operational units. I will refer to these operational units as "shops," but they are also called departments, divisions, and other names. Each shop faces systematic as well as idiosyncratic risks, and the cost of producing outputs for the market will depend upon how information relevant to those risks is processed and utilized for the purpose of coordinating the firm's activities.

It is useful to categorize the possible risks. The effect of a manager's action is subject to the influence of an uncertain "macro" environmental variable, which may include output and factor market uncertainties. Each shop is subject to the influence of an individual "micro" environmental variable, which may include uncertainty involved in the operation of machinery at a particular shop. Finally, the effect of activities of both the manager and the shops are subject to the influence of *systematic* risk (albeit in possibly different degrees), which may include the uncertainty involved in the operation of an assembly line connecting actions of various operational units.[1]

---

1. Some readers may find it easier to follow parts of this discussion if the terms are expressed in notation. Thus, the firm can be composed of one manager and n shops indexed by i ($= 1, \ldots, n$). The "macro" environmental variable is θ, the micro environ-

We make the safe assumption that rationality is bounded. This means that information errors inevitably occur in collecting information about these risks. Moreover, assume that it is impossible for the manager and shops to perfectly process, communicate, and utilize information concerning relevant stochastic events because of their bounded capabilities in observations, communications, and calculations. In the tradition of Hayek, we exclude even the possibility that imperfect observations of idiosyncratic micro environmental variables (on-site information) of the shops can be centralized and utilized by the management for the purpose of coordinating activities of the shops.

To make the discussion of organization more concrete, let me propose three prototype modes of organizational coordination: hierarchy, the shared (information) system, and the decentralized (information) system. Notice that this classification is solely from the perspective of how information moves, and should be distinguished from classifications based on a personnel administrative perspective. For example, the participants of an organization may coordinate their tasks based on shared information, but be differentiated in status and wages. The discussion here focuses only on the former aspect of the organization. Of course, there may be other varieties. Also in large organizations, the three prototype models may be combined in various manners. But in this discussion, it offers a useful simplicity to focus on these three distinct approaches.

In the hierarchical mode, management collects information regarding macro and systematic risks (subject to some observation error, of course). Utilizing this information, the management chooses its own activity level and the level of activity for each shop to minimize the expected cost. Management instructs each shop to follow the chosen level of activity for it. The shops receive and implement the instructions, again with some errors.

In the sharing mode, the management and the shops jointly process information regarding the systematic risk. They ignore idiosyncratic macro and micro risks. On the basis of this *common* knowledge, the management and the shops choose the levels of activity which would minimize the expected cost.[2]

---

mental variable is γ_i (indexed by the particular shop involved), and the systematic risk is a common stochastic variable A, with γ and $1 - \gamma$ representing its degree affecting the outcome of the activities of the management and the shops, respectively. Assume the values of those stochastic variables are independently distributed with means zero and variances σ_θ^2, σ_γ^2, and σ_A^2, respectively.

2. This corresponds to the "undifferentiated structure" in the modeling of a firm's information structure by Cremer (1990). The information in the decentralized organization, immediately following this note, corresponds to the "differentiated structure" in the modeling of a firm's information structure by Cremer.

In the decentralized mode, management collects information regarding macro and systematic risk, while each shop collects information regarding its own micro and systematic risks (allowing for observation error in both cases). The management and the shops select their activity levels independently on the basis of *differentiated* knowledge according to an organizational rule, which is chosen beforehand to minimize the expected cost.[3]

In this approach, the cost conditions of the firm are determined by the joint effects of actions of management and shops on one hand, and uncertain macro, micro, and systematic events on the other. In addition, the information processing capacity of agents helps determine the level of expected cost.[4] As a benchmark of comparison, we first assume that the information processing capacity is identical for each observer in each mode. In the next main section of this chapter, we consider the situation where information processing capacities may differ.

In the remainder of this section, I wish to identify four factors which will affect the relative "informational efficiency" of various modes of organization.[5] We say that one organizational mode is informationally more efficient than another mode if it leads to lower expected costs.

The first three factors are relatively obvious—they are simply the three forms of risk already identified. First, if systematic risk affects the actions of shops to a large extent, the sharing mode becomes relatively informationally more efficient than the hierarchical or the decentralized mode. Second, as macro risk becomes relatively large, the hierarchical mode becomes informationally more efficient than the sharing mode, provided that shop errors in implementing management command are low. Third, if micro risks become large, the decentralized mode becomes relatively more efficient.

---

3. In terms of the notation first introduced in note 1, in the hierarchical mode, the management collects aggregate information $\nu A + \theta + \epsilon_m$ regarding macro and systematic risks with observation error ϵ_m. The management information also serves as an incomplete substitute for the shops environment $(1 - \nu)A + \gamma_i$. In the sharing mode, the management and the shops jointly process information $A + \epsilon_s$ regarding the systematic risk with a common observation error ϵ_s. In the decentralized mode, management collects aggregate information $\nu A + \theta + \epsilon_m$ regarding macro and systematic risk with observation error ϵ_m. Each shop collects aggregate information $(1 - \nu)A + \gamma + \epsilon_i$ regarding its own micro and systematic risks with observation error ϵ_i.

4. Information processing capacity may be technically defined as the ratio of the variance of true value of relevant risk variable to the variance of observed value including observation errors.

5. In the following comparison, it is assumed that the management action and the shop actions are separable in that the marginal cost of management action does not depend upon shop actions and vice versa.

The fourth factor is not as obvious; it involves the issue of complementarities versus resource competitiveness. When the marginal cost of the action undertaken by a shop decreases if the actions of other shops simultaneously increase, we say that there are complementarities among actions of those shops. On the other hand, if the marginal cost of the action undertaken by a shop decreases when the actions of other shops simultaneously decrease, we say that those shops are competing for internal resources. If shops are resource competitive, the decentralized mode is informationally more efficient. If actions of shops are complementary, the sharing and hierarchical modes are informationally more efficient than the decentralized mode. It is because the use of common knowledge stabilizes coordination when the complementarity is important. On the other hand, when the flexible reallocation of corporate resources is important, the utilization of idiosyncratic information becomes essential.

The above claims are based upon a formal model which is too abstract and generic to derive any definite inference regarding the superiority of particular business organizations for particular industries. Yet, the model is sufficient to suggest that business organization should not be taken as an exogenous technological data for economists, but rather as the object of economic choice. When the management needs to change the variety of products produced from a single plant in response to volatile market conditions (large macro risk), while the operation of the plant can be engineeringly controlled with high accuracy (small micro risk), the hierarchical mode may be the informationally most efficient. If the breakdown of machinery or the failure of timely delivery of supplies at one spot can easily disrupt the smooth operation of the entire production line (large systematic risk), the sharing mode may be the informationally most efficient. If internal units of the firm are independently engaged in highly uncertain information processing activities (like R&D or high-level software design), the decentralized mode may be the most efficient. The technological characteristics of complementarity and resource competitiveness among the internal units are quite relevant. Therefore, it seems unlikely that any one form of organization is always and everywhere the best.

If some diversity in organizational forms is appropriate, the economy needs to embrace diverse types of business organizations fitting individual characteristics of industries. Indeed, the constellation of business organizations in the United States offer some observations that seem congruent with this framework. Large chemical plants and steel plants are operated in the traditional hierarchical mode, while the automobile industry has begun to adopt new practices, such as the just-in-time inventory method and team-oriented product development, which require a higher degree of cross-functional information sharing. Along these lines, a recent econometric study of nuclear power plants by Geoff Rothwell (1995) reports that less hierarchy and a high level of horizontal interactions and communications are associated with higher productivity, by shortening the time needed for repairs. The emergent multimedia industry is experimenting with various decentralized organizational forms, such as spin-offs, joint ventures, and entrepreneurial ventures, each dealing with certain components of a yet-to-be-born large system (high micro risks).

This emergence of organizational diversity is relatively new. Up until about two decades ago, the dominant mode of business organization had been closer to the hierarchical mode, in which information processing was highly centralized at the management level. That seems to be still the case in most of continental Europe. In the transitional economies of eastern Europe and Russia, an even stronger form of managerial centralization seems to be currently establishing itself. On the other hand, the dominant mode of business organization in Japan seems more akin to the sharing mode, regardless of the industry or the size of the firm. The evolution of the decentralized mode, which may turn out to be more consonant with knowledge-intensive industries, seems still to be hard to come by there.

Despite the insight that different organizational forms would seem appropriate for different types of industries, it seems clear that organizational forms in a given country seem to cluster around a certain norm, at least for long periods of time. It seems thus useful to explore why an organizational mode tends to become conventional in one economy before exploring further the possibility of gaining from organizational diversity.

The Evolution of Different Organizational Conventions

Whether a particular type of organizational mode is economically viable depends on the availability of information processing capacity (skill) relevant to that mode (perhaps even unique to that mode), which in turn depends on the extent to which economic players have been investing in that skill. Further, the decision about which type of information processing capacity to invest in (often a costly and irreversible decision) is heavily influenced by whatever is the prevailing organizational mode. Thus, the equilibrium selection of an organizational mode is expected to be path dependent; that is, economic actors invest in a particular sort of information processing because they expect its use to be widespread, and its use continues to be widespread because so many people have invested in it.

To see this interaction more clearly, consider the following thought experiment (based on Aoki, 1993). Suppose that there are two populations of individuals, entrepreneurs and workers. Entrepreneurs choose an industry in which the firms are organized in an information system following either the sharing, the hierarchical, or the decentralized mode. There are two industries whose products are complementary in consumption; say that one is industry M (multimedia software) and the other is V (the VCR industry).

Workers invest in either individualistic-oriented information processing (I strategy) through formal training, or group-oriented information processing (G strategy) through formal training as well, such as on-the-job training. Further, let me assume that skills possessed by individualistic strategists are specialized ones geared toward processing of particular idiosyncratic (macro and micro) risks, although they have generic values across firms for that particular purpose. On the other hand, it is assumed that skills possessed by group-oriented strategists are geared toward effective information sharing in a particular organizational context (firm-specific skills). Firms are put in operation by being matched with workers. Entrepreneurs adopting the sharing mode of organization are better matched with group-oriented strategists, while those adopting the hierarchical and decentralized modes are better matched with individualistic strategists.

The cost matrices in Figure 1 should be helpful in spelling out the possible interactions in this situation. In the figure, the three modes of organization are referred to by their initial letter: H is hierarchical, D is decentralized, and S is sharing. The two sorts of strategies for investing in information processing are identified in the same way: I for individualistic,

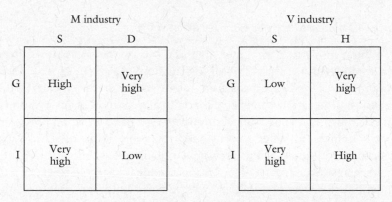

Figure 1. Cost matrices. S = sharing; D = decentralized; H = hierarchical; G = group-oriented strategy; I = individualistic strategy.

G for group-oriented. And the two industries are identified by two letters chosen mainly for convenience: M for multimedia, V for VCR.

Now, suppose that the M industry is characterized by the importance of macro and micro risks. Therefore, the decentralized mode can produce a unit output at a lower cost than either the sharing or the hierarchical mode if it is matched with individualistic strategists. Suppose, in contrast, that the V industry is characterized by strong complementarities among workers' tasks and/or the importance of systematic risk. In this industry, it will be the sharing mode matched with group-oriented strategists which can produce a unit output at the lowest cost. In this industry, individualistic strategists are more productive under the hierarchical mode than the decentralized mode, because individual tasks are complementary and coordination is more important in this industry, but not as productive as group-oriented strategists operating under the sharing mode. If the hierarchical or the decentralized mode is operated by group-oriented strategists, the cost is too high because of the mismatching of the organizational mode and required skills. By the same token, the matching of the sharing mode and individualistic strategists yields a very high cost.

Suppose that firms are formed by entrepreneurs who draw workers randomly from the population of workers.[6] What constellation of organizational modes would emerge in an economy? Would the M industry be served by the agents who have invested in individualistic strategy and the V industry by those who have invested in a group-oriented strategy? Well, maybe and maybe not.

Begin by considering an economy in which the majority of the population of workers have invested in individualistic strategy. The majority of entrepreneurs then initially perceive it as profitable to enter the M industry where the decentralized mode, taking advantage of these individualistic skills, can be efficiently organized. However, the product of the V industry is necessary to derive utility from the consumption of the M product. As a result, the relative price of the scarce V product would rise. Would the workers then switch to the group-oriented strategy, which may have comparative advantage in the V industry? Or perhaps the next generation of workers will adopt the group-oriented strategy?

If the workers are bounded in rationality and they imitate the strategy of the fittest with some inertia (because investment in different information

---

6. The following reasoning does not change fundamentally even if we change the assumption to state that the sharing-mode entrepreneur is matched with group-oriented strategists with higher probability and the hierarchical or decentralized mode entrepreneur is matched with individualistic strategists with higher probability.

processing capacity either takes time or is irreversible), they may very well *not* switch to the group-oriented mode. In fact, entrepreneurs in the V industry might have adopted the hierarchical mode because it is more efficient *given the initial availability of individualistic strategists*. In this situation, workers won't switch to a group-oriented strategy, because few are using it. And because of the relative scarcity of group-oriented strategists, entrepreneurs would find it unprofitable to enter the V industry on the basis of the sharing mode. In this sort of Darwinian economic competition, it is better to be a conformist.

The same reasoning can be applied to an economy where the majority of the workers have earlier adopted the group-oriented strategy or where entrepreneurs have adopted the sharing organizational mode.

Thus, two equilibria can evolve. In one, every worker adopts the individualistic strategy and every entrepreneur adopts the hierarchical or the decentralized mode, depending upon the industry. At the risk of caricature, let us call this the A equilibrium, since it captures some aspects of the American economy. In the second equilibrium, every worker adopts the group-oriented strategy while every entrepreneur adopts the sharing mode, regardless of the industry. I will call this the J equilibrium, since it captures some aspects of Japanese business organization. Of course, the logic of the model and the argument does not depend on whether one accepts that the American or the Japanese economy actually looks this way.

There are many other equilibria—actually nine altogether in the full model—but these two equilibria are both "evolutionarily stable," which simply means that if a relatively small number of workers and entrepreneurs were to try an alternative strategy, they would not be economically successful, and the alternative strategy would die out rather than spread (Aoki, 1993).[7] We can conceptualize that uniform organizational modes emerge at evolutionarily stable equilibria as "organizational conventions." Organizational conventions would arise when a particular combination of organization and information processing becomes a dominant one in an economy. In other words, conventions describe a situation where conforming is better. This philosophy is sometimes captured in popular proverbs. In Australia they say, "The tallest poppy is cut first." In Japan, it's "A nail sticking out is hammered down."

7. Even if we relax the assumption of random matching and replace it with a more reasonable assumption that group-oriented strategists have a higher probability of being matched with a sharing-mode entrepreneur than with a hierarchical- or decentralized-mode entrepreneur, the same proposition holds, although the number of mutants who try the alternate strategy has to be contained in a smaller number to make those equilibria stable.

There is another evolutionarily stable equilibrium that is (Pareto) superior to both the A and J equilibria already described. In this equilibrium, entrepreneurs in the V industry adopt the sharing mode and match themselves with group-oriented strategists, while entrepreneurs in the M industry adopt the decentralized mode and match themselves with individualistic strategists. However, the very meaning of "evolutionarily stable" means that this equilibrium is not easily reachable once an A or J equilibrium has become established in an economy.

Of course, under certain conditions, the new equilibrium may be possible. If a certain proportion of the population of entrepreneurs has foresighted insight that switching to a non-conformist strategy would pay off in the long run (despite short-term losses) and starts to act according to such expectations, and if a large enough portion of the workers started to respond to it by investing in non-conformist information processing capacity, then a shift could occur. Aoki (1993, especially prop. 5) presents a dynamic analysis of such a switchover, in the style of Krugman (1991) and Matsuyama (1991).

The early stage of capitalist development may be characterized by the skewed distribution of information processing capacity in the population. There may be a small number of entrepreneurs who have invested in individualistic information processing capacity, while the majority of the population may be limited in the scope and depth of information processing capacity. In such a situation, the centralized hierarchical mode is likely to emerge, across industries, as the dominant mode of firms in which the workers are specialized in narrow tasks and exercise little, if any, discretion. As the education system becomes more inclusive, the accumulation of information processing capacity within the economy expands in depth and scope. Yet if the individualistic ethos has been prevalent in the economy, the dominant strategic orientation would continue to involve investing in individualist information processing capacity.[8]

The accumulation of more widespread individualistic information processing may lead to greater diversity in organizational mode. The prototype hierarchical mode may be combined with a variant of the decentralized mode, leading to the formation of a multidivisional corporate form.[9] Further, a subgroup of agents who have invested in higher levels of infor-

---

8. Immigration seems likely to intensify this process. As the education base of a society expands, it becomes more likely that a steady flow of educated immigrants will seek to enter the country. And if immigrants tend to be those who are already strong individualists, then their presence will only strengthen the individualistic tendencies of the society.

9. Chandler (1977) would refer to this as the M form of corporate organization.

mation processing capacities may come to interact with higher probability among themselves—for example, through regional concentrations like Silicon Valley—leading to the emergence of new entrepreneurial firms of the decentralized mode. In addition, the efficiency of the hierarchical mode may be enhanced through the development of communications technology and increased information processing capacity at the lower levels of hierarchies.

In this description, multiple variations of the hierarchical and decentralized modes would be observed. However, individualist information processing capacity would, by its very nature, be specialized in a certain well-defined function within organizations. For that particular function, the individualist information processing capacity would have generic value across firms. From the societal point of view, the flexible coupling and decoupling of individualistic strategists through the development of the competitive labor and capital market institutions would then contribute to increased allocative efficiency under changing market and technological conditions.

This is the American-style equilibrium described earlier. However, the very development of competitive market institutions that facilitates the efficiency of this A equilibrium may make it harder for the economy to make the transition to the more (Pareto) efficient equilibrium, which has a mix of organizational forms and information processing. A transition to the superior equilibrium, the reader will recall, would require that the critical mass of the population of workers convert to the group-oriented strategy, while entrepreneurs in the V industry convert to the sharing mode of organization. However, group-oriented information processing capacity may be organization-specific by its very nature, nurtured to a great extent by on-the-job training within a particular organizational context. If the labor market is competitive, there would be no credible commitment by the workers to remain with particular firms, and thus there is no incentive for the firms to invest in such a firm-specific information processing capacity. Also, if the competitive market for corporate control is active, there can be no credible commitment by the firms to long-term employment; management may be taken over by outsiders who have not made such a commitment. The workers would then prefer to invest in marketable, generic skills rather than relational, specific skills. The A equilibrium thus would be perpetuated.

There can be an alternative historical path. Consider an economy where the development of individualistic-oriented information processing capacity is at an infant stage, but the pace of economic expansion is rapid because of exogenous reasons (such as high export opportunities), endogenous reasons (such as high entrepreneurial spirit or high savings of the population), or both. Facing growing demands, firms may not be able to afford sticking to the rigorous demarcation of tasks among the workers. To respond to continually changing markets, the firm may find it imperative for the workers to help each other on an ad hoc basis, and to solve a succession of problems as they emerge in a collective way. The demarcation of job responsibilities may become rather obscure. But some aspects of ad hoc, collective problem solving may be found to work well, particularly when complementarity among tasks is high. Workable practices may be identified, standardized, and diffused throughout the organization as routines that guide individual behavior.[10] For such organizational learning, the long-term association of the workers would become more effective. Under such pressures, a group-oriented segment of the economy might emerge.

Another possible story for the evolution of group-oriented information processing may be found in the transition from a traditional economy to the modern market economy. In the traditional model of economic development à la Arthur Lewis, industrial workers were supposed to be recruited from a massive pool of immigrants uprooted from rural areas. However, it is also possible that the transformation of the rural community to the modern industrial sector may be incremental. In such a situation, some entrepreneurs may play an active role in linking the rural workforce to the urban markets, while trying to use the traditional community bonds as a means of reducing transactions costs, organizing production, and enforcing contracts. If the workforce is relatively homogeneous, peer monitoring may become more efficient than hierarchical monitoring.[11] Yujiro Hayami (1993) recently argued that such "rural-based entrepreneurs" have played essential roles in East Asian development. They may take various forms ranging from the rural merchants in the putting-out system in the proto-industrial period of Japan, to the market middlemen in Indonesian commercialization of rural products, to the organizers of the township-village enterprises in China. Even in the modern industrial sector, the workers who carry over traditional hierarchical values may aspire to be recognized as "members" of the firm, rather than as isolated individuals whose collec-

10. Fujimoto (1994) shows that the Toyota production and development systems originally evolved from ad hoc adaptations of the organization to the rising demands within the limited organizational resources.

11. See Itoh (1993) for the efficiency of peer monitoring under the condition of the homogeneity of agents in terms of risk attitudes.

tive interests may be expressed only through adversarial industrial union-ism (Gordon, 1986).[12]

Once the majority of the population have subscribed to a group-oriented strategy, various complementary institutions would then evolve to save costs of running the sharing mode. For example, a seniority wage system may develop as a device to facilitate the accumulation of firm-specific group-oriented information processing capacity through on-the-job training. The enterprise union may also serve as a device for an entre-preneur to commit to mutually beneficial long-term employment, curbing its otherwise discretionary ability to terminate employment contracts.

A bank-oriented financial system ("main bank" system) and the asso-ciated corporate governance system may also develop in a manner consis-tent with the accumulation of group-oriented information processing ca-pacity. In this system, a particular bank (the "main bank") closely monitors the performance of the firm, but does not intervene in the internal man-agement as long as the financial state of the firm is healthy. The prospect of management autonomy provides a setting where internal members of the firm (managers and workers) can invest in firm-specific information pro-cessing capacity. Yet the main bank credibly threatens to punish members of the firm if they perform badly. The incentive effect of this threat is amplified when other firms commit to lifetime employment as well, so that displaced workers would suffer greater difficulty if forced to seek re-employment. Firms are credibly committed not to hire workers in the middle of their career paths as it may discourage the motivation of younger workers to invest in firm-specific information processing capacity. Thus, the main-bank system and the permanent-employment system do not exist independently, but together form a cluster of complementary institutions (Aoki, 1994a, b).

While such an institutional framework strengthens the strategic com-plementarity between the group-oriented strategy and the sharing mode, it represses investment in individualist information processing capacity and the formation of the decentralized mode. When existing firms commit to lifetime employment, investing in marketable generic skills is not likely

---

12. The attentive reader will have noted that I am distinguishing two types of hierar-chies here. One may be called a "vertical" or "functional" hierarchy. It is based on func-tional division, like the hierarchical mode discussed throughout this paper. The second might be called a "horizontal" or "status" hierarchy. A modern form of the latter type is found in the seniority wage system as an incentive device for long-term association of the workers with the firm. The status hierarchy may exist without being accompanied by a functional hierarchy. In fact, as I have argued elsewhere, the seniority wage system can function as an incentive mechanism for non-hierarchical sharing-mode organization.

to pay off as highly. Financing for entrepreneurial ventures may be difficult to come by from banking institutions which commit only to long-term relationships. The institutional story thus reinforces an earlier lesson: once the group-oriented information processing strategy and the sharing mode of organization become entrenched, the individualistic strategy and the decentralized mode may not be viable.

In short, institutional developments will often come into being to facilitate the efficient operation of a particular organizational convention. This phenomenon of "institutionalization" means that once an equilibrium comes into being, equilibrium strategies may be transformed into "rules of the game" and higher costs may be imposed on those mutants who try an alternate strategy. In this way, institutionalization often hinders the transition to the (Pareto) superior situation of optimal organizational diversity.

Are There Ways to Realize Gains From Diversity?

Let us now consider a parable between two fictitious economies—the A economy and the J economy, as already described. The A economy is larger and has established the decentralized mode convention in the M industry and the hierarchical mode convention in the V industry. The J economy is relatively smaller, and the group-oriented convention has evolved there in both industries.

Both economies become open to free trade, and the J economy finds itself to have absolute cost advantage in the V industry. However, the J economy is so small that it can supply only a small quantity of the V product relative to the total productive capacity of the A economy. A portion of the V product (which is, remember, complementary in consumption to the M product) must therefore be forthcoming from the A economy. Of course, the A economy will produce the V product using the less efficient hierarchical mode. If such production is to be economically viable in the V industry of the A economy, the price of the V product needs to be maintained relatively high. Under this situation, the V industry of the J economy could earn rents (excess profits) from its absolute cost advantage. However, no gain from trade is available for the larger A economy at this stage. After all, those in the A economy are still paying for the V product what it cost to produce it in the domestic economy.

Now imagine that the J economy and the A economy are integrated in a big-bang manner, and economic agents from both economies start to be randomly matched to form firms. In other words, assume factor mobility.

The Darwinian parable would predict that the sharing mode of the small J economy would become extinct, *in spite of its absolute cost advantage in the V industry*. The relative size of individualistic strategists in the integrated economy is so large that the agents from the former J economy would convert to the individualistic strategy, out of fear that they would find themselves with information skills that don't fit the prevalent organizational form, or with an organizational form based on very scarce informational skills.

To prevent its sharing niche from being wiped out, suppose that the J economy erects a barrier to discourage factor mobility. As a result, the sharing-mode industry continues to grow in size, and ploughs back the rents available from protection into development of the V industry. At a certain threshold point, the V industry from the J economy would be able to capture the whole market. Then the J economy would be specialized in the V product and the A economy would be specialized in the M product. Can this international specialization realize full gains from organizational diversity? In other words, can the Pareto-efficient equilibrium for the entire world economy be realized?

Beyond the point where the V industry of the J economy captures the entire world market for that product, the price of the V product starts to decline. The population of the A economy finally begins to enjoy benefits from free trade, while rents available to the V industry in the J economy begin to be squeezed. However, unless the relative sizes of the populations of the two economies happen to be precisely equal to those which would be necessary for the production of Pareto-equilibrium output composition, full gains from organizational diversity cannot be realized. Furthermore, because of transportation costs, conventional attachment to local goods, and some other reasons, commodity trade may not become so ubiquitous as to warrant complete specialization among nations.

At least theoretically, the big-bang integration of the two economies of relatively equal size could eventually lead to the approximation of Pareto equilibrium through the Darwinian dynamics of random matching (Aoki, 1993). But this approach creates another problem: the convention in each economy is supported by a corresponding institutional framework, and it is not clear at all how different institutional frameworks can be consistently merged.

A feasible approximation for the optimal organizational diversity may be to create a "sub-institution" which is able to support a mutant organizational mode in each economy and insulate non-conventional strategists from the costs of mismatching. For example, one might transplant the sub-institution of long-term employment to part of the A economy, and transplant the sub-institution of a competitive labor market to part of the J economy. The interpenetration of direct foreign investment by both economies may be a most effective vehicle for this purpose. Foreign firms are known to commit to a different type of employment system through reputation effect. They are also comparatively free from the constraints imposed by the financial systems of host economies. Remember, once a certain critical mass of the population is attracted to a mutant organizational form, then it may be able to sustain itself. In this way, the Pareto-efficient equilibrium may evolve in each economy through Darwinian dynamics.

This story is only a parable, and it would be unwise to draw too-definite public policy implications from it. Yet the parable is suggestive: if an economy has developed an organizational convention which is efficient in certain industries but not in others, that economy may benefit itself, as well as contribute to global welfare, by deregulating the entry of foreign organizations—at least once that economy achieves a certain development stage. From such a perspective, advocating "leveling of playing fields" may be misplaced, if it means that business organizations, including inter-firm relationships, should become alike everywhere—which in U.S. public rhetoric usually means that foreign firms should be structured like American ones. Organizational diversity could be a source of higher global welfare. It is an interesting twist of history that such diversity seems to be at last within our reach only after different conventions have evolved first in different economies.

PART IV

The Institutional Setting
for Economic Growth

Liability Reforms and Economic Performance

THOMAS J. CAMPBELL, DANIEL P. KESSLER,
AND GEORGE B. SHEPHERD

In two waves, the first in the mid-1970s and the second in the mid-1980s, state legislatures and courts adopted reforms that sought to control liability. Debate continues at state and federal levels over adoption of additional reforms. However, despite decades of contention over liability reforms, no study has examined the impact of liability reforms on general economic performance.

This chapter attempts to fill the gap. We provide empirical evidence on one of the bottom-line policy issues that should motivate the liability reform debate: using a data set that includes each of the 50 states from 1969 to 1990, we examine whether liability reforms influence states' productivity and employment in a number of industries.

One reason that earlier research has not addressed this issue is that no reliable data existed on when liability reforms occurred, and where. The liability reform data set that we have assembled permits us to overcome this obstacle. For each year in our sample, we have carefully identified, by reference to statute books and judicial decisions, each state that has adopted each of eight liability reforms.

Similarly, we exploit a new data set that the U.S. Department of Commerce's Bureau of Economic Analysis has created, which describes output by state and industry for the last several decades.

We thank James Alt, Randall Bovbjerg, Gerald Carlino, Morris Fiorina, Robert Hall, Gary King, Keith Krehbiel, Ralph Landau, Roger Noll, Al Pross, Robert Rabin, Scott Stern, and Stanford seminar participants for generously providing comments and data. Campbell and Shepherd are grateful for support from the Center for Economic Policy Research at Stanford University. Kessler received generous support from the Harvard/ MIT Research Training Group in Positive Political Economy, the John M. Olin Foundation through the Olin Program at MIT, and the State Farm Companies Foundation.

Our central finding is that liability-reducing reforms can offer economic benefits. A state's adoption of more liability-reducing reforms tends to enlarge productivity and employment in most industries that we studied. In contrast, a state's adoption of more liability-increasing reforms generally causes productivity and employment to decline.

Liability Reforms in the 1970s and 1980s

Until recently, judge-made common-law rules governed most states' liability systems. The traditional rules, which had remained relatively unchanged for many years, governed most aspects of procedure, burdens of proof, and damages. However, in recent years, states have changed several common-law rules. Both legislation and judicial decisions caused the reform tide to begin to rise in the late 1960s. Then the deluge came: state legislatures flooded the statute books with two waves of liability reforms, the first in the mid-1970s and the second in the mid-1980s.

Rising rates for liability insurance triggered both waves, although other political and economic forces contributed. Most reforms in the first wave applied only to medical malpractice actions: in the 1970s, some legislatures responded to doctors' claims that excessive legal judgments had caused their malpractice insurance rates to rise. The second wave was more general. In the 1980s, a broader group of doctors, manufacturers, and other producers asserted that a lawsuit deluge had increased their insurance and liability costs, and threatened their competitiveness and survival. Again, some legislatures responded.[1] Below, we discuss patterns of adoption for eight individual reforms.

Eight Liability Reforms

Caps on Contingency Attorney Fees

Traditionally, a client and his or her attorney were free to agree to any size attorney fee. For example, the U.S. common law placed no constraint on contingency fee agreements, under which the plaintiff's attorney receives as payment a fraction of the plaintiff's judgment or settlement. The law placed no limit on the fraction to which client and attorney could

---

[1]. Several reports argue that increased liability caused insurance rates to increase (U.S. Department of Justice, 1986; ABA, 1987). In contrast, Abraham's (1988) and other studies indicate that the causes of insurance rate increases were declines in interest rates; in other words, insurance firms raised insurance rates not because of increased liability, but instead to compensate for the lower returns on their assets from lower interest rates.

agree. Several states have altered this rule by imposing limits on the contingency fee fraction.

Reform of the Collateral Source Rule

At common law, insurance payments that a plaintiff had received to cover an injury did not reduce the plaintiff's recovery for the same injury in a legal action. Indeed, evidence of insurance payments was inadmissible. For example, even if a plaintiff's private insurance reimbursed the plaintiff fully for a $100 injury, the plaintiff could nonetheless recover an additional $100 from the injurer at trial; evidence of the $100 insurance payment was not admitted. The rule's rationale was that an injurer should not fortuitously benefit from having injured a plaintiff who had had the foresight to purchase insurance. Reforms of the rule either have required reduction of damage awards by the amount of insurance payments or, at minimum, have permitted the juries to consider insurance payments. Sometimes the plaintiff receives credit for insurance premiums that she or he has paid.

Caps on Damages

Several states have placed dollar limits on the amount that a plaintiff can recover. For example, a reform statute might state that regardless of either the severity of a plaintiff's injuries or the culpability of a defendant, the plaintiff can recover no more than $250,000.

Periodic Payments

At common law, a plaintiff would receive compensation for all damages at the end of the trial, even for damages that the plaintiff would incur only in the future. For example, a plaintiff whose personal injury required him or her to obtain future medical care would, at the time of judgment, receive a lump-sum payment for the estimated cost of the future care. Reforms of this rule permit defendants to pay future damages as they occur, rather than as a lump sum. Several statutes require a defendant to purchase an annuity that will fund the future damages payments. Defendants' groups have generally supported the passage of this reform.

Reform of Joint and Several Liability

Traditionally, if several defendants' acts combined to injure a plaintiff, then each defendant was liable for the judgment's full amount, regardless of how minor a defendant's contribution was to the injury. For example, if a first defendant was 95 percent responsible for a plaintiff's injury and a second was only 5 percent responsible, the rule required the second defendant to pay the entire judgment if the first defendant lacked sufficient re-sources to pay her or his share. The rule's rationale was that if a defendant became insolvent, then other culpable defendants should suffer, not the innocent plaintiff. Corporations and the wealthy disliked the rule; it often required them to pay more than their shares. Several states have eliminated the rule, either completely or for defendants whose culpability is lower than a percent threshold.

Punitive Damages Reform

A judge or jury awards punitive damages not to compensate a plaintiff for his or her injuries—compensatory damages do that—but instead to punish the defendant, or to make an example of the defendant to other potential injurers. Several states have sought to control punitive damages by eliminating them completely, or by means either of dollar limits or of maximum ratios of punitive to compensatory damages. For example, a stat-ute might limit punitive damages to $250,000, or might limit them to three times the amount that the jury awards in compensatory damages. Although we have tracked other punitive damages modifications, for clarity, in this study we catalog as reforms only those statutes that either eliminate punitive damages or impose dollar or ratio limits on them.

Contributory Negligence to Comparative Negligence

Regardless of a defendant's culpability, the common-law doctrine of contributory negligence completely denied recovery to a plaintiff who had been at all negligent. Comparative negligence modified this sometimes-harsh result so that the negligent plaintiff's recovery would not decline to zero, but would decline only by the plaintiff's fraction of the total negli-gence: if the plaintiff had been 15 percent negligent and the defendant had been 85 percent negligent, then the plaintiff would recover 85 percent of her damages.[2]

Prejudgment Interest

The common law entitled a plaintiff to interest on the value of a loss only from the date of judgment, not from the time of the loss. If a plaintiff did not receive judgment until two years after a loss, the plaintiff received no interest on the loss for the two-year period. Several states have altered

---

2. Some states adopted "pure" comparative negligence: the plaintiff would recover the defendant's share of the negligence regardless of the plaintiff's share. Other states enacted "modified" comparative negligence, which denies recovery to a plaintiff whose negligence exceeds 50 percent.

this rule to entitle the plaintiff to interest either from the time of the injury or from the time the plaintiff filed the suit.

Increase and Decrease Reforms

Liability reforms are of two kinds. Theory predicts that certain reforms will increase the sizes of trial judgments, and thus also will increase settlement amounts. We call these reforms "increase" reforms. In contrast, "decrease" reforms are predicted to decrease the sizes of judgments. The liability reforms that we use in this study are shown by category in Table 1.

Some states have enacted decrease reforms that apply only to medical malpractice tort actions; other states have enacted decrease reforms that apply to all legal claims. In contrast, the increase reforms that we track apply to all claims; none applies only to medical claims. We studied fourteen reforms: two generally applicable increase reforms; six general decrease reforms; and six decrease reforms that apply only to medical malpractice claims.

Patterns of adoption differed among the liability reforms. The fraction of states that had enacted the two increase reforms, comparative negligence and prejudgment interest, increased gradually over the entire period, except for a 20 percentage-point jump in the number of states with comparative negligence in 1973–74.

The fraction of states that had generally applicable attorney fee caps also increased gradually. In contrast, the remaining decrease reforms occurred in the two waves that we described above, in the mid-1970s and the mid-1980s. Many states enacted reforms that applied only to medical malpractice suits in 1975–76: fractions for medical malpractice fee caps, col-

TABLE 1

Categorizing Liability Reforms

Decrease reforms[a]	Increase reforms[b]
Contingency fee limits	Comparative negligence
Reform of collateral source rule	Prejudgment interest
Limits on damage awards	
Periodic payments	
Reform of joint and several liability	
Punitive damages reform	

[a] Reforms hypothesized to decrease judgment size.
[b] Reforms hypothesized to increase judgment size.

lateral source rule reform, damages caps, and periodic payments jumped during those years. The second surge hit in 1985–86 and continued through the decade's end. In the second surge, some states enacted general reforms; others chose reforms that controlled only medical malpractice actions. Fractions for each general reform increased. Fractions of states that had enacted general *or* medical malpractice reforms increased even more.

Models of the Influence of Liability Reforms on Employment and Productivity

We now investigate the influence of liability reforms both on productivity, as measured by output per worker, and on employment. To understand the impact of liability reforms on economic performance, we employed four different models. The first two models examined how productivity in a given state in a given year in a given industry was affected by the state's number of increase and decrease liability reforms and by other factors, and how employment in a given state, year, and industry can be described as a function of the state's number of increase and decrease reforms and of other factors. The second two models, rather than considering how these factors affected the level of productivity and unemployment, looked at how the liability reforms and other factors affected productivity and employment growth.

The models acknowledge the important impact on productivity and employment of influences other than liability reforms by means of econometric devices known as "state fixed effects" and "time fixed effects." The fixed effects permit the models to recognize econometrically that states may systematically differ in productivity and employment, and that all states' productivity and employment may follow similar trends from year to year.[3]

We estimate the four models—the factors influencing productivity, employment, productivity growth, and employment growth—for seventeen industries. We selected most of these industries because production and consumption of their output largely occur in the same state, so that the state in which production occurs is the same as the state in which liability accrues. One would expect that liability reforms in a given state would have the greatest impact on those industries in which liability and

---

3. We lag the legal reform variables one year; we assume that a liability reform's impact on productivity and employment will occur with a delay of at least one year. In addition, we have adjusted the variables for differences in reforms' effective dates. All employment and productivity levels are in logs.

production are both located in that state. For example, Michigan's tort law would not be especially relevant to Michigan's automobile manufacturers. Instead, California law might be more important, because the Michigan manufacturers sell more cars in California than in Michigan, and so California law would apply to many product liability actions against the manufacturers. In contrast, Michigan law will govern most all of a Michigan construction contractor's business; the structures that the contractor builds are all within Michigan (Epstein, 1988).

The legal industry is a special case, since liability reforms may impose two opposing forces on a state's legal industry. First, reforms that decrease liability will tend, at least initially, to reduce the legal industry's output; that is, decrease reforms that reduce judgments, reduce lawyers' fees, and deter lawsuits will reduce lawyers' income and employment. Second, it is possible that the decrease reforms will increase other industries' efficiency, and so permit the state's economy to expand. The economy's expansion could expand legal income and employment. Our model permits us to determine the outcome of how these two forces interact.

We also include the manufacturing sector as a check. The impact of liability reforms on manufacturing should be less pronounced than their impact on more local industries; because goods often sell in many states, the law of the state where a good is manufactured often does not govern a product liability action that involves the good. Accordingly, we expect that the coefficients on the reform variables will be less substantial and less statistically significant for this industry than for other industries.

Ordinary least squares estimates of the two models may yield inaccurate results because liability reforms may not be exogenous: although liability reforms may influence output and employment, output and employment may also influence the adoption of liability reforms. A state that suffers a particularly deep recession may blame lawyers, and so enact decrease liability reforms.

To correct for this possible inconsistency, we estimate the models by means of a standard statistical technique called "instrumental variables." This involves using predictors of the enactment of liability reforms as "instruments" for the liability reforms themselves. For our instruments, we used variables that theory suggests will influence states' propensity to enact liability reforms but will not influence employment or productivity.[4]

---

4. See Campbell, Kessler, and Shepherd (1994). We find that several, but not all, liability reforms that tend to reduce legal liability are correlated with political indicators: the more politically liberal a state, the less likely it is that the state would adopt these

TABLE 2

Estimates of Effects of Liability Decrease Reforms

	Effects of decrease reforms			
Industry	Productivity	Employment	Productivity growth	Employment growth
Construction	+	+++	–	–
Local and interurban passenger transit	–	+++	+	+
Transportation services	++	–	+	– – –
Electric, gas, and sanitary services	– –	++	+	+++
Wholesale trade	+++	+++	+	+
Retail trade	+++	+++	+	– – –
Insurance agents, brokers, and services	+++	+++	++	– – –
Hotels and lodging places	+++	+++	+	+
Personal services	–	+++	–	+
Business services	+++	– –	+	–
Auto repair, services, and garages	+++	+++	+	–
Misc. repair services	+++	+++	+	–
Motion pictures	++	+++	+	– – –
Amusement and recreation services	+++	+++	–	+
Health services	+	+	+	– – –
Legal services	+	–	+	+
Manufacturing	–	+	+	–

Triple + or − indicates significant at 0.05 level.
Double + or − indicates significant at .10 level.
A single + or − is not statistically significant.

Results

Tables 2 and 3 present a summary of results for the four models. The models address each of the seventeen industries separately and include statistical adjustments for state and time fixed effects. We use two aggregate measures of liability reforms as explanatory variables: Table 2 focuses on each state's number of decrease reforms, while Table 3 focuses on the number of increase reforms. The variables reflect each state's commitment to attempting to control liability. For example, a state that has adopted few increase reforms and many decrease reforms has demonstrated its commitment to reducing liability. Each row in each table reports the

reforms. In addition, the study produces two results that may, at first glance, appear surprising. The more lawyers per capita in a state, the more likely it is that the state will adopt liability-reducing reforms. In contrast, the higher a state's relative number of doctors, the lower the likelihood of liability-reducing reforms.

TABLE 3

Estimates of Effects of Liability Increase Reforms

Industry	Effects of increase reforms			
	Productivity	Employment	Productivity growth	Employment growth
Construction	− − −	− − −	− − −	− − −
Local and interurban passenger transit	− − −	−	−	−
Transportation services	− − −	−	−	−
Electric, gas, and sanitary services	+ + +	−	+	− − −
Wholesale trade	− − −	− −	− − −	− − −
Retail trade	− − −	− −	−	−
Insurance agents, brokers, and services	− − −	+	−	−
Hotels and lodging places	−	− − −	− − −	− − −
Personal services	− − −	−	+	− − −
Business services	− − −	+	−	− − −
Auto repair, services, and garages	− − −	−	−	−
Misc. repair services	− − −	− − −	−	−
Motion pictures	−	− − −	−	−
Amusement and recreation services	+	−	−	−
Health services	−	−	−	−
Legal services	+	− − −	− − −	− − −
Manufacturing	− −	− −	− −	+

Triple + or − indicates significant at 0.05 level.
Double + or − indicates significant at .10 level.
A single + or − is not statistically significant.

influence of the reforms on an industry's productivity, employment, productivity growth, and employment growth.[5]

For simplicity, the tables report both the direction and the statistical significance of the reforms' impact. For example, in Table 2, a plus at the intersection of the construction row and the productivity column would indicate that additional decrease reforms tend to increase manufacturing productivity; in contrast, a minus would indicate that decrease reforms reduce productivity. The number of pluses or minuses indicates the level of statistical certainty for each effect. For example, three pluses indicate that the effect is positive and different from zero at a 95 percent level of statistical significance. Two pluses or minuses indicate significance at the 90 per-

---

5. To save space and add clarity, we do not report results for the state and time dummies. Those interested in more detailed reporting of methods and results should begin with Campbell, Kessler, and Shepherd (1994).

cent level. A single plus or minus is not statistically significant, given our sample size and methods.[6]

As the first column of Table 2 indicates, reforms that decrease the size of judgments generally increase productivity. In thirteen of the seventeen industries, the coefficients for decrease reforms are positive. Ten of the thirteen positive coefficients are statistically significant at a 90 percent level, eight of the ten at a 95 percent level. If one looks only at the eleven industries out of seventeen where the results are statistically significant, the relationship is positive in all but one of the eleven.

In contrast, the first column of Table 3 shows that reforms that enlarge judgments generally decrease productivity. In fourteen of the seventeen industries, the coefficients for increase reforms are negative. Of the fourteen negative coefficients, eleven are statistically significant, ten of them at the 95 percent level. Or, looked at another way, the coefficients for increase reforms are statistically significant in twelve of the seventeen industries. Of the twelve significant correlations, eleven are negative.

As economic theory predicts, the estimated impact of reforms on productivity was relatively small and less significant in the health care and manufacturing industries. For the health care industry, the coefficients for both decrease reforms and increase reforms were small and insignificant. This is consistent with doctors' responding to increased liability not by reducing output, as in other industries, but by performing additional procedures to protect themselves from liability—that is, by increasing output. Some doctors may be willing to increase output in this manner because they may be able to pass on the additional costs to insurers.

In contrast to strong effects in other industries, the impact of decrease reforms on manufacturing output was insignificant. Increase reforms depress productivity in manufacturing, even though much manufacturing output travels to other states, and thus is not subject to local tort law. However, as predicted, increase reforms' depressing effect is smaller in manufacturing than in many other industries.

The impact of both decrease and increase reforms on productivity in the legal industry is positive, but insignificant. The reforms affect legal productivity little, if at all. At least in the short run, decrease reforms may reduce legal income, as judgments shrink and plaintiffs file fewer suits. However, the positive sign and statistical insignificance of the coefficient on decrease reforms for the legal industry suggests that the reforms' beneficial impacts on other industries may, in the long run, also benefit the legal

6. Campbell, Kessler, and Shepherd (1994) report the regression coefficients in detail.

industry. As output rises in other industries, they use more legal services. The two opposing forces combine to leave legal productivity unaffected by reforms. The results suggest that lawyers have little to fear from reforms to decrease liability. If anything, the reforms expand lawyers' productivity. Rising productivity in other industries causes legal productivity also to rise or, at minimum, prevents it from falling. Likewise, lawyers taken as a broad group have little to gain from reforms that increase liability.[7]

According to the third column of Tables 2 and 3, the impacts of liability reforms on productivity growth are generally consistent with their impacts on productivity levels, in both magnitude and direction. Reforms that decrease the sizes of judgments spur productivity growth. For fourteen of the seventeen industries, the decrease reform coefficients are positive, although only one coefficient is significant.

In contrast, reforms that increase judgments retard productivity growth. Fifteen of the seventeen increase reform coefficients are negative. Of the five statistically significant coefficients, all were negative. The coefficient for legal services is negative and significant: although reforms that increase judgments had an insignificant impact on legal services productivity levels, the reforms appear to retard the industry's growth.

Estimated effects of liability reforms on employment follow the pattern of the productivity models. Reforms that reduce judgments, shown in Table 2, tend to expand employment. For fourteen of the seventeen industries, the decrease reform coefficients are positive. Twelve of the fourteen positive coefficients are significant, eleven of the twelve at the 95 percent level. As theory helps to explain, the coefficients for legal services and manufacturing are insignificant.

In contrast, reforms that enlarge judgments tend to reduce employment, as shown in the second column of Table 3. For fifteen of the seventeen industries, the coefficients for increase reforms are negative. Eight of the negative coefficients are significant, six of the eight at the 95 percent level. Increase reforms reduce employment even in the legal industry; the industry's coefficient is negative and significant.

Results for employment growth follow a slightly different pattern. The impacts on employment growth of reforms that decrease judgments differ among industries, as shown in the fourth column of Table 2. The coeffi-

---

7. A state's number of lawyers per capita might influence adoption of liability reforms in another manner. If all changes in the law, whether they increase or decrease liability, require lawyers to interpret and implement them, then lawyers may favor both increase and decrease reforms more than they otherwise would. Lawyers benefit from any change in legal regime if the change increases demand for lawyers' expertise.

cients for seven industries are positive, with one significant coefficient. The coefficients for ten industries are negative, with five significant coefficients.

As with the pattern in our other models, reforms that enlarge judgments decrease employment growth. For sixteen of the seventeen industries, the coefficients for increase reforms are negative. Seven of the negative coefficients are significant, all of them at the 95 percent level. Every statistically significant coefficient is negative. Even in the legal services industry, increase reforms retard employment growth; the coefficient for legal services is negative and significant.[8]

The magnitudes of liability reforms' estimated impacts on economic performance are substantial. For example, in a state with the average level of liability, the adoption of an additional decrease reform would cause an increase in output per worker of 3.1 percent in the retail trade industry, 7.6 percent in the miscellaneous repair services sector, and 8.9 percent in amusement and recreation. The impacts on productivity of increase reforms were equal or greater, although in the opposite direction. Likewise, in several industries, reforms' impacts on employment were large. Further research is necessary to establish whether the liability reforms alone are responsible for the changes in economic performance, or whether other forces that might have coincided with the reforms might also have played a part.

In addition, we estimated the four productivity and employment models with eight individual liability reforms as explanatory variables: instead of examining the impact on a state's economy of the overall number of reforms that the state has enacted, we examined the separate impact of each individual reform. Several estimation methods yielded inconclusive estimates. Comparative negligence reforms tended to depress levels and growth of productivity and employment, for all industries, for all estimation techniques. However, results for other reforms varied among industries and estimation methods. Results for variables that indicate whether a state had enacted any increase or decrease reforms were similarly inconclusive.

---

8. To ensure that our instrumental variables approach improved upon simple ordinary least squares estimation, we calculated F tests. For most industries, the tests rejected the consistency of ordinary least squares estimation with 95 percent confidence. Our results are generally robust to changes in estimation method. We estimated our four productivity and employment models using ordinary least squares, without instrumental variables. We did this only as a check; F tests had indicated that for most industries, ordinary least squares estimates were inconsistent. Ordinary least squares estimates of the impact of the number of decrease and increase reforms on productivity and employment were generally similar to our instrumental-variables estimates.

In short, the impact of liability reforms appears to be cumulative. The important influence on a state's economic performance is the *number* of decrease or increase reforms that the state has adopted. The state's choice among individual reforms influences economic performance less; the impact of an individual reform varies among different industries and different economic indicators. Our study suggests that a state can achieve a consistent impact only by committing to a portfolio of reforms.

Conclusion

Using a new data set that we have assembled of the times and states in which liability reforms were adopted, this chapter estimates empirically the impact of liability reforms on economic performance. A state's adoption of additional liability-reducing reforms generally enlarges levels of output per worker and employment, in a broad range of industries. In contrast, a state's adoption of liability-increasing reforms generally causes lower productivity and employment. Similarly, liability-decreasing reforms tend to increase productivity growth, while liability-increasing reforms generally restrict growth in productivity and employment.

Liability reforms' impact appears to be cumulative. The important influence on a state's economic performance is the *number* of decrease or increase reforms that the state adopts. The state's choice among individual reforms influences economic performance less; the impact of an individual reform varies among different industries and different economic indicators. Our study suggests that a state can achieve a consistent impact only by committing to a portfolio of reforms.

Our findings indicate that lawyers have little to fear from liability-reducing reforms. Such reforms do not decrease productivity or employment in the legal services industry. Liability-reducing reforms may initially reduce the sizes of judgments and deter lawsuits, and so reduce lawyers' income and employment. However, the reforms then appear to cause productivity and employment expansions in other industries that eventually induce increased demand for legal services. The eventual increase balances the initial reduction. The reforms cause a rising tide of business activity that lifts all ships, including boats with lawyers aboard.

Our finding that a state's adoption of decrease reforms tends to improve economic performance in many industries does not necessarily establish that liability reforms benefit the state or the country as a whole. Liability reforms can influence a state's productivity or employment in three ways. First, a reform can alter costs and incentives in the state so that the state's existing producers operate more efficiently and the welfare of the state's citizens improves. For example, the liability reform movement argues that limits on liability will reduce manufacturers' costs, increase output and employment, and benefit all citizens.

Second, a state's liability reforms might decrease costs for some of a state's industries, but reduce welfare for the state as a whole. Liability reforms might permit certain industries to thrive only by shifting costs from the industries to other industries and to consumers: by externalizing the industries' costs. The reforms might induce substantial increases in productivity and employment for some industries, but only by imposing still greater costs on consumers and other industries. The costs that the reforms impose—for example, smaller recoveries for injured consumers, and products with fewer safety features—might exceed the benefits from greater productivity and employment. Moreover, our results address neither distributional concerns nor issues of fairness and justice. It is conceivable that liability-reducing reforms might improve economic performance either by causing unfair transfers among groups or by allowing other injustices.

Third, a state's reforms might merely cause companies to relocate from other states. Delaware's favorable corporate law may induce some firms to incorporate there. Similarly, a state's favorable tort law could lure corporations and investment, which would, in turn, elevate productivity and employment.

A state will not necessarily benefit by engaging in competitive federalism to become the Delaware of tort law, attracting producers by means of favorable liability laws. The "Delaware effect" will improve a state's general welfare if the reforms attract firms because the reforms permit the firms to operate more efficiently than in their original locations. In contrast, the Delaware effect will reduce welfare if the reforms merely permit the immigrant firms to externalize costs onto the state's population and existing producers.

In addition, a liability-reform Delaware effect that improves welfare for the state that adopts reforms may reduce other states' welfare. Although productivity and employment might flow to the state to which the companies relocate, other states would suffer.

Financial Infrastructure and Economic Growth

MYRON S. SCHOLES

The last ten to fifteen years have witnessed an explosive growth in financial innovation and new financial products. For example, ten years ago, automatic teller machines were rarely used to facilitate transactions processing. Today, almost all commercial entities accept credit cards. Financial intermediaries such as banks, insurance companies, and investment banks have created many new financing alternatives to facilitate large-scale projects by corporations and other entities on a global basis. The explosive growth of mutual funds in the United States and other investment programs abroad has provided vehicles for individuals to save either directly or indirectly through pension accounts. These vehicles allow individuals not only to transfer resources through time but also to allocate resources globally.

New and innovative risk-sharing mechanisms have also been developed over the last ten years to allow individuals and corporations to pool risks and to share them efficiently with other parties. For example, ten years ago, corporations rarely used derivative contracts to hedge risks. Organized financial markets have experienced growth on a global scale. The Asian and European markets, along with the United States, are active in trading bonds, stocks, and commodities. Listed futures and options exchanges have flourished around the world. Without the development of these markets in standardized contracts, many of the over-the-counter innovations fostered by financial institutions could not have been developed. These listed markets provide important price signals to investors and corporations as to how to allocate resources among competing ends.

Each of the above examples of financial innovation and change stresses the functions of a financial system. Merton (1993) and Sanford (1993) emphasize that a focus on the functions of the financial system will provide a road map to future innovations in financial techniques, services, and products. Financial infrastructures will develop that provide more efficient alternatives to: (1) facilitate transactions; (2) supply funding for large-scale projects; (3) transfer savings into the future and across markets; (4) provide for more efficient risk-sharing and risk-pooling mechanisms; and (5) transmit more efficient price signals to market participants.

These developments are hindered by market frictions. Transaction costs are a necessary part of all financial interactions. These costs include asymmetric information costs, as well as the hidden information and action costs of dealing with other entities. For example, an investment bank incurs expenses not only to design a new financial product, but also to inform customers that the product provides the stated functions and that the price of the product is not too high. This is a hidden information cost. Investment fund managers and their investors incur deadweight costs when fund managers act as agents for investors. This is a hidden action cost.

Financial innovation tends to reduce the friction costs of providing financial services. The successful financial innovators are those that provide financial services at lower friction costs. Although the functions of a financial system have been fairly static for many generations, the costs and faculty to provide financial services change over time.

Surprisingly, many practitioners and regulators focus not on the financial functions but on the institutions that serve market participants. The manner in which financial services are provided, however, is less important than the types of financial services that financial institutions provide. In recent years, financial regulators have tried to save many financial institutions—like the savings and loan industry in the United States—even when other entities provided their products more efficiently. A whole new infrastructure had developed to repackage mortgage contracts, the former mainstay of the savings and loan industry. Mortgage buyers no longer needed to go to a full-service institution to secure a mortgage. Now it is just as likely that a mutual fund investor, a pension fund, a hedge fund, a bank, or any other entity buys and sells mortgage pools. Banks, mutual funds, and other entities provide secure mechanisms for investor savings.

Regulation has aimed to shore up financial institutions and to prolong the life of financial infrastructure by delaying the growth of more efficient competition. At times, these attempts have hindered the growth of the protected financial institutions. Regulators appear to compete with the financial institutions and markets that they regulate. To protect themselves, financial institutions prefer to select among several different regulatory options. Moreover, with competition, regulators expend more effort to understand the financial functions and the competitive forces faced by the entities that they regulate. For example, the Commodity Trading Commission regulates financial futures and options on futures, and the Securities and Exchange Commission regulates securities and options on securities. Yet functionally, these instruments prove to be close substitutes for one another.

Institutions change while financial functions remain stable. The development of efficient infrastructure necessarily follows from the functions of a financial system—a need to satisfy investor and corporate demands for products and services—not from a need to preserve particular institutions. The financial functions define institutional changes. Moreover, the functional approach is relatively culture free. Investors and institutions have the same demand for financial services and products around the world.

Telecommunications and computing technology have created more efficient channels through which entities can provide financial services. These new channels reduce the importance of particular financial institutions. As Sanford (1993) has argued, even without further technological advances, current computing and telecommunications technologies can completely transform the infrastructure through which financial institutions provide services in the next two decades. Further reduction of frictions and restrictions will enable investors and corporations to transact, to save, to shift and pool risks, and to reduce information asymmetries more efficiently.[1] Although today's institutions will survive, the forms in which they provide services will change dramatically.

The evolution of financial infrastructure into the next century can be illustrated by how derivative instruments will play a large and expanding role in reducing frictions involved in providing financial services. First, we describe derivative contracts and their function in the investment process and corporate financial management. Then, we turn from the demanders of financial services to the providers—the financial institutions—and their concerns about managing the transformation. This leaves the last word to the topic of regulation and the academic research agenda.

Derivative Contracts

A derivative is an instrument whose payoff depends on the performance of an underlying asset, index, or security. The payoff pattern can

---

1. Miller (1986, 1992) argues that all financial innovation results from a desire to mitigate the effects of regulations, be they tax rules, accounting rules, or regulatory frictions imposed by government entities. Reducing the importance of other frictions, however, plays a large role in fostering new financial innovations. Miller could be correct, however, if in a second-best world, regulations and frictions are not separable because inefficient regulations arise from other frictions.

depend linearly on the performance of the underlying asset, as in the case of a futures or a forward contract, or the payoff pattern can be non-linear, as in the case of an option contract. These contracts are not new; they have existed in various forms for centuries. But their use has exploded recently for many reasons: computing and telecommunications technology has made them less costly, regulators and monitors now understand their efficiency, in a global economy they provide flexibility, and academic research has furthered the understanding and valuation of these contracts.

Most financial instruments are derivative contracts in one form or another. Black and Scholes (1974) pointed out that the equity holders of a firm with debt in its capital structure have an option to buy back the firm from its debtholders on maturity of the debt. The high-yield bond (the so-called "junk bond") is a riskier option contract than more highly rated corporate debt. Corporate debt and equity contracts are derivative to the underlying investments. Researchers have pointed out that firms undertaking investment projects use option theory to decide whether to invest in new projects or to change the investment levels of existing projects.

It is easy to forget that a firm's capital structure is derivative to the underlying investments of the firm. Debt and equity are like boxes that provide particular cash flows to investors. They evolve over time as investor demands change. Investors might prefer cash-flow patterns that differ from those given by underlying investment instruments. Corporations might prefer to make payments based on patterns other than those available in the standard boxes. This allows for intermediaries to offer derivative contracts of various forms to match more closely the needs of demanders and suppliers of funds. Investment projects are coarse bundles of cash flows; corporations are combinations of these coarse bundles of cash flows. They issue securities to finance their activities, claims that represent bundles of coarse cash flows. As frictions are reduced or to reduce frictions, however, entities break cash flows into finer gradients through the use of derivatives. This process gives issuers the cash flows that they want. This in turn reduces the cost of capital to firms. Institutional boxes evolve and change their form and shape.

Alternative Ways to Invest in Contractuals: The Building Blocks

Figure 1 illustrates four financial forms. The top panel depicts the performance of a standard, simple swap contract. In a swap contract, parties agree to exchange cash flows depending on various indices based on a notional or stated amount. Unlike a bond contract, the parties do not exchange any principal amounts. For example, Bank X might agree to pay Corporation Z a floating rate of interest based on LIBOR (the London Interbank Offering Rate in dollars, R) on $100 million notional amount, while Corporation Z in turn agrees to pay Bank X a fixed rate of interest on the same notional amount periodically for a set number of years. If the floating rate exceeds the fixed rate, when a cash flow should be exchanged, Bank X makes a payment to Corporation Z. For example, if at the end of the year the floating rate is 7 percent and the fixed rate is 6 percent, the bank pays the corporation $1 million (that is, 1 percent of $100 million).

In the top panel of Figure 1, one party agrees to receive the change in value of a total-return Government Bond Index (such as a discount bond),

---

Illustration of a Swap Contract on Government Bond Index

		Return
Receive:	Return on bonds	$B^* - B$
Pay:	LIBOR	$-RB$
	Total payment	$B^* - B - RB$

Illustration of a Leveraged Government Bond Investment

		Return
Buy bonds:	B	$B + B^* - B$
Borrow:	$-B$	$-RB - B$
	Total payment	$B^* - B - RB$

Illustration of Futures Contract

	Return
Buy futures: $F = B(1 + R)$	$B^* - F$
Total payment	$B^* - B - RB$

Illustration of Option Contracts
Buy a Call Option and Sell a Put Option with Exercise Price (K) equal to the Forward Price; that is, $K = B(1 + R)$

	Return	
	$B^* < K$	$B^* > K$
Buy call: C	0	$B^* - B - RB$
Sell put: $-P$	$B^* - B - RB$	0
Total payment	$B^* - B - RB$	$B^* - B - RB$

CONCLUSION: Without frictions, a swap contract is functionally equivalent to a leveraged contract, a futures contract, and a long call and short put option contract.

Figure 1. Alternative ways to invest in contractuals: The building blocks

B* − B on a notional amount B, and to pay at the LIBOR rate, R, on the same notional amount. If B* − B − RB is positive, the index has appreciated by more than RB, and the party agreeing to receive the return on bonds receives the payment. If B* − B − RB is negative, that party must make this payment to the counterparty paying the return on bonds.

The second panel depicts a more conventional debt contract. An entity buys long-term bonds and finances its position. This is called a repurchase agreement.[2] The bond buyer realizes gain or loss on the bond position and must repay the loan at the end of the period. The net payment received is B* − B − RB, exactly the same as for the swap contract.

The third panel illustrates the investment returns from buying futures contacts on the total-return Government Bond Index. To prevent arbitrage, the futures price, F, generally sells above the spot price of a commodity by an amount equal to interest on the notional amount but minus the present value of any carrying charges on the underlying instrument. Since, in this illustration, the futures contract has no carrying charges—the index does not pay coupons—the futures price, F, will be equal to the current spot price of the index, B, multiplied by one plus the interest rate.[3] The return on the futures contract is equal to B* − B − RB, the same return as for the swap and the financed bond position.

The final panel illustrates the investment returns available from buying call options and selling put options on the total-return Government Bond Index. The exercise price was selected to be the forward price of the underlying bond index to illustrate that the swap contract, financed bond position, futures contract, and options position can provide investors with exactly the same total payoff pattern. If B* − K is greater than zero, the call option will be exercised and the put option will expire unexercised. If B* − K is less than zero, the put option will be exercised and the call option will expire unexercised. Buying the call and selling the put is equivalent to holding a financed bond position as in the second panel.

Economically, these alternatives provide functionally equivalent pay-

2. Although the illustration assumes that the borrower can attain financing of the entire position, in reality, financial intermediaries that finance these government bond positions require borrowers to post and maintain capital of approximately 2 percent to guard against default.

3. As shown in the third panel of the illustration, if F > B(1 + R) by an amount X, market participants would sell their futures and hedge their positions by buying government bonds (financed as in panel two). Market participants would receive B* − B − RB on their bonds and pay B* − B − RB − X on their futures, realizing a sure profit of X. If futures were selling for a price of X below this amount, market participant would follow the opposite strategy and make a sure profit of X.

offs, which means that in a world without frictions, there is no need for swap contracts and futures contracts. Investors participate in the returns on the bond index by either buying or selling a financed bond position.[4] Option contracts are created to provide non-linear payoff patterns. As Black and Scholes (1974) demonstrated, however, investors can create their own options by using financed-bond positions.

Once we move to the world of frictions, however, each of these contracts plays an important role in the evolution of the financial infrastructure. The swap or forward market is generally an over-the-counter market frequented by large financial institutions such as banks, investment dealers, insurance companies, and corporations. Here dealers fashion contracts that contain combinations of options and forwards to suit a counterparty's particular needs. Most likely, the contractual terms are idiosyncratic. Since the contract is tailored to the client, the dealer must take the other side of the contract. Dealers, however, tend to avoid general market risks. For example, they prefer not to hold the risk associated with a change in the value of the underlying bond index, a risk for which they had no comparative advantage. The dealer's risk of entering into a particular contract is partially offset by the risks of other contracts in the dealer's portfolio. Most dealers, however, enter the underlying market to hedge remaining risks. For example, they buy (sell) bonds to hedge out risks of promising to pay (receive) the returns on bonds to counterparties. Alternatively, the dealer might sell or buy futures (options) to hedge the inherent risks of the idiosyncratic contract's component pieces.

To stay competitive, the dealer is forced to select the least costly alternative to divide the cash flows on particular contracts. With well-functioning financing markets, futures markets, and options markets, dealers can provide idiosyncratic contracts to corporations and investors at lower cost than in the absence of these markets.

Dealers use the standard-form contracts in listed futures and options markets to hedge parts of the risk of idiosyncratic contracts. It is often too costly for dealers to hedge all of the contract risks. They retain some risk, so-called "basis risk." Although corporations and investors cover the dealers' costs to provide these contracts, the dealers provide the payoff patterns at much lower cost than other alternatives.

---

4. It is not necessary to finance any of these positions at the 100 percent level. Any other fixed level of capital illustrates the same functional equivalence. A sale of bonds with a promise to repurchase them is a financing trade called a repurchase agreement. The seller receives the bond rate on the proceeds of the sale. A direct financing trade on a long position is sometimes called a reverse repurchase agreement.

The put-call relationship in the last panel of Figure 1 brings out another important point about swap, financed bonds, and futures contracts. The buyer of a call option must rely on the seller of the call option to fulfill the obligation to pay the difference between the market price and the exercise price in the event that the buyer exercises the option. The buyer assumes the seller's credit risk. The buyer of options is exposed to the possibility of a seller's default on the contract. The seller, however, is not worried about the default risk of the buyer since the option is the buyer's asset in the event of the buyer's bankruptcy.

Although each of these contracts is a zero-investment contract at inception—no money is exchanged—their value does change as the underlying asset value changes because the options are only settled periodically. Since these contracts involve the sale of put options in addition to the purchase of call options, each party is exposed to the other's credit risk. As the value of the bond index increases, the call option becomes more valuable and the put option less valuable. As a result, the receiver of the returns on the bond index has a receivable and is exposed to the credit risk of the writer of the call (the entity paying the return on bonds). As the value of the bond index falls, the put option becomes more valuable and the call becomes less valuable; the receiver of the returns on the bond index owes money on the contract. The credit risk has swung in the other direction.

It has become common practice to advertise the size of the market in these derivative contracts in terms of the notional amount outstanding. Loomis (1994) and the General Accounting Office (1994) indicate that the size of the derivative market exceeds $15 trillion of notional amount outstanding. The notional amount, however, provides a meaningless estimate of market size. Although Chemical Bank and Bankers Trust each have over $2 trillion of outstanding notional contracts, this figure gives no indication of their credit exposure. The cash-settled value of their receivables is probably less than 3 percent of these stated amounts.[5]

Investment Process and Derivative Contracts

A fundamental question is whether derivative contracts are a fad or destined to be the fundamental building blocks of the new financial infrastructure. We have seen only the first steps in financial innovation using derivative contracts. Using the elemental building blocks described in the last section, financial intermediaries will more clearly define the cash-flow

---

5. Remember that the dealer in swap contracts does not lose the value of the principal as is the case with a standard debt contract.

patterns demanded by investors and corporations. This will create more tailor-made investment products to suit investor needs around the world.

Recent years have seen movements from individual securities to portfolios, to international diversification, and to broader classes of securities in investor portfolios. Investors from around the world have become willing to select from a broad class of mutual fund offerings. The entire mutual fund and investment product industry has grown dramatically in response to investor demand for alternative investment products and services.

Although the products have grown in number, there are few tools available to investors to make educated allocation decisions. This generates deadweight costs, which discourage savings and increase the cost of capital to corporations. Investors want to save to meet future consumption needs. They want to insure against contingencies. They want to control risks. Investment products will be developed that combine these mutual fund inputs efficiently to target investor needs over the life cycle. This repackaging of investments will, in turn, reduce the cost of capital to corporations.

Individuals reduce risk in three primary ways. In the 1960s and early 1970s, other than investments in a home and in human capital, individuals held a small number of stock issues and savings accounts of various kinds. To reduce their risk, they held more in savings accounts and less in stock. In the late 1970s through to the present, investors learned that diversification reduces risk and does not sacrifice expected return. They moved away from individual stock selection to save through institutionalized diversified investments for both savings on own account and savings through retirement. The costs to provide these products have fallen dramatically over time.

A third way to reduce risk is to hedge. The hedge can be linear or nonlinear in its payoff structure. For example, an investor who holds a portfolio of mutual funds might want to reduce his risk. He can sell his holdings, but this might be more costly than offsetting his risks by using futures contracts or swap contracts. Individuals have acquired insurance against contingencies such as death and accident for many years. The financial infrastructure will develop to allow investors to buy financial insurance through contracts that provide non-linear payoffs. For example, investors might prefer to participate in the appreciation in the underlying market at a reduced rate in exchange for a guaranteed floor.[6]

---

6. Recently, the government of France has allowed individuals to invest up to the equivalent of approximately $100,000 in an equity account. The account allows French investors to buy French equity without paying any tax at either the corporate or the shareholder level if they hold their funds in the account for five years. Although

Financial infrastructure will be built to provide investors with pay-off patterns that are more in line with their needs. Investment programs will insure investors against financial contingencies at extremely low cost through the use of derivative instruments. As long as the risks that the investor wants to hedge are highly correlated with a traded instrument, entities will provide financial insurance to meet investors' idiosyncratic needs.

Derivatives are not a fad, because they provide a less costly alternative to direct investment. For example, many academics have argued that international diversification of investments provides higher returns for risk compared to domestic investments. Investors can expand their opportunity set through international diversification. The degree of international diversification in practice is far less than predicted by theory. An explanation is that the frictions associated with international investing have exceeded the benefits. The cost of learning how to invest internationally is quite high. Even sophisticated entities incur substantial costs to invest internationally because of regulations, stamp duties, withholding taxes, and broker and custodian fees. Even for passive institutional index accounts, these costs can approximate from .75 to 2.0 percent a year. Many institutions find it more efficient to invest the money that they would have invested abroad in home-country bonds (for example, at LIBOR) and enter into a swap contract with an intermediary to receive the returns on a foreign index in return for paying LIBOR.

Entities that are more efficient should make the foreign-country direct investment and then swap the returns on that direct investment with the entity that finds it more costly to invest abroad. Transportation costs are reduced. This lowers the cost of capital to corporations around the world. There may be considerable economies of scale because only a few entities need acquire the expertise to invest in these markets. The systematic returns to investing internationally can be transferred efficiently through swap (or other derivative) contracts. This reduction in costs improves global economic efficiency and more closely links the world economy. The use of derivatives allows for growth of efficient infrastructures to provide less expensive international investing.

It is inappropriate to limit the definition of derivatives to listed options

---

the account offers significant tax advantages to investors, many French investors fear the potential losses of investing in the market. To overcome this fear, many French banks have established programs to ensure that the investor receives the maximum of the appreciation in a French market index and the return of his money at the end of five years. With this form of insurance, many French citizens have entered the program.

and futures contracts or to swap and option contracts entered into with a financial intermediary. Investors can acquire equity-linked notes or structured bonds to achieve similar results. For example, a foreign investor who wants to invest in the U.S. market as represented by the Standard and Poor's 500 can: (1) buy the stocks in the index; (2) buy a mutual fund that replicates the returns on the index; (3) invest in U.S. Treasury instruments and buy a futures contract on the index; (4) invest in U.S. Treasury instruments and receive the returns on the index though an over-the-counter swap contract; (5) buy an equity-linked note that provides this payoff structure; (6) buy a structured bond which provides for protection in case the market falls in value in return for only partial participation in the growth in the index; (7) buy a structured bond that provides for a truncated participation in the upside for more income in case the market falls in value; (8) buy put options to protect against a market decline in any of the above products; and (9) buy protection against currency price fluctuations. With frictions and restrictions, only a limited subset of these alternatives might be suitable for particular classes of investors.

Investors demand significantly higher returns for investing in illiquid investments. The bid-offer spreads are quite large; and since investors might be forced to sell quickly, they demand a premium in expected return to overcome the expected costs of the illiquid investment. Derivatives have been used to provide liquidity to the market, which attracts investors to these investment classes. For example, we have seen the transformation of a very illiquid market in mortgages into a much more liquid market through the securitization of mortgage pools. This "pool" concept revolutionized mortgage finance by improving liquidity. Securitization broadened the market and resulted in reduced costs of securing mortgages for many households. Emerging market investments provide another example. By pooling illiquid emerging-market securities into a fund, investment bankers have offered various tranches to different classes of investors. Investors in the debt-like tranches do not need to know the particular assets in the pool; they only need to know the value of the pool standing behind their claim. As a result, these derivatives trade with very low bid-offer spreads even though the underlying assets in the pool have high bid-offer spreads. Investors with greater knowledge about the underlying assets in the pools hold the riskier tranches.

Pooling investments and allocating more of the direct risk of the investment to those investors closest to the underlying investments has been an integral part of the venture capital industry. The venture capitalist finds underlying investments and provides outside investors with return patterns that are more secure than its own. This tends to align the interests of insiders and outsiders. If information differences between insiders and outsiders are large, outsiders might require insiders to guarantee a higher level of return in exchange for less of a participation in the upside. Information differences are likely to be greater when outsiders are potential investors from foreign countries. Many in the venture capital industry do not have sufficient capital to provide such guarantees. The market will broaden to allow entities to provide the requisite guarantees to attract outsiders.[7]

Derivative contracts play a large role in the compensation policies of firms. For example, most start-up ventures require employees to forgo salary in the start-up phase in return for a share of the success of the business. The payoff patterns are similar to those of an option. Not only do these contracts align the interests of outsiders and insiders, but they also help lower the cost of capital to the venture by reducing information differences. Because employees are most knowledgeable about the operations of the venture, they might be the lowest-cost providers of funds.

As Scholes and Wolfson (1992) explained, if employee tax rates remain unchanged and employer tax rates increase, which is the likely case for start-up ventures that become successful, deferred compensation is a tax-efficient contract. Employees, however, might prefer a grant of shares to future increases in salary, because capital gains tax rates might be lower than personal tax rates and because future increases in salary appear more uncertain than a grant of shares. The corporation, however, cannot deduct the realized capital gains. Under U.S. tax rules, therefore, the optimal arrangement most likely rewards employees in the successful firm with increased salary. These payments are taxed only once at the personal level. These compensation arrangements reduce the cost of capital to the start-up venture.

Derivatives foster the growth of private corporations. A public market allows investors to share risks with other investors around the world. The private investor has a higher cost of capital than the global well-diversified investor. The public market also provides liquidity and valuable market price signals to investors. The cost, however, of a public market is the loss of voting control, the need to disclose information about the operations of the firm, and higher agency costs with outside investors. Moreover, as reported in National Research Council (1994) and many other places, managers of public corporations, particularly in the United States, forgo some

---

7. Many business ventures are financed by family members for similar reasons.

long-term investments at the margin because outside investors demand short-term performance.[8]

If private investors and employees have too much of their wealth in a particular corporation, they can hedge those parts of the risk that arise from exogenous factors such as changes in the general level of the market. The cost here, however, is that these investors might not have enough liquidity to carry the investment in their firm and use listed futures (options) to hedge market risks. If the value of their firm increases by more than the market, the increased value arises in an illiquid asset and the loss on the hedge in futures or options that must be paid immediately. In the United States, under the current tax system, the loss is a deferred tax deduction, but any gain is immediately taxable. These costs reduce the demand for hedging. New financial infrastructure is being built using deferred swap contracts with either investment intermediaries or foreign institutions to reduce these market frictions.

Moreover, as we will see in more detail below, the private corporation can hedge the risks of those aspects of the business in which it lacks expertise, such as currency, interest rate, and commodity price fluctuations. As frictions are reduced, entrepreneurs can shed those business aspects that are really market risks and retain only those risks that add extra value and are specific to their business. By reducing risks at low cost, more entrepreneurs will remain private or do so for longer time periods, fostering the growth of new businesses in the United States.

By breaking its cash flows into finer gradients, the private corporation can provide liquidity to its owner-employees, and design ways to obtain valuation signals. As frictions are reduced, new institutions arise that address these specific concerns.

Hedging allows many entities to remain private. Entering the public markets for shares provides many benefits in addition to financing activities. The functions include, among others: (1) the provision of an external valuation for shares; (2) liquidity for entrepreneurs to borrow against their holdings; (3) assurance money; and (4) a ready market to sell the company. But there are many costs to being a public corporation.[9] As these costs

---

8. This might reduce the deadweight costs of certain managers acting to reduce shareholder value by engaging in long-term investments that have exaggerated claimed benefits at some distant future point, maybe beyond the retirement of current management. Although not all managers engage in such activities, outsiders cannot separate the manager types. If this view is indeed correct, financial innovations will reduce the asymmetries.

9. For example, corporations are subject to shareholder suits, to constraints on their business activities, and to compliance and disclosure costs.

increase and the market for derivatives expands, many of the functions provided by the public issuance of shares will be provided by derivative contracts.

Investors might have expertise in a particular market. For example, a high-technology stock manager at a financial institution might have spent considerable effort to analyze and acquire the best portfolio of high-technology stocks. If she now believes that the general level of the market is too high, she can hedge the risks of her portfolio by selling futures or swap contracts. Moreover, the successful high-technology stock manager can provide superior stock market returns in general. She concentrates her direct investment in particular high-technology stocks to provide enhanced returns. Then she enters into a swap contract: she agrees to pay the general level of high-technology stock returns to another entity and to receive the return, say, on a stock market index. For example, assume that her expertise in the high-technology market generates a return of 15 percent while high-technology stocks, in general, produce a return of only 12 percent. She receives 15 percent on her specific stocks and pays 12 percent on her swap. Her net return is 3 percent plus the return on the stock index. As a result, she has outperformed other stock index managers by 3 percent.

In the future, strategic investment management will evolve to combine the best of selectivity (market expertise) with risk reduction through derivatives. This serves to complete the market. Foreign investors have no particular advantage in investing in selected stock issues; they find it difficult to select superior managers. Information differences, however, can be resolved through derivatives. As in the example, the high-technology manager sells the foreign investor a participation in the returns on an index of high-technology stocks (through a financial intermediary) at less cost than the foreign investor can acquire the assets directly. Foreign investors might require lower rates of return on investments than U.S. investors because of lower capital gains taxes; they might require higher rates of return on investments because of higher friction costs to buy U.S. securities. Derivatives (including the ability to hedge currency returns) reduce the friction costs to foreign investors and reduce the cost of capital to U.S. corporations. The same is true for U.S. investors. The U.S. investor does not need to reduce the risk of investment by liquidating positions. The investor can transfer the risk to other investments without incurring a capital gains tax.[10]

---

10. It might be less costly for the United States to reduce the capital gains tax on the realized returns on investments. On the other hand, it has been politically expensive for members of congress to enact legislation that reduces the capital gains tax on investments. Even if the capital gains tax were reduced for U.S. investors, foreign investors

The current investment management process is geared to require managers to concentrate in specific investment regions or categories. For example, the manager is deemed to be a bond manager, a money market manager, an index manager, and so on. Once a manager is an expert in any one area, however, he becomes superior in other areas as well though the indirect method of derivative contracts. This tends to equate risk-adjusted required rates of return on investments around the world. In the extreme, because of lower rates of return demanded by foreign investors, U.S. investors facing higher capital gains tax rates might be induced to hold other than U.S. stock investments. U.S. investors would channel investments into partnership structures and obtain and hedge other risk exposures through other tax-efficient mechanisms.[11]

Corporations and Financial Infrastructure

Some corporations use derivative contracts to hedge their exposure to movement in interest rates, foreign currency prices, and commodity prices. Other companies use derivative contracts to attempt to beat the market.[12]

During the 1990s, we will see a dramatic change in the way corporations manage their risks. The nature of bonds and stocks will also change, with standard distinctions being blurred over time. The thrust will be towards a financial infrastructure that reduces the systematic risks of those parts of the business in which the corporation lacks expertise and that levers the returns to its core business activities—activities that add economic value.

In the past, equity capital and retained earnings have been the prime means by which corporations financed large projects. Equity capital has played another important role. It has served as assurance money against unforeseen events. By having enough assurance money or permanent financing, firms mitigate the deadweight costs associated with reorganizing their businesses in the event of an unexpected downturn. Moreover, if a highly leveraged firm's debt-to-equity ratio increases because of market

would still want to invest in U.S. stocks to diversify their holdings. Derivatives might be the lowest-cost alternative.

11. With the reduction of market frictions, tax rule differences between the United States and other countries are harder to sustain. Fiscal policies and regulatory policies become integrated though capital flows.

12. As one recent example, see the story in the July 25, 1994, issue of *Fortune*, which discusses Procter and Gamble's reported $145 million loss in derivative contracts.

forces, it often cannot expand its business activities. To do so would most likely transfer its resources to debtholders at the expense of equityholders.

Equity is an all-purpose cushion, a reserve that guards against unforeseen downturns. The firm "dips" into the cushion to protect itself from incurring reorganization costs that result from too heavy a debt load. If equity capital were costless, the firm would have a small amount of debt and a large amount of equity to finance its activities. By equity being costless, we mean that there are no deadweight financing costs (such as taxes or agency costs) to produce goods and services in corporate form. However, there are other deadweight costs. For example, equity has been taxed more heavily than debt in the United States. It would not be economic, for example, for a corporation to buy a portfolio of bonds with the proceeds from issuing equity. The returns on the bonds would be taxed once at the corporate level, and the remainder would be taxed again at the shareholder level after the shareholder liquidated the position. It is expensive for corporations to hold cash reserves (assurance money) in the form of bonds.

When personal tax rates are far above corporate tax rates and capital gains tax rates are low, as was the case prior to the 1980s, the corporate form is tax advantageous compared to the partnership form. In the 1980s, the reverse was true: personal tax rates were below corporate rates, and capital gains rates were quite high. More formally, as Scholes and Wolfson (1992) have shown, if t_c is the corporate rate, t_p is the personal rate, and t_s is the annualized capital gains rate,[13] then \$1 earned in corporate form results in $\$1(1 - t_c)(1 - t_s)$ after both corporate and shareholder-level taxes. Producing the same goods and services in partnership form results in $\$1(1 - t_p)$. If t_c were 40 percent, t_s were 20 percent, and t_p were 40 percent, the advantages of partnership form over corporate form would be 25 percent; that is, the partner would retain 25 percent more of the profits after all taxes than the corporate shareholder producing the same goods and services. These tax rates are close to current U.S. tax rates. This encourages the firm to use more debt financing: like partnership income, debt interest payments are tax deductible and taxed only once at the same rates as partnership income.

Moreover, to issue shares to the public involves other agency costs resulting from the separation of ownership and control. As Jensen (1989) argues, public shareholders demand higher returns to induce them to in-

---

13. Shareholders pay taxes on dividends when received at ordinary rates and on realized capital gains when they sell shares. Therefore, t_s is an annualized equivalent shareholder-level tax rate that includes the investor's ability to defer payment of the tax on gains.

vest in corporate form. These agency costs increase the cost of capital to corporations. Those corporations that align shareholder and manager interests enhance value and reduce their cost of capital.

Since equity is expensive, firms will attempt to economize on using equity capital both to finance their activities and to provide assurance money for unforeseen events. The growth of derivative instruments has allowed firms to substitute debt (or debt-like forms) for equity in their capital structures. If it were costless for firms to hedge such risks as interest rate risk, foreign exchange risk, and commodity price risk, all firms would hedge these risks. By hedging these risks, firms reduce the volatility of their earnings. Without the hedge, exogenous market price movements cause windfall gains and losses. Most firms add value by producing goods and services—not by forecasting the movements in interest rates, foreign exchange prices, and commodity prices.

A firm that does not hedge these exogenous risks is forced to hold more equity to ensure against the eventuality that random price movements might result in losses that would cause a costly reorganization of its activities. Both equity and hedging activities are not costless. As the costs to hedge activities through the use of derivative contracts and securities fall, however, the financial infrastructure will change. More and more entities will use hedging as part of their strategic financial activities.[14]

To remain competitive, corporations will be forced to hedge these exogenous risks. For example, if a utility can issue a bond whose interest rate is tied inversely to its fuel costs, it may be able to reduce its equity capital. As fuel costs increase, its interest costs decrease. Without the hedge, if profits were inversely related to fuel costs, the utility would need more equity capital to buffer the increase in fuel prices. A natural candidate to buy such a contract is the fuel supplier or producer.[15] These firms can offer contract terms that other corporate customers and direct customers want and then hedge systematic risks through derivative contracts.

---

14. Many corporations use derivatives to attempt to add value for shareholders. Some treasury departments are able to add value because they do have expertise at forecasting the direction of interest rates (or other prices) more efficiently than other market participants. Derivative instruments are one way in which they can take directional risks. Unlike this tactical approach to the use of derivatives (and any other market instrument), a strategic approach uses derivatives as any other financial tool for long-term strategic planning.

15. For an illustration of a change in financial infrastructure in natural gas distribution, see "Enron Gas Services," Harvard Business School, N9-294-076. For an application to the extraction industry, see "American Barrick Resources Corporation Managing Gold Price Risk," Harvard Business School, N9-293-128.

The theory is simple. Reducing exogenous systematic risks reduces the need for equity. As a result, corporations substitute less expensive debt for equity in their capital structures. Shareholders bid up the stock prices of these firms because they receive more valuable cash flows. This reduces the cost of capital to corporations.

To use derivatives to hedge risks, corporations must understand the specific risks of the sub-parts of their businesses. This ties industrial organization more closely to the finance function. Derivatives allow corporations to separate various risks into risks they understand and that add value for owners (such as supplying clients with power) and risks that are exogenous and provide no excess value to owners (such as changes in interest rates). Corporations can mitigate the risks that add no excess value to owners and "fine tune" their activities.

Generally, corporations must estimate after-tax cash flows associated with long-term investments to decide whether to undertake them. As discussed in the National Research Council (1994) report, corporations employ a higher hurdle rate than the cost of capital to discount these cash flows. Option theory, which is contingent claims pricing, would suggest that this is a short-hand method to protect the firm against unforeseen costs that depend on the success or failure of the project. Most present value analysis depends on the assumption of symmetry in the payoffs on projects to discount the expected value of each period's distribution by the cost of capital. In practice, this assumption is seldom appropriate. In a real investment decision, the payoffs in each state/date pair must be valued. Investments are undertaken that, on net, add value for the firm. These payoffs are contingent not only on the firm and market forces but also on regulatory and other conditions. While regulations often tend to bound the payoffs, they seldom support failed investments. Moreover, through time, information uncertainties as to the state/date payoffs are resolved.

Those countries that support (or at least don't add uncertainty to) the investment process of their corporations could reduce the costs of investments, which makes more investments profitable to undertake. The longer the investment horizon, the more uncertain are the regulatory costs of investment. These costs reduce the investment horizon and change the nature of investments. In the extreme, with great regulatory uncertainty, firms make no long-term investments. It might not be possible to hedge these regulatory risks. Corporations apply option pricing theory to value complex investment decisions and, given the costs of hedging, to understand what risks to hedge.

Regulation and Financial Infrastructure

Technological improvements have reduced the costs of controlling risks. More tools to understand derivatives and to price risk have become available to investors, corporate managers, investment intermediaries, accountants, lawyers, rating agencies, and others. Financial institutions have developed sophisticated risk management reports and controls to manage risk. Accountants have become more familiar with control problems associated with derivatives. The rating agencies have increased their understanding of derivative instruments through their rating of structured bonds, collateralized mortgage obligations, contingent corporate debt, and myriad other contracts. Tax and corporate lawyers have become involved in the structuring of derivative contracts, and in general, users of derivatives have become better educated.

As the market broadens, costs of using these instruments fall. More investors understand how to value and use them in their global activities. Investment intermediaries convert contracts from one form into another to satisfy demands. For them, the costs of producing these contracts fall as futures and options markets develop worldwide.

Because of the uncertainties associated with new infrastructure, there are regulatory implications. Do investors and corporations know how to price and hedge risks? Do banks and other intermediaries know how to price these contracts? Are they hedging their risks and providing proper risk controls? Do they have operational controls in place? Do these entities control and price the credit risk in the contracts?

The press, the public, and regulators fear derivatives because they are new and complex. Although pervasive and growing, derivatives are still mysterious to the general public. Many regulators argue that the growth of derivatives has led to an increase in the amount of systemic risk, the chance of a financial system meltdown at a great cost to taxpayers. Maybe the cost is a cost not to taxpayers but to regulators, who must learn to understand the new financial infrastructure. It may be just as likely that derivatives have reduced the chance of a financial meltdown because they have reduced the need for banks and other entities to carry illiquid positions.

There is an important concern associated with the changing financial infrastructure. The speed of institutional change has increased in recent years. As new financial innovations have succeeded, regulatory conventions have become obsolete, or lagged behind the new innovations. New finance does not easily fit into the old regulatory boxes. Tax laws have been strained. The definitions of securities and contracts have been tangled. The roles of the various regulatory bodies have been changing.

Because of the dynamics of innovation, it has become very difficult for Congress to draft specific rules to regulate institutions. The half-life of the regulations is very short. As a result, regulators must rely more on the industries, which are motivated by their own self-interests, to provide the appropriate economic level of risk controls and management.

Systemic risk is not well understood. What is the cost to taxpayers? Who should stand by to reduce systemic risk if not government agencies? If there is a chain reaction of some sort that leads to potential defaults, should the government provide liquidity to the system? What is the externality? It is that market chaos causes bankruptcies and destroys valuable infrastructure that is costly to rebuild. The argument goes as follows: If market participants had had more time to sort out and incorporate information into new valuations, prices would have rebounded and society could have prevented these bankruptcies, avoiding their consequential deadweight costs. On the other hand, even after the time needed to assess information had passed, if market prices had not rebounded, businesses would have failed at no further deadweight cost to society.

The regulatory agencies can supply liquidity on a secured basis to financial entities. This provides only a short-term facility. The provision of secured financing does not create incentives for institutions to undertake activities that are subsidized by taxpayers, as is the case with specific banks or insurance companies being afforded government protection because they are "too big to fail." With secured financing, the loss, if any, resides with the stockholders of the financial entity.

Specific financial contracts do not necessarily increase systemic risk to the system. As we have seen, new innovations reduce the costs of providing financial services. As institutions develop many more ways to provide financial services to different entities more efficiently, no one mechanism has as large an impact on the global market in financial services. As a result, we reduce systemic risk by reducing the importance of any one mechanism in the provision of financial services.

Research Agenda and Conclusions

For many in economics and finance, the new strategic financial organization requires the answers to questions such as what should be hedged; how to decompose the cash flows of the firm; how a change in structure affects incentives within the organization; how much it costs to implement these changes; and how corporations, investors, regulators, rating agencies, customers, and employees are affected.

The future research agenda is rich for financial institutions, who must continue to understand how to provide products and services at lower friction costs to satisfy the functions of the financial system. On a micro level, they must build more efficient pricing mechanisms and risk-control systems. They must model and price credit risk. There is an untapped research vein in the regulatory arena.

The remainder of this decade and beyond should be an exciting time for investment managers to provide products and services. Corporate managers have an opportunity to go back to basics and determine an optimal investment and financial program. Emerging companies and companies with long-term investment projects will marry physical technology with financial technology. The new infrastructure allows corporations to design what they want at lower cost. Corporations will change the ways in which they manage their economic balance sheets. The regulatory process can serve to attempt to monitor the divergence of innovation from the development of infrastructure. As the pace of innovation accelerates, the gap between products and controls might widen. The system might be more vulnerable at these times. In response, regulators serve to warn the financial industry that it is time to develop controls.

Regulatory effort must be aimed at fostering the functions of the financial system, not at preserving its institutions. With global competition in the provision of goods and services, including financial services, it is not profitable for agencies to concentrate on narrow institutional definitions. The entity that provides services at lower cost—and potentially in far different ways than anticipated—will succeed despite the regulatory protection of other entities.

PART V

Structural and Supportive Policies—Technology

Privatizing Public Research:
The New Competitiveness Strategy

LINDA R. COHEN AND ROGER G. NOLL

Beginning in the late 1980s, the U.S. government initiated significant changes in the fundamental purpose and structure of federal research and development (R&D) policies. Since World War II, the dominant theme in federal R&D has been national security. Over half of the federal R&D budget was devoted to advancements in defense technology. Much of the rest—including fundamental research in mathematics and physical sciences—was supported because of its historical connection and potential relevance to national security. But the end of the cold war has weakened national security as the basis of political support for federal research policies. The emerging new theme, intended to substitute for the military security rationale, is international competitiveness. Its proponents argue that the federal government should support R&D to increase productivity in trade-sensitive segments of American industry to assist business in global economic competition and hence provide "economic security" for the nation.

The present efforts to change the basic rationale for R&D policy come at a time when possibilities for major new spending initiatives for discretionary programs appear remote. During the 1980s, the increasing proportion of the population that is elderly and the rising costs of publicly financed medical care shifted budget priorities in favor of entitlement programs and away from most forms of domestic discretionary spending. For most of this period, federal support for R&D fared relatively well, as the cold war arms race formed the basis for a strong defense-research coali-

The authors thank Richard Nelson and Timothy Taylor for insightful and useful comments on the first draft of this essay. Noll gratefully acknowledges research support from the Markle Foundation.

TABLE I

Federal R & D and Total Discretionary Budget, 1993

Item	Billions of dollars	Percent of total budget	Percent of discretionary budget
Total federal budget	1,467	100	—
Discretionary programs	554	38	100
Defense	292	20	53
Domestic	240	16	43
All R & D programs	69	5	12
Defense	41	3	7
Civilian	28	2	5

SOURCE: Office of Management and Budget (1993, Tables 8.1, 10.1).

tion.[1] As a result, the fraction of the federal discretionary budget accounted for by R&D programs continued to grow until only a few years ago.

In the late 1980s, Congress adopted institutional changes that were intended to impose budgetary discipline, the most recent of which was the budget agreement between Congress and President Clinton in 1993 to cap discretionary expenditures at approximately the fiscal 1993 level in nominal (not inflation-adjusted) dollars. (Initially, the primary effect of tighter budget controls was on defense expenditures; however, by fiscal 1994 the defense budget had been cut by as much as either Congress or President Clinton believed was prudent.) Consequently, the cap on total expenditures, in the teeth of ever-higher expenditures on entitlement programs, has caused much larger reductions in discretionary programs than in the previous decade. After their rapid growth in the 1980s, R&D programs have become an obvious target, for they account for about one-eighth of total discretionary spending (Table 1).

The aggregate data indicate that political support for federal R&D effort is beginning to unravel. One important indicator is the decline in the fraction of GDP that is accounted for by R&D expenditures, as shown in Figure 1. Real R&D expenditures (corrected for inflation) by the federal government have fallen since 1987, as shown in Figure 2. Real R&D in the private sector is still increasing, but its growth has fallen below the rate of increase in real output. Because a substantial fraction of private R&D is directed at defense technologies, the fall in private R&D as a fraction of output is at least partially due to cuts in defense spending.

Thus far, the new competitiveness rationale has led to a few new pro-

---

1. To emphasize the connection between defense and government R&D, the only other periods to witness a decline in federal R&D activities were during the war in Vietnam and the Nixon-era détente with the Soviet Union.

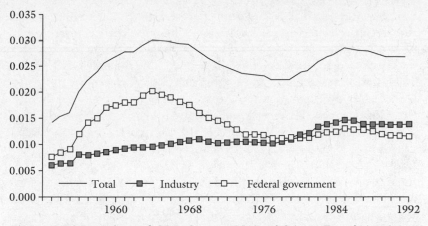

Figure 1. R&D as share of GDP. Sources: National Science Foundation (1992, Table B-2) and Office of Management and Budget (1993, Table 1.2).

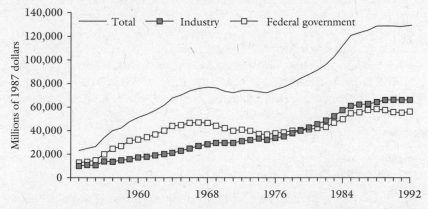

Figure 2. Support for R&D (constant 1987 dollars). Sources: National Science Foundation (1992, Table B-2) and Office of Management and Budget (1993, Table 1.2). Data deflated by the GDP deflator given in National Science Foundation (1992, Table 1).

grams, and succeeded in reducing the budget cuts of a few more; however, it has not offset the decline in total R&D spending. For fiscal 1994, President Clinton initially proposed an increase in federal R&D budget authority that would have matched inflation; however, Congress cut the president's request by $4.4 billion, mostly for the purpose of providing more funds for other domestic programs than the president had requested (a small amount of the cut was transferred to disaster relief after the January 1994 Northridge earthquake). The actual budget outcome was a cut of

$1.9 billion in nominal dollars from the fiscal 1993 budget and of over 5 percent in real dollars.[2] For fiscal 1995, the president has given up the quest for a significant increase in the R&D budget, having proposed only a modest 0.5 percent real increase; however, as in the previous year, the administration's target is the most optimistic possible outcome.

Recent budget trends give rise to a serious question as to whether the new rationale is an effective substitute for the cold war in forming the basis for a durable support coalition for federal research programs and R&D budgets that equal the federal R&D effort in the preceding twenty years. On the basis of our analysis of trends in federal R&D spending, the economic case for the new programs, and the base of political support for programs based upon the competitiveness rationale, we are pessimistic about these initiatives. In particular, we foresee three major problems: (1) in some cases the government is pursuing projects with gloomy prospects for a significant economic payoff; (2) the new rationale, even if successful, is very likely to cause a significant reduction in more fundamental, long-term research and to weaken significantly one of the few remaining strengths in the American educational system, the research university; and (3) the political coalition supporting federal R&D programs is fragile, and likely to weaken as some questionable projects fail and other successful ones create powerful enemies because, by succeeding, they will create losers as well as winners. Hence, we conclude that the competitiveness rationale will not succeed in maintaining a quantity and quality of national R&D effort that compares to the levels of the past 30 years.

The New Competitiveness Rationale

The new theme in federal research programs, intended to be the basis for reversing the decline in R&D effort, is a broad-based policy to assist business in developing technologies that will make U.S. industry more competitive in international markets. An illustration of the new argument is the following description of AMTEX, the new government-industry partnership for commercial R&D in the textile industry (Lawrence Berkeley Laboratory, 1994b, p. 24):

This industry currently provides 12 percent of all manufacturing jobs in the U.S. (including 176,000 in California). In recent times, however, imports have been re-

---

2. The best source for up-to-date information about the federal R&D budget is the series of publications by the Intersociety Working Group of the AAAS, as referenced in the bibliography. The data reported here are taken from their FY 1994 and FY 1995 reports.

placing domestic goods at an alarming rate with commensurate loss of jobs. The purpose of the AMTEX partnership is to develop high technology that can successfully compete with cheap foreign labor. This will not only save thousands of jobs but should also generate thousands of new jobs.

At the most fundamental level, the competitiveness theme as expressed in this quotation is economically irrational. As many economists have observed, most notably Paul Krugman, increased productivity is valuable regardless of whether the commodity in question is traded internationally, and is not valuable in an industry in which, regardless of feasible productivity growth, wages will remain low and costs will remain higher than the costs of imports. Reallocating R&D away from its most productive applications on the basis of the importance of the product in U.S. trade will almost always reduce national welfare, and the rhetoric for such expenditures reveals a gross misunderstanding of the economic causes and consequences of international trade. As a case in point, the textile R&D program seems motivated primarily by the possibility that NAFTA will cause a reallocation of U.S. employment away from textiles and into products in which the U.S. is a relatively more efficient producer. In fact, a textile R&D subsidy only makes sense if the net effect of this investment is to increase U.S. national product, which will not be the case if all that it does is achieve its stated objective: to make U.S. textile manufacturing costs equal manufacturing costs in Mexico and other developing countries.

The competitiveness rationale for R&D programs is new, but many recent initiatives have their roots in activities having a more defensible economic rationale that were begun during the Carter administration (Advisory Committee on Industrial Innovation, 1979; Office of the White House Press Secretary, 1979). At that time, concerns with flagging U.S. industrial productivity led to the Domestic Policy Review, a broad-based effort undertaken by Congress and the Department of Commerce that led to several major pieces of legislation: the Bayh-Dole Act of 1980, which liberalized patent policies for inventions arising from federal grants and contracts; the Stevenson-Wydler Act of 1980, which provided a legislative basis for redirecting federal laboratory activities towards a more commercial focus; and proposals for changes in tax and antitrust policies that led eventually to the National Cooperative Research Act of 1984 (relaxing antitrust enforcement for research joint ventures) and the research and development tax credit, initiated in 1982.[3]

These policies reflected four propositions about commercial R&D pol-

---

3. For a concise discussion of the major technology policy legislation, see Larson (1993).

icy, which are incorporated in the new programs as well. First, private control of research results (that is, privately owned intellectual property rights) yields greater incentives to innovate and commercialize research results. Second, efficient technical choices for commercial products require that private participants, rather than government managers, strongly influence technical choices. Third, cooperation among businesses can provide a basis for the efficient conduct of research activities but requires encouragement by government. Fourth, government resources—most important, the laboratories and publicly supported universities—can play an important role in developing technology primarily for private use, rather than accidentally yielding commercial applications as essentially serendipitous spin-offs from government missions.

Although President Carter proposed federal programs to accomplish these structural reforms, his proposals led to virtually no changes in federal R&D priorities or budgetary allocations. Whereas Carter succeeded in obtaining appropriations for many specific R&D projects, these programs were aimed at matters of traditional national concern (defense and energy). His more universal proposals, justified as weapons to attack stagflation by reversing the decline in productivity growth, did not produce new spending programs. Recently, the end of the cold war and the new competitiveness theme (although a less defensible rationale for federal spending) have provided the impetus to back up a broader commercial R&D policy with well-financed programs, despite a decline in total federal R&D spending.

Several features of the new environment have contributed to wider acceptance of these programs. The downsizing of the defense effort led the federal laboratories to search for a new role, to market actively their research expertise for the purpose of assisting in the development of commercial products, and to emphasize their value to the U.S. economy under the "technology transfer" rubric. Reductions in the defense budget gave rise to new R&D expenditures for developing technologies that would serve a "dual use" in that products used for national security purposes would be created in part out of the same parts used in related civilian products. Furthermore, the goal of supporting effective competition with foreign firms through technological pre-eminence led logically to privatizing research results emanating from federally financed projects, rather than leaving technical innovations in the public sector, where they are more accessible for exploitation by foreign firms. Finally, the increased penetration of foreign firms into U.S. markets has led to a shift in attitudes about the importance of an anticompetitive downside to collaboration among domestic firms.

Although the actual size of all of the programs that emphasize this theme has not been published by the government, from congressional and executive branch budget documents we estimate that in fiscal 1994 at least $3 billion was spent in one way or another to subsidize private R&D consortia, with plans announced by the Clinton administration to double or even triple this amount in three years. Thus, based on the data in Table 1, these programs already account for about 10 percent of federal support for civilian R&D, are scheduled to grow to perhaps one-third in a few years, and are the only component of federal R&D expenditures that is experiencing significant growth. Moreover, because less than 2 percent of industrial R&D involves inter-firm collaboration (U.S. Congressional Budget Office, 1990, p. xiv), these programs already constitute more than a doubling of industrial consortia, with the prospect of accounting for an order-of-magnitude increase within a few years.

Some Prominent Examples of the New Approach

One form that the new approach can take is exemplified by SEMA-TECH, a consortium of semiconductor manufacturing firms that receives an annual subsidy of about $100 million.[4] Projects are chosen by a board composed of SEMATECH members with a representative from the Advanced Research Projects Agency and SEMI-Sematech, an association of equipment and supplier manufacturers. The Department of Defense also plans a similar distancing of subsidies from federal management in its new program to support the development of flat-panel displays, whereby a firm or production consortium can qualify for a matching grant for its R&D by winning a procurement contract and building new production capacity. These projects represent the extreme in delegation of management from government to private R&D performers.

A more common approach to program management, with somewhat greater government involvement in the choice of projects, is represented by the Advanced Technology Program (ATP), run by the National Institute of Standards and Technology (NIST) in the Department of Commerce. In this approach, program management is similar to the traditional operation of the basic research programs in the National Science Foundation. Organizations seeking support submit detailed proposals to NIST, which subjects them to technical reviews and makes awards for projects that are judged to be most promising. Although proposals are solicited from all

---

4. For more information about SEMATECH, see Congressional Budget Office (1990) and Cohen and Noll (1992).

industries, nearly all projects to date have been from "high-tech" industries, such as microelectronics, superconducting materials, and biotechnology.[5]

ATP was authorized in the 1988 Omnibus Trade and Competitiveness Act and received its first appropriation, for $10 million, in fiscal year (FY) 1990. ATP is one of the fastest-growing programs in the federal government. Its budget increased from $68 million in FY 1993 to $200 million in FY 1994. President Clinton has requested over $400 million for the program for FY 1995, and advocates expanding ATP's budget to $750 million annually by FY 1997. Thus far, Congress has enthusiasatically gone along with the president. With the increase in its budget, NIST has taken a more active role in defining the technologies that it will support, and plans to allocate most of its budget to a handful of program areas, while continuing to leave the design and supervision of the projects to private firms. ATP requires cost matching by industry. Furthermore, the organization receiving a grant, or the lead entity in a consortium, must be a for-profit U.S. company.

The efforts to redirect defense-related R&D programs follow a similar structure. Most prominent of these is the Technology Reinvestment Program (TRP), administered by the Advanced Research Projects Agency (ARPA), the successor agency in the Department of Defense to DARPA. TRP received $472 million in FY 1993, and $575 million for FY 1994. Half of TRP's budget goes to developing "dual use" technologies for both defense and civilian applications.[6] TRP also awards funds in its "deployment category" for technology transfer and engineering education. In the former category, many of the projects involve government laboratories and the manufacturing extension services run by state agencies and NIST. For engineering education, the grants have favored joint programs by engineering schools, community colleges, and manufacturing firms, and have focused on retraining private defense industry employees. Like ATP, all TRP projects require 50 percent cost sharing by participants. About a third of the budget is restricted to "eligible firms"—commercial enterprises that conduct significant research and manufacturing activities within the United States (which means that some foreign-owned firms can qualify).

Initially, the TRP program has proved to be almost embarrassingly popular with industry, for in 1994 proposals were submitted for a total of $8.5 billion in project costs. If ARPA paid 50 percent of the costs of these

5. For a discussion of ATP program requirements and descriptions of supported projects, see National Institute of Standards and Technology (1994).

6. A description of TRP is contained in Advanced Research Projects Agency (1993). A list of FY 1994 awards can be found in *New Technology Week*, Oct. 25, 1993; Nov. 19, 1993; Dec. 13, 1993; and Feb. 28, 1994.

projects, as envisioned by TRP, this amounts to over eight times the agency's budget. Because of its size, the dearth of alternative pork-barreling opportunities in the federal budget, and the low success rate of proposals, the program has attracted criticism as exhibiting political favoritism. Over a fourth of the fiscal 1994 TRP budget was "earmarked" during the appropriations markup in Congress. Although the program's authorization requires all funds to be allocated competitively, the committee report accompanying the appropriations bill designated a list of projects, many in California, that the agency was required to support. The head of the program succeeded in inducing Congress to rescind the earmarked provisions of the appropriations bill by supporting these projects out of other funds (Intersociety Working Group, 1994), and claimed that "no credit was given [to proposals] for proximity to a seismic structure with a Spanish surname."[7]

Extra credit aside, three factors conspired to concentrate the initial set of TRP awards in California. First, the program has an explicit dual-use purpose, and California contains a disproportionate share of defense manufacturing. Second, the program favors consortia and hence, especially in the initial round, firms with pre-existing collaborative efforts. Established defense contractors have unusually great experience with collaboration because of the proclivity for subcontracting in the defense sector. Third, the application and financial reporting requirements are least onerous for firms (and universities) that have substantial experience with government contracting procedures. Consequently, the development awards favor defense contractors and subcontractors, many of whom are indeed located in seismically active parts of the country.

The other major new federal effort is the Cooperative Research and Development Agreement (CRADA) program, whereby a federal laboratory engages in collaborative commercial R&D projects with one or more companies. NASA and the Department of Agriculture have longstanding authority to enter into such contracts; this authority was expanded to other agencies and almost all types of labs by the 1980 Stevenson-Wydler Act and its subsequent amendments in 1986 and 1989. CRADAs increased dramatically in 1990, when the Department of Energy's contractor-operated labs were allowed to enter into such agreements. Several thousand CRADAs are now in effect, led by the DOE and NIH labs, with NIST, the defense agencies, and NASA accounting for a substantial number of projects as well (Office of Technology Assessment, 1993a, b).

While many CRADAs focus on rather narrow projects, some are de-

7. "Q&A with Lee Buchanan," in *Defense Week*, Apr. 11, 1994, pp. 8–11.

signed to develop an entire new technology base for an industry. One example is the National Battery Consortium, which seeks to improve the prospect for an economically attractive electric vehicle. Another is the program to develop a more fuel efficient automobile, a billion-dollar collaborative effort with automobile manufacturers that has been dubbed the "swords into fenders" program. Still a third is AMTEX, the textile consortium involving several national laboratories. As with ATP, CRADA projects are proprietary, and the legislation allows for (and encourages) patent ownership by private participants. Moreover, these proprietary products can be extensions and applications of purely governmental research initiatives. An example is a CRADA involving Amgen, the genetic engineering company, in which a discovery by a scientist at Lawrence Berkeley Laboratory about the biochemical process that triggers growth of tendon cells is being developed into a commercial product at a cost of only $1.8 million (25 percent paid by the Department of Energy); the product will be the property of Amgen (Lawrence Berkeley Laboratory, 1994a, p. 25).

The cost of CRADAs is difficult to ascertain because the government's contribution of shared lab facilities and personnel is not separately budgeted. Nevertheless, the program is comparable in importance to ARPA and ATP. For example, in FY 1994, the federal government is estimated to be spending $350 million for CRADAS at Department of Energy laboratories, and another $135 million on cooperative ventures at NASA labs (Intersociety Working Group, 1994, p. 14). President Clinton has proposed allocating 10 to 20 percent of the DOE lab budget, along with significant shares for other agencies, to CRADAS (Council of Economic Advisers, 1994, pp. 194–204). The nation's 700 laboratories spend about $25 billion annually (over 30 percent of federal R&D), so CRADAs could grow to several billion dollars in federal spending if the labs succeed in finding private firms willing to share costs.

Universities in the New System

The new policy has produced changes even at universities. Historically, universities have performed about half of the basic research conducted in the United States, as shown in Table 2. Since 1980, the government has allowed universities to patent the results of research performed under federal grants and, with a few exceptions, to sign exclusive licensing agreements with domestic manufacturing firms.[8] The effect has been dramatic: the income of major research universities from patent royalties has in-

8. For a discussion of current university patent policies and licensing trends, see U.S. General Accounting Office (1992).

TABLE 2

R & D Support and Performers by Type of Project

(*billions of 1987 dollars*)

Type of entity	Total expenditures							
	R&D support from own funds				Amount of R&D performed			
	1978	1983	1988	1993	1978	1983	1988	1993
Federal government	39.8	46.9	59.1	55.1	11.4	12.2	13.8	13.5
(% share)	(50)	(46)	(46)	(42)	(14)	(12)	(11)	(10)
Industry	37.2	51.9	64.6	67.5	55.2	74.8	94.2	90.7
Universities	1.7	2.2	3.3	4.9	7.8	9.1	13.0	16.7
University FFRDCs	0	0	0	0	2.9	3.1	4.4	4.3
Nonprofits	1.3	1.3	1.8	2.6	2.8	3.1	3.4	4.8
Total	80.1	102.3	128.8	130.1	80.1	102.3	128.8	130.1

Type of entity	Expenditures on basic research							
	Basic R&D support from own funds				Amount of basic R&D performed			
	1978	1983	1988	1993	1978	1983	1988	1993
Federal government	7.9	8.9	11.2	13.4	1.7	1.9	2.0	2.4
(% share)	(71)	(66)	(62)	(63)	(15)	(15)	(11)	(11)
Industry	1.6	2.4	4.0	3.8	1.7	2.5	4.1	3.8
Universities	1.0	1.3	2.0	2.9	5.3	6.1	8.6	11.0
(% share)	(9)	(10)	(11)	(14)	(48)	(48)	(48)	(52)
University FFRDCs	0	0	0	0	1.5	1.7	2.1	2.3
Nonprofits	.6	.7	.9	1.3	1.0	1.1	1.3	1.8
Total	11.1	13.4	18.1	21.3	11.1	13.4	18.1	21.3

Year	Sources of university research funds					
	Federal government	Other government	Industry	Nonprofits	Internal	Total
1968	5.0 (72%)	.6	.2	.4	.7	6.9
1978	5.1 (65%)	.7	.3	.6	1.0	7.8
1983	5.7 (63%)	.7	.4	.7	1.5	9.1
1988	7.9 (61%)	1.1	.8	.9	2.5	13.0
1993	9.3 (56%)	1.5	1.2	1.3	3.4	16.7

SOURCE: U.S. National Science Foundation (1993, pp. 332–35).

creased a hundredfold since the early 1980s. In addition, federally sponsored research at universities increasingly emphasizes commercial applications and cost sharing. For example, the Engineering Research Centers
Program in the National Science Foundation provides federal grants to
projects undertaken with the collaboration of private businesses. NSF is
under pressure from Congress to support more applied research; in the
FY 1994 budget, Congress required that NSF allocate 60 percent of its
budget for supporting "strategic projects," a poorly defined concept generally thought to involve near-term economic payoffs.

The new commercialization initiative is having a significant effect on the pattern of support for universities.[9] During most of the 1980s, the real research budgets of universities grew dramatically, with rapid rates of growth from all sources. Since 1988, this growth has slowed substantially, especially from federal support. Although real federal expenditures for university research grew by approximately 3 percent per year between 1988 and 1993, this growth was only about half the rate for the previous five years, and as a result the share of university R&D that is supported by the federal government fell from 61 percent to 56 percent. The decline is dramatic when compared to the high-water mark for the federal share of university research support: 74 percent in 1966. Over the past twenty years, the share of university research that NSF classifies as "basic" fell from 77 percent to 64 percent, while the share of "applied" research rose from 23 percent to 36 percent. The federal share of university research has now returned to the share that existed in the pre-Sputnik era, although the levels, of course, differ enormously. In 1958, the federal government paid for 56 percent of university research, and 62 percent of university research was basic while 38 percent was applied.

The Economic Foundation of the New Rationale

The link between technological innovation and productivity has a firm foundation in theoretical and empirical research in economics. A rich line of research, including work by Moses Abramovitz (1956), Robert Solow (1957), Edward Denison (1985), Zvi Griliches (1984), Richard Nelson (1964), F. M. Scherer (1984), and many others, concludes that more than half of the historical growth in per capita income in the United States is due to advances in knowledge, and that the total economic return to investment in R&D is several times as high as the return to other forms of investment.[10]

The fact that R&D is an important source of improvements in economic welfare is not, by itself, sufficient reason to justify a major role for the federal government in financing it. Nevertheless, here, as well, economics research has developed a rationale for government subsidies of R&D. Although research on the issue has produced widely differing estimates of the distribution of the economic benefits of technological change,

---

9. Data on the distribution of university R&D are taken from various issues of *Science and Engineering Indicators*, compiled by the National Science Foundation.

10. Lawrence Lau's chapter in this volume reports an important new advance in this line of research.

the consensus view is that most of the benefits of innovation accrue not to innovators, but to consumers through cheaper and/or better products and to workers in higher wages arising from higher labor productivity.[11] Because the benefits of technological progress are broadly shared, innovators lack the financial incentive to engage in as much investment in improved technology as is socially desirable. Profit-oriented businesses can be expected to evaluate R&D projects on the basis of their private profitability, not total social benefits, so businesses are not likely to pursue some projects that produce significant benefits to consumers and labor. As a result, from a societal perspective, business will underinvest in R&D.

More recently, a second rationale for public R&D policies has emerged in the economics literature, following a line of argument developed by, among others, Richard Nelson and Sidney Winter (1982), and Nathan Rosenberg (1982; this volume). This view flows from three observations about the process by which businesses identify and develop potentially beneficial new technology. One observation pertains to the uncertain process by which scientific knowledge is assembled into new technologies. A technical innovation typically embodies many advances in knowledge, some of which arose from solutions to seemingly unrelated problems and which were completely unanticipated by the original researchers and their sponsors. A researcher may not know all the promising uses of a new advancement in knowledge, and a research manager may be unaware of technical information that would be very useful to an ongoing project. The second observation is that R&D is not best conceptualized as a unidirectional flow (the "pipeline" model) from basic to applied to developmental research, but instead as a mutually interactive process in which potentially useful ideas about any one stage of the R&D process can emerge at any other stage (the "chain link" model).[12] The third observation is that the cost of transferring knowledge from one project to another is likely to be lower among researchers who work in teams or at the same location than among researchers who are physically and organizationally separated.

An important implication of these observations is that R&D is likely to exhibit economies of scale and scope—that is, a given R&D expenditure is likely to produce a greater return in terms of advancement in technology if it is performed in the same organization rather than divided among several. Moreover, these economies are especially likely to occur at the earlier stages of innovation, when a new technology is being designed and the details of its application are being worked out. Of course, these economies

---

11. For an excellent survey of this research, see Griliches (1992).
12. For a detailed explanation of this idea, see Kline and Rosenberg (1986).

can be offset by organizational diseconomies and greater risk aversion in large corporations.

The significance of these observations for policy hinge on possible conflicts between efficiency in conducting R&D and protecting proprietary information. A collaborative R&D venture among companies with overlapping but in some ways distinct technical capabilities and knowledge can increase the productivity of research because it reduces the costs of learning about and transmitting new technical information while reducing the organizational diseconomies associated with large firms; however, for parallel reasons a firm that participates in a research collaboration will be less likely to protect its own valuable proprietary knowledge, and so risks losing some of the appropriability of its own research. The latter factor then leads to underinvestment in collaborative efforts.

Policies to Increase Commercial R&D

In principle, government can solve the problem of underinvestment in R&D in two ways: by increasing the profits of innovators, or by undertaking R&D in areas where the private sector underinvests.

Making Innovation More Profitable

The first approach to R&D policy, which tends to be emphasized by political conservatives, is accomplished by making intellectual property rights more secure, by providing tax subsidies to innovative activity (such as the R&D tax credit), or by permitting, or even encouraging, mergers and acquisitions of horizontal competitors when the combined entity is likely to be more effective in research. In the last case, greater appropriability is obtained by creating concentrated or cartelized industries.

Historically, the most important policy has been to protect intellectual property rights: patents, copyrights, and trade secrets. More secure intellectual property rights increase the incentive to innovate, but they also have three major drawbacks (Nordhaus, 1969). First, intellectual property rights increase profits by establishing monopolies, and thus lead to economic inefficiency due to excessive prices and restricted production. Second, in some cases intellectual property rights can inhibit follow-on innovations by others who combine an older technology with a new idea. Extreme privatization of information can prevent one entity from understanding the technology invented by another well enough to recognize a useful extension of it. And when two holders of potentially compatible intellectual properties are aware of each other's technology but each is uncertain about their combined value, the firms can fail to reach an agreement to collaborate even when collaboration is beneficial to both. Third, intellectual property rights limit diffusion of research results. Because research can have applications in many products and industries, its potential benefits are realized only if results are diffused broadly and other companies have an incentive to find new applications for them. The fact that diffusion costs are higher across than within organizations does not imply that interorganizational diffusion is not important in the innovative process and so can be safely ignored without disadvantageous consequences. For these reasons, the economically optimal system of intellectual property rights is not one which maximizes the extent to which all commercially relevant technical information is durably protected.

Tax policies have the virtue of simplicity, but they present problems as well. One problem is the accounting and auditing costs associated with monitoring compliance with the tax code. Tax subsidies increase tax complexity, and thereby the collection costs of the tax system. Another problem is that tax subsidies cannot easily be constructed to be focused on the R&D activities that produce the largest spillover benefits and that suffer the greatest underinvestment by the private sector. In fact, tax subsidies do not alter the fundamental incentive of private industry, which is to invest in technologies that generate the greatest private profit, as contrasted to the highest social return.

Policies to encourage significant concentration of research-intensive industries have been advocated in the United States, but with little success. The United States has a more vigorous antitrust policy than other advanced industrialized nations. The only change in antitrust policy regarding R&D was legislation in 1984 that reduced the exposure of firms collaborating on R&D from triple to single damages if their collaboration is first registered with the government. Whereas several hundred collaborations have been registered since the act was passed, the importance of this change is debatable, because antitrust complaints focusing on research collaborations were exceedingly rare before the change was made. In fact, approximately two-thirds of the antitrust registrations have involved three industries in which research-related antitrust concerns have been raised in the past: the telecommunications industry, where the various divested components of the old AT&T have filed numerous registrations; the computer industry, where the old antitrust suit against IBM contained allegations regarding IBM's research policies; and the automobile industry, stemming from when the Big Three undertook a collaborative program in the 1960s to invent methods to reduce emissions from autos that was later alleged to have been an industry-wide conspiracy to slow down the rate of technological progress in this area (Clearinghouse for State and Local Initiatives, 1993).

Targeted Correction of Market Failures

A second type of solution to the problem of underinvestment in R&D, one which tends to be emphasized by political liberals, is for the government to subsidize it through grants for specific projects. In this case, the government selects specific technologies and areas of basic research to support, either subsidizes them in the private sector or undertakes them in government research laboratories, and then attempts to disseminate the new technologies by making the research results freely available to anyone who can make use of them.

Subsidization policies have drawbacks as well. One source of problems is the effect of subsidies on the incentives of those undertaking the research. Without the opportunity to profit from applications, researchers may not pursue topics that have the greatest potential economic payoff, and may be prone to make promises that government officials want to hear, rather than those that are based on a sober assessment of technical and market realities.

Another drawback of subsidization policies is the system of federal procurement. The federal government's methods for procurement of products that are not widely available in the private market are extremely detailed, complex, and inflexible, leading to an inordinately large administrative cost in managing federal contracts and great difficulty in redirecting effort as one proceeds in fulfilling a contract. Whereas this tendency for elaborate and costly contractual arrangements may well reflect general public skepticism about the propensity of government to be wasteful and corrupt, and the concomitant political payoff to elected officials who uncover scandals and punish the perpetrators, the problem is deeply rooted in the nature of a broad class of procurement activities, including R&D projects.

Efficient contracts for technology development across organizational boundaries are especially difficult to write, which is why private firms virtually never attempt to procure R&D from other organizations rather than to undertake it in house. The cause of the problem is uncertainty about both the costs and results of R&D, which must be imperfectly known or else the research would not have to be undertaken in the first place. Because of this uncertainty, the government faces difficulties in specifying realistic technical approaches and objectives, and in monitoring the performance of the contract. Moreover, as work proceeds, the government is quite likely to change its mind about the kind of product it wants, based on new information that arises in the early stages of a project. Consequently, R&D contracts usually are based on some form of cost-reimbursement formula, despite the notorious tendency of such contracts to produce cost overruns.[13]

Because whether a contractor is putting forth best effort and managing a project wisely is extremely difficult to detect, the government's traditional solution to the contracting problem is to impose elaborate cost-accounting and audit requirements on R&D contractors, and to put forth great effort to find even a tiny amount of waste, fraud, or lax management. This system of monitoring is far more complex, costly, and inflexible than the monitoring systems that are used in private organizations for conducting their own research, and as a result, R&D undertaken under federal contract is inherently more costly and less effective than R&D undertaken with internal funds. Indeed, federal contractors for R&D and other sole-source products often engage in "walling off" the government work—that is, they carry out private activities in separate facilities, using separate employees and an entirely different management and accounting system, to make sure that the rigidities and monitoring expenses of the federal activities do not carry over into the private work.[14]

A third source of problems with subsidization policies is that the government may not be very adept at picking promising technologies, particularly if the goal is a commercial product rather than one that supports a government mission, and in any case is prone to allocate funds according to political criteria rather than strictly the technical and economic merit of a proposal.[15] Because technical information is difficult and costly to transmit across organizational lines, federal officials are likely to know less about technical opportunities, market requirements, and a contractor's capabilities than the contractor knows. Because federal sponsors are trying to cure a market failure by inducing contractors to pursue projects that they have insufficient private incentive to undertake, a contracting agency faces a fundamental dilemma: Is the contractor's reluctance to pursue the agency's plans without modification based on the contractor's superior knowledge, or the result of the incentive operating upon the contractor to bend the project more towards activities that promise greater appropriability of the research outputs and so higher long-run profits for the contractor?

13. For analysis of the incentive effects of procurement contracts in the development of defense weapons systems, see Demski and Magee (1992) and Rogerson (1992).

14. See Markusen and Yudken (1992) on how defense procurement rules can undermine converting defense firms to civilian production.

15. These issues are examined in the context of six major government R&D programs in Cohen and Noll (1991).

A fourth source of problems with the subsidization policies is adverse political incentives for maintaining an efficient portfolio of commercially oriented projects. The portfolio problem arises from two distortions caused by political control. Historically, the government has had extraordinary difficulty in abandoning large development projects that were clearly failing efficiency tests. Unfortunately, technical and economic failure does not necessarily lead to the timely demise of a government program, for, unlike the private sector, government officials are sensitive to the effects of project cancellation on employment at the facility and profits of contractors. Alternatively, some projects that are successful run into another problem: they are perceived as unfair by non-participating firms on the grounds that the government is determining the pattern of success and failure among companies in the industry (Cohen and Noll, 1991).[16] In brief, the government is prone to abandoning worthwhile projects while continuing poor ones, so that even if it were as adept as industry in picking worthwhile projects initially, its portfolio of projects overall would tend to be weaker.

The Role of the Two Strategies: History and the New Rationale

Historically, the two basic approaches to R&D policy—measures to increase the profits of innovators, and subsidies of specific types of R&D to offset private underinvestment—have been regarded as substitutes. Technologies in which private industry could hold a reasonably secure intellectual property right were expected to be supported by business. Government supported this private R&D only indirectly, through preferential tax treatment, the system of intellectual property rights, and grants for fundamental research at universities and national labs that was available to the private sector for free—if businesses could figure out where to look. Government also supported some developmental R&D, but argued that it did so only when the benefits were likely to be widely dispersed. In all cases, the government insisted that the results of its projects be disseminated.

---

16. A recent example was an unsuccessful attempt to block a CRADA at an EPA lab through a lawsuit. The district judge found that the plaintiff lacked standing to challenge the CRADA, because: "Nowhere in the legislative history of the Act [enabling the establishment of CRADAs] is there any indicia of a Congressional concern for the interests of individual businesses qua competitors. Rather, the Act is concerned with improving the nation as a whole so that it may compete globally, not with ensuring the competitive rights of individual companies" (*Chem Service Inc. v. EPA, et al.*, Civil Action 92–0989, U.S. District Court for the Eastern District of Pennsylvania). Notwithstanding the legal issue, this type of program is vulnerable politically. In 1993, a highly publicized $70 million CRADA to develop supercomputing technology signed between Cray Research and two DOE laboratories was unceremoniously shelved after other domestic supercomputer manufacturers complained to Congress.

Even in defense technologies, where national security considerations led officials to retain maximal confidentiality about some research results, the government frequently called upon one contractor to produce technologies that were developed by another, encouraged (and sometimes required) defense firms to disseminate firm-specific technical knowledge through subcontracting, and welcomed commercial adoption of technologies that were not closely related to highly confidential defense products, such as advances in computers, microelectronics, and telecommunications.

The use of direct federal subsidies of commercially relevant R&D is more than 100 years old, dating from the development of the telegraph and hybrid seeds in the nineteenth century. Nevertheless, direct federal support of R&D did not become a significant component of national R&D effort until World War II, and even then it was confined almost exclusively to defense-related technologies. Not until the 1960s did the federal government undertake a broad array of research programs for primarily civilian purposes, at that time initiating important new programs in biomedical technology, supersonic commercial aircraft, and geosynchronous communications satellites, and smaller programs in several other areas, including synthetic fuels from coal, environmentally benign automobile engines, and new construction methods.

Even after the new initiatives of the 1960s, the federal government lacked anything remotely resembling a coherent, economy-wide strategy for civilian R&D. The majority of federal R&D dollars were still spent on defense or fundamental knowledge that was relevant to defense, and the remaining civilian programs were a series of largely unrelated, targeted responses to much narrower public issues than the overall long-run performance of the economy. Examples were the "War on Cancer," the desire for more environmentally benign production methods and products, the perceived threat to the national pre-eminence of the U.S. aircraft industry after defense aerospace technologies significantly diverged from commercial technologies, the persistent decline of the eastern coal-mining industry, and, in the 1970s, the search for an effective technological response to the rise of the worldwide oil cartel.

By contrast, the new approach is essentially economy-wide, and owes its appeal both to productivity justifications and to the common belief that the dominance of international markets by U.S. manufacturers can be reclaimed (or strengthened) through innovation. The new approach rejects the prior view that policies to make commercially relevant technical knowledge more proprietary are alternatives to direct federal support. Proponents of the new theme argue that by making the products of federally supported research the property of the private entity that undertakes it, research organizations will have a greater incentive to bring new technical knowledge to commercial practice. Moreover, foreign companies will face greater costs and delays in trying to make use of the products of this research, giving American firms a competitive edge in international markets. Proponents buttress their case by pointing to the similar approach to R&D undertaken in Japan (computers and microelectronics) and Europe (Airbus), where governments have created and subsidized collaborative, proprietary R&D projects in the private sector that have led to important gains in the international market shares of domestic industries.

The combination of a proactive role in selecting and paying for commercial R&D and giving proprietary rights in research products to private industry has appeal to both conservatives and liberals, and so, like defense prior to the demise of the Soviet Union, can command bipartisan political support. This advantage is exemplified by the fact that the Clinton administration's R&D policy is primarily a continuation and expansion of the R&D policy of the Bush administration, which in turn has roots in the Carter policy and attained budgetary significance through relatively nonconflictual collaboration with a Democratic Congress.

Economics, Politics, and the Future of the New Strategy

Despite its advantages, there are good reasons to believe that the new approach to U.S. R&D policy will not succeed either economically or politically. Because the political problems are rooted in the economic consequences of the policy, it is useful to begin by examining the economics of the new theme.

Fundamental Research and Privatization of Knowledge

An important economic consequence of encouraging privatization of knowledge is that it works far better at encouraging the more developmental end of research than at encouraging more fundamental advances in knowledge. The U.S. system of R&D is unique in the role it assigns to universities in performing basic research. The historical U.S. policy of supporting university research and encouraging open and free dissemination of the results not only accommodates diffusion of research across organizations, but also permits an integration of teaching and research that is uncommon elsewhere and that facilitates the diffusion of new knowledge to industry through students. Even basic research at national laboratories has been carried out in a similar fashion because many labs are managed by universities, and most have numerous faculty and students in residence undertaking experiments.

Economics research indicates that the economic payoff to basic research is higher in the United States than in other nations, and the most plausible cause is the unique American emphasis on research universities (Griliches, 1986; Mansfield, 1980, 1988). Making the dissemination of basic research more difficult is likely to reduce its economic payoff to society—albeit probably not to the university. Furthermore, research that is motivated by its profitability is far more likely to focus on projects with a predictable application, causing university research to be more applied and focused, and hence to generate less foundational knowledge with widespread application across a variety of industries.

Encouraging universities and national laboratories to make the results of their research proprietary, either by giving universities exclusive rights to the products of government-financed research or by subsidizing more extensively proprietary collaborations with industry, sets a troubling precedent for the institutional structure of basic research in the United States. Some of these changes may be inevitable. The historical generosity of government in supporting basic research apparently is no longer sustainable. Nevertheless, the new policies are not substitutes for the old, and are likely to have economic significance because the social payoff to basic research in the United States has been so high.

The Profit-Inducement Strategy: Property Rights and Cartelization

A very important element of the economics of privatized and collaborative research is that it can reduce competition in domestic industries. Obtaining maximum security of intellectual property rights requires eliminating market competition, which, if innovations cannot be durably protected by their creators, requires domestic cartelization of industry and permanent, impermeable barriers to import competition.

Industry cartels and protectionism are far more common in Japan, the newly industrializing countries of Asia, and, to a lesser extent, western Europe than in the United States. The postwar history of Japan illustrates especially well the dilemma inherent in this trade-off. By facilitating the formation of cartels, Japan has produced a system that ranks first in the world in the fraction of gross domestic product (GDP) that is spent on R&D and other forms of investment, that produces a higher rate of sustained economic growth than any other advanced, industrialized economy, and that has persistently low unemployment. Moreover, in Japan a far lower proportion of R&D is financed by government than in the world's other leading economies, and defense plays virtually no role in motivating public or private R&D.

The other side of Japan's remarkable performance is that the standard of living of the ordinary Japanese citizen is far below living standards in other nations with approximately the same per capita GDP. Although the average Japanese employee works substantially more hours per year than the average American worker, the real purchasing power of average annual take-home pay in Japan is approximately 75 percent of the real value of the average American's take-home earnings—a remarkable fact considering that the real value of wages for average American workers essentially has not increased for twenty years. Moreover, many Japanese are not pleased with their own economic system. The recent political upheaval in Japan, while sparked by scandals among members of the ruling party, has been brewing for more than a decade, and was rooted in the increasing dissatis-faction engendered by the inability of the ordinary Japanese to attain a standard of living that is roughly equal to living standards in North America and western Europe.[17] A key lesson from the experience of Japan is that policies that provide especially sharp financial incentives for private investment will produce rapid economic growth, but the economic bene-fits of that growth will not be as widely shared.

Limits to the Economic Rationale for Promoting Collaboration

For programs subsidizing industrial R&D, the new theme for federal research is based on an incomplete conception of the incentives affecting the innovative process. A ubiquitous element of the new research policy is that the government should encourage industry-wide research consortia to pool the resources of otherwise competitive companies, perhaps by subsi-dizing such ventures, but also by granting antitrust immunity to them. But industry-wide collaboration does not necessarily increase overall research effort and the rate of technological progress.

Whether collaboration is beneficial depends on the details regarding the nature of the work that is undertaken and the role of domestic industry in the international economic system. R&D collaboration among domestic competitors is unlikely to produce the undesirable effects of a domestic cartel in either of two circumstances. First, if trade in the products of the industry is free and several nations are efficient producers, even a complete merger of all domestic companies will create simply another competitor in

---

17. For a comparison of the political context of economic policy in Japan and the United States, see Kernell (1991), especially the chapter by Shimada.

the world market. In this case, domestic collaboration can be beneficial if it enables the domestic industry to capture scale economies in R&D, to exchange specialized expertise across companies, or to avoid duplicative research. Second, a collaboration is likely to be beneficial if it is limited in scope to expanding the technological base of the domestic industry, enabling each firm in an industry to make use of this research to develop its own proprietary products. In this case, collaboration in more fundamental research does not inhibit domestic competition among the collaborators.

Centralized "technology base" research is likely to be beneficial across a wide spectrum of industries. Unfortunately, changes in the technology base of an industry typically are difficult to protect with intellectual property rights. Consequently, such programs are unlikely to be effective in confining their new knowledge to U.S. firms. Furthermore, separate efforts by competing domestic companies to apply the new technology base will dissipate the private profitability of the technology-base research. Thus, industry-wide technology-base programs, while attractive as an efficient means to develop new technology, are neither very effective as part of a national competitiveness strategy nor likely to generate a great deal of enthusiasm from business—unless, as was the case in Japan, they are married to a domestic production cartel and effective trade barriers.

Industry-wide R&D programs are likely to take one of two directions. If they retain a generic technology-base focus, the public sector is likely to be called on to provide most of the financial support. This option appears unlikely in these penurious times, particularly if the project lacks strong industry support. Alternatively, industrial participants are likely to press for a reorientation towards work on more focused developmental research projects, which can be more effectively protected by patents and hence offer greater profits to the domestic industry. The problem then becomes the possibility of domestic cartelization. By contrast, research on innovation demonstrates that a large proportion of technological progress comes from new, upstart entrants or firms from outside an industry. Hence, if the national interest rests on increasing the rate of technological progress, industry-wide R&D cartels with government R&D subsidies are very likely to be counterproductive (Jewkes, Sawers, and Stillerman, 1969).

Collaboration on applications research can be socially beneficial if the domestic industry faces competition at home from foreign producers; however, as a practical matter, centralization of domestic R&D beyond the technology base is almost always dangerous. Even when the domestic market is open to relatively free imports, poor performance by the domestic industry usually leads to trade barriers, such as the import quotas that were adopted by the United States for steel, autos, semiconductors, and numerous other products when the domestic industry began to lose significant market share to foreigners. Hence, industry-wide centralization of more applied R&D gives domestic consumers something of a Hobson's choice. If the venture is successful in making U.S. industry more productive than its foreign competitors, the domestic industry will retain most of the benefits of its improved productivity by cartelizing the domestic market. If the venture is unsuccessful, and the domestic industry loses market share to foreigners, import restrictions are likely to be imposed, leading again to a domestic cartel—but in this case one that is inefficient as well as monopolistic. In either case, the main effect of centralized R&D is to transfer wealth to the domestic industry, not to improve the economic welfare of most citizens.

If centralization of applications research for an entire domestic industry is dangerous, another possibility is to support projects undertaken by one or a few firms that account for only part of the domestic industry. Supporting only some firms in an industry, especially one that has numerous but technologically differentiated firms, can be attractive because it enables the government to capture economies of scale and scope without supporting all technical ideas and creating a cumbersome decision process that accommodates a large number of players. This has been the approach taken to date by the National Institute of Standards and Technology in its ATP program, although whether this strategy can survive a vastly expanded budget is doubtful. In principle, such a strategy can preserve technological competition among domestic companies while increasing overall R&D effort. However, in competitive industries these kinds of programs quickly run into the claims by disgruntled displaced firms that the government is unfairly helping their competitors.

Another form of the "picking winners" problem arises because of the strict policy of focusing subsidies on U.S. firms. In some of the most visible high-technology industries—most notably, computers—few final products are composed entirely of components from a single nation, and some research collaborations across national boundaries are already in place. For example, in the non-impact printer industry (with $5.5 billion of U.S sales in 1989), the dominant firms are both American: Apple and Hewlett-Packard. The active optoelectronic components, accounting for less than 15 percent of the cost of these products, are mostly manufactured in Japan, although Texas Instruments (TI) is also in this business. The DRAM chips in the printer are manufactured in Japan; however, the integrated circuits that control the Japanese optoelectronic component tend to be manufactured in the United States, mainly by Motorola.[18] A U.S. cooperative research venture in non-impact printers that barred Japanese participation would threaten at least some U.S. firms, either the dominant printer manufacturers if they did not want to end their procurement of Japanese optoelectronics, or Motorola if manufacturers agreed to switch to the TI component.

The laser printer example demonstrates the fundamental dilemma of the competitiveness rationale, and its accompanying prohibition against foreign collaboration. Specialization based on firm-specific expertise can lead to products for which the most efficient distribution of manufacturing responsibilities crosses international boundaries. Attempts to overcome these international cooperative relationships in the name of trade flows waste R&D resources, cause a loss of sales by domestic manufacturers who efficiently use some foreign components, and increase prices to purchasers of the product by eliminating the cheapest alternative.

Problems with Public/Private Collaboration

Programs encouraging more coordination and collaboration between public and private research efforts are also likely to face significant problems. With respect to collaborations between industry and either national laboratories or universities, the main issues are the degree of interest overlap and the extent of synergistic capabilities. Certainly both exist to some degree, but the issue is whether the present plans for expanding these collaborations are consistent with the magnitude of potentially fruitful complementarities. The basic problems are that the missions of these organizations—defense weapons development and basic scientific research—have a limited commonality with the commercial objectives of industry. Although the Clinton administration is a leading advocate of these collaborative efforts, its Office of Technology Assessment (1993a, b) has expressed some important limitations to these programs. One report offers the following synopsis of its findings (Office of Technology Assessment, 1993a, pp. 2–3):

For the longer term future, R&D partnerships with industry, *per se*, are not likely to provide a satisfactory central mission for the weapons labs. As public institutions, the labs' existence is best justified if they serve missions that are primarily public in nature. The lab technologies that are currently exciting high interest from industry are drawn from the well of public missions of the past half century, especially nuclear

---

18. Several examples of U.S.-foreign collaboration on high-technology products, including details about laser printers, are discussed in Congressional Budget Office (1990, chap. 3).

defense. . . . There is also growing interest in expansion of the labs' public missions into newly defined areas. . . . However desirable they may be, it is not likely that any of these [new opportunities] would create nearly enough jobs at the right time and in the right places to compensate for the hundreds of thousands of defense jobs being lost.

The dual-use programs raise similar concerns. Here the form of the cooperative objective is different, in that the purpose is to bring greater commonality among components of defense and civilian products. The problem arises because the problem of picking the optimal point on the cost/performance trade-off can have a very different solution in defense and civilian systems. In some cases, defense accounts for a very small part of total industry output, so an attempt to bend R&D for a dual-use technology for defense purposes could undermine the much more important position of domestic firms in the civilian part of the industry. For example, consider the potential future market of high-resolution display devices, including HDTV and flat-panel displays. Annually, over 100 million computer display terminals and television sets are produced worldwide. In the United States, about 10 million cathode ray tubes are used for computer terminal displays, 8.9 million of which are imported. But the United States is a leader in the high end of cathode ray displays, producing 2.4 million and exporting 1.1 million of the most expensive versions. Another 1.0 million flat-panel displays are sold as parts of newly manufactured laptop computers. In this market, the motivation for the defense dual-use program in this industry is an annual use of 76,000 high-resolution flat-panel displays for government aircraft and 220,000 high-performance displays for computers (Congressional Budget Office, 1990, pp. 47–50). Obviously, at this scale, there is a serious question whether it is necessary or desirable for the government to try to bend the technology of domestic display devices for dual-use purposes, and whether in the post–cold war era the government's total funds in this area—R&D plus procurement—will be adequate to influence the technology should government try to do so.

The Procurement Dilemma

As discussed above, direct federal support for commercial R&D seems inevitably to lead to onerous accounting and audit processes. In fact, most of the new programs have adopted the same procedures for submitting proposals and monitoring performance that are used for defense procurement and other government R&D programs. These methods for increasing the accountability of federal recipients of grants and contracts undermine the effectiveness of federally sponsored R&D programs. The more obvious effect is on costs: the procedures for defining the details of a project, developing the substance and budget of a proposal, and monitoring progress and expenditures lead to substantially higher costs of research. Both universities and private companies, when left to their own devices, develop far less complex procedures than the government requires—and so incur lower expenses while retaining greater flexibility in carrying out projects.

Federal procurement procedures have another undesirable effect on the overall effectiveness of R&D policy in that they create a selection bias in projects. Specifically, participation is going to be more difficult for industries that are not involved in federal procurement activities, and that would have to develop such procedures and negotiate accounting and operating agreements with the government before being eligible to participate. Some prospective recipients of support may not find it worthwhile to develop ways to adhere to required federal procedures. Even if they do develop such procedures, a likely consequence is "walling-off" federally supported work from other research in the organization, reducing the ease of technology transfer between public and private projects.

Cutting Losses—and Not Winners

The new programs were explicitly designed to subsidize commercial development while avoiding the "pork barrel" problems that have plagued previous large commercial R&D efforts. In particular, management choices for the programs are decentralized to a much greater degree than on previous programs, and program characteristics are intended to incorporate private incentives. As the focus of the programs is commercial development, rather than government missions, their emphasis on private selection of projects is probably wise. However, we are not sanguine that the programs can avoid the subsequent selection problems that have distorted previous government programs.

For example, the programs require cost sharing by industry, in part to avoid continued support of failed projects. The logic of the argument is that poor projects will die when private participants bail out. This logic may work for small projects, but frequently a big project—one with substantial employment—becomes too important politically for the government to abandon. Instead, Congress is likely to revise the program so that government assumes a greater financial burden. Some of the most celebrated federal technology turkeys, including the Clinch River Breeder Reactor and the supersonic transport project, started out in life with apparently iron-clad cost-sharing requirements. One wonders whether a substantial failure by ventures such as SEMATECH and the flat-panel display project would lead to the demise of the program rather than an increase in the federal financial contribution. Moreover, even the very limited experience with the new programs suggests that the claims of unfairly subsidized successes will have equal applicability to these programs as to previous federal efforts.[19]

These arguments do not imply that government should never support commercial R&D; instead, it means that proactive government subsidization is unlikely to prove to be an effective mechanism for enhancing productivity across a broad spectrum of industries. Moreover, it also explains the attraction to both government and industry of supporting industry-wide R&D collaboration. Because industry-wide projects do not create losers, they are unlikely to be killed because they might succeed. Furthermore, historical precedents suggest that if such a program is a technological failure, not only will information not be forthcoming that would allow the timely cancellation of the project, but the government is likely to "buy out" the private participants and continue the effort. Once again, the logic of the economics and politics of R&D programs implies a tendency towards complete centralization—and the problems it creates.

What Works: Are Economics and Politics Compatible?

The preceding review of U.S. R&D policy leads inexorably to the conclusion that the United States has not yet found a politically viable and economically attractive solution to the problem of encouraging beneficial technological progress. Both economic research on R&D and historical experience with government programs suggest that the most effective combination of policies is likely to be a proactive program to subsidize fundamental and technology-base research, partly in basic research facilities like universities and national labs and partly in collaborative centers for particular technologies, and to make the results of such research broadly available rather than proprietary. Additional incentives for applications research can be beneficial, but they are likely to be more effective if they are implemented through an indirect, broadly based program such as the R&D tax credit. Targeted subsidies for specific commercial applications can sometimes be effective, but only if they are limited to special cases where the government as a user or producer has a major stake in the product of research (as was the case for defense) or where the technology and economic structure of the industry make the risks of cartelization minimal.

---

19. See note 16 and the surrounding argument, and the discussion of SEMATECH in Cohen and Noll (1992).

Unfortunately, this more effective approach has significant political liabilities. The benefits of such a program will accrue primarily to consumers, yet most of the active political support for R&D programs is from industry. Moreover, because the results of technology-base programs usually cannot be confined to the entities that undertake the research, the benefits of this approach cannot be confined to U.S. firms, vitiating the competitiveness rationale for the policy. Thus, the economically preferred approach from the standpoint of maximizing the growth in productivity does not respond to the sources of a political demand for domestic R&D policy. In this sense, domestic R&D policy has an interesting parallel to education policy in that whereas there is widespread agreement that a change in policy is necessary, no effective means has been developed for mobilizing the political system to tackle the problem. In the case of R&D, until a replacement is found for national security as the consensus-creating theme, federal R&D support, especially in more fundamental areas that contribute to the technological base of industry, is likely to continue to decline, with a debilitating long-term effect on economic growth. Thus far, historical experience seems to provide only negative lessons: neither an appeal to the goal of enhancing overall national economic performance, as attempted by President Carter, nor the economically less attractive call to arms based on international competitiveness, as developed in the Bush and Clinton administrations, has yet proven effective as a political rallying cry.

Uncertainty and Technological Change

NATHAN ROSENBERG

I would like to begin with two generally accepted propositions about technological change: it is a major ingredient of long-term economic growth, and it is characterized by a high degree of uncertainty. Understanding the nature of these uncertainties and the obstacles to surmounting them is not a trivial matter. Rather, it goes to the heart of how new technologies are devised, how rapidly they diffuse, the ultimate extent of that diffusion, and their eventual impact on economic performance and welfare.

In view of the great uncertainties attached to the innovation process, it is hardly surprising that innovating firms have, historically, experienced high failure rates. Quite simply, the vast majority of attempts at innovation fail. But to describe the high failure rate associated with past innovation is to tell only a part of the story, and perhaps not the most interesting part. Indeed, I want to suggest that the more intriguing part of the story, with which I will be mainly concerned, has been the inability to anticipate the future impact of successful innovations, even after their technical feasibility has been established. This statement remains valid whether we focus upon the steam engine 200 years ago or the laser within our own lifetimes.

I will suggest that uncertainty is the product of several sources and that it has a number of peculiar characteristics that shape the innovation process and therefore the manner in which technological change exercises its effects on the economy. Since I will be primarily concerned with what has shaped the trajectory and the economic impact of new technologies, my

The author wishes to acknowledge valuable comments on earlier drafts by Moses Abramovitz, Victor Fuchs, Ralph Landau, Roberto Mazzoleni, Richard Nelson, Richard Rosenbloom, Scott Stern, and members of the Program on Economic Growth and Policy of the Canadian Institute for Advanced Research.

focus will be confined to technologies that have had significant impacts. A study that included unsuccessful as well as successful innovations might yield insights of a very different nature.

I should also say at the outset that while I am not primarily concerned with the recent formal literature on growth theory (specifically the "new growth theory"), I am surprised that that literature has, so far at least, omitted any mention of uncertainty. While the rate of innovation is surely a function of the degree to which investors can appropriate the gains from their innovation, a number of central features of the innovation process revolve around uncertainty. At the very least, there is a risk/return trade-off to be considered when evaluating projects that reflects the uncertainty attaching to appropriability. But the kinds of uncertainties that will be identified here go far beyond the issue of appropriability.

One further caveat seems appropriate. The discussion that follows is "anecdotal" in nature. However, the anecdotes have been deliberately selected to include many of the most important innovations of the twentieth century. Thus, if the characterizations offered below stand the test of further scrutiny, the analysis of this chapter will have captured distinct features of the innovation process for technologies whose cumulative economic importance has been immense.

It is easy to assume that uncertainties are drastically reduced after the first commercial introduction of a new technology, and Schumpeter offered strong encouragement for that assumption. His views have proven to be highly influential. In Schumpeter's world, entrepreneurs are compelled to make decisions under circumstances of very limited and poor quality of information. But in that world the successful completion of an innovation resolves all the uncertainties that previously existed. Once this occurs, the stage is set for imitators, whose actions are responsible for the diffusion of a technology. Perhaps it should be said that the stage is now set for "mere imitators." Schumpeter was fond of preceding the noun "imitators" with the adjective "mere." The point is one of real substance, and not just linguistic usage. In Schumpeter's view, life is easy for the imitators, because all they need to do is to follow in the footsteps of the entrepreneurs who have led the way, and whose earlier activities have resolved all the big uncertainties.

It is, of course, true that some uncertainties have been reduced at that point. However, after a new technological capability has been established, the questions change and, as we will see, new uncertainties, especially uncertainties of a specifically economic nature, begin to assert themselves.

The purpose of this chapter is to identify and to delineate a number of important aspects of uncertainty as they relate to technological change. These aspects go far beyond those connected with the inventive process alone. In addition, as we will see, they reflect a set of interrelated forces that are at the heart of the relationship between changes in technology and improvements in economic performance.

Some Historical Perspectives

Consider the laser, an innovation that is certainly one of the most powerful and versatile advances in technology in the twentieth century, and one that is still surely in the early stages of its trajectory of development. Its range of uses in the 30 years since it was invented is truly breathtaking. A list of uses would include precision measurement, navigational instruments, and a prime instrument of chemical research. It is essential for the high-quality reproduction of music in compact discs (CDs). It has become the instrument of choice in a range of surgical procedures, including extraordinarily delicate surgery upon the eye, where it is used to repair detached retinas, and gynecological surgery, where it now provides a simpler and less painful method for removal of certain tumors. It is extensively employed in gall bladder surgery. When this chapter was being revised in manuscript, its pages were printed by a laser jet printer. Lasers are widely used throughout industry, including textiles, where it is employed to cut cloth to desired shapes, and metallurgy and composite materials, where it performs similar functions.

But perhaps no single application of the laser has been more profound than its impact on telecommunications, where, together with fiber optics, it is revolutionizing transmission. The best trans-Atlantic telephone cable in 1966 could carry simultaneously only 138 conversations between Europe and North America. The first fiber optic cable, installed in 1988, could carry 40,000. The fiber optic cables being installed in the early 1990s can carry nearly 1.5 million conversations (Wriston, 1992, pp. 43–44). And yet it is reported that the patent lawyers at Bell Labs were initially unwilling even to apply for a patent on the laser, on the grounds that such an invention had no possible relevance to the telephone industry. In the words of Charles Townes (1968, p. 701), who subsequently won a Nobel Prize for his research on the laser, "Bell's patent department at first refused to patent our amplifier or oscillator for optical frequencies because, it was explained, optical waves had never been of any importance to communications and hence the invention had little bearing on Bell System interests."

Let me cite some further major historical instances where the common theme is the remarkable inability, at least from a later perspective, to foresee the uses to which new technologies would soon be put. Western Union, the telegraph company, was offered the opportunity to purchase Bell's 1876 telephone patent for a mere $100,000, but turned it down. In fact, "Western Union was willing to withdraw from the telephone field in 1879 in exchange for Bell's promise to keep out of the telegraph business." But if the proprietors of the old communications technology were myopic, so was the patent holder of the new technology. Alexander Graham Bell's 1876 patent did not mention a new technology at all. Rather, it bore the glaringly misleading title "Improvements in Telegraphy" (Brock, 1982, p. 90).

Marconi, who invented the radio, anticipated that it would be used primarily to communicate between two points where communication by wire was impossible, as in ship-to-ship or ship-to-shore communication. To this day the British call the instrument the "wireless," precisely reflecting Marconi's early conceptualization. Moreover, the radio in its early days was thought to be of potential use only for private communication: that is, point-to-point communication, rather like the telephone, and not at all for communicating to a large audience of listeners. Surprising as it may seem to us today, the inventor of the radio did not think of it as an instrument for broadcasting. Marconi in fact had a conception of the market for radio that was the precise opposite of the one that actually developed. He visualized the users of his invention as steamship companies, newspapers, and navies. They required directional, point-to-point communication, that is, "narrowcasting" rather than broadcasting. The radio should therefore be capable of transmitting over great distances, but the messages should be private, not public (Douglas, 1987, p. 34).

The failure of social imagination was widespread. According to one authority, "When broadcasting was first proposed . . . a man who was later to become one of the most distinguished leaders of the industry announced that it was very difficult to see uses for public broadcasting. About the only regular use he could think of was the broadcasting of Sunday sermons, because that is the only occasion when one man regularly addresses a mass public" (Martin, 1977, p. 11).

The wireless telephone, when it became feasible in the second decade of the twentieth century, was thought of in precisely the same terms as the wireless radio. J. J. Carty, who was chief engineer of the New York Telephone Company, stated in 1915, "The results of long-distance tests show clearly that the function of the wireless telephone is primarily to reach inaccessible places where wires cannot be strung. It will act mainly as an extension of the wire system and a feeder to it" (Maclaurin, 1949, pp. 92–93).

The computer, in 1949, was thought to be of potential use only for rapid calculation in a few scientific research or data processing contexts. The notion that there was a large potential market was rejected by no less a person than Thomas Watson, Sr., at the time the president of IBM. The prevailing view before 1950 was that world demand could probably be satisfied by just a few computers (Ceruzzi, 1987).

The invention of the transistor, certainly one of the greatest inventions of the twentieth century, was not announced on the front page of the *New York Times*, as might have been expected, when it was made public in December 1947. On the contrary, it was a small item buried deep in the newspaper's inside pages, in a regular weekly column titled "News of Radio." It was suggested there that the device might be used to develop better hearing aids for the deaf, but nothing more.

This listing of failures to anticipate future uses and larger markets for new technologies could be expanded almost without limit. We could, if we liked, amuse ourselves indefinitely at the failure of earlier generations to see the obvious, as we see it today. But that would be a mistaken conceit. For reasons that I propose to examine, I am not particularly optimistic that our ability to overcome the ex ante uncertainties connected with the uses of new technologies is likely to improve drastically. If I am right, a more useful issue to explore is what incentives, institutions, and policies are more likely to lead to a swifter resolution of these uncertainties.

Much of the difficulty, I suggest, is connected to the fact that new technologies typically come into the world in a very primitive condition. Their eventual uses turn upon an extended improvement process that vastly expands their practical applications. Thomas Watson, Sr., was not necessarily far off the mark when he concluded that the future market for the computer was extremely limited, if one thinks of the computer in the form in which it existed immediately after the Second World War. The first electronic digital computer, the ENIAC, contained no less than 18,000 vacuum tubes and filled a huge room (it was more than 100 feet long). Any device that has to rely on the simultaneous working of 18,000 vacuum tubes is bound to be notoriously unreliable. The failure in prediction was a failure to anticipate the demand for computers after they had been made very much smaller, cheaper, and more reliable, and when their performance characteristics, especially their calculating speed, had been improved by many orders of magnitude; that is to say, the failure was the inability to anticipate the trajectory of future improvements and the economic consequences of those improvements.

If space permitted, the history of commercial aviation could be told in similar terms, as could the history of many other innovations. With respect to the introduction of the jet engine, in particular, the failure to anticipate the importance of future improvements occurred even at the most eminent scientific levels. In 1940 a committee of the National Academy of Sciences was formed to evaluate the prospects for developing a gas turbine for aircraft. The committee concluded that such a turbine was quite impractical because it would have to weigh fifteen pounds for each horsepower delivered, whereas existing internal combustion engines weighed only slightly over one pound for each horsepower delivered. In fact, within a year the British were operating a gas turbine that weighed a mere 0.4 pounds per horsepower (U.S. Navy, 1941, p. 10).

This is an appropriate place at which to make a very simple, but nonetheless fundamental observation: most R&D expenditures are devoted to product improvement. According to McGraw-Hill annual surveys over a number of years, the great bulk of R&D (around 80 percent) is devoted to improving products that already exist, rather than to the invention of new products. Thus, it is incorrect to think of R&D expenditures as committed to the search for breakthrough innovations of the Schumpeterian type. On the contrary, the great bulk of these expenditures need to be thought of as exhibiting strongly path-dependent characteristics. Their main goal is to improve upon the performance of technologies that have been inherited from the past. A moment's reflection suggests that this should not be surprising. The telephone has been around for more than 100 years, but only recently has its performance been significantly enhanced by facsimile transmission, electronic mail (e-mail), voice mail, data transfer, on-line services, conference calls, and "800" numbers. The automobile and the airplane are each more than 90 years old, the camera is 150 years old, and the Fourdrinier machine, which is the mainstay of the papermaking industry today, was patented during the Napoleonic Wars. Clearly the improvement process deserves far more attention than is suggested by Schumpeter's frequent recourse to the derisory term "mere imitators." Equally clearly, a world in which most R&D expenditures are devoted to improving upon technologies that are already in existence is also a world in which technological change can hardly be characterized as exogenous.

So far it has been suggested, by citing important historical cases, that uncertainty plays a role in technological change that goes far beyond the uncertainty associated with technological feasibility alone. Indeed, the uncertainty associated with the eventual uses of the laser or the computer might, more appropriately, be characterized as "ignorance" rather than as "uncertainty." That is to say, along any particular dimension of uncertainty, decision makers do not have access to an even marginally informative probability distribution with respect to the potential outcomes. It is not difficult to demonstrate that ignorance plays a large part in the process of technological change! However, rather than arguing over the differences between Arrovian and Knightian uncertainty (which is how economists phrase this distinction between measurable and unmeasurable uncertainty), the next section of this chapter will outline a number of important dimensions along which uncertainty plays a role in the rate and direction of inventive activity and diffusion. Taken together, we have very little information, even retrospectively, about the relationships among these different dimensions. If uncertainty exists along more than one dimension, and the decision maker does not have information about the joint distribution of all the relevant random variables, then there is little reason to believe that a "rational" decision is possible, or that there will be a well-defined "optimal" investment or adoption strategy.

Dimensions of Uncertainty

Why is it so difficult to foresee the impact of even technologically practicable inventions? Much of the relevant literature emphasizes the huge uncertainty that has attached to the question "Will it work?" This is clearly a major source of uncertainty, but the fixation upon workability has served to distract attention from several other, more subtle and overlapping sources. We turn now to a consideration of these sources.

First, it is not only that new technologies come into the world in a very primitive condition; they also often come into the world with properties and characteristics whose usefulness cannot be immediately appreciated. It is inherently difficult to identify uses for new technologies. The laser (Light Amplification by Stimulated Emission and Radiation) represents, at one level, simply a light beam formed by the excitation of atoms at high energy levels. It has turned out that laser action can occur with a wide range of materials, including gases, liquids, and solids. The uses to which this capability has been put have been growing for 30 years, and will doubtless continue to grow for a long time, just as it took many decades to explore the uses to which electricity could be put after Faraday discovered the principles of electromagnetic induction in 1831.[1]

An essential aspect of both electricity and the laser is that neither represented an obvious substitute for anything that already existed. Neither had a clearly defined antecedent. Rather, each was a newly discovered phenomenon that was the outcome of pure scientific research.[2]

In the field of medical diagnostics, it has frequently happened that after some new visualization technology has been developed, it has taken a long time to learn how to translate the new observational capability into clinically useful terms. This has been the case with respect to CAT scanners, magnetic resonance imaging (MRI), and most recently echo cardiography. Often a great deal of time-consuming additional research has been required before it was possible to make a reliable, clinically helpful interpretation of what was already being visualized in terms of the diagnosis of a disease condition in the heart, lungs, or brain.

This is presently the case with respect to PET—positron emission tomography. PET scanners are powerful tools for providing a quantitative analysis of certain physiological functions, unlike CAT and MRI, which are valuable for anatomical observation. Thus, it has a great potential for providing useful information on the effectiveness, for example, of drug therapy for the treatment of various diseases, such as brain tumors. But quite aside from the huge cost of this technology, its clinical application in such fields as neurology, cardiology, and oncology has so far been limited by the continuing difficulties of translating observations and measurements of physiological functions into specific, meaningful clinical interpretations.

There is a related point in the currently burgeoning field of medical innovation. The inherent complexity of the human body and, perhaps equally important, the heterogeneity of human bodies have rendered it extremely difficult to tease out cause-effect relationships, even in the case of medications that have been widely used for long periods of time. Aspirin (acetylsalicylic acid), probably the world's most widely used drug, has been

---

1. It is recorded that a skeptical MP turned up at Faraday's laboratory shortly after his discovery of electromagnetic induction and asked him in a rather supercilious tone what it was good for. Faraday is supposed to have replied, "Sir, I do not know what it is good for. But of one thing I am quite certain: some day you will tax it."

2. In fact, Einstein had already worked out the pure science underlying laser action in 1916, in a paper on stimulated emission. From the point of view of the history of science, it might be said that there was "nothing new" when laser technology was developed some 45 years later, although in fact a Nobel Prize was awarded for the achievement. From the point of view of technological change and its economic and social impact, the development of the laser was, of course, a major event.

in use for very nearly a century, but only in the last few years has its efficacy been established for reducing the incidence of heart attacks as a consequence of its blood-thinning properties.

Although the discovery of negative side effects has received far more public attention, the discovery of unexpected beneficial new uses for old pharmaceutical products is a common, and often serendipitous, experience. Another significant case in point has been the applications of andrenergic beta-blocking drugs, one of the more significant medical innovations of our time. These compounds were originally introduced for the treatment of two cardiovascular indications, arrythmias and angina pectoris. Today they are used in the treatment of more than twenty diverse conditions, largely as a result of new uses that were uncovered after they had been introduced into cardiology. These include such non-cardiac indications as gastrointestinal bleeding, hypertension, and alcoholism (Gelijns, 1991, pp. 121, 269). Similar experiences could be related with respect to AZT (currently employed in the treatment of AIDS patients), oral contraceptives, RU-486, streptokynase, alpha interferon, and Prozac. More generally, the widespread "off-label" use of many drugs is a good indication of the pervasiveness of ex ante uncertainty in medical innovation.

Second, the impact of an innovation depends not only on improvements of the invention, but also on improvements that take place in complementary inventions. For the lawyers at Bell Labs to have had some appreciation of the importance of the laser for telephone communication, they would have required some sense of the technology of fiber optics, and the ways in which lasers and fiber optics might be combined. The laser was in fact of no particular use in telephone transmission without the availability of fiber optics. Telephone transmission is being transformed today by the combined potential of these two technologies. Optical fibers did in fact exist in a rather primitive form in the early 1960s, when the first lasers were developed, but not in a form that could accommodate the requirements of telephone transmission. In fact, it is interesting to note that an excellent book on the telecommunications industry, published as recently as 1981, provides no discussion whatever of this new fiber optic technology (Brock, 1982). As is often the case, it took a number of years for some of the attractive properties of fiber optic technology to become apparent: the lack of electromagnetic interference, the conservation of heat and electricity, and the enormous expansion in bandwidth that fiber optics can provide— the last feature a consequence of the fact that the light spectrum is approximately 1000 times wider than the radio spectrum.

The general point is that the impact of invention A will often depend upon invention B, and invention B may not yet exist. But perhaps a more useful formulation is to say that inventions will often give rise to a search for complementary inventions. An important impact of invention A is to increase the demand for invention B. The declining price of electricity, after the introduction of the dynamo in the early 1880s, stimulated the search for technologies that could exploit this unique form of energy. But the time frame over which such complementary innovations could be developed turned out to vary considerably. The search gave rise almost instantly to a burgeoning electrochemical industry, employing electrolytic techniques (aluminum), but a much longer period of time was required before the development of the complementary electric motor that was to become ubiquitous in the twentieth century. Similarly, a main reason for the modest future prospects that were being predicted for the computer in the late 1940s was that transistors had not yet been incorporated into the computers of the day. Introducing the transistor, and later integrated circuits, into computers were, of course, momentous events that transformed the computer industry. Indeed, in one of the most remarkable technological achievements of the twentieth century, the integrated circuit eventually became a computer, with the advent of the microprocessor in 1970. The world would be a far different place today if computers were still being made with vacuum tubes.

The need to develop complementary technologies may have a great deal to do with the apparent failure of computer technology in the last couple of decades to raise the level of U.S. productivity growth above its rather dismal recent levels. Robert Solow has made the observation that we see computers everywhere today except in the productivity statistics. But it appears to be typical of truly major innovations that they take a long time to absorb. The historical experience with respect to the introduction of electricity offers many earlier parallels. If we date the beginning of the electric age in the early 1880s, with the invention of dynamos, it was fully 40 years—into the 1920s—before the electrification of factories began to show up in terms of significant measured productivity growth (Du Boff, 1967; Devine, 1983; Schurr, 1990).

Major new technological regimes take many years before they replace an established technology. The delay is due partly to having to develop numerous components of a larger technological system—an issue that will be addressed shortly. Restructuring a factory around an electric power source, in place of the earlier steam engine or water power, commonly required a complete redesign and restructuring of a factory facility. It represented, among other things, a revolution in the principles of factory organization. The layout of the machinery in the factory now had far more flexibility than it did with the old power sources. Learning how best to exploit a new, highly versatile power source with entirely different methods of power transmission inside the plant involved decades of experimentation and learning. Indeed, such technological innovations commonly require significant organizational changes as well.

Moreover, firms that had huge investments in manufacturing plants that still had long productive lives ahead of them were naturally reluctant to discard a facility that was still perfectly usable. As a result, if we ask who were the early adopters of electricity in the first twenty years of the twentieth century, it turns out that they were mainly new industries that were setting up production facilities for the first time, like producers of "tobacco, fabricated metals, transportation equipment and electrical machinery itself." In the older, established industries the introduction of electric power had to await the "physical depreciation of durable factory structures," and the "obsolescence of older-vintage industrial plants sited in urban core areas" (David, 1990, p. 357).

The general point is that a radical new technology such as a computer must necessarily have a very long gestation period before its characteristics and opportunities are well understood and can be thoroughly exploited. In 1910 only 25 percent of U.S. factories used electric power. But twenty years later, in 1930, it had risen to 75 percent. History suggests that we should not be terribly surprised. For comparison, if we date the beginning of the modern computer (a much more complex general-purpose technology than electricity) from the invention of the microprocessor in 1970, we are still only a quarter-century into the computer age. It took some 40 years or so before electric power came to play a dominating role in manufacturing. History strongly suggests that technological revolutions are not completed overnight. If this is correct, it should be a source of optimism. The great economic benefits of the computer may still lie before us!

Third, as a closely connected point, major technological innovations often constitute entirely new technological systems. But it is difficult in the extreme to conceptualize an entirely new system. Thus, thinking about new technologies is likely to be severely handicapped by the tendency to think of them in terms of the old technologies that they eventually replace. Time and again, contemporaries of a new technology are found to have thought about it as a mere supplement that would offset certain inherent limitations of an existing technology. In the 1830s and 1840s, railroads were thought of merely as feeders into the existing canal system, to be constructed in places where the terrain had rendered canals inherently impractical (Fogel, 1964). This is precisely the same difficulty that was later encountered by the radio. Similarly, the telephone was originally conceptualized as primarily a business instrument, like the telegraph, to be used to exchange very specific messages, such as the terms of a prospective contractual agreement. This may, of course, explain why Bell's telephone patent was, as mentioned earlier, titled "Improvements in Telegraphy."

It is characteristic of a system that improvements in performance in one part are of only limited significance without simultaneous improvements in other parts. In this sense, technological systems may be thought of as comprising clusters of complementary inventions. Improvements in power generation can only have a limited impact on the delivered cost of electricity until improvements are made in the transmission network and the cost of transporting electricity over long distances. This need for further innovation in complementary activities is an important reason why even apparently spectacular breakthroughs usually have only a slowly rising productivity curve flowing from them. Within technological systems, therefore, major improvements in productivity seldom flow from single technological innovations, however significant they may appear to be. At the same time, the cumulative effects of large numbers of improvements within a technological system may eventually be immense.

Fourth, an additional and historically very important reason why it has been so difficult to foresee the uses of a new technology is that many major inventions had their origins in the attempt to solve very specific, and often very narrowly defined, problems. However, it is common that once a solution has been found, it turns out to have significant applications in totally unanticipated contexts. That is to say, much of the impact of new technologies is realized through intersectoral flows. Inventions have very serendipitous life histories (Rosenberg, 1976, chap. 1).

The steam engine, for example, was invented in the eighteenth century specifically as a device for pumping water out of flooded mines. In fact, it was, for a long time, regarded exclusively as a pump. A succession of improvements later rendered it a feasible source of power for textile factories, iron mills, and an expanding array of industrial establishments. In the course of the early nineteenth century, the steam engine became a generalizable source of power and had major applications in transportation: railroads, steamships, and steamboats. In fact, before the Civil War, the main use of the steam engine in the United States was not in manufacturing at all but in transportation. Later in the nineteenth century, the steam engine was, for a time, used to produce a new and even more generalizable source of power—electricity—which, in turn, satisfied innumerable final uses to which steam power itself was not directly applicable. Finally, the steam turbine displaced the steam engine in the generation of electric power, and the special features of electricity—its ease of transmission over long distances, its capacity for making power available in "fractionalized" units, and the far greater flexibility of electricity-powered equipment—sounded the eventual death knell of the steam engine itself.

Major innovations, such as the steam engine, once they have been established, have the effect of inducing further innovations and investments over a wide frontier. Indeed, the ability to induce such further innovations and investments is a reasonably good definition of what constitutes a major innovation. It is a useful way of distinguishing between technological advances that are merely invested with great novelty from advances that have the potential for a major economic impact. But this also highlights the difficulties in foreseeing the eventual impact, since that will depend on the size and the direction of these future complementary innovations and associated investments.

The life history of the steam engine was shaped by forces that could hardly have been foreseen by British inventors who were working on ways of removing water from increasingly flooded coal mines in the eighteenth century. Nevertheless, the very existence of the steam engine, once its operating principles had been thoroughly understood, served as a powerful stimulus to other inventions.

I have been stressing here the observations that innovations often arise as solutions to highly specific problems in a particular industry, and that their subsequent inter-industry flow is bound to be highly uncertain. This is because the uses of a new technology in a quite different industrial context are especially difficult to anticipate. Yet in some cases a new technological capability may have multiple points of impact on another industry.

Consider the impact of the computer upon the air transportation industry. I would suggest that the changing performance of commercial air transportation has been influenced at least as much by the application of the computer to new uses in this industry as by the R&D spending that has taken place within the industry itself. Consider seven substantial impacts of computers on the airline industry:

1. Supercomputers now perform a good deal of fundamental aerodynamic research, including much of the research that was formerly performed in wind tunnels.

2. Computers have been a major source of cost reduction in the design of specific components of aircraft, such as wings. They played an im-

portant role in the wing designs of the Boeing 747, 757, and 767, as well as the Airbus 310.

3. Computers are now responsible for much of the activity that takes place in the cockpit, including, of course, the automatic pilot.

4. Computers, together with weather satellites, which routinely determine the shifting locations of high-altitude jet streams, are now widely used in determining optimal flight paths. The fuel savings for the world commercial airline industry is probably well in excess of $1 billion per year. (Note that this is yet another important case of the economic impact of a technology, the computer, depending upon a complementary technology that was developed many years later, weather satellites.)

5. Computers and computer networks are at the heart of the present worldwide ticketing and seating reservation system.

6. Computer simulation is now the preferred method of instruction in teaching neophytes how to fly.

7. The computer, together with radar, has become absolutely central to the operation of the air traffic control system, which would be difficult to imagine without it.

One important implication of this discussion is that R&D spending tends to be highly concentrated in a small number of industries. However, each of these few industries needs to be regarded as the locus of research activity that generates new technologies that may be widely diffused throughout the entire economy. Historically, a small number of industries have played this role in especially crucial ways: steam engines, electricity, machine tools, computers, transistors, and so on. This reinforces the earlier suggestion that we may even define a major or breakthrough innovation as one that establishes a new framework for the working out of incremental innovations. In this sense, incremental innovations are the natural complements of breakthrough innovations. Breakthrough innovations, in turn, have often provided the basis for the emergence of entirely new industries.

The fifth and final constraint is rather less precise than the rest but, I believe, no less important. It is that the ultimate impact of some new technological capability is not just a matter of technical feasibility or improved technical performance; rather, it is a matter of identifying certain specific categories of human needs and catering to them in novel or cost-effective ways. New technologies need to pass an economic test, not just a technological one. Thus, the Concorde is a spectacular success in terms of flight performance, but it has proven to be a financial disaster, costing British and French taxpayers several billions of dollars.

Ultimately, what is often called for is not just technical expertise but also an exercise of the imagination. Understanding the technical basis for wireless communication, which Marconi did, was a very different matter from anticipating how the device might be used to enlarge the human experience. Marconi had no sense of this. On the other hand, an uneducated Russian immigrant to the United States, David Sarnoff, had a lively vision of how the new technology might be used to transmit news, music, and other forms of entertainment and information into every household (and eventually automobile) in the country. Sarnoff, in brief, appreciated the commercial possibilities of the new technology. Sarnoff's vision, of course, eventually prevailed under his leadership of RCA after the First World War (Bilby, 1985).

Similarly, Howard Aiken, a Harvard physics instructor who was a great pioneer in the early development of the computer, continued to think of it in the narrow context in which its early development took place—that is, purely as a device for solving esoteric scientific problems. As late as 1956 he stated, "If it should ever turn out that the basic logics of a machine designed for the numerical solution of differential equations coincide with the logics of a machine intended to make bills for a department store, I would regard this as the most amazing coincidence that I have ever encountered" (Ceruzzi, 1987, p. 197). That is, of course, precisely how it turned out, but it was hardly a coincidence. A technology originally invented for one specific purpose—the numerical solution of large sets of differential equations—could readily be redesigned to solve problems in entirely different contexts, such as the making out of bills for department stores. But it obviously was not obvious!

The essential point, of course, is that social change or economic impact is not something that can be extrapolated out of a piece of hardware. Rather, new technologies need to be conceived of as building blocks. Their eventual impact will depend on what is subsequently designed and constructed with them. New technologies are unrealized potentials that may take a very large number of eventual shapes. What shapes they actually take will depend on the ability to visualize how they might be employed in new contexts. Sony's development of Walkman is a brilliant example of how existing technologies—batteries, magnetic tapes, and earphones—could be recombined to create an entirely new product that could provide entertainment in contexts where it could not previously be delivered—where, indeed, no one had previously even thought of delivering it, like to joggers and walkers. To be sure, the product required a great deal of engineering redesign of existing components, but the real breakthrough was the identification, by Akio Morita, of a market opportunity that had not been previously identified.

Although many Americans continue to believe that the VCR was an American invention, that is simply an unsupportable perception. The American pioneers in this field, RCA and Ampex, gave up long before a truly usable product had been developed. Matsushita and Sony, on the other hand, made thousands of small improvements in design and manufacturing after the American firms had essentially left the field. These developments were closely connected to another point. A crucial step forward in the development of the VCR was the realization that there was a potential mass market in households if certain performance characteristics of the product, especially the size of its storage capacity, could be sufficiently expanded. Although the initial American conception of the VCR had been of a capital good to be used by television stations, some American as well as Japanese participants were aware of the much larger home market possibilities. The crucial difference seems to have been the Japanese confidence, based upon their own manufacturing experience, that they could achieve the necessary cost reductions and performance improvements. The rapid transformation of the VCR into one of Japan's largest export products was therefore an achievement of both imagination and justified confidence in their engineering capabilities (Rosenbloom and Cusumano, 1987).

The limited view once held by Americans of the potential for the VCR bears some parallels with the disdain of the mainframe computer makers toward the personal computer as it began to emerge about fifteen years ago. It was then fashionable to dismiss the PC as a mere "hacker's toy," with no real prospects in the business world, and therefore no serious threat to the economic future of mainframes (*New York Times*, Apr. 20, 1994, p. c1).

Reviving Old Technologies—or Killing Them Off

My analysis has focused on barriers to the exploitation of new technologies. But of course, in highly competitive societies where there are strong incentives to innovation, those incentives apply to improving old technologies as well as to inventing new ones. In fact, innovations often appear to induce vigorous and imaginative responses on the part of firms which find themselves confronted with close substitutes for their traditional products. It is not at all uncommon to find that the competitive pressure resulting from a new technology leads to an accelerated improvement in the old technology. Some of the greatest improvements in wooden sailing ships took place between 1850 and 1880, just after the introduction of the iron-hull steamship and the compound steam engine, which were to displace sailing ships by the beginning of the twentieth century. Included were drastic improvements in hull design that allowed greater speed, more cargo in proportion to the tonnage of the ship, and, above all, the introduction of labor-saving machinery that reduced crew requirements by no less than two-thirds. Similarly, the greatest improvements in gas lamps, used for interior lighting, occurred shortly after the introduction of the incandescent electric light bulb (Rosenberg, 1976, chap. 11).

A major feature of the postwar telecommunications industry is that research has increased the capabilities of the already-installed transmission system, in addition to leading to the development of new and more productive transmission technologies. Every major transmission system—a pair of wires, coaxial cables, microwaves, satellites, fiber optics—has been subject to extensive later improvements in message-carrying capabilities, often with only relatively minor modification of the existing transmission technology. In some cases, there have been order-of-magnitude increases in the message-carrying capability of an existing channel, such as a ⅜-inch coaxial cable, and such productivity improvements have frequently led to the postponement of the introduction of new generations of transmission technologies. For example, time-division multiplexing allowed an existing pair of wires to carry 24 voice channels or more rather than the single channel that it originally carried. The same pattern is observed in fiber optic technology. When AT&T began field trials with fiber optics in the mid-1970s, information was transmitted at 45 megabytes per second. By the early 1990s, the standard for new fiber optic cables had reached 565 megabytes per second, with reliable sources predicting capacities of nearly 1,000 megabytes per second in the near future.

But it is not only the case that the introduction of new technologies often has to await the availability of complementary technologies and that, in the meantime, established technologies may achieve renewed competitive vigor through continual improvements. New technologies may also turn out to be substitutes rather than complements for existing ones, thus drastically shortening the life expectancy of technologies that once seemed to warrant distinctly bullish expectations. The future prospects for communication satellites declined quite unexpectedly during the 1980s with the introduction of fiber optics and the huge and reliable expansion of channel capacity that they brought with them. In turn, fiber optics, whose first significant application was in medical diagnostics in the early 1960s, may now be approaching the beginning of the end of its useful life in that field. Fiber optic endoscopes had made possible a huge improvement in minimally invasive techniques for visualizing the gastro-intestinal tract. Recently, new sensors from the realm of electronics, charged couple devices (CCDs), have begun to provide images with a quality of resolution and degree of detail that could not possibly be provided by fiber optic devices. The CAT scanner, certainly one of the great diagnostic breakthroughs of the twentieth century, is giving way to MRI, which possesses an even more powerful diagnostic capability. Uncertainties of this sort impart a large element of risk to long-term investments in expensive new technologies. The competitive process that eventually resolves these uncertainties is not the traditional textbook competition among producers of a homogeneous product, each seeking to deliver the same product to the market at a lower cost. Rather, it is a competition among different technologies, a process that Schumpeter appropriately described as "creative destruction." Thus, it is no paradox to say that one of the greatest uncertainties confronting new technologies is the invention of yet newer ones.

The simultaneous advances in new technology, along with the substantial upgrading of old technology, underlines the pervasive uncertainty confronting industrial decision makers in a world of rapid technological change. One would have to be very optimistic, as well as naive, to think that some intellectual paradigm can be developed to handle all the relevant variables in some neat and systematic way. But it may be plausible to believe that a more rigorous analysis of the issues that have been raised here may lead to a considerable improvement in the way we think about the innovation process.

We can now return to the point made earlier: the lack of knowledge about the relationships between these different dimensions of uncertainty prevents us from understanding the total effect of uncertainty upon technological change. For example, two dimensions of uncertainty, discussed above, concern the refinement of complementary technologies and the potential for any technology to form the core of a new technological system. Even at the simplest level, it is difficult to be precise about the interaction between these different effects. The existence and refinement of complementary technologies may exercise a coercive and conservative effect, forcing the novel technology to be placed inside the current "system." Alternatively, however, complementary technologies may be exactly what is necessary for the practical realization of an entirely new system. My point is not to decide one way or the other on these issues; instead, it is to argue that a research program that neglects these interactions may be missing a very large part of how uncertainty has shaped the rate and direction of technological change and, by extension, the historical growth experience.

Conclusion

It is not part of my warrant to offer policy recommendations. However, a few closing observations may be in order.

The research community is currently being exhorted with increasing force to unfurl the flag of "relevance" to social and economic needs. The burden of much that has been said here is that we frequently simply do not know what new findings may turn out to be relevant, or to what particular realm of human activity that relevance may eventually apply. Indeed, I have been staking the broad claim that a pervasive uncertainty characterizes not only basic research, where it is generally acknowledged, but also the realm of product design and new-product development—that is, the D of R&D. Consequently, early precommitment to any specific, large-scale technology project, as opposed to a more limited, sequential decision-making approach, is likely to be wasteful. Evidence for this assertion abounds in such government-sponsored projects as weapons procurement, the space program, research on the development of an artificial heart, and research on synthetic fuels.

The pervasiveness of uncertainty suggests that the government should ordinarily resist the temptation to play the role of a champion of any one technological alternative, such as nuclear power, or any narrowly concentrated focus of research support, such as the War on Cancer. Rather, it would seem to make a great deal of sense to manage a deliberately diversified research portfolio, a portfolio that is likely to illuminate a range of alternatives in the event of a reordering of social or economic priorities or the unexpected failure of any single, major research thrust. Government policy ought to be to open many windows and to provide the private sector with financial incentives to explore the technological landscape that can only be faintly discerned from those windows. Thus, my criticism of the federal government's postwar energy policy is not that it made a major commitment to nuclear power that subsequently turned out to be problem-ridden. A more appropriate criticism is aimed at the single-mindedness of the focus on nuclear power that led to a comparative neglect of many other alternatives, including not only alternative energy sources but also improvements in the efficiency of energy utilization.

The situation with respect to the private sector is obviously different. Private firms may normally be expected to allocate their R&D funds in ways that they hope will turn out to be relevant. Private firms are very much aware that they confront huge uncertainties in the marketplace, and they are capable of making their own assessments and placing their "bets" accordingly. Bad bets are, of course, common, indeed so common that it is tempting to conclude that the manner in which competing firms pursue innovation is a very wasteful process. Such a characterization would be appropriate were it not for a single point: uncertainty. In fact, a considerable virtue of the marketplace is that in the face of huge uncertainties concerning the uses of new technological capabilities, it encourages exploration along a wide variety of alternative paths. This is especially desirable in the early stages, when uncertainties are particularly high and when individuals with differences of opinion (often based upon differences in access to information) need to be encouraged to pursue their own hunches or intuitions. Indeed, it is important that this point should be stated more affirmatively: the achievement of technological progress, in the face of numerous uncertainties, requires such differences of opinion.

Finally, a further considerable virtue of the marketplace is that it also provides strong incentives to terminate, quickly and unsentimentally, directions of research whose once-rosy prospects have been unexpectedly dimmed by the availability of new data, by some change in the economic environment, or by a restructuring of social or political priorities. For a country that currently supports more than 700 federal laboratories with a total annual budget of over $23 billion, more than half of which is devoted to weapons development or other defense-related purposes, that is no small virtue.

PART VI

Performance of
Key Industries

The Competitive Crash in Large-Scale Commercial Computing

TIMOTHY F. BRESNAHAN AND

SHANE GREENSTEIN

The appearance of a new technology offering lower costs or superior capabilities rarely leads to instant replacement of the old technology. Many important historical examples display this pattern: steam ships versus sailing ships; diesel locomotives versus steam locomotives; equipment for the basic oxygen process for steel versus the open-hearth process; jet engines in commercial aircraft versus propeller engines; numerically controlled machine tools replacing those that were not numerically controlled; and many others (Mansfield, 1968; Rosenberg, 1982; Rogers, 1983; Ray, 1984; Stoneman, 1988). In each case, it is not surprising that the old technology stayed in use; users may be reluctant to retire capital that continues to offer a flow of useful services, even if technical change apparently depreciates the market value of those services. What is surprising is that the old technology continued to sell and to compete viably long after the introduction of the new.

The equilibrium pace of diffusion of a new technology depends not only on developments within that new technology but also on the behavior of customers and older competitors. Buyers may delay their purchase of the new technology until anticipated price/performance improvements materialize. Often buyers need to become informed or to make other investments to take advantage of "enabling" technologies.[1] Sellers of the old

We would like to thank participants at many seminars for their comments. Ken Brown, Denise Chachere, and Harumi Ito provided outstanding research assistance. Kathryn Graddy, Tom Hubbard, Scott Stern, Garth Saloner, and the editors provided many useful comments. We also thank the Institute for Government and Policy Analysis at the University of Illinois, the Center for Economic Policy Research, the Sloan Foundation, and the National Science Foundation for funding.

    1. See, inter alia, Bresnahan and Trajtenberg (1995) for the widespread importance of this phenomenon in connection with general-purpose technologies.

technology may find their competitive circumstances changed, and react with new pricing or technology strategies. Clearly, the pace of adoption of the new technology, the pace of retirement of the old, and the competition between old and new determine average practice in the economy and, ultimately, the equilibrium pace of creation of social returns.

This historical pattern is reappearing in contemporary information technology. Large complex computer installations are in the process of shifting to a new technological base. For many years, large organizations were forced to rely on expensive mainframe and supermini computers and the proprietary system software and networking technology that accompanied them. More recently, microprocessor-based smaller systems have begun to compete for use in these very large applications. The process of transition has been called many things, but we will call it "downsizing" to "client/server architectures." A transition from old to new has clearly begun. Only its pace and character are still somewhat sketchy.

This transition is more than just a story about the speed of technology diffusion. It also coincides with a major change in information technology firm and industry structure, where the contrasts between old and new structure are hard to miss (Grove, 1990). Most of the old suppliers maintain vertically integrated organizations, with proprietary rights over their technologies. A single firm, the system supplier, influences the development of all hardware and software technologies. It is widely anticipated that the industry structure associated with the new technology will resemble the current structure of the personal computer industry. Competing specialized supplier firms influence different hardware, software, and networking technologies, and no single firm monopolizes the rate and direction of technical change. The anticipation that all of these changes are a serious possibility has already led market observers to devalue the property rights over technologies held by vertically integrated suppliers.[2] This is the "competitive crash" of our title.

The pace of creation of social gains to the new technology has been slow. This is due primarily to slow buyer adoption of the new technology, which contrasts with the rapid advance in the capabilities of that technology (Caldwell, 1994; Ambrosio, 1993). Again, there is (recent) historical precedent for this contrast—it is just an exaggerated version of normal relations in information technology. The information technology industry contains some of the most rapid sustained technical progress in modern economies

2. See "Hardware and Tear" (1992) about destruction of rents at IBM, and Sherman (1991) about DEC. Also, see Hall (1993) for estimates of the decline in the private return to R&D at incumbent large-system vendors in the computer industry.

(consider the integrated circuit) as well as somewhat slower technical progress (consider software) and some very slow progress (consider organizational change and systems development to make full use of computer and data telecommunications technologies). We investigate the competitive crash to understand the forces underlying buyers' slow movements.

The goal of this chapter is to examine the factors underlying buyer demand for large information technology solutions. This goal takes advantage of the natural experiment embodied in the current choice between old and new: recent choice behavior illuminates what demanders really value. Understanding what buyers value not only illuminates the factors underlying the competitive crash, but also the factors underlying the slow realization of the social gains to information technology in large complex applications more generally. We use systematic statistical methods and focus on the early period of diffusion of client/server architectures, through 1991. In this early period, there is very little actual choice of the new technology. Yet it is not competitively irrelevant. Buyers chose, in very substantial numbers, to wait for the new technology to mature. This very substantially lowered demand for the old technology. Demand behavior regarding the old technology is the best available observable information about the early competition between old and new.[3]

Demand for the old technology is well documented in large data sets. Our investigations are based on individual user site data on mainframe hardware and software collected by Computer Intelligence Corporation. We contrast two periods to learn about the competitive crash. The first is in the mid-1980s, late in the period of a mature and stable large-systems market. The other period is the early 1990s, very early in the diffusion of the new client/server technology. Our study provides the first systematic statistical analysis of buyers of large computer systems confronted with the new technological opportunity.

There is controversy about the appropriate theory for understanding the buyer behavior behind the slow diffusion of client/server technology. All reasonable views explain the slow transition as a balance between forces moving buyers forward and other forces holding them back. In the dominant view, the forward-moving forces are the lower costs of the microprocessor-based systems used in client/server architectures. The backward-looking forces are the slow development of client/server software and the sunk investments large users have made with old, proprie-

---

3. More anecdotal but less consistent and comprehensive information is available from interviews and from the trade press. We take up the relationship between our results and the results of the 1992 and 1993 Bresnahan-Saloner (1994) interview study below.

tary architectures. Yet there are other views as well. Another important hypothesis about the new technologies is that they themselves will alleviate the bottlenecks in information technology commercialization. This view emphasizes the superior features, not lower costs, of microprocessor-based computing. Many buyers would say that the full benefits of client/server architectures, like those of most networking and software technologies, will be difficult to achieve and therefore very slow. We will attempt to clarify the testable implications of these different theories of the competitive crash and then test them.

We do not see this as a backward-looking study of the death of an old technology. We expect a reversal of some of the trends of the late 1970s and 1980s, when small-systems solutions to individual or small-group business problems were the cutting edge and a smaller fraction of total information technology spending went to solving large-business information problems. Networking today, especially over wide areas, is driving a new secular increase in the importance of organization-wide or even inter-organization computing. Understanding the economic process underlying demand for those large-scale computer projects has lasting value.

Investment in Large-Scale Information Technology Solutions

To model the demand for large-scale computing, in either mainframe or client/server form, we begin with the observation that many user organizations have business needs calling for large, complex hardware and software systems. Typically, these systems are not merely purchased from outside the organization, but involve substantial programming at the user's site and even substantial redesign of business practices (Friedman and Cornford, 1989). These projects can be quite large, so that adjustment of the stock of information technology capital is costly. There is a normative literature advising managers how to minimize these adjustment costs, but little quantitative work on their size or origins.[4] In this section, we review

4. Most quantitative literature on the demand for computing uses hedonic measurement in an attempt to quantify the value of computers in use. Triplett (1989) summarizes the literature covering mainframes; more recent evidence in this area comes from Dulberger (1989), Gordon (1989, 1990), and Oliner (1993). Stavins (1996), Berndt and Griliches (1993), and Berndt, Griliches, and Rappaport (1993) have conducted hedonic microcomputer studies. A second branch of the literature on demand for computing focuses on the relationship between computerization and productivity, as in Berndt and Morrison (1991). Loveman (1994) and Brynjolfsson (1993) review this literature. Another branch tries to estimate the aggregate marketwide value of different forms of computerization by demand analysis (Bresnahan, 1986; Flamm, 1987; Brynjolfsson, 1993), sometimes using micro data (Trajtenberg, 1990; Greenstein, 1995).

the investment process for large projects in general. The next section turns to several specific theories of the adjustment from mainframe to client/ server architectures in particular.

We use the Friedman and Cornford "map" (1989, p. 46f) of the position of computer systems in large organizations. It speaks to four distinct complementary assets which are part of adjustment of useful computing capacity. The "computer system core" consists of hardware *and* software acquired from outside the using organization. The "uses of computer applications" are large organization-wide demands for data processing services. These are backbone financial applications such as payroll or accounting, or operations support applications like reservations systems in airlines or accounts processing in banking.[5] The "mediating process" between usage and the computer systems core is undertaken by employees of the using organization (or consultants to it) to make the computer systems core useful. Typically, most of the mediating functions are done by a specialized management information systems (MIS) staff.

They undertake three main kinds of activities. The least frequent and most expensive are whole new applications. End-user departments and MIS jointly work out what broad applications are needed. Then MIS undertakes detailed systems analysis and programming to realize those goals in part. This process is typically denominated in years, not months, and is undertaken by very large teams. More frequently, users and MIS discover problems with existing applications, or request new kinds of reports based on existing data. The maintenance and new-report programming backlog is typically months rather than days. An intermediate category arises when systems usage presses against systems capacity, and MIS manages the tran-

---

Only a few papers look at the theory of demand, and those are confined to very special groups of demanders (Greenstein, 1991, 1992).

Non-statistical literature on the value of computers in use is largely normative. A positive analysis has been provided by Friedman and Cornford (1989). Scott-Morton (1991) and Allen and Scott-Morton (1994) contain essays that are good examples of the positive and normative literature.

5. This definition excludes personal productivity applications running on personal computers or workstations. The usage category boundaries are hard to define precisely in a technical way. Small systems, for example, replaced many time-sharing usages of mainframes over a decade ago. The same applications that require mainframe power in larger areas can be mini-computer "departmental computing" or even micro-computer "small business computing" in other contexts. So the definition of the category boundary depends on both the size and complexity of the user organization and the business purpose of the application. Our definition is pragmatic, the kinds of applications for which mainframes were deployed in the mid-1980s. Our description of them, and our language, closely follows the standard systems-choice doctrine of that era (Inmon, 1985).

sition to new (frequently compatible but involving work to install) higher-capacity systems. This third category is often caused by the second—better systems get more use, and more reports eat up more computing resources. The third category often merges into the first—increased purchases of hardware and software capacity will often be the occasion for increasing an application's features. These upgrades/improvements also can take significant time to build.[6]

As a result, most important expansions of capacity, whether new systems or major upgrades/improvements, involve changes in hardware, externally acquired software, on-site technical work, and changes in business procedures together. For this reason, we feel confident that using changes in hardware capacity offers a good way to observe large projects. As long as we catch both major upgrades and whole new systems, hardware expansions and new projects should largely overlap.

These expansions and upgrades obviously involve investment costs which are irreversible in part. While mainframe hardware can be leased, and mainframe software typically has annual license fees, the costs of in-house and consultant programming typically are irreversible. From reports on the budgets of a typical MIS staff in our time period, it seems clear that the latter, irreversible budget category is well under a half and probably no more than a third of total investment costs.[7] In earlier work with Harumi Ito, we quantified the fraction of project investment costs which sites appear to treat as irreversible. That led to a much larger estimate, around four-fifths.[8] The discrepancy in the two estimates is probably explained by irreversible investments in changed business practices accompanying projects, suggesting that these internal investments are roughly as large as hardware, acquired software, or local programming.

The analytical literature on investment (Dixit and Pindyck, 1994) and recent theoretical work on competition, standard setting, and the rate of technical progress in information technology industries has highlighted several distinct roles that buyer inertia or caution may play.[9] These are re-

---

6. Friedman and Cornford (1989) offer an excellent summary of both anecdotal and quantitative research on these processes.

7. See, for example, data processing budget stories in *Datamation* on April 1, 1986, and May 1, 1993. Friedman and Cornford (1989) also have useful information on this topic.

8. The source of this estimate is in a distinct treatment of increases in capacity versus decreases in capacity. (The present chapter examines only increases in capacity.) The decrease in demand that leads to capacity reduction is approximately four times as large as the increase in demand that leads to capacity expansion. Hence the four-fifths sunk estimate.

9. See David and Greenstein (1990) or Besen and Saloner (1988) for reviews.

flected in competing engineering and business theories of buyers' slow response to client/server architectures. In the next section, we attempt to organize these competing theories of the slow switch to client/server. That work emphasizes that the appropriate theory of the irreversible adjustment costs is as important as the size of the irreversible costs themselves.

Technological and Economic Theories of Slow Diffusion

Each of the currently available competing theories, as we shall see in this section, embodies an important truth about technical forces. Hypotheses about which of these forces are most important, however, are necessarily hypotheses about demand. In this section we go on to illuminate the testable implications of a variety of specific theories of the competitive crash.

The dominant view of the new competition contrasts an old, inferior technology with a new, superior one. Mainframes and other large computer systems, in this view, embody old hardware and software technologies. By contrast, microprocessor-based computer systems are the wave of the future. They are based around technologies that offer lower costs per unit of performance, and that promise more rapid technical progress in the future. In this view, the date of replacement of old systems by new is determined by the timing of technical advance. In particular, two main classes of technical advance were needed. The first was the emergence of a "mainframe on a chip." For some time, microprocessor-based computer systems offered cheaper price/performance, certainly cheaper measured by cost per millions of instructions per second (MIPS) and also by broader performance measures. Now the largest microprocessor-based systems have begun to offer these low costs at levels of performance comparable to large systems. The second advance needed was the emergence of fundamental software technologies such as operating systems, databases, and networks which would permit new systems to perform the traditional tasks of the old. The slow changeover is explained by the difference in technical progress between software and hardware. Throughout the period from 1989 to 1992, the hardware technical progress was typically described as recent, the software technical progress as imminent.[10]

This view is extremely attractive to technologists, in large part because of its compact and compelling description of technical progress. We call this view "competitive MIPS arbitrage." Obviously, it suggests a rosy fu-

---

10. Compare, for example, Kador (1992) to Keefe (1990) or Radding (1989). All describe the near-term possibilities in much the same terms.

ture for the social gains to information technology once a difficult period of adjustment has passed.

This first view explains the destruction of private rents in the old computer industry as an anticipated increase in replacement of old hardware by cheaper new hardware. That there are potential future substitution opportunities due to different hardware costs is not in serious dispute.[11] When they can actually perform this arbitrage, buyers will destroy the market power of sellers of old technologies—that is, they will flatten the demand curves for mainframe and supermini hardware and software. This is a powerful testable implication. It implies not only that the old system business was unprofitable overall, but also that it was unprofitable in the price-cost margin sense. Since over 80 percent of our sites use IBM mainframe architectures, it is probably appropriate to view our tests of this hypothesis as primarily about IBM mainframe market power.

Another very important technologists' view of recent changes emphasizes the different technical characteristics of traditional large and small systems. Large systems to solve large business problems are very powerful, but very difficult to use. The specialist programmers and others who use these systems, in this view, have also not been organized in a way that makes them very responsive to business end users. Programming backlogs are better measured in quarters than in weeks. This has been an ongoing frustration to computer-using organizations. A change occurred when business people in the organizations saw how quickly and easily easy-to-use microcomputers could solve real (but small) problems. There began to be very substantial demand for business computer systems that were as powerful as traditional mainframes yet as responsive and easy to use as micros. Client/server architectures attempt to accomplish this through the use of linked heterogeneous systems. In the second technologists' view, one should understand the competitive threat to traditional systems as coming from these superior technical features, not just lower costs. This view, too, is broadly held in the technical community.[12] It has even spilled over into the business strategy community. We summarize this view as "client/server best of both worlds."

The "best of both worlds" view is important because it captures some-

---

11. See interview with John F. Akers, IBM Corp. Chairman, in the July 15, 1991, issue of *Fortune* magazine.

12. See the same articles as in note 10 for journalists' views of this. This view tends to be held more by systems integrators, consultants, and client/server software engineers rather than by technologists from the small-systems world exclusively. An important version of this view links the payoff from information technology to a broader "reengineering of business processes." See, for example, Hammer and Champy (1993, chap. 5).

thing fundamental in the demand for large-systems, and links it to the successes of different technologies in the marketplace before the competitive crash. User organizations are deeply unhappy with the clumsiness of central MIS as an organizational solution.[13] Further, the theory is testable because there is considerable variety in the extent of this unhappiness. Under the best of both worlds theory, the kinds of sites for which professionalized MIS is a particularly unsatisfactory organizational solution should be those most eager to switch to client/server.

There is another theory based on much the same facts and history.[14] This theory agrees that the largest *potential* gains from client/server come in the organizations least satisfied with existing MIS. There is, however, an equilibrium reason for the dissatisfaction. These organizations are those in which the adjustment costs of change to use new information technology for business purposes have been the largest historically. In this story, these sites are simply those for which the problem of coordinated change in business practices and information technology is the most difficult. If the adjustment costs to client/server are very large at these same sites, they may find the switch both more attractive and more difficult than other sites. They could be, counting costs and benefits together, the least rather than the most interested in switching.

The relationship between the best of both worlds and adjustment costs theories is that they are opposites. Both order site organizations according to the degree to which there is dissatisfaction with existing MIS as an organizational solution in the mainframe era. In Figure 1, the horizontal axis captures this. As we move to the right, the existing internal organization of large-scale computing grows more complex and correspondingly less satisfactory. The existing set of information technology solutions is less satisfactory to, or less controlled by, the business organizations using them. Now, as we move to the right, both the benefits (best of both worlds) and difficulties (adjustment costs) of moving to new solutions rise. Under the best of both worlds theory, it is the benefits curve which rises more steeply, so the organizations to the right are the most interested in switching to client/server. Under the adjustment costs theory, we get the reverse. The cost curve rises more steeply than the benefits, and it is those organizations on the left switching to client/server.

---

13. Friedman and Cornford (1989) devote several chapters to the long history of this unhappiness.

14. This view is argued by Bresnahan and Saloner (1995) in connection with their interview study. It is clearly consistent with the theory of adjustment costs advanced by Friedman and Cornford (1989) for an earlier era. By late 1993 or early 1994, the trade press began to pick up these gripes from users. For example, see Caldwell (1994).

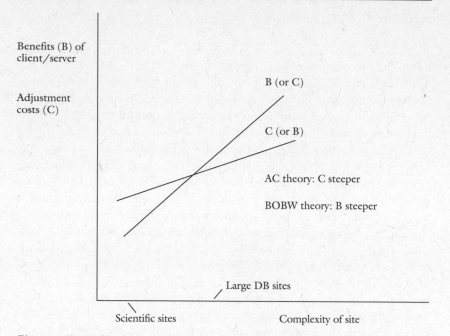

Benefits (B) of
client/server

Adjustment
costs (C)

B (or C)

C (or B)

AC theory: C steeper

BOBW theory: B steeper

Large DB sites

Scientific sites

Complexity of site

Figure 1. Best of both worlds theory versus adjustment cost theory.

Finally, the diffusion of new technologies may have been slowed by the possible lock-in of proprietary systems vendors at particular sites. The costs of existing ("legacy") applications may be not only irreversible, but irreversibly tied to the systems of a particular vendor. More plausibly, sites may vary in that some of them have very high costs of migrating away from their existing systems vendor, others lower costs. Similarly, the MIS department itself may have locked in a powerful internal political position and be resistant to change.

All of these stories have in common that there are powerful forces pulling demanders forward toward client/server. None of the theories suggests that client/server will not prevail in the long run. The stories differ in whether the client/server attractions are costs or features. More important, the stories differ in the nature of the forces holding back the diffusion of client/server—though clearly every theory must have such a force as well. Some posit a "lock-in" to existing assets: that is, the inertia of already sunk costs is holding back the diffusion. Others posit caution as a source of high forward-looking adjustment costs to new opportunities. Note that the theories do not differ in their predictions for the pace of diffusion in the early phases. Instead, they differ in the kinds of sites they predict to be faster or slower adopters.

Sample and Data

What kinds of sites change their demand for the old technology? Our strategy focuses on differences between large-system users who continue to add capacity to their installations and those who choose not to do so. We wish to identify which large-system users waited for client/server rather than expand the stocks of their general-purpose mainframes. To accomplish this goal, we use a database of many large-system users in the United States.

We examine individual site locations as measured by Computer Intelligence Corporation in their year-end surveys. We use two "triads" of data, 1984–85–86 and 1989–90–91. While the first triad is the oldest available to us, it also has the virtue that it represents a period of mature mainframe demand. The latter triad represents the beginning of the diffusion of client/server alternatives.[15] Characteristics of a site in a "base" year, 1984 or 1989, predict capacity expansion. We will interpret the kinds of sites with the largest otherwise unexplained downturns in mainframe demand (in a richly specified model) between the two triads as those who are waiting.

Our sample begins with all Computer Intelligence Corporation survey participants with at least one general-purpose mainframe in any of the six years. This is the most complete and richest panel data available on the use of large computing equipment. Roughly 14,000 sites appear in the Computer Intelligence Corporation sample in each year, which comprises somewhere between 70 and 80 percent of all general-purpose mainframe computer users, according to Computer Intelligence Corporation estimates. Each year new sites enter and some old sites exit; turnover is about 10 percent of the sample of sites each year. To be included in our analysis, the site can exit in the third year but not the second of each triad. Also, the site must have general-purpose mainframes and must have filled in the soft-

---

15. Investigation of periods after this very early one is going to call for more complex models than the simple ones reported here. We have acquired the more recent data for 1992 and 1993 and are in the process of analyzing it. Other issues arise in these periods. For example, sites that decided to wait during our current sample period may later decide not to keep waiting. To many sites, it became clear that client/server applications for their purposes would arrive after 1992 or 1993, not as soon as predicted. Accounting for such dynamically complex behavior calls for more subtle empirical models than the ones we are treating here.

ware as well as the hardware survey. Finally, we must be able to determine the industry of the site.[16] We are left with over 10,000 sites in each triad, over 50 percent of all mainframe users in the United States.

We use Computer Intelligence Corporation's definition of a "site," which corresponds with a unique company address and senior data processing manager. Since Computer Intelligence Corporation designs its database for direct marketing campaigns by value-added peripheral and software vendors, a site corresponds closely to the organization within which decisions are made about acquisition of systems. Thus, it is likely that the same factors influence decisions at the same "site." However, this correspondence may be weaker at the largest sites, such as those devoted to varied research tasks in campus-like settings in private industry. At these sites, Computer Intelligence Corporation's site definition may only partially embed decentralized authority.[17]

We also employ Computer Intelligence Corporation's definition of a *general-purpose mainframe* computer. The advantage of Computer Intelligence Corporation's definition is the accuracy and completeness of Computer Intelligence Corporation's data for large systems. This definition, like any other, is unavoidably arbitrary at the smaller end, where general-purpose mainframes compete against general-purpose superminis. Though we could quibble with some of Computer Intelligence Corporation's choices about what systems to include and exclude as general-purpose mainframes, they tend to follow industry conventions about what is and is not a mainframe. The most important problem arises in limiting the scope of our conclusions. We cannot say, on current evidence, whether proprietary supermini systems have been affected in the same way as have proprietary mainframe systems.

Endogenous Variables

Our dependent variables should capture increases in mainframe capacity, taking into account lumpiness and the time taken to make changes. We construct three different variables with partially overlapping definitions of capacity increases.

We begin with increases in the number of systems in use at the site that persist for at least two years. In each triad, we say that there is an increase

---

16. We have used the name of the firm or other institution owning the site matched to public sources to increase the coverage and accuracy, especially for government sites.

17. As in many marketing databases, there is some information about the locus of decision making. For the years 1987–91, we know whether large technical decisions are made at the site or at a central authority elsewhere in the company. We have not yet used this information to examine our definition of "site" as decision locus.

in capacity if there are more mainframe systems the second year than there were the first. We say that the increase is persistent if there continue to be more systems in the third year than in the *first*; transitory, if the number of systems falls back to or below the original level. We believe that the persistent increase in the system counts variable, hereafter Systems, measures large increases in the stock of mainframes. Our interpretation is that increases in the *number* of mainframes in use represent significant increases in mainframe capacity and reveal large increases in desired capacity. To capture smaller changes in computing capacity, such as those associated with upgrades or system replacements, we turn our attention to the total processing power of a site's mainframes, measured in MIPS. Here, a persistent increase is more MIPS on the site in the second year than the first, and still more MIPS on the site in the third year than in the first.

In Table 1, we present descriptive statistics on these and closely related variables. Note that persistent capacity increases are much less frequent for Systems than for MIPS. In both triads, persistent capacity reductions outnumber persistent increases for Systems but not for MIPS. This reflects the mature state of the mainframe market, where revenue stays high through selling larger systems, in spite of selling fewer of them. Consistent with the description of the difficulty of large capacity projects above, the most frequent outcome in each of our triads is "other," which consists mostly of sites that do not change their stock of mainframe computers.

Another fact in Table 1 also has some implications for the amount of time the investment in large new computer projects takes. There is a dramatic difference in the MIPS and Systems measures. In both triads, half of the increases in Systems counts are transitory—that is, half of the increases are reversed after one year. Only a very small portion of MIPS increases are

TABLE I

Net Changes in Large Computing Capacity

(*percent*)

	Persistent capacity increase	Transitory capacity increase	Persistent capacity reduction	Site exit	Other (mostly no change)
Counting systems					
First triad	8	8	14	6	64
Second triad	5	5	12	8	70
Counting MIPS					
First triad	33	2	11	6	48
Second triad	25	1	10	8	55

NOTE: Total sample size for the first triad was 10,778 sites; for the second triad, 11,776 sites. Rows may not sum to 100 percent due to rounding error.

reversed in the second year. This is evidence for the quantitative importance of dual systems operation. The investment process for new data processing projects must take a very great deal of time, at least a very substantial fraction of a year, to explain these numbers.

Now let us consider changes over time in demand behavior looking at the raw facts in Table 1. First, consider *reductions* in capacity. There are always some; but there is very little change over time in the fraction of sites that reduce either mainframe MIPS or Systems. If anything, the fraction of sites reducing capacity is slightly smaller later on. On the other hand, far fewer sites *expanded* mainframe capacity in the second triad. Measured by Systems, the rate of capacity expansion fell from 8 percent to 5 percent, by MIPS, from 33 percent to 25 percent. The larger drop in MIPS means that there was a decline in upgrades and replacements above and beyond the decline in whole new systems.

A variety of evidence makes clear that this decline in mainframe expansion is not actual switches to client/server. First, the trade press and the Bresnahan-Saloner interviews (1994) make clear that there is not much downsizing to client/server until 1993, at least not in the sense of switching over real production applications (Caldwell, 1994; Ambrosio, 1993). The switch to massively parallel computers is trivial, despite persistent rumors.[18] About one-fourth of total expected mainframe demand has gone away ($[33-25]/33$). It is not the case that these are needs met with new technology, but instead unmet needs.

One possible explanation is the recession during our second triad. But this explanation is far from sufficient. First, despite the broader recession, MIS budgets continued rapid growth into our second triad's decision times.[19] Moreover, using our econometric estimates of the impact of demand growth on capacity expansion, we still see a substantial downturn above and beyond the effects of the recession. Finally, we have demanders' frequent statements in the trade press or in interviews that this was a period of "evaluation" or of "wait and see" for downsizing opportunities. Using either the MIS budgets or the econometric estimates, we can calculate the extent of the decline in mainframe-based projects above and beyond recession effects. Both calculations suggest that there are over 1,400 "missing" mainframe projects nationwide, including upgrades as well as new systems.

---

18. This question is very common in seminars. But the evidence is that there was little replacement, even as late as 1993. Even then, massively parallel systems were typically deployed as complements to, not substitutes for, mainframe systems (Boughten, 1993).

19. MIS budgets continued to grow in 1990 only slightly slower than in the first triad. By 1991, there were clearly decelerations in the growth of MIS budgets. But they continued to have positive nominal growth. For example, see *Datamation*, April 15, 1991.

TABLE 2
"Brand" Switches

	Count of brand switches	As fraction of persistent increases in system counts	As fraction of sites
First triad	93	0.10	0.0086
Second triad	171	0.31	0.0145

NOTE: Definition of "brand switch": If the main system is IBM-compatible, a permanent increase in the count of non–IBM-compatible systems is a switch. Otherwise, a permanent increase in the count of IBM-compatible systems is a "switch." In 1984 the main-system question was not asked, so we use the 1985 reported main system. At one-system sites, we often impute a main-system brand.

Within our sample, which covers about half of the installed base, there are over 700 missing projects. There was very substantial waiting for client/ server even though there was little actual adoption of the new technology in this period.

The economics literature on product pre-announcement has for some years posited the importance of this kind of anticipatory demand behavior (Farrell and Saloner, 1986). The strength of the behavior, given that client/ server architectures were definitely "vaporware" at this stage, is impressive.

We also report simple statistics on brand switches among vendors of mainframe technology. We consider only two "brands" of mainframes, IBM (and compatibles) and all others. As can be seen in Table 2, switches are very infrequent in our first triad and, while increasing, still rare in our last. Some alternative brand-switch definitions, like changes in the reported main system, would be even rarer. So we do not pursue analysis of brand switches further.

Finally, we add a continuous-valued capacity increase variable, the persistent increase in MIPS at the site. Because of the importance of dual system operation, we define the persistent increase in MIPS as the minimum of the increase from the base year to the first year or to the second year. The simple first difference double-counts the MIPS of the systems in dual system operation, and we know from Table 1 that this double-counting applies to about half of capacity expansions. So that the first and second triad figures will be comparable, we deflate the MIPS figures using a main-frame computer price index from Dulberger (1989).

We will proceed by estimating cross-section models for increases and decreases in capacity, measured by both number and MIPS. These will be probits in the first analyses. Similarly, we will estimate a tobit for the continuous-valued increase in MIPS.

Exogenous Variables in Cross Section

We predict each of these three dependent variables with a long list of regressors. This section defines the regressors. In each triad, the regressors are observed in the "base" year (1984 and 1989). We use them to predict persistent net increases in capacity over the next two years. We begin this section with variables which are included primarily to ensure we capture much cross-section variation in large computing demand. We then describe variables closely linked to our hypothesis.

We use employment data for each industry (two- or three-digit SIC) to proxy for changes in the derived demand for computer systems output. We also include SIC dummies for a more limited set of unusual cases.[20] Employment has several useful properties: though it is an input in production, it is a cyclical indicator of computer systems output and therefore desired computer system investment. Moreover, user institutions in our sample are both public and private, for-profit and not. Thus, employment is probably the best unifying measure of the derived demand for inputs. We would prefer company or institution data rather than industry data, but this is only available for a subset of users.

The maximum and minimum age of the general-purpose mainframe computing systems at a site measure, crudely, the distribution of times since upgrades. As a result, they are related to the gap between the technical frontier embodied in new equipment and the level embodied in the equipment at the site. Of course, these variables are endogenous in a dynamic sense. They are likely determined by (among other things) the site's past history of computing power needs, which could be correlated with current needs. Here and elsewhere, we use lagged technical choices as proxies. We do not make causal inferences about these variables. Their task is to capture much of the cross-section variation in the state of the replacement cycle at the site. If they also pick up persistent heterogeneity in the valuation of computer services, or in "lock-in" to particular systems, we are untroubled by that.

Similarly, we use the MIPS rating of the largest and smallest general-purpose system as an indicator of the maximum and minimum demands on computing capacity. Use of a large-capacity system correlates with a

---

20. In preliminary research we tried regional dummies interacted with time and a more complete list of SICs than shown in the present results. We found that our results were not qualitatively influenced by dropping or including these variables. Hence, we only show the shorter results below. In work in progress, we have linked many of these sites to microdata sources (Bresnahan, Greenstein, and Ito, 1994).

demand for systems performing a large maximum feasible task (Bresnahan and Greenstein, 1992). Use of a small-capacity general-purpose system ought to correlate with a need to employ mainframes instead of the next smallest alternative, a general-purpose supermini. That is, it may suggest that the buyer anticipates increasing capacity along well-understood mainframe growth paths as user needs grow (instead of the more limited growth paths associated with superminis). So these variables may capture the site's past assessment of the pace of upgrading and replacement.

We include a count of general-purpose systems, with several possible interpretations. First, it may signal that the computing core serves a large end-user community. The coordination problems associated with a large community may slow the pace of change. Second, a large site is likely to realize the economies of scale and scope necessary to try technical solutions with high fixed costs. Therefore, we expect to observe a large portfolio of technical solutions to computing needs.

We also include a dummy variable showing whether the site's "major" system is not from IBM or from an IBM plug–compatible manufacturer. Because of the rarity of vendor switching, this will help us measure differences in the demand facing IBM relative to the other mainframe vendors.

We now describe the variables closely linked to our hypotheses. Using standard descriptive analyses of large computer installations, we identify the kinds of environments associated with organizational dissatisfaction with large systems. To obtain proxies for these environments, we construct a series of variables based on the software in use on mainframes at the site. Computer Intelligence Corporation provides lists of software programs and their provider, categorization of its functionality, and the number of copies in use at a site. This information is rich in detail. Software information captures important activities inside the mediating process at the site. Different software categories point to a more or less costly, complex, localized, or locked-in mediating process.[21]

We categorize software programs into two different sets of dummies. The first uses the software *author* to identify the importance of the vendor-user interface for large-system demand. If sites' investments lock them into their hardware vendor, as switching cost theory suggests (Klemperer, 1992), then a site that uses much software written by its general-purpose hardware vendor will be particularly locked in. Switching will require aban-

---

21. In general, while we use software variables as proxies for the sites' adjustment costs, none of these uses of software variables is a calculation of investment in complementary software, per se.

doning any idiosyncratic investments tied to the software provided by the hardware vendor. A similar argument applies to software that Computer Intelligence Corporation designates "in-house," meaning where the user is also the designer. Such software may incorporate idiosyncratic features of the user and the computing platform, which makes it virtually unportable. However, in-house expertise in software programming may ameliorate some of these lock-in effects. These users may be able to overcome portability difficulties themselves, instead of relying on vendors.

The rest of the software, not written in-house and not from the hardware vendor, is either from consultants or from third-party software firms. We somewhat arbitrarily categorize software as "third-party" if we find more than twenty programs in all the sites in our sample. Under the lock-in theory, users with much third-party software find it less costly to move to new platforms. We further divide third-party software. If the apparent strategy of the software author company was to make its product portable across different brands of mainframe system, we put it in the "multiplatform" category. If the author company appears dedicated to only one type of computer, we put the software into an IBM-specific or other-specific category.

The test of both the vendor lock-in and MIS lock-in theories comes from the behavior of buyers with more specific software. More specific software—that from the proprietary systems vendor or from a third-party software firm writing only for one type of computer—is interpreted as revealing a mediating process with costs more sunk to a relationship with a specific mainframe vendor. Similarly, under the MIS lock-in theory, software that is more local to this site is interpreted as revealing an opportunity for foot-dragging by MIS should it wish to preserve the value of its skill base in the old system. Being tied to a vendor occurs either because vendors force such sunk costs on the buyer who cannot successfully resist, or because managers of information systems prefer their incumbent and have the power to enforce these preferences, even if these conflict with broader organizational goals.[22]

We calculate the fraction of software packages that fall into each author category at each site. The results are in Table 3, along with descriptive statistics of all our other regressors. Note that the fractions are essentially the same in our two triads.

The second set of software variables focuses on the use of software and

---

22. The MIS lock-in and the vendor lock-in theories are not completely distinct, as this sentence suggests. Outsourcing of the entire MIS function in connection with downsizing is often suggested as a way to solve the two linked problems.

TABLE 3

Site Characteristics in Selected Summary Statistics

Variable label	Definition/categories	Mean	Std. dev.	Mean	Std. dev.
		First triad		Second triad	
Software usage variables (proxies for organizational complexity)					
SCI	% scientific & number crunching s/w	0.037	0.062	0.037	0.085
TS	% technical support required s/w	0.009	0.068	0.008	0.045
STD	% standard business application s/w	0.256	0.209	0.219	0.224
DB	% database & application oriented s/w	0.206	0.149	0.201	0.144
COMM	% communication & network s/w	0.259	0.163	0.243	0.169
MIPCM	% comm * maxmip (defn. below)	0.812	1.502	1.208	2.176
MIPDB	% db * maxmip (defn. below)	0.687	1.361	1.161	2.131
Software author variables (lock-in theories)					
INHOUS	% software written in-house	0.198	0.198	0.189	0.248
PROP	% s/w from a proprietary systems vendor	0.445	0.244	0.451	0.252
PROPDB	% s/w prop and db	0.139	0.132	0.121	0.129
PROPCM	% s/w prop and comm	0.183	0.147	0.172	0.158
TPBLUE	% s/w from a third-party vendor, all IBM	0.285	0.207	0.291	0.224
TPNONB	% s/w from a third-party vendor, one brand	0.002	0.043	0.009	0.047
MPLAT	% s/w from a multiplatform third-party vendor	0.061	0.147	0.062	0.111
Replacement cycle or background variables					
EMPGRW	% employment growth in 1–3 digit SIC	0.024	0.080	0.004	0.033
MINAGE	Age of the newest system	1.724	2.108	2.046	2.137
MAXAGE	Age of the oldest system	3.116	2.538	3.264	2.566
SYSSUM	# of systems	1.733	1.242	1.697	1.337
MMBLUE	Major system is IBM or compatible	0.853	0.353	0.834	0.372
MAXMIP	Maximum MIPS of systems	3.142	5.378	5.545	9.141
MINMIP	Minimum MIPS of systems	1.655	2.540	2.955	5.366
Dependent variable not shown in Table 2					
ΔMIPS	Increase in MIPS (if positive) (deflated)	5.430	11.14	8.749	18.95

the kinds of system it is running on. Here, we make use of Computer Intelligence Corporation's evaluation of the purpose of the software. We group their very detailed categories based on a close reading of the similarities and differences between each market niche. Our reading focused on attempting to predict the horizontal axis in Figure 1 under the best of both worlds and adjustment costs theories.

One category is what we call "scientific computing and other numerically intensive methods." This includes such software as CAD/CAM and standard large spread-sheet applications. Years before client/server, these uses were first to move to workstations because these users tend to possess a high degree of computer sophistication and do not require frequent use of a large centralized database. Another category is what we call "technical support necessary," which includes applications such as manufacturing. These applications are technically demanding—where "technically" means the computing is complementary to technologies other than computer technology—and require frequent interaction between user and vendor. A site with a high percentage of these products will be populated with engineers and will contain needs that are organizationally simple to address. So these first two categories are to the left in Figure 1. Earlier, these users were the first to anticipate leaving large computing platforms and taking advantage of advances in alternative smaller platforms like minicomputers. These users tend to be among the most successfully resistant to centralized management of computing resources, frequently using junior scientists rather than MIS professionals.

A third category of software is what we call "communications and other multiuser tools." This includes many system programs designed to enable mainframe-micro links, and many system programs designed to control communications. A large community of users will exist at sites with a large percentage of these programs. This may signal difficult mediating processes associated with essential computing tasks or costly processes of adjusting applications to new technical alternatives.

Our fourth and fifth categories examine the type of database programs in use. Computer Intelligence Corporation designates these as either "system" or "application" programs. System database programs include software such as file management programs. Database applications include such software as standard financial analysis and large accounting packages. Sites that make use of many application database programs may find it marginally easier to shift, since many of these types of programs are available on different computing platforms. The omitted category includes software that we find on nearly all large computers, like operating systems. These programs should provide little information about a large-system user, since virtually every computing core makes use of similar programs.

Finally, we interact some software variables with other measures to highlight where the mediating process has been problematic. We interact our database application variable with the size of the maximum MIPS system on site. We also treat database software from the systems vendor as a separate category. We do a similar interaction of our communication software variable with the measure of maximum MIPS and treat this software differently if it is proprietary to the system vendor. We think that the interactions with the largest MIPS should capture sites to the right in Figure 1. Under adjustment cost theory, these sites are least likely to move out of mainframes because these users are taking advantage of system size and vendor-specificity in applications using large databases and frequent real-time communication with computing resources. Under best of both worlds theory, these are many of the users who express the most unhappiness with large-system solutions and are the most likely to move.

These variables, too, can be seen in Table 3. Once again, the figures reported come after a calculation of the fraction of mainframe software packages at the site falling into the category.

Econometric Models

Our econometric models focus on identifying changes in mainframe capacity expansion behavior between our two triads. We have three dependent variables; the persistent capacity increase dummies for MIPS and for systems described above, and continuous-valued increases in MIPS. The capacity expansions are measured in the second two years of each triad (1985/86 or 1990/91). The three dependent variables are treated separately; the first two are estimated by probit, the third by tobit.

The regressors are all measured as of the first year of each triad, 1984 or 1989. We interact all of the X's with a second triad dummy. Call the first-triad coefficients of all the regressors in one of the analyses β_{85}. The second-triad coefficients are $\beta_{85} + \beta_2$. Our specification leaves the β_2, which measure how behavior changes over time, unrestricted.[23] All of the regressors are positive. Thus, negative β_2 identifies the types of sites that tended to expand mainframe capacity less in the second period. Our interpretation of negative β_2 is that it identifies the sites that waited for client/server.

The interpretation is slightly more complicated for the two mutually exclusive sets of software dummies. We include separate intercepts for each year, and we also include the employment variable. Between these two variables, they should capture much of the business cycle effects. Since the software variables within each category sum to one, we must exclude one variable in each category. As a result, they have relative interpretations. A negative β_2 identifies kinds of sites that tended to wait more for client/server; a positive β_2 identifies kinds of sites that tended to wait less.

Specifications Estimated and Results

Results are reported in Tables 4 and 5; the format is that all three estimations are reported together, with the change parameters β_2 in Table 4 and the baseline from the first triad in Table 5.

---

23. In an obvious notation, we will call $\beta_{90} = \beta_{85} + \beta_2$ below.

TABLE 4

Changes in Behavior Over Time

Variable label	Definition/categories	MIPS tobit	MIPS probit	Systems probit
Software usage variables (proxies for organizational complexity)				
SCI	% scientific & number crunching s/w	-12.4085 (4.53918)	-.543227 (.302894)	-.642352 (.420265)
TS	% technical support required s/w	-6.71945 (6.23987)	-.525692 (.397538)	-.917339 (.649192)
STD	% standard business application s/w	-3.47132 (2.41683)	-.247190 (.157595)	-.370071 (.217556)
DB	% database & application oriented s/w	-3.86638 (4.04167)	-.311132 (.266800)	-.601025 (.378115)
COMM	% communication & network s/w	-6.71316 (4.79685)	-.565845 (.316349)	-1.14444 (.468129)
MIPCM	% comm * maxmip	-.392041 (.381483)	-.014073 (.029606)	-.005754 (.032770)
MIPDB	% db * maxmip	1.55301 (.416548)	.059314 (.031260)	.027342 (.034424)
Software author variables (lock-in theories)				
INHOUS	% software written in-house	-5.65120 (7.39035)	-.553258 (.475507)	1.47796 (.918601)
PROP	% s/w from a proprietary systems vendor	-7.42648 (7.36940)	-.729804 (.473940)	.746187 (.919417)
PROPDB	% s/w prop and db	-4.80366 (4.52567)	-.185774 (.297639)	.263288 (.427679)
PROPCM	% s/w prop and comm	-4.99698 (5.24249)	.621137 (.344654)	1.74229 (.510188)

TPBLUE	% s/w from a third-party vendor, all IBM	−6.06387 (7.34379)	−.475147 (.473252)	1.20520 (.919225)
TPNONB	% s/w from a third-party vendor, one brand	−7.49751 (10.1583)	−.571061 (.657678)	1.80417 (1.15012)
MPLAT	% s/w from a multiplatform third-party vendor	−2.94401 (7.68936)	−.429298 (.494201)	1.23953 (.938708)
Replacement cycle or background variables				
C-1990	Constant (change over time)	−21.0692 (4.52015)	−.946986 (.295153)	−3.26459 (.777093)
EMPGRW	% employment growth in 1–3 digit SIC	5.59733 (9.83675)	−.18431 (.654021)	−.126910 (1.05055)
MINAGE	Age of the newest system	.743663 (.213215)	−.010190 (.014706)	.008400 (.022147)
MAXAGE	Age of the oldest system	−.672842 (.172217)	.006289 (.012177)	−.014566 (.018369)
SYSSUM	# of systems	1.81999 (.301390)	.027313 (.023934)	.022627 (.031137)
NONIBM	Major system not IBM-compatible	5.16814 (1.18211)	.517137 (.078230)	.484600 (.108700)
MAXMIP	Maximum MIPS of systems	−.053739 (.140150)	−.003765 (.010458)	.0067614 (.011645)
MINMIP	Minimum MIPS of systems	−.444075 (.107141)	−.001209 (.007970)	−.046341 (.009200)

NOTES: These results are drawn from three separate analyses and are a subset of the total parameter vector in each. In particular, each coefficient reported here is a change over time between the first and second triad in the impact of the variable. The rest of the coefficients are in Table 5. The first column has units d(MIPS)/d(variable). In the second column, multiply each coefficient by .37 to get units d(probability of increasing MIPS)/d(variable). In the third, multiply by .15 to get units d(probability of increasing Systems)/d(variable). Estimated standard errors are in parentheses.

TABLE 5

Variety in Behavior in First Triad

Variable label	Definition/categories	MIPS tobit	MIPS probit	Systems probit
Software usage variables (proxies for organizational complexity)				
SCI	% scientific & number crunching s/w	.389712 (.297245)	−.004630 (.237877)	.389712 (.297245)
TS	% technical support required s/w	.182191 (.278786)	−.004600 (.243933)	.182191 (.278786)
STD	% standard business application s/w	−.082500 (.151175)	−.046636 (.116685)	−.082500 (.151175)
DB	% database & application oriented s/w	−.036402 (.251937)	−.158785 (.195033)	−.036402 (.251937)
COMM	% communication & network s/w	.253666 (.291834)	−.367987 (.221719)	.253666 (.291834)
MIPCM	% comm * maxmip	.006777 (.027698)	.037635 (.024987)	.06777 (.027698)
MIPDB	% db * maxmip	−.025255 (.028623)	−.039224 (.025703)	−.025255 (.028623)
Software author variables (lock-in theories)				
INHOUS	% software written in-house	−.168724 (.491378)	.015557 (.374191)	−.168724 (.491378)
PROP	% s/w from a proprietary systems vendor	.334697 (.484176)	.258297 (.369084)	.334697 (.484176)
PROPDB	% s/w prop and db	−.041529 (.272438)	.342716 (.210215)	−.041529 (.272438)
PROPCM	% s/w prop and comm	−.708612 (.324029)	.042241 (.242506)	−.708612 (.324029)

TPBLUE	% s/w from a third-party vendor, all IBM	.328231 (.484904)	.807962 (.371453)	.328231 (.484904)
TPNONB	% s/w from a third-party vendor, one brand	-.177615 (.701146)	.757258 (.493164)	-.177615 (.701146)
MPLAT	% s/w from a multiplatform third-party vendor	.442619 (.499505)	.363190 (.382307)	.442619 (.499505)
Replacement cycle or background variables				
C	Constant	-23.9410 (5.79986)	-.8177 (.370131)	-1.7601 (.485662)
EMPGRW	% employment growth in 1–3 digit SIC	4.88205 (2.55363)	.420278 (.172980)	.933320 (.227801)
MINAGE	Age of the newest system	.201929 (.147617)	.007889 (.010322)	.025299 (.014457)
MAXAGE	Age of the oldest system	.500196 (.116371)	.037131 (.008432)	.001795 (.011836)
SYSSUM	# of systems	.090544 (.022566)	.096111 (.017483)	.090544 (.022566)
NONIBM	Major system not IBM-compatible	-.142170 (.078144)	-.444534 (.058747)	-.142170 (.078144)
MAXMIP	Maximum MIPS of systems	.342612 (.118147)	.003132 (.008730)	.008892 (.009519)
MINMIP	Minimum MIPS of systems	.616223 (.094417)	.013679 (.007025)	.057616 (.007935)
Summary statistics				
	Log (likelihood)	-32777.9	-11382.3	-4714.7
	Observations	18567	18567	18031

NOTES: These results are drawn from three separate analyses and are a subset of the total parameter vector in each. Each coefficient reported here is the estimated first triad impact of the variable. Changes over time are reported in Table 4.

The first column has units d(MIPS)/d(variable). In the second column, multiply each coefficient by .37 to get units d(probability of increasing MIPS)/d(variable). In the third, multiply by .15 to get units d(probability of increasing Systems)/d(variable).

Estimated standard errors are in parentheses.

Before we turn to the hypotheses, we note that these tables reveal quite a bit about how much information there is in the data. In particular, the probits are able to determine the coefficients of the replacement cycle variables reasonably precisely. They are, however, not able to determine the coefficients of very many individual software author or usage variables with much precision at all. We can reject, at extremely high degrees of confidence, the hypothesis that either set of software variables taken as a group has constant coefficients over time, or that the coefficients are zero in the second triad. We cannot, however, say much about individual coefficients. Nor is there much difference—in a statistical sense—between the MIPS and Systems probits. On the other hand, the tobit, with its continuous-valued dependent variable, clearly has information to tie down many of the coefficients. Accordingly, we focus discussion on it, noting the few cases where the probits might lead to a different conclusion.

Which Version of Figure 1 Is Correct?

We begin with changes over time in the coefficients of the software usage variables. These are the first panel in Table 4. We have ordered the coefficients so that going down the page corresponds to movements to the right in Figure 1.

The first coefficients show that intensive users of scientific and numerically intensive software reduced their demand for mainframe hardware in the second triad, relative to other kinds of sites. First read the first row of coefficients, those relating to scientific and other number-crunching software, literally. The -12.4 coefficient in the first column means that a 100 percent increase in the percentage of this kind of software would lead to just over 12 fewer MIPS being bought at the site in the second triad. The standard error of about 4.5 suggests that we can estimate this coefficient reasonably precisely. Now, that is not a within-sample change in the variable—a 100 percent SCI mainframe is rare (recall that the operating system and similar management tools are counted in these percentages). But a 50 percent change in this variable is well within the sample range. It corresponds roughly to the difference between a purely data-processing computer and a mostly dedicated number-crunching computer. So the coefficient means that the number-crunching site would decrease its mainframe acquisitions by about 6.2 MIPS ($12.4 \times .5$) deflated between the two triads, compared to other kinds of sites. That is a huge decrease in demand, corresponding to delaying a very large replacement/upgrade project.[24]

---

24. In the second triad the mean increase in capacity among expanding sites was only a little over 8 MIPS (deflated).

The next two columns refer to the probability of increasing MIPS (rather than the amount of MIPS increase) and the probability of permanent increases in the number of systems. The $-.54$ in the "MIPS probit" column means that the same 50 percent increase in SCI would lead to a decrease in this probability of 10 percent ($.54 \times .37 \times .5$) for a site in the middle of the sample on all the other variables. (The .37 is the probability derivative from the probit evaluated at the sample mean.) Once again, this is the predicted change in behavior between triads for this kind of site in relation to others. Since about a third of the sites upgrade or expand (increase MIPS), 10 percent is a lot of waiting behavior. We are not, however, able to estimate this coefficient with all that much precision, as the large standard error suggests. Finally, the same logic implies that the 50 percent increase in SCI would lead to a decrease in the probability of permanently increasing the number of systems of almost 5 percent ($.64 \times .15 \times .5$). Since the sample average for that probability is about 8 percent, this, too, is a huge change in behavior. Once again, the estimate is statistically imprecise.

The coefficient of TS, the technical and engineering software usage, is similar to that of SCI but less precisely estimated in all analyses.

For the rest of the software usage variables, all three specifications tell much the same story. After SCI, the other reasonably precisely estimated coefficient is that of MIPDB—that is, database and dbms (database management systems) tools software running on very large systems. The rest of the coefficients are, on average, negative and not significantly different from zero. Our choice of omitted category (which is, after all, arbitrary) only hides one statistically significant difference: The coefficient of MIPCM is clearly larger than any of the SCI, TS, STD, or DB. Once again, we only have much in the way of statistical precision with the MIPS dependent variable. Finally, the coefficient of COMM is of the same general size as SCI, but much less precisely estimated.

Relying first on only the statistically significant results, there seem to be two facts here. First, the scientific and number-crunching software sites seem to be waiting for new computer architectures, compared to other sites. Second, sites running very large applications on very large computers, those with large MIPCM or large MIPDB, seem to be waiting less than other sites.[25] In between those two extreme groups, there is little informa-

---

25. In the first triad, a select number of heavy users of database and communication software show accelerated, not slowed, demand, particularly in the MIPS tobit. This period was well into the diffusion of relational databases and real-time query capabilities, as reflected in the DB and COMM coefficients.

tion in the data to tell the rest of the sites apart.[26] They form a large "middle."

In terms of overall waiting for client/server, the number-crunching kinds of sites do not have too much to contribute. Individual sites' behavior is predicted to change a lot, and at least for the scientific categories we can have a good deal of statistical confidence in the size of that change. There are not, however, many of these sites left in the mainframe world by the 1980s, and their aggregate contribution to the downturn in demand is small. The big contribution comes from the difference between the "middle" category and the non-waiters. There is a smaller but still significant difference in behavior between the large MIPCM and MIPDB sites and the "middle" sites. The "middle" category contains many sites, so the aggregate amount of waiting for client/server that it represents is substantial.

These results argue that the right version of Figure 1 is the one in which the adjustment cost curve is steeper; in other words, the adjustment cost theory rather than the best of both worlds theory is true. The important caveat to remember for this result is that it is based on the early part of the competition between the two technologies. There could be differences in expectations between the different kinds of sites about future standardization or software developments.[27]

Lock-In?

In the second part of Tables 4 and 5, the comparable results for the vertical relations software variables appear. For these, the coefficients are estimated far less precisely and the sign pattern varies between the analyses of MIPS and Systems. In the MIPS tobit specification, where there appears to be the most information in the data, the signs are surprising. The negative coefficient on in-house software means that sites which had written their own applications tended to wait for client/server. This is exactly the opposite of what would happen with defensive and powerful MIS. It is

---

26. To a large extent, this is caused by the nature of the cross-section distribution of computer usage rather than by behavior in this time period. The scientific-computing sites and the MIPDB or MIPCM sites tend to be quite distinct from other sites. The former are typically doing primarily number crunching (rather than a mix of it and other things). The latter are typically using a "transactions processing" kind of application or something like it. If we remove these two groups of sites, it is very hard to see any clear pattern in the remainder of the software usage in the data. The remaining sites tend to do some of all the remaining categories, and not to vary all that much.

27. All of our results could be turned around by appropriate coincidence theories. The large sites which we say have large adjustment costs might instead be those for whom future standardization and future software developments are the most valuable, for example.

further (and weak statistically) evidence against MIS power in organizations (Lucas, 1984).[28]

Similarly, with one exception the vertical relations variables are insignificant and of the wrong sign given the vendor lock-in theory. Sites that have acquired software from their proprietary systems vendor or from single-platform third-party vendors tended to wait more, not less, for client/server than those buying multiplatform software or using consultants. Once again, these effects are quite weak statistically and the sign pattern changes in the systems probit. Overall, the results offer little support for the vendor relations theory.

An important exception is the positive sign on usage of communications software from the proprietary systems vendor. While the coefficient is not statistically significant, the size of the coefficient is consistent with considerable vendor lock-in for this kind of software. Since this important category of software is numerically dominated by IBM products that differ radically from industry-wide data communications products, it is not surprising that this is one area where we detect vendor lock-in. Recent innovation in this area is important enough that users of these services, even as late as the early 1990s, may still be making long-term commitments to mainframes in order to exploit these innovations.

Overall, however, we must conclude that vendor and MIS lock-in are an unimportant explanation of behavior in this period. It simply is not true that the most backward-looking sites are those with a lot of in-house or systems-vendor proprietary software. We were quite surprised by these results. One possible interpretation is that these sites are indeed locked in but expect that their downsizing to client/server will go forward within the client/server products families that are compatible with the products of their historical mainframe vendor.

IBM

We draw attention to one result from the rest of Table 4 because it is so large. In the probits, the coefficients on the non–IBM-compatible sites are large and positive. If we look at Table 5, we see that the same coefficients are negative in the first triad. What this means is that non–IBM-compatible sites used to purchase mainframes less frequently, but that they catch up in our second triad.

---

28. In more restrictive specifications we tried, the sign is not reversed but the coefficient is estimated much more precisely. There is thus some fragile statistical evidence that in-house measures MIS capability to undertake large, forward-looking (as opposed to defensive) projects. That this effect does not appear in the systems probit underscores its fragility.

This shift in behavior has many possible interpretations in theory, but only a few plausible ones in practice. Given the choice between interpreting this as either "IBM's fortunes got worse" or "its rivals got better," we are tempted more by the former. Here is why:

There is little to suggest that shifts in the competitive position of IBM's mainframe rivals were responsible. For example, little industry evidence suggests that the non-IBM firms innovated dramatically more.[29] We note, as well, that the non-IBM variable could account for characteristics that we have not successfully measured with either the software variables or the other derived demand variables.[30] The variable shift can potentially stand in for any of a number of changes to the non-IBM or IBM network of suppliers, for changes to the software supported by IBM or non-IBM firms, to the quality of the hardware, and so on.

Though we are not out of theoretical possibilities, they seem less plausible than the simple theory that users anticipated a smaller alternative to mainframes: the increasing reliable and capable open system alternatives associated with microprocessor-based systems. The new open alternatives had developed many standard applications by the late 1980s, and the levels and directions of advance were predictable and understood by professionals. In this view, IBM and non-IBM users alike anticipated a future alternative. Both behaved similarly, resulting in similar demand behavior in the latter triad (in contrast with the earlier triad).

Other Determinants of Demand

Many of the rest of the variables are statistically significant in Table 5 but not in Table 4. The magnitude of coefficient estimates for all the other

29. Control Data's attempts at revival were a well-publicized failure. Unisys's victories were largely measured by the ability to stay out of the red. Honeywell, now part of the Bull group, provided no real competition for IBM in general-purpose mainframes by the late 1980s. Despite being swallowed by AT&T, NCR continued its steady, but unspectacular, advances in niches in which it already specialized. DEC's high-flying days were at a well-publicized end by the early 1990s. The advance in systems using vector processors, which came from several high-profile new firms, had hardly dented the mainframe world by 1990. IBM would only feel such an effect for a few select users of extremely large systems. It is unlikely that the imminent diffusion of vector-processor mainframes would affect behavior at more than several score sites at most. Makers of plug-compatibles will feel this demand shift as much as IBM, since they sell exclusively to sites where we record IBM as the dominant supplier.

30. Even with as much data as we have for these sites, there are many possible interpretations of this coefficient, because IBM is both the largest proprietary software vendor and hardware vendor in the mainframe world. Moreover, IBM has the largest user third-party network—that is, an enormous third-party peripheral and software vendor market, large user group communities, its own magazine, and so on.

variables change very little over time. We conclude that these demand factors continued to be a force in the second triad, even though the frequency of capacity increases dropped off considerably. We briefly summarize the site-specific factors.

While employment growth predicts both systems and MIPS growth, these effects do not change over time. It appears that computer systems expand to meet current needs. The age coefficients also do not change much, and illustrate important features of demand. First, there is obsolescence. A newer system appears more sunk because it has had less time to become obsolete, while an older one is less sunk because it has become technically obsolete. Obsolete systems tend to be retired. This sunkness story explains why the coefficients are irrelevant, as the sunkness of existing investments is irrelevant to further expansion. A second interpretation refers to a slow-moving valuation of the stock of capacity. As for MINAGE, sites that have recently invested have a high desire for capacity. Sites that have not invested for some time have not had any needs for a while. As for MAXAGE, sites with a very old system have not felt the need to expand the capacity of some of their applications for some time. For the second interpretation to be the right one, it requires some further explanation about why the age variables do not matter. The likely source of a story is that the lagged endogenous variables have already been put into the stock. Thus, a low "minage" means that the site has already adjusted to desired capacity.

The size of the smallest system is also statistically and economically important. The larger the smallest system, the most likely the user will increase capacity. Inmon (1985) observes that sites whose smallest system is large have placed themselves on a mainframe growth path and rarely deviate. These users are most likely to resist moving away from these long-term commitments. The size of the *largest* system does not predict behavior nearly as well, which is noteworthy in light of its predictive abilities when interacted with software variables.

How Did New Choices Shift Demand for Old Systems?

The future opportunity to downsize cut the rate of (systems) capacity expansions between our two triads. It is by now standard to interpret this as an increase in competition. Yet sellers of the old technology did not act as if they were now in a more competitive industry. Mainframe price/performance ratios, for example, continued to fall at about the same rate as before (Brown and Greenstein, 1994). The largest vendor, IBM, continued to announce ambitious R&D initiatives closely complementary to its existing proprietary products, and resisted until quite recently portability to open systems for its more important software products.[31] It is by now typical to interpret these actions as evidence that mainframe vendors are stupid, or at least backward.[32] An alternative, economic explanation of the pricing and technology behavior is available in our estimates. This explanation turns on a shift inward but not a flattening of the demand for mainframe systems.

The adjustment-cost results of the last section suggest such a story. Traditional inframarginal mainframe customers (for example, those with large MIPDB) *stayed*, while traditional marginal customers (for example, those with large SCI) *moved* or waited. In this section, we examine the implications of our estimates for shifting mainframe demand more systematically.

We order sites by predicted $X\beta$ in each year. Since all sites face the same prices, this should also be their ordering by (the observable portion of) the value of expanded capacity. High $X\beta$ sites will systematically be inframarginal purchasers, for example.

As a first calculation very close to the data, we ask how general the SCI versus MIPDB anecdote is. Has demand fallen because there are fewer high-value, inframarginal customers? That would be demand-curve flattening. Or has it fallen because low-value, marginal customers have shifted away? That would be demand-curve steepening. In Figures 2 and 3, we use $X_{85}\beta_{85}$ and $X_{90}\beta_{90}$ from the MIPS-capacity increase model reported in Tables 4 and 5. On the vertical axis, we graph $X\beta$; on the horizontal axis, the percentage of sites in the sample that have a higher predicted valuation in each year. As can be seen from examination of the graph, particularly from the marked bars, the shift over time in demand appears to be of the demand curve–steepening variety. There is no tendency for inframarginal customers to be the ones who left the market over time. In percentage terms, the decline in high-value sites is somewhat less than the decline in low-value sites. This is the generalization of the SCI versus MIPDB anecdote, and suggests a decline in quantity demanded but not a flatter demand curve.

In an Appendix, we report calculations that move the analysis closer to a theoretical demand curve. The distributional assumptions behind the

---

31. On the first point, see, for example, the ongoing importance of the SAA and AD/Cycle initiatives. On the second, it was not until spring 1993, for example, that IBM announced a credible policy of moving key database software tools (like CICS) to open systems.

32. See the extensive discussion on the inadequacy of IBM's organizational form, for example.

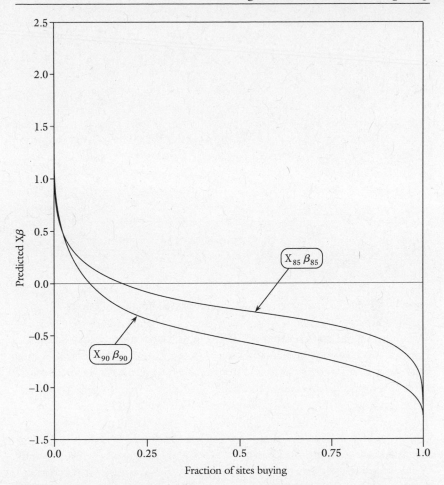

Figure 2. Demand curve implied by probit—fraction of buyers.

probit are relaxed, and the better definitions of predicted quantity demanded and implicit price change are used. The resulting pictures are quite
similar to those in Figures 2 and 3.

What changed over time to move the demand curves is closely linked
to the increased importance of the outside option, client/server. A simple
variance calculation illuminates this. We use the sample distribution of X
from the second triad. We take coefficients from the probits and calculate
variance statistics with each parameter vector. We find that $X_{90}\beta_{90}$ varies
more than $X_{90}\beta_{85}$. The effect of the outside option was not to make the

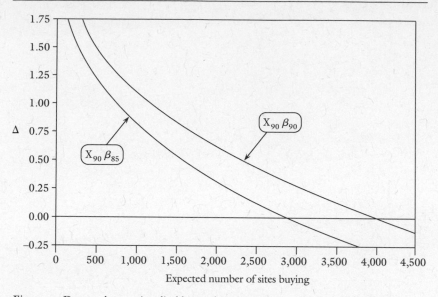

Figure 3. Demand curve implied by probit—expected number of buyers.

sites more alike (reduce variance) as the MIPS arbitrage theory suggests. Instead, the reverse. The demand curves in the figures get steeper because high-value mainframe customers tended not to wait for client/server, while low-value customers waited.

Upshots

While these results are drawn from the early phases of the diffusion of client/server, they resonate with what users think. We propose three interpretations of our results. These relate to the dynamics of investments in large information technology solutions, the commercialization of information technology, and the competitive crash in computing. In each, the technologically active role of the buyer leads to a new interpretation.

The Large-Scale Computing Project as an Investment

We started from the view that expanding capacity for large-scale computing is complex. It calls for new hardware, which is how an expansion project leaves observable tracks in our data set. It calls for new software expenditures. It calls for complementary investments at the site, both within MIS and in the end-user business organization. There is a large body of literature on the management of these investments, but positive studies of them have been scarce. Our quantitative study of them examines their degree of irreversibility and adjustment costs.

We have found that a large fraction of the investment cost of a large-scale computing project is sunk. Should the need for the project's output disappear (or never appear), reversal of the project will not lead to recovery of these sunk costs. One should expect all the general results about sunk investments, especially the inertia and caution they induce, to hold.

The obvious candidate sunk costs are expenditures on installation and local programming at the site rather than acquired hardware and software. (Hardware can be leased or resold in this market, and software has substantial annual license fees.) Our estimate (in earlier work) of the fraction of investment costs sunk, about four-fifths, is much larger than the fraction of expenditures of a typical MIS department on installation and local programming.[33] Economists frequently draw the distinction between "internal" and "external" adjustment costs. The "external" costs are money spent in the course of making the investment, while the "internal" costs are the disruption to regular business routines that have to be borne while the investment is being made. Since our estimates have the sunk costs too large to be explained in terms of external costs, they suggest internal costs as well.[34] What is interesting about our findings is not that we believe that these costs exist, as that was well established in the descriptive literature. Instead, we emphasize their quantitative importance, roughly as large as the programming expenditure on a large-scale project.

The introduction of a new technological generation, in our case the networked small systems alternative to mainframes, offers an opportunity to study the sources of the adjustment costs. All sites face uncertainty about the future path of technology. When a site shifts from an old technological base to a new one, "legacy" applications matter a good deal. Sites have very different kinds of legacy applications, and as a result can have very different adjustment costs.

We examined two different sets of measures of how legacy applications matter. First, we use software at the site as an indicator of the degree to

---

33. Surveys of MIS departments reveal that externally acquired hardware and software are well over half the total budget. If we assume (conservatively) that MIS employees and consultants do nothing but big projects, we still get too small a fraction.

34. Some analysts use internal political power language rather than costs language to describe these phenomena. Projects may be difficult to reverse because MIS holds a favored position in the organization after an expensive project is completed, for example. For our purposes, this alternative language is not particularly different. Obviously, the distinction matters a great deal for the practical marketing of downsizing solutions, and so on.

which the site is tied to a particular systems vendor's technology and of the possibility of MIS lock-in. We contrast, for example, sites using much software acquired from their systems vendor with those using third-party software. To our very considerable surprise, the sites more closely tied to the vendor do not appear to be more reluctant to move forward to the new technology. Neither does MIS lock-in appear to be an important problem.[35] In contrast, variation in the application of software does predict failure to adjust quickly. The pattern closely follows that suggested by the organizational adjustment costs model. More complex organizations (like those using big database management system applications) adjust much more slowly than simple ones (like number-crunching sites). We conclude that many of the sources of slow adjustment are in the adjusting organization. User relations problems, not vendor relations problems, appear to be the source of slow adjustment.

While these results refer to mainframe-based computing, we suspect that they apply with little alteration to large projects based on wide-area network or client/server technology. (These are much harder to study in a systematic way at the present time.) To the extent that these newer enabling information technologies gain their value in use by changing business practices, they will be characterized by sunk internal adjustment costs.

The Commercialization of Information Technology

In information technology, as in many other areas, a sustained high rate of technical progress by inventors is not the same as large continuing social gains from use of the technology. The problem of commercialization intervenes. Computer and networking hardware and software are enabling technologies, and the costs of bringing them into use will affect behavior. For information technology, the commercialization problem can be summarized as a very high rate of technical progress in hardware, a reasonably high rate of return in marketed software, and often painfully slow complementary investment in new software and business practices at end-user sites. The last portion has limited economies of scale because of the variety of business practices in a highly decentralized economy and is also characterized by sunkness.

The primary behavioral implications of sunk costs are inertia and caution. We see both in the demand for large-scale computing. All these are rational responses to sunk costs: caution before moving to a new tech-

---

35. This confirms the general finding in the organizational literature since Lucas (1984) that MIS has little internal political power.

nology, inertia in staying with an old technology, and even caution in making new commitments to an old technology when a new one may be arriving. All of these behaviors are evident in the late period of mainframe usage. The inertia and caution in this case must ultimately break and permit movement to new technologies, at least with regard to hardware. It appears that the transition era is characterized by great technological uncertainty; the theory suggests that this will lead to more caution.

A variety of market responses to this problem are in evidence. Consider the recent market successes of system integrators and consultants. Expertise in making the adjustment to new technological opportunities certainly lowers external adjustment costs.[36] In this regard, system integrators and consultants are a mechanism for gaining economies of scale in the on-site portion of information technology investments. In the old industrial organization of information technology, this expertise often could be found in the systems vendor. As information technology moves to a more open-systems arrangement, that source becomes correspondingly less important. This leaves a market opportunity for system integrators and consultants, and quite possibly for sellers of proprietary software.

Yet system integrators, consultants, and the sellers of systems, networking, and database management system software cannot make the internal adjustment costs less sunk, nor can they fundamentally reduce uncertainty about future technical developments. The internal adjustment costs arise from the need to make valuable organizational changes to get the biggest advantages of information technology, a problem that is not going away.[37] This view implies that the current transition era in information technology is not just a time of technical change and the emergence of new standards. Instead, it is a period of definition of new market institutions for commercialization.

Once again, there is every reason to believe that the shift to wide-area network and client/server technologies will increase these forces rather than make them go away. The span of cutting-edge information technology investments is increasing to cover more technologies, more vendor companies, and more markets.

---

36. It may lower the internal (disruption) costs as well, though this assertion is more controversial.

37. The degree of future technological uncertainty will certainly decline with time as standards for the post–competitive crash era are set. This will reduce the purely technical role of system integrators and consultants, but probably not their adjustment cost–lowering role.

The Competitive Crash

Two technological/economic stories of nascent competition between old and new types of computer systems and between the kinds of companies that sell them have circulated widely among technologists and in the trade press. Both are wrong. What is instead right is not yet completely clear, but the behavior of customers in the early stages of the competitive crash gives many useful clues.

The "MIPS arbitrage" theory correctly identifies an important driver behind the competitive crash, increases in the capabilities of the largest microprocessor-based systems and in networks of microprocessor-based systems. Yet the theory is seriously incomplete in that it ignores a product-differentiation advantage of mainframe software. In our estimates, the size of the market for mainframe systems declines with competition but the degree of market power does not. Most mainframe brands continue to be monopolies, albeit over a smaller body of inframarginal customers.[38] The best of both worlds theory expected that client/server architectures would quickly solve the long-standing user relations problem. To be sure, the user relations problem is more likely to be solved sometime in the future than it was in the past. Yet the view that it was going to be solved quickly by combining the strengths of servers with the strengths of clients was more a fond hope than a technological and organizational reality. At least in the early going, exactly the sites that would benefit least from these advantages were the fastest to switch.[39] Buyers appear to have viewed the advanced claims for client/server architectures with real suspicion.

What instead is actually true? The dynamics of user behavior affected the early competition between the old and new computer systems in a variety of ways. First, the readiness of buyers to wait for new technologies they could not yet use was a huge revenue and public relations shock to old-system suppliers. This was partially offset by their continued ability to

---

38. By late 1993, the trade press had caught on to this, as discussed in a number of citations above. It does not speak particularly well of client/server vendors that they needed to be berated this late in the transition for using MIPS arbitrage arguments for marketing purposes. The falsity of that view was evident in buyers' behavior as early as 1990, and could be clearly heard in the first phase of the Bresnahan-Saloner (1995) interviews with buyers in late 1992.

39. Seeing whether this persists into the 1990s is one very good reason for our current investigation of more recent data. As of the second wave of Bresnahan-Saloner (1995) interviews in spring 1993, there were some interesting exceptions, but this described the overall pattern quite well. The exceptions, for example in the marketing departments of telecommunications companies, related to the value of best of both worlds–style solutions as a reaction to a radical change in competitive circumstances.

command a substantial price premium for their products—the market power alluded to above. A more important offset was the very slow pace of the transition to the new world. This left sellers of the old technology a number of years to come to interpret events and to organize technology and marketing for a competitive response. This "breathing space" may well be important for the future structure of the information technology industry.

Further evidence of a very different kind comes from the supply behavior of vendors. First, the failure of the vertical-relations model as an explanation of preference for specific old vendors is an important part of our story. If we are correct, then old-line vendors should be abandoning the "account management" marketing strategy. That strategy focuses on extracting rents from the existing base of locked-in customers. The switch of most old-style vendors to a somewhat more open-systems approach, while late, suggests that they see the same environment we do. Most current discussion of the old-line vendors discusses the inefficacy and slowness of their decision making. The slow transition to a new technological base is "breathing space" to them and permits these changes of strategies to be visible despite how slowly they have occurred.

Second, the adjustment costs appear to be inherent in the problem of making effective use of the new technologies in large applications. If this is correct, it suggests that old vendors' behavior should change; they should now see the source of their rents in service and in software products that run on large systems or networks. The same argument suggests that new vendors—of database management systems and tools, and (especially) systems integration services—may pursue the same rents. Once again, this is a recognizable description of parts of the technology strategy of old-line vendors, their competitors in open-systems software markets, and systems integrators. Supply behavior as well as demand behavior is consistent with the story.

Our analysis of all three topics is limited by essentially the same problems, and these await further research. We study the very early period in the diffusion of client/server technology. We have little to say about technological expectations, in particular about waiting for software tools and the setting of new standards. Yet we want to finish by emphasizing the element of continuity in behavior we observe, which leads us to believe that the world will not quickly change to make us wrong. A long series of technical initiatives have dramatically increased the potential range of useful information technology applications. Achieving that potential has always been difficult and therefore slow.

APPENDIX   *Statistical Models*

Our statistical models for increases in capacity at the site (s) level take the form:

$$V_{s85} = X_{s85}\beta_{85} + \epsilon_{s85}. \tag{1}$$

$$V_{s90} = X_{s90}\beta_{90} + \epsilon_{s90}. \tag{2}$$

So the expected aggregate demand for systems expansion in each triad is calculated by first predicting the probability that each site will expand, then adding them up:

$$Q_{85} = \Sigma_s \text{ Prob (Expand)}_{s85} = \Sigma_s \text{ } F_{s85} \text{ } (X_{s85}\beta_{s85}). \tag{3}$$

$$Q_{90} = \Sigma_s \text{ Prob (Expand)}_{s90} = \Sigma_s \text{ } F_{s90} \text{ } (X_{s90}\beta_{s90}). \tag{4}$$

It is clear from this definition that the predicted aggregate demand curve shape is determined by two forces. The first is the shape of the distribution function for unobserved heterogeneity, as has been emphasized much in recent modeling work.[40] The second force is the distribution of *observed* heterogeneity in valuation, $X\beta$. Since our data do not contain variation in prices, we can say very little about the first force. Instead, we will try to make inferences that are robust to assumptions about the shape of $F\epsilon$, and to changes in its shape over time. Our estimates do contain a good deal of information about the changing distribution of $X\beta$ over time.

First, assume for a moment that the statistical assumption behind Tables 4 and 5 is correct—that is, that the shape of $F\epsilon$ is unit normal for both 1985 and 1990. Then, we can calculate (3) and (4) to get predicted demand. To hypothetically change prices, we add a fixed "value deviation," Δ, to the valuation of all customers. We recalculate (3) and (4) for a wide variety of Δ, using

$$Q_y(\Delta) = \Sigma_s \text{ } \phi(X_{sy}\beta_y + \Delta).$$

Now, since we do not estimate a price coefficient, we do not know whether Δ has units of pennies or billions of dollars. Yet it does correspond to a hypothetical price change. We could show the results with Δ on the vertical axis and $Q_y(\Delta)$ on the horizontal axis for $y = 1985, 1990$. The shape of this is the same as Figure 3, and the tendency to steeper demand over time is preserved.

This analysis relies heavily on the assumption that the errors are known to have a specific shape, the normal, and that the shape is the same over time. Neither assumption can be defended on a priori grounds. To relax them both, we move to semi-nonparametric estimation. In particular, we approximate $F\epsilon_{85}(X_{85}\beta_{85})$ and $F\epsilon_{90}(X_{90}\beta_{90})$ by a fifth-order series approximation around the unit normal. This allows quite different shapes, and we also allow the approximation to vary between the two triads. This body of reported demand curve findings changes very little if we replace the MIPS definition of capacity changes with the coarser systems definition. These figures are available from the authors.

---

40. See, for example, Berry, Levinsohn, and Pakes (1993) for the importance of this in determining the demand elasticities.

Also, the body of results changes little if we use different conditioning assumptions. Obviously, the distribution of X across sites is an important determinant of $X\beta$. The distribution of X changes quite little between our two triads. The important changes are that the macroeconomic downturn is reflected in smaller employment growth figures and that the sites have more powerful mainframe computers but slightly fewer of them five years later. We have redrawn the figures using the same Xs for both years, and this, too, makes little difference.

Strategy for Economic Growth: Lessons from the Chemical Industry

RALPH LANDAU

During my business career in the chemical industry, spanning nearly four decades from the mid-1940s to the early 1980s, I spent little time thinking about issues of economic growth and competitiveness. Instead, I focused on running Halcon International, a specialized engineering firm that developed several innovative chemical processes which the industry is still using to produce various intermediate and consumer goods. When issues of industrial competitiveness did cross my mind, I generally assumed that the market would help support and generate new technologies and growth, and left it at that.

The chain of events that led me to question this simple orthodoxy began—although I had no way of knowing it at the time—in the mid-1960s, when Halcon established a partnership with the Atlantic Richfield Company (Arco) to exploit our invention for production of propylene oxide, a key ingredient for making polyurethane plastics and foams. The venture proved commercially successful, soon becoming one of the two major world producers of propylene oxide. By the mid-1970s, the latest of seven plants which used this technology was financed in part by a bank loan geared to the prime rate, which was then 11 percent. Up to that point, federal economic policy had not had a notable effect on the venture's activities.

But then inflation roared in during the 1970s; by 1979, it had reached 13 percent. President Jimmy Carter appointed Paul Volcker to be chairman of the Federal Reserve, and Volcker proceeded to fight inflation by limiting the money supply. The prime rate shot up to 21 percent. Since the loans had adjustable interest rates, suddenly all of Halcon's cash flow was going to the banks. Technological strategy, which had built Halcon's past successes, gave way to concerns for sheer survival: could the next interest payment be met? Arco reopened the original partnership agreement, and I vividly remember Arco's financial head saying, "I'll teach you the value of money." In such unfavorable macroeconomic conditions, Arco had much deeper pockets and a greater ability to make the interest payments. Finance was decisive over even great technology. These circumstances forced Halcon to sell out its 50 percent interest to Arco.

With the taste of this experience in my mouth, my original orthodoxy—that market forces would inevitably lead to new technology and growth—no longer seemed to apply as well. Halcon had been a technological and commercial success; for example, novel processes, such as for terephthalic acid and propylene oxide, were singled out for special plaudits by Peter Spitz (1988). But sheer size and the availability of finance had proved decisive.

I realized that I had just lived through something important, although at the time I wasn't yet able to identify and describe fully the factors at work. However, I became determined to investigate these issues after joining the economics community at Stanford and Harvard in the 1980s. I undertook a survey of the chemical industry from its beginnings in the 1850s, and then broadened my work to the interaction of technology and economic growth. The chemical industry proved a fortuitous choice. Chemicals were the first science-based industry, and the more familiar high-technology industries of the post–World War II era are essentially similar to it in their dependence on innovative science and the commercialization of technology. Thus, lessons gleaned from the development of the chemical industry are broadly applicable in considering policies that will nurture the long-term health of the U.S. economy.

This combination of industry and academic background has left me well-positioned to see the connections between the microeconomic world, as exemplified by the chemical industry, and the broader macroeconomic context of economic growth, competitiveness, and trade. It has helped me understand how technological advantages are created and maintained, from time to time and place to place, and the relationship of technology to economic growth and the wealth of nations. Much of the material contained in the introduction to this volume summarizes my understanding of these processes. This chapter is a step further along this path; a book on these subjects is in preparation.

Competitiveness in the Chemical Industry

The history of the chemical industry offers clear illustrations of the interdependence between the government-created economic policy envi-

TABLE I

1990 and 1991 R&D Expenditures of Major R&D Investment Industries

(*billions of dollars*)

Industry	1990	1991	Privately financed	Percentage privately financed
Aerospace	25.36	21.69	6.59	30
Electrical machinery and communications	17.72	17.28	12.46	72
Machinery	14.70	15.09	14.03	93
Chemicals	12.34	13.18	13.09	99
Autos, trucks, transportation	10.66	10.40	9.29	89
Professional and scientific instruments	6.19	6.62	6.52	98
Computer software and services	4.63	4.78	3.23	68
Petroleum	2.13	2.25	2.23	99
Total	93.73	91.29	67.44	

SOURCE: National Science Foundation (various years).

NOTE: Total R&D estimated (by Batelle Memorial Institute) at $150.8 billion for 1991, of which industrial R&D was $106.8 billion so the above are the bulk of investors in R&D. These figures for 1993 are estimated at $164.5 billion and $114.8 billion, respectively. In real terms, R&D spending is flat.

ronment and the actions of individual firms. The chemical industry is useful to consider for three reasons. First, it was the first science-based, high-technology industry, with its research and development financed almost solely by private investment, as shown in Table 1. Second, chemical processing has played a central role in generating technological innovations for other industries, such as autos, textiles, consumer products, health services, cosmetics, household cleaners, construction, and photography. In this regard, the chemical industry is evidence of the more general fact that the benefits of internationally competitive industries spill over to other industries. Third, the chemical industry is a U.S. success story. Chemicals are one of only two major high-technology industries (aerospace is the other) where the United States has maintained its competitive lead in international trade, and the growth rate has exceeded that of the economy since World War II.

To understand why comparative advantages in the chemical industry changed, it is useful to summarize briefly the essential historical facts, before offering a more detailed analysis for the reasons that underlay the changes. In 1856, William Henry Perkin discovered the first synthetic dye (mauve), which launched the modern organic chemical industry and led to British dominance in this industry until the 1870s. England in the mid-1800s was rich; it had the know-how, the largest customer base (textiles), and the largest supply of raw material (coal). But it let its advantages slip away, and by the end of the 1880s the Germans dominated the chemical industry. By 1913, German companies produced 140,000 tons of dyes, Switzerland produced 10,000 tons, and Britain only 4,400 tons. The American industry depended mainly on German dyestuff and other chemical imports, although it was a large producer of basic inorganic chemicals.

The First World War changed the relative positions completely, at least for a few years. The United States built its own organic chemical industry, and the German industry fell on hard times. Britain sought to take advantage of its victory at the expense of Germany, by creating a national standard bearer, Imperial Chemical Industries (ICI), through a merger of smaller entities. The relative positions shifted again as a postwar recession and subsequent political unrest led to formation of a European cartel, in which the Germans through the I. G. Farben company soon regained dominance, especially as Germany under Adolf Hitler began preparations for the Second World War. At the same time, the United States was gaining strength through the development not only of a large petroleum refining base, but also of skill in designing large-scale continuous-processing plants through the use of expert chemical engineering tools. This skill, largely in the hands of specialized engineering firms (like Halcon), was readily transferable to the burgeoning petrochemical industry, which was based on the cheap petroleum and natural gas feedstocks in which the United States was rich. However, the European chemical industry still used coal, rather than petroleum, as its main feedstock.

World War II resulted in the physical destruction of the German chemical industry. The U.S. industry was now using petrochemicals to produce fibers, plastics, and many other products while dyestuffs shrank in importance.[1] America's chemical industry grew enormously and dominated the market at least until the 1970s. As world prosperity returned, however, so did a successful chemical industry in Germany, and Europe more generally. Petrochemical industries were soon well-established in Asia, in the oil-rich countries, and elsewhere. No longer did one country dominate; the industry's growth had made it a major worldwide economic success story. Comparative advantage at the firm level truly came to the fore, with different companies in different countries excelling at what they did best. Japan was the exception. Although the Japanese chemical industry grew to become the second largest in the world, it never became a major player in international markets for products or technology.

What led to these shifting patterns? To analyze the lessons from the chemical industry, it is essential to examine systematically the context in

---

1. In 1993 only one major domestically owned dyestuff manufacturer remained in the United States—Crompton and Knowles.

which firms must operate. For this purpose, I have found it useful to start at the most general national characteristics of key industrial countries and then proceed through various less aggregate layers of governmental, institutional, and social factors to the individual industry and its firms, as illustrated in the "Levels of Comparative Advantage" table in the Introduction to this volume. Comparing these levels of aggregation across national and temporal boundaries makes it easier to draw more general conclusions about what makes for comparative advantage. The emphasis in the discussion that follows is primarily on the United States, Germany, the United Kingdom, and, to a somewhat lesser extent, Japan. From these accounts, it is evident that countries don't compete; firms do. But it all adds up at the top.

This discussion should illustrate that comparative advantage is dynamic and ever-changing. Moreover, it is not a zero-sum game—all countries can benefit, even if advantage shifts from time to time, from place to place, and from industry to industry. Moreover, growth paths are often distinct for each country, depending on the internal behavior and structure of firms, as well as on their ability to manage their own affairs—for example, their skill in exploiting the findings of scientific research in a commercial context. Firms, of course, can be considerably aided or hindered by the economic climate that the government creates for them to work in. In this way, for better or for worse, a nation's economic fate is in its own hands to shape. The chapter by Moses Abramovitz and Paul David in this volume illustrates well the complexity of the growth process.

At the National Governance Level

Although all four of the countries considered here are now democracies, that was not always the case. Germany flourished from 1871 until 1914 as an authoritarian government, primarily under the Iron Chancellor Otto von Bismarck and two Kaisers, with a strong national goal of industrializing rapidly so as to overtake Britain, then the strongest European power, with a worldwide empire rich in resources and markets. This national goal was more than achieved by 1914, when Germany had become the strongest nation in Europe. The chemical industry was one of a handful of industries encouraged by the government to grow rapidly and help propel the rise of the German economy. From 1870–1913, the German rate of growth per capita averaged 1.8 percent per year, while Britain's was only 1.3 percent. The British government, influenced by the teachings of Adam Smith, took no particular initiative to strengthen the nation's infrastructure or its chemical industry, but concentrated instead on developing its empire and its overseas investments, and allowing its domestic industries to grow without any special intervention.

Likewise, the U.S. government made no special effort to foster industry during this period (or later, for that matter), but the combined effect of its policies resulted in a growth rate per capita of an average 2.2 percent during the same period. Compounded over many years, these differences became decisive in relative wealth and influence. Until the Second World War, Japan was also governed by authoritarian and ultimately militaristic measures; its chemical industry was quite insignificant on the world scale. After the Second World War, Japan followed the earlier German precedent of a national "catch-up" goal, and achieved growth rates as high as 5 percent per year, but did not especially favor the chemical industry.

Socio-Political Climate

Both Britain and Germany in the nineteenth century were aristocratic and class-structured, but the landed aristocracy of Prussia gave high social status to learning, science, and scholarship. Industrialists were well respected. Engineers, however, were accorded second-class status, which prevented the Germans from developing a chemical engineering discipline until long after the discipline was established in the United States. In Britain, industry and industrialists ranked in social status well below the armed forces, the foreign and civil service, law, politics, the clergy, and medicine. In short, the British social order was not well-positioned to support a science-based industry.

The lack of an aristocracy may have been one of the basic factors behind the greater U.S. economic growth. Furthermore, by encouraging widespread immigration, the United States generated a powerful brew of motivated workforces and a blend of cultures. The United States prided itself on its pragmatism, and engineers often had a higher social status than scientists.

In Germany, the basic strength of science-based industries, such as chemicals, contributed to the nation's confidence in its military superiority. German scientists, for example, had developed the first process for the synthetic production of fertilizers and explosives ingredients from air (the Haber-Bosch process). The military disasters of the two world wars set back the German economy for many years, but its chemical industry recovered quickly, aided by the benign policies of the victorious allies, and Germany again became a world-class competitor.

After the Second World War, Britain had a long period of social redistribution and dissolution of empire under the Labor Party, along with a government policy less favorable to industry. Nevertheless, ICI and others grew and competed. This is an excellent illustration of the thesis propounded by Harvard's pre-eminent business historian, Alfred D. Chandler (1990): companies that make the necessary three-pronged investment in technology, distribution, and management can remain leading factors over extended periods of time because of economies of scale and scope.

Japan's rise from the ashes of defeat in the Second World War was accomplished with strong national discipline under a U.S.-imposed constitution and for a long time with a single dominant party. However, the Japanese chemical industry was not a major world competitor for several reasons. One was that to maintain power, the Liberal-Democratic Party dictated that domestic heating fuel should be subsidized at the expense of raising prices on the petroleum naphtha used to make petrochemicals. Oil companies were given the exclusive right to import petroleum or its major refinery products, no doubt to improve their bargaining position vis-à-vis the Middle Eastern oil producers. Such policies prevented Japanese chemical companies from purchasing feedstocks in world markets at prices lower than those of the government-supported monopolistic oil companies. Conversely, the United States has had abundant and cheap petroleum and natural gas resources. Britain has also possessed these, but the Germans have been somewhat less fortunate. Another was the fierce desire of every Japanese *keiretsu* group to have its own petrochemical division, which led to non-world-scale sizes, and also to frequent overcapacity by overbuilding.

Macroeconomics, Trade, and Exchange Rates

Britain, for most of the chemical industry's history, has practiced some version of free trade, and this laissez-faire macroeconomics has meant that some industries gain and some lose. Many economists believe that Britain's free trade policies had a positive effect on growth. The pound sterling, until the depression in the early 1930s, was the international reserve currency, maintained on a gold standard. As Ronald McKinnon and David Robinson (1992) have shown, this period of monetary stability contributed substantially to British and world growth. Since then, international currency exchanges have become much more volatile. These currency fluctuations inflicted substantial damage on the chemical industry in Britain, which depended heavily on exports to pay for its essential imports. Since World War II, Germany has favored free trade, and it has flourished under the free market economic policies introduced by Chancellor Ludwig Erhard in 1948. It vies with the United States for the position of the world's largest exporter. German chemical companies have been affected unfavorably by the high value of the esteemed D-mark, resulting from Germany's tight monetary policy to restrain the inflation arising from German unification. U.S. chemical companies are less subject to currency effects because of their large domestic activities, but the recession of 1981–82 and the high real interest rates resulted in virtually no profits in 1982 for the U.S. industry. The volatility of U.S. economic policies from about the mid-1960s has been frequently described in the press and economic literature, and has been accompanied by sharply reduced growth rates in productivity.

In recent years, the United States has been the strongest advocate of free trade, abolishing its American Selling Price tariffs on some chemicals in the 1970s. Japan remains the most protectionist. Part of the reason is that the Japanese do not want to depend on faraway supply lines for important materials. Imports of chemical intermediates clearly fall into this category. At certain times, Halcon's joint venture with Arco could have supplied propylene oxide to Japanese polyurethane consumers at a lower price than Halcon's joint venture with Sumitomo in Japan could offer, but the shipping distance from Texas and the shortage of storage facilities at Japan's ports made logistics difficult and justified continued operations of the higher cost product.

Structural and Supportive Policies

Tax and regulatory policies have played an important role in determining whether innovation and technology flourish. The United States had no income tax until 1913, which permitted the accumulation of great wealth and contributed to the establishment of the professionally managed modern corporation. Germany legalized cartels in the 1890s, and a strong cartel philosophy has always been present in its chemical industry, culminating in the establishment of I. G. Farben in the 1920s and its leadership of a European cartel, which, while preserving the industry during the turbulent 1920s, also helped pave the way for the 1939 war. In Europe generally, the culture of enduring monopolies and cartels has been dismantled too slowly, old industries have been heavily subsidized, and growth in the economy as a whole has been inhibited. Around the turn of the century, the United States began adopting its series of antitrust acts, which have remained the dominant factor in encouraging vigorous competition.

Britain never much emphasized antitrust policies, as witness its governmental encouragement of the formation of ICI. Japan purports to have an antitrust policy, but strong government bureaucracies such as the Ministry for International Trade and Industry (MITI) help coordinate industrial activities. MITI seeks to encourage vigorous domestic competition at the same time that it acts in the best long-term interests of Japanese business. During recessions, MITI has encouraged the emergence of "recession cartels" among certain groups (including chemicals) which permit necessary industrial restructuring to happen in an orderly fashion.

In the modern era, every country has extensive environmental regulations, which affect the chemical industry profoundly, often for good reason (technology does have its darker side) but sometimes based on poor evidence and varying country necessities. The worldwide industry has accordingly been compelled to allocate perhaps a quarter of its annual investments for pollution mitigation, and to refocus some of its research on developing processes that pollute less and products that can be recycled. The German government has been particularly severe in this area, and the major German chemical companies have incurred heavy costs to clean up their operations, especially those polluting the Rhine River. Recently, Germany has imposed harsh product recycling laws, which (although they are not working very well and may be modified) pose additional problems for its chemical companies. This climate of super-zealous regulation has been forcing German companies to consider moving even more aggressively into the United States, Asia, and other European countries—an ironic twist to the nineteenth-century success story, when the German government strongly supported the growth of its chemical industry.

Dr. Gottfried Plumpe, assistant to the chairman of the Bayer Company, provided a startling example of this in commenting on this chapter. Bayer, he said, is moving its biotechnology center to the San Francisco Bay Area in California, rather than leaving it in Germany. He argued that California, and the United States more generally, have a comparative advantage in this major growth area of the 21st century, because they have a less hostile media and public opinion than in Germany. For example, the United States has no equivalent of the Green Party in Germany's parliament, which opposes all such technology. Furthermore, the Bay Area is populated with great research centers in biology at Stanford and the University of California, and shares the "can-do" entrepreneurial spirit of Silicon Valley and its venture capital industry. In many ways, this close regional strength and industrial-university linkage resembles the nineteenth-century situation in the German chemical industry along the Rhine, which permitted it to grow to world dominance by 1914. The Germany of today is quite different. BASF has taken similar steps, and Hoechst may well follow suit.

The German government recognized the importance of protecting its intellectual property as early as its patent act of 1877, and thus greatly encouraged its chemical industry in its competition with the British, who paid less attention to patents. The United States also developed a strong patent system, open to all countries under rules somewhat favoring domestic companies, whereas in Japan foreign companies have been subject to long delays in patent issuance.

Some national differences are most pronounced in education. In Britain, technical education and scientific research were not accorded the support that applied in Germany, and as early as the 1850s, most important chemical research and education was performed on the Continent. German university chemical research dates from the early 1840s, and served as a model for the United States, which until nearly the end of the nineteenth century had no research universities. Oxford and Cambridge neglected science education in favor of the classics, language, religion, and literature. The aristocratic ideals of what makes a gentleman dominated the social structure (Bernal, 1939). It was in the American universities, particularly at MIT, that the science of chemical engineering was created and developed, in synergy with the evolution of the petroleum refining and chemical industries (Landau and Rosenberg, 1992). As mentioned above, engineers have been respected in the United States for a long time, as witness the passage of the Morrill Act of 1862, which laid the foundation for the establishment of colleges for the agricultural and mechanical arts. Chemical engineering in Germany was always subordinated to the chemists at the tops of their companies, so the educational system was slow to respond. To a considerable extent, this has also been the situation in Britain and Japan. In general, university-industry relations have been much warmer in the United States, as Rosenberg and Nelson (1993) have recently shown.

In science and technology, the United States has had a variety of defense-related federal laboratories, but the bulk of the post-1945 support has come from federal grants to universities for research in basic science and engineering. More recently, efforts are being made to achieve federal support for generic research. This now extends to some direct industrial help, like SEMATECH (a consortium of companies to develop manufacturing techniques for semiconductors), which has been funded 50 percent by government. The United States is by far the largest supporter of university-based research and education in science, and whereas the German universities were once the model, it is now the United States which welcomes students from all over the world.

In labor policies, Bismarck's Germany led the way with social security measures, like introducing a retirement age of 65 years. The chemical industry in Germany during the last part of the nineteenth century also provided workers with housing and other benefits. This policy was further embellished after 1945 by labor-management participation in German company supervisory boards, and by other generous unemployment and health provisions which produced labor peace. More recently, this century-old consensus that provided the world's most generous social cushion (with concomitant high taxes and regulations) is proving more difficult for German industry and the economy to swallow. Compulsory company charges and benefits, including lavish vacations, holidays, and shorter work weeks, nearly double hourly wage costs, making them the highest in the world. The rest of Europe, hitched to the German economic wagon, is also seeing higher wage costs.

The United States has fewer labor market rigidities than either Europe or Japan, where the previously successful lifetime employment policy of large companies is proving very costly in difficult economic times. (In fact, lifetime employment never covered the 70 percent of the workforce in manufacturing companies of less than 300 employees.) In the twentieth century, as the chemical industry in the United States became more capital intensive and automated, it became relatively immune to labor disturbances, but has paid relatively high wages.

Institutional Setting

Since the chemical industry (along with most high-technology industry) is so dependent on capital, financial institutions can have a powerful effect. Britain had the freest and largest financial market in the nineteenth century, which helped finance the growth of many overseas countries and dominions. Perversely, this worked against the chemical industry, because British investors found opportunities for lower risk and higher financial returns overseas in the empire, as well as in the more traditional fields of iron, coal, steel, and textiles. Britain's banking system encouraged growth in commerce and trade.

By contrast, German investors were latecomers on the industrial scene, forcing them to look for new opportunities, which they found in exports and in domestic industries based more heavily on scientific research and newer technologies (including a drive for military self-sufficiency). Shut out of the easy opportunities for short-term profit or colonizing resource-rich countries, the Germans appear to have adopted longer time horizons than the British in their industrial undertakings, assisted by cooperative banks that retained significant ownership interests in the companies they financed.

The U.S. financial system evolved along different paths, as described by Myron Scholes in this volume. Porter (1992) compares the capital allocation systems of the United States and its competitors. The brief summary is that Japan's has resembled Germany's more, while the United Kingdom's is more like that of the United States, with widespread public ownership by many institutions and individuals. Porter shows, reinforced by the work of Hatsopoulos and Poterba (1993), that higher equity capital costs in the United States as compared with Japan have favored shorter-term horizons of managers, since there is financial pressure to get a reward sooner.

That this is also true in the United Kingdom is demonstrated by the recent breakup of Imperial Chemical Industries—the United Kingdom's largest industrial company and chemical standard bearer—into two companies, namely Zeneca (agrochemicals and pharmaceuticals) and ICI. A higher overall stock valuation resulted, yielding enhanced shareholder value, and management of each could better focus on their business and core competences. It should be remembered that this harsh market judgment in turn reflects the impact of an over-valued pound sterling due to U.K. efforts to remain within the European currency band for too long, thereby pricing many chemical exports out of the market.

In the United States, this pressure led to many acquisitions and mergers in the 1980s. The chemical industry was not often a target of many hostile investors, since corporate raiders know enough to be wary of risky science-based industries like chemicals. More often, changes in the chemical industry were due to restructuring or foreign acquisition. However, Union Carbide, one of the big three United States chemical companies in the early 1980s, was taken over and broken up. The Halcon experience does apply generally: finance *is* more important than technology in an era of low savings rates and escalating demand for social services. Even the friendly German big bank system is fraying as the bank owners themselves seek more diversification and higher returns to shareholders. Hence, market values of the large German chemical companies stagnate or fall along with their earnings.

A striking illustration of the present financial situation was provided in comments on this chapter by Dr. Albert D. Richards of Credit Suisse–First Boston, London, an expert analyst of the chemical industry. He used the case of Dow Chemical and BASF. Common opinion among analysts and industry observers has been that Dow is better managed than BASF. Yet BASF has been able to achieve an identical performance when measured by growth in company size, growth in earnings per share, share price performance, and growth in real book value per share. Nevertheless, the total market value for Dow is more than twice that of BASF. Why is this? Because Dow has been much kinder to its shareholders and debtholders, who have received almost five times as much of the operating cash flow as BASF's shareholders. BASF retained much more of its cash flow in order to grow as fast as Dow, but at the expense of its shareholders. Is it any wonder then that shareholders everywhere are becoming more active, putting managements under increasing pressure, and increasing the scrutiny over fund managers? The whole issue of corporate governance has been a very live subject of debate for some years, as Porter (1992) has illuminated.

Much has been written about the great litigiousness of the American legal system; the chapter by Thomas Campbell, Daniel Kessler, and George Shepherd in this volume deals with this issue. It has affected the U.S. chemical industry in two ways: in forcing greater attention to product safety, and expending large sums for disappointing results in toxic waste cleanup under the Superfund legislation. As illustrated in the comments from Plumpe, however, it has not yet, at least, impacted the growing biotechnology industry in a major way, partly because the U.S. government and the industry are careful to observe the necessary precautions and test procedures for approval.

A number of intermediating institutions have formed over the years to aid industrial development and growth. Thus, Germany has its Max Planck Institutes and its Fraunhofer Institutes to help bridge scientific-commercial interfaces. Although there are some pan-European research organizations for other sciences, few have much pertinence for the chemical industry. The United States developed the system of specialized engineering firms that handled much of new chemical plant construction, as well as provided technology transfer. These firms, and the chemical industry more generally, pioneered among industries the fusing of process manufacturing and product. Halcon, for example, developed a worldwide licensing and design business based on proprietary process technology for important petrochemical derivatives, such as the key intermediates for polyester and nylon fibers, plastics, and rubbers. These helped in the extensive buildup of a vibrant chemical industry, both here and abroad.

Professional and industrial organizations also flourished in the four countries, with the American Institute of Chemical Engineers and the American Chemical Society as models of their kind. No pan-European organizations of this type yet exist, and hence the Americans attract much interest and attention from Europe as well as other regions.

The Industry Level

The chemical industry became international early, well before any other high-technology industry, and most major chemical companies are also significant players and investors in the major industrial markets. Thus, the industry has had to become highly competitive, and there is relatively little any one government can do to control the transnational activities of so many technologically powerful companies. As Porter (1990) has written, the surest way for governments to encourage the growth of an industry is to provide for strong competitive pressure, while creating a suitable domestic climate.

But the industry has had to respond to the macroeconomy's financial pressures by paying much closer attention to its shareholders' interests. One index of this has been the recent rise of financially oriented top management in companies traditionally dominated by scientists or engineers. This year, for the first time ever, the CEOs of all the big-three German companies (Bayer, BASF, Hoechst) will not be scientists. However, it seems likely that as technologists become more financially and economically sophisticated, they will return to the top (Landau, 1992). This is one lesson the Halcon-Arco experience certainly illuminated. Another major trend has been the shift of basic petrochemical manufacture (the largest component of the chemical industry) to companies or countries rich in resources, while many chemical companies moved to products with more value-added. For example, the pharmaceutical segment of the chemical industry, never dependent on cheap feedstocks, continued to be among the most innovative industries in the United States.

Despite the financial and regulatory pressures described above, but partially also because of them, the U.S. industry has retained its traditional research intensity, where it is distinctive in being virtually all privately financed. The moderate R&D decline in the last several years reflects the severe financial pressures mentioned above, as well as a worldwide recession, which has affected European industry as well. As a consequence, the U.S. industry has, since World War II, maintained a favorable trade balance (in 1992 over $16 billion) and a growth rate greater than that of the economy. It is the country's largest export sector (with $44 billion), surpassing the aerospace industry in 1992. The chemical industry is also the largest in Europe. However, the world's current slack economic environment has emphasized to the Europeans that they still have much reorganization and rationalization to accomplish, which the American industry has already largely accomplished.

In the United Kingdom, companies in 1992 spent only one-third the percentage of sales devoted to R&D as did the average of the 200 top R&D spenders around the world. They prefer to pay out dividends to shareholders, whereas the average spending of the top 200 was 2.5 times as much on

R&D as on payouts. ICI ranks 47th in this list, and only ten other British companies are in it. The United States and Japan dominate the list with 75 and 59 companies. Germany has much lower representation, which suggests weakness ahead.

As in other industries, the chemical industry is watching the decline of the conglomerate in favor of the more highly focused company. Europe suffers from considerable redundant capacity, which is exacerbated by some European state-owned companies (particularly in France and Italy) that do not have the same profit-making constraints as does private industry, and strong environmental regulations, particularly in Germany.

The Firm Level

Firms display great differences in strategy and performance. For example, DuPont, Dow, Monsanto, Exxon, and Union Carbide in the United States have all adjusted to changing world conditions more rapidly than have the German big three. DuPont bought an oil company (Conoco) but sold off its commodity chemical businesses and focused on its fiber and specialized chemicals strengths (in agrochemicals, electronic and photographic products, and so on)—lately swapping its lagging acrylic fibers with ICI's nylon to strengthen each one. It has been engaged in heavy cost reduction and has lowered its capital investment rate. Dow remains a major international factor in petrochemicals, and has acquired a pharmaceutical company; Monsanto has bet its future on biotechnology. Exxon, the third largest American chemical company, is primarily a worldwide producer of petrochemical intermediates and plastics. Union Carbide has returned to its roots as a pioneer in petrochemical technology, having shed its consumer products divisions to fend off takeover bids and raise stock prices.

In Germany, the big three never ventured completely into petrochemicals. Bayer partnered with BP, and BASF with Shell. Bayer and Hoechst fortified their positions in pharmaceuticals and many other differentiated chemicals, but have gradually relinquished their traditional dyestuff interests to less developed countries such as India and China. The Japanese have their unique *keiretsu* system in which related companies organized around a main bank (like Mitsui, Mitsubishi, Sumitomo) own substantial blocks of stock in each other and also have cross-bank ownerships. Thus, the companies have little or no fear of takeover or bankruptcy. Large dividends have never been traditional, and close relationships between suppliers and customers provide continuous revenues and reduce pressures on top management to compete globally. However, the internal competition between *kei-*

retsu is intense. Each insisted on its own chemical complex, thus losing the scale advantage of world-class plants. The Japanese chemical companies are only one-third to one-tenth the size of the large western companies. Combined with other factors, this *keiretsu* pattern has prevented the Japanese chemical companies from being factors in the international market. They have also lagged in technological advances. In fact, they were avid purchasers of Halcon technology.

What Lessons Can Be Learned?

History's lessons are rarely transparent, but they clearly matter; how else can one explain the astonishing survival of strong chemical companies in the United States and Germany, despite many discontinuities? This is well illustrated by the fact that the three largest chemical companies in the world in 1929, and of roughly equal size and scope, were DuPont in the United States, ICI in England, and I. G. Farben in Germany. Despite a world war, and many changes in the world and national economies, they still survive as major factors in the industry (I. G. being decomposed into its three successor companies: Bayer, BASF, and Hoechst, each larger than I. G.). Chandler's thesis still holds: the key to long-term success in managerial capitalism is making an essential investment. It may be especially difficult to apply lessons from the past to younger high-technology industries like computers, communications, and aerospace. Still, with the passage of time, certain powerful themes recur.

The preceding analysis emphatically demonstrates that dynamic comparative advantage is not just technology; instead, it exists at a variety of levels, from the type of governmental structure down to the individual firm. The United States should organize itself to identify the best features at each level that have historically been shown to confer advantage, and adapt them to the U.S. conditions. Such a policy will not eliminate national differences, which will endure for a long, long time. But such differences as remain will make for competition and comparative advantage, and foster trade which benefits all the participants. Lawrence Lau's words, in his chapter of this volume, are particularly helpful in arriving at generalizations: "A pro–economic growth policy must therefore have three parts—it should be pro-investment, pro-technology, and pro-education."

Clearly, not every government and nation has been equally effective in promoting growth. This fact matters, since small differences in growth rates, compounded over several generations, make a vast difference. The United Kingdom today is but a mediocre economic member of the European Community. West Germany served as a locomotive of growth after the Second World War—until reunification with East Germany derailed it in the past few years. Moreover, the German economy alone seems too small to sustain the large, capital-intensive, newer high-technology industries, and its social conditions and high costs have made it uncompetitive even within Europe. Germany is in danger of becoming a second-class technical power. Japan, on the other hand, has grown rapidly by astute national policies and national discipline.

It would increasingly appear that the world is moving into a new global economic era (as Henry Rowen points out in his chapter for this volume), where a key focus of intelligent governments must be to assure a supply of the ingredients of growth: capital, skilled labor, and technology. Lawrence Lau (with Jong-Il Kim in 1992 and in his chapter for this volume) has shown in careful studies of postwar industrial growth that technical progress over much of the period was the most important source of economic growth for the United States, at 34 percent, followed by labor quantity (30 percent), physical capital (23 percent), and human capital (quality of labor) at 13 percent. In Japan and the United Kingdom, human capital was relatively less important than physical capital, but in Germany, physical capital was just as important as technical progress. Other researchers have confirmed these findings (DeLong, 1991; Durlauf, 1992; Wolff, 1992). These factors of growth are not independent of each other, but are complementary. Thus, technology is largely embodied in physical and human capital. Indeed, physical capital and its embodied technology contributed well over half of the growth of the U.S. postwar economy. The chemical industry history illuminates these findings. Of the key factors, the greatest shortage for the foreseeable future will be in capital of all kinds.

Some will say that this focus on growth ignores the main problem—a lack of good jobs. One irony that emerges from Lau's studies is that Europe invested more and gained higher productivity, but created virtually no new jobs in the private sector in almost twenty years, while maintaining a generous social safety net. Conversely, in the United States, low productivity gains and low investment saw over 20 million jobs created, at the cost of stagnant living standards and a widening wage distribution. Bosworth (1994) and Solow (1994) also discuss this situation. The unemployment rate in the United States is around 6 percent; united Germany's is probably over 9 percent; Britain's is about the same; Japan's is less—but many firms retain redundant workers in make-work projects as a social policy, even when losing money. In the United States, it is the entrepreneurial small and particularly the rapidly growing businesses in both manufacturing and services that are the net job creators, expecially in services but also in manufacturing companies, such as those that supply larger companies that are increasingly outsourcing. There is no magic cut-off definition for a small company; size is a continuum. It is true, however, that the smaller-company jobs are less well compensated and often associated with lower skills.

As an illustration of these effects, during the 1980s the Fortune 500 companies lost four million workers but the economy gained eighteen million jobs. Smaller companies are also the most rapidly increasing source of exports. In "How America Sees the World" (1993), the *Economist* states that such companies now total three times the size of the exports of those of the top 50 exporting companies (which are growing very slowly). They are also often the initiators of important new technologies. However, smaller companies are increasingly threatened by mandatory expenditures, excessive regulations, and higher taxes, as well as reluctance of banks to lend to them. Halcon generated in its own businesses several thousand new jobs, but in derivative plants and abroad (including U.S. investments) many times that number. Furthermore, this was accomplished in an era of much less impact of government on business decisions.

Jobs policies can no longer depend on simple macroeconomic stimuli, like government spending programs or tax cuts, but must look at the underlying structures down to the industry and firm levels of the microeconomy. Edmund Phelps (1994) and others have been emphasizing that to reduce the natural non-inflationary rate of unemployment, or to achieve it, many labor regulations need to be reviewed, especially in Europe. Furthermore, the growing requirements of a knowledge-based economy for greater skills in the workforce add to the problems of job creation. These are potential forces for political and social turmoil.

The Proper Role of Government

Nowadays, government policy toward growth seems to be largely discussed in the most simplistic and misleading terms as a choice between industrial policy and protectionism, or no government action at all. But the issue of whether government intervention helps or hurts is far from settled by this history. For example, the German government had much more direct influence on the success of its chemical industry prior to 1945, using tariffs, patents, cartels, educational systems, and wartime controls to foster it. The United States, to the contrary, had little direct intervention.

Yet both grew well, albeit in different directions. The U.K. chemical industry was more like that of the United States, the Japanese chemical industry more like that of Germany, but with much less success.

The challenge, it would seem, is to sort out useful intervention from less useful. This task may be more difficult than it used to be; maturing industrial societies have greater difficulty in exerting direct government influence because of their much greater complexity. To illustrate how governments can do harm as well as good, consider that the Japanese government discouraged Honda from trying to enter international markets, and supported an already obsolete analog-type high-definition television. Japan has also placed rigid price controls on pharmaceuticals, putting the goal of restraining public spending on health care ahead of encouraging its pharmaceutical companies to be world-class in innovation. This has left the field clear for the United States and also some western European countries. Linda Cohen and Roger Noll, in both a 1991 Brookings Institution study and this volume, have documented some expensive American failures in supporting commercializable projects. Nathan Rosenberg's chapter in this volume also deals with the uncertainties inherent in technological evolution. The recent triumph of the privately developed personal computer (PC) in the United States over the long-dominant mainframe and minicomputers, the penetration of American PCs into the Japanese market, and the rise of Microsoft show that creativity and risk taking are required for the most successful firms.

Indeed, history shows that previous reliance on government can be damaging, as the recent German chemical stagnation brought about by excessive regulation and taxation shows. The U.S. chemical industry, with almost no reliance on direct government support, not only continues but also attracts foreign investment. In Japan, the government at first failed to restrain the pride of the various *keiretsu* and thus permitted an uncompetitive chemical industry to evolve, then later protected the status quo by cartels and import restrictions on goods and technology, so as to weaken their competitive drive abroad. And of course, the former Soviet Union offers a supreme example of the failure of government control. When watching the U.S. political process at work, with its constitutional checks and balances, its weak party discipline and bureaucracy, its widespread politicization of Congressional actions, and its excessive litigiousness, it's easy to doubt that many of the technology policies actually being carried out will make even a modest difference for growth, especially in an age of rapid technological developments.

Having expressed these reservations, it remains true that government sets the climate within which companies can grow and compete internationally, thereby feeding back to successful macroeconomic growth. For better or worse, that climate may be crucial for both large and small companies, as in the cases of ICI and Halcon. Recent research suggests that broad government policies are much more important to industrial success than incentives or actions targeted on a particular industry or technology.

The recent recession and slow recovery have made such broad actions more difficult. In political discussions, free trade and open competition are often equated with job losses; if that statement finds public approval, it seems inevitable that protectionist trends will strengthen. Despite the economic and historical arguments which show that trade promotes growth, the recently negotiated General Agreement on Tariffs and Trade (GATT) for lessening trade barriers was still far from ideal, and still faces ratification hurdles in some states. Here is one important warning signal for the world: between the First and Second World Wars, international trade and growth stagnated as countries turned more isolationist. Now that the cold war is over, could a vicious circle of trade restrictions happen again?

How Government Can Maintain a Pro-Growth Climate

In view of these considerations, what is the proper government climate for sustainable and improved growth? The problem can often be phrased as an inadequacy of successful "commercialization," the process whereby technology is converted into commercially salable products and services. Much of recent research has focused on how the government can create a regime favorable to this sort of commercialization and high productivity growth. The United States should seek as its growth strategy to raise its annual rate of growth in real GDP from what seems to be the current maximum of $2-2\frac{1}{2}$ percent to $3-3\frac{1}{2}$ percent (Landau, 1988). That this would be quite feasible industrially if America's savings/investment imbalance could be corrected is well illustrated in a recent *Business Week* article (Farrell and Mandel, 1994), which, however, does not treat this financial dilemma.

Specifying the elements of such a policy both relies on the specific experience of the chemical industry, and to some extent reaches beyond the experience of that particular industry, examining what has worked well for Germany and Japan. The elements of a plan for growth involve creating a stable backdrop for businesses to plan, the right incentives to invest, a flexible supply of capital and skilled labor, and the opportunity to compete worldwide.

Germany and Japan have largely managed in the postwar era to keep inflation low, with a less volatile macroeconomic policy, and to encourage private saving, thus reducing the need for business to worry about either the financial risks of inflation or the chance of a high-interest-rate policy to fight that inflation. This stable pro-investment macroeconomic background by government is essential if business is to focus all of its attention on commercializing new technology, and be held accountable to society for its performance. The United States has been much less successful in this regard. In addition, the United States had to deal in the 1970s with enormous additions to the workforce as the baby boomers entered the labor market, a wave of new workers that is now diminishing. John Taylor's chapter in this volume describes how stabilization policies can also be favorable for a long-term growth strategy.

New technology requires new ideas, and economists have long argued that in free markets companies will tend to underinvest in research and development. When government subsidizes research and development through tax credits to private industry and direct support, society as a whole reaps benefits. But the current R&D tax credit has been allowed to expire over and over during the last eight years, before receiving temporary renewals—hardly a policy that leads business to base long-term plans on the existence of the credit. Yet the importance of sustained substantial industrial research has been amply demonstrated, in the chemical industry and elsewhere. In addition, the federal R&D budget is overdue for a shift from defense-driven to civilian-driven projects, which could well include more experiments like SEMATECH or the Advanced Research Projects Agency's support of flat display panel development in the absence of private market production. Such government support should not seek to "pick winners." The recent failures in Europe and Japan to develop an advanced high-definition television system show that the American approach of setting high standards and encouraging strong competition is effective. However, government should see to it that trading partners do not use technology standards setting to hinder imports of even better products, or those at lower prices.

Finding these new ideas, and making use of them, will require a skilled workforce. The education of youth from kindergarten to twelfth grade requires continuing improvement. The German emphasis on education, including their apprentice schools, has paid rich rewards. While U.S. research universities remain supreme in the world, it is also true that a declining proportion of U.S. citizens is receiving engineering degrees at U.S. universities, leading to fears of a shortfall of skilled personnel. More education and training are increasingly vital for the United States in view of the job issues described above.

If the skilled workers and managers are to put their ideas into effect, they will require sufficient low-cost capital, and capital comes from maintaining a high-savings economy, as Germany and Japan have done in recent decades. This is the weakest component of the United States growth strategy, as Michael Spence describes in his chapter for this volume and in the recent report by the Board on Science, Technology and Economic Policy (STEP) for the National Research Council (1994). The chapter in this volume by Sylvester Scheiber and John Shoven also sounds the alarm in savings trends. Remember that research has shown technology and capital investment to be mutually reinforcing: technology works better with more investment; more investment facilitates more rapid technology improvements. The increase in national savings should come from all available sources: government, households, and industry. This saving must be allocated to the investors by an efficient financial system in which incentives for both lenders and users are aligned and favor longer term investments for greater growth. The direction is clear—move toward consumption taxes and away from capital taxes to achieve greater investment now, and a higher standard of living in the future.

The interlocking systems of tax policy, regulation, and law need to be examined to assure that they encourage commercialization of new technology. In the past, tax incentives for investors in young and growing firms, or for encouraging more risky investment, have filled this role. It may be especially important to offer a higher return to those who hold an equity investment for a relatively long time, as the STEP report recommends; the German and Japanese systems use strong bank ownership of individual firms to encourage more patient investment. A certain number of environmental and other regulations are inevitable, even welcome, but they should be examined to be sure that the costs they inflict on business are as light as possible, given society's goals.

Finally, as noted, postwar economic history does show that trade promotes growth, as Anne Krueger argues in her chapter for this volume. Real U.S. gross domestic product has tripled since 1950, income per capita nearly doubled. Over that same time, world trade grew sevenfold, with fourfold growth in real GDP as the war recovery and development took place. No country has completely free trade, but increasing the freedom to buy and to sell abroad is tremendously important to growth of the U.S. economy. In an era of high structural unemployment, better policies for improved domestic growth rates are essential for free trade to flourish; otherwise, extensive "cheating" will take place by various countries to maintain their jobs. Opening barriers to trade also requires good domestic pro-growth policies.

Of course, a complete agenda for raising the standard of living and quality of life would include many other items: matters related to families and child rearing; to health care and the environment; to justice and crime, equity and liberty. But whatever one's wish list of social policies, there is no free lunch. Policies and benefits must be paid for, and it is far easier to enact such policies in a growing economy than a stagnant one. Finally, greater growth is also a prerequisite for more satisfactory division of the wealth created. In the words of the *Economist* (in "How America Sees the World," 1993), "America needs to recognize that nothing on earth but fast economic growth has the power to shift whole societies for the better more or less overnight." If such greater growth is not attained, there is a real danger of great world social and political upheavals, unfortunately already present today in many areas, even the United States.

Reference Matter

References

Landau, Taylor, and Wright, Introduction

Abramovitz, Moses, "Resource and Output Trends in the United States Since 1870." *American Economic Review*, May 1956, 46, 5–23.
——, *Thinking About Growth*. Cambridge: Cambridge University Press, 1989.
Arrow, Kenneth, "The Economic Implications of Learning by Doing." *Review of Economic Studies*, June 1962, 29, 155–73.
Baily, Martin Neil, Garry Burtless, and Robert Litan, *Growth with Equity*. Washington, D.C.: The Brookings Institution, 1992.
Barro, Robert J., "Economic Growth in a Cross Section of Countries." *Quarterly Journal of Economics*, 1991, 106, 407–43.
Barro, Robert J., and Jong-Wha Lee, "Losers and Winners in Economic Growth." National Bureau of Economic Research Working Paper No. 4341. Cambridge, Mass., 1994.
Barro, Robert J., and Xavier Sala-i Martin, "Convergence." *Journal of Political Economy*, 1992, 100, 223–51.
Baumol, William J., "Productivity Growth, Convergence and Welfare: What the Long-Run Data Show." *American Economic Review*, Dec. 1986, 76, 1072–85.
Baumol, William J., Richard R. Nelson, and Edward N. Wolff, eds., *Convergence of Productivity*. Oxford: Oxford University Press, 1994.
Beason, Richard, and David Weinstein, "Growth, Economies of Scale, and Targeting in Japan (1955–1990)." Harvard Institute of Economic Research Discussion Paper No. 1644. Cambridge, Mass., 1993.
Board on Science, Technology, and Economic Policy, National Research Council, *Investing for Productivity and Prosperity*. Washington, D.C.: National Academy Press, 1994.
Boskin, Michael, and Lawrence J. Lau, "Capital, Technology, and Economic Growth." In Nathan Rosenberg, Ralph Landau, and David Mowery, eds., *Technology and the Wealth of Nations*, pp. 15–55. Stanford, Calif.: Stanford University Press, 1992.

Chandler, Alfred D., "Organizational Capabilities and the Economic History of the Industrial Enterprise." *Journal of Economic Perspectives*, Summer 1992, 6, 79–100.

Council of Economic Advisers, *Economic Report of the President*. Washington, D.C.: GPO, 1993.

———, *Economic Report of the President*. Washington, D.C.: GPO, 1994.

Dixit, Avinash, and Joseph E. Stiglitz, "Monopolistic Competition and Optimum Price Diversity." *American Economic Review*, June 1977, 67, 297–308.

Durlauf, Steven N., "International Differences in Economic Fluctuations." In Nathan Rosenberg, Ralph Landau, and David Mowery, eds., *Technology and the Wealth of Nations*, pp. 121–47. Stanford, Calif.: Stanford University Press, 1992.

Frame, J. Davidson, and Francis Narin, "The United States, Japan, and the Changing Technological Balance." *Research Policy*, Oct. 1990, 19, 447–55.

Griliches, Zvi, "Productivity, R&D, and the Data Constraint." *American Economic Review*, Mar. 1994, 84, 1–23.

Hatsopoulos, George N., and James M. Poterba, "America's Investment Shortfall: Probable Causes and Possible Fixes," Report to the Board on Science, Technology, and Economic Policy, National Research Council. Washington, D.C., 1993.

Helpman, Elhanan, and Paul Krugman, *Market Structure and Foreign Trade*. Cambridge: MIT Press, 1985.

Jorgenson, Dale W., Frank Gollop, and Barbara Fraumeni, *Productivity and U.S. Economic Growth*. Cambridge: Harvard University Press, 1987.

Jorgenson, Dale W., et al., "Bilateral Models of Production for Japanese and U.S. Industries." In Charles R. Hulten, ed., *Productivity in the U.S. and Japan: Studies in Income and Wealth*, vol. 5, pp. 59–83. Chicago: University of Chicago, 1990.

Krugman, Paul, "Does Third World Growth Hurt First World Prosperity." *Harvard Business Review*, July–Aug. 1994a, 113–21.

———, "European Jobless, American Penniless?" *Foreign Policy*, Summer 1994b, 95, 19–34.

Landau, Ralph, and Nathan Rosenberg, *The Positive Sum Strategy*. Washington, D.C.: National Academy Press, 1986.

Lucas, Robert, Jr., "On the Mechanics of Economic Development." *Journal of Monetary Economics*, 1988, 17, 3–42.

———, "Why Doesn't Capital Flow from Rich to Poor Countries?" *American Economic Review*, 1990, 90(2), 92–96.

Nadiri, M. Ishaq, and Jeffrey I. Bernstein, "Interindustry R&D Spillovers, Rates of Return, and Production in High Tech Industries." *American Economic Review*, May 1988, 429–34.

———, "Research and Development and Intra-industry Spillovers, an Empirical Application of Dynamic Duality." *Review of Economic Studies*, Apr. 1989, 56, 249–67.

Nelson, Richard, and Sidney G. Winter, *An Evolutionary Theory of Economic Change*. Cambridge: Harvard University Press, 1982.

Nelson, Richard, and Gavin Wright, "The Rise and Fall of American Technological Leadership." *Journal of Economic Literature*, Dec. 1992, 30, 1931–64.

Pack, Howard, "Endogenous Growth Theory: Intellectual Appeal and Empirical Shortcomings." *Journal of Economic Perspectives*, Winter 1994, 8, 55–72.

Porter, Michael E., *The Competitive Advantage of Nations*. New York: Free Press, 1990.

Putnam, Robert D., "The Prosperous Community." *American Prospect*, Spring 1993.

Romer, Paul, "Increasing Returns and Long-Run Growth." *Journal of Political Economy*, 1986, 94, 1002–37.

———, "Endogenous Technological Change." *Journal of Political Economy*, 1990, 98, S71–S102.

Rosenberg, Nathan, "The Impact of Technological Innovation." In Ralph Landau and Nathan Rosenberg, eds., *The Positive Sum Strategy*, pp. 17–32. Washington, D.C.: National Academy Press, 1986.

———, *Exploring the Black Box*. Cambridge: Cambridge University Press, 1994.

Rosenberg, Nathan, Ralph Landau, and David Mowery, eds., *Technology and the Wealth of Nations*. Stanford, Calif.: Stanford University Press, 1992.

Schumpeter, Joseph, *Capitalism, Socialism, and Democracy*. London: George Allen & Unwin, 2d ed., 1943.

Solow, Robert, "A Contribution to the Theory of Economic Growth." *Quarterly Journal of Economics*, 1956, 70, 65–94.

———, "Technical Change and the Aggregate Production Function." *Review of Economics and Statistics*, Aug. 1957, 39, 312–20.

———, "Perspectives on Growth Theory." *Journal of Economic Perspectives*, Winter 1994, 8, 45–54.

Stiglitz, Joseph E., "Endogenous Growth and Cycles." National Bureau of Economic Research Working Paper No. 4286. Cambridge, Mass., 1993.

Stokes, Bruce, "Immovable Mandarins." *National Journal*, Apr. 30, 1994, 1005–8.

U.S. Department of Commerce, *Survey of Current Business*, various years. Washington, D.C.

Abramovitz and David, Convergence and Deferred Catch-up

Abramovitz, Moses, "Rapid Growth Potential and Its Realization: The Experience of the Capitalist Economies in the Postwar Period." In Edmond Malinvaud, ed., *Economic Growth and Resources*, vol. I. London: Macmillan, 1979.

———, "Catching-Up, Forging Ahead and Falling Behind." *Journal of Economic History*, 1986, 46(2), 385–406.

———, *Thinking About Growth*. Cambridge: Cambridge University Press, 1989.

———, "The Search for the Sources of Growth: Areas of Ignorance, Old and New." *Journal of Economic History*, 1993, 53(2), 217–43.

———, "Catch-Up and Convergence in the Postwar Growth Boom and After." In William Baumol, Richard Nelson, and Edward Wolff, eds., *The Convergence of Productivity: Cross-National Studies and Historical Evidence*. Oxford: Oxford University Press, 1994.

Abramovitz, Moses, and Paul A. David, "Reinterpreting Economic Growth: Parables and Realities." *American Economic Review*, 1973a, *63(2)*, 428–39.

———, "Economic Growth in America: Historical Parables and Realities." *De Economist*, May/June 1973b, *121(3)*, 251–72.

Amable, Bruno, "Endogenous Growth Theory, Convergence and Divergence." In G. Silverberg and L. Soete, eds., *The Economics of Growth and Technical Change: Technologies, Nations, Agents,* chap. 3. Aldershot, Hants.: Edward Elgar, 1994.

Antonelli, Cristiano, *The Economics of Localized Technological Change.* Norwell, Mass.: Kluwer Academic Publishers, 1994.

Arrow, Kenneth J., "The Economic Implications of Learning by Doing." *Review of Economic Studies,* June 1962, 29, 155–73.

Atkinson, Anthony B., and Joseph E. Stiglitz, "A New View of Technological Change." *Economic Journal,* Sept. 1969, 79, 573–78.

Barro, Robert J., "Economic Growth in a Cross-Section of Countries." *Quarterly Journal of Economics,* 1991, *106(2)*, 407–43.

Barro, Robert J., and Xavier Sala-i-Martin, "Convergence." *Journal of Political Economy,* 1992, *100(2)*, 223–51.

Baumol, William, "Productivity Growth, Convergence and Welfare: What the Long-Run Data Show." *American Economic Review,* 1986, *76(5)*, 1072–85.

Baumol, William, Sue Anne Batey Blackman, and Edward Wolff, *Productivity and American Leadership: The Long View.* Cambridge: MIT Press, 1989.

Broadberry, Stephen N., "Technological Leadership and Productivity Leadership in Manufacturing Since the Industrial Revolution: Implications for the Convergence Debate." Warwick Economic Research Paper, Department of Economics, University of Warwick, Feb. 1993.

Cain, Louis P., and Donald G. Paterson, "Factor Biases and Technical Change in Manufacturing: The American System, 1850–1919." *Journal of Economic History,* June 1981, *41(2)*, 341–60.

Chandler, Alfred, *Scale and Scope.* Cambridge: Harvard University Press, 1990.

Darmstadter, Joel, "Energy Consumption: Trends and Patterns." In Sam Schurr, ed., *Energy, Economic Growth and the Environment,* Appendix. Published for Resources for the Future. Baltimore: Johns Hopkins University Press, 1972.

David, Paul A., *Technical Choice, Innovation and Economic Growth, New York: Essays on American and British Experience in the Nineteenth Century.* Cambridge: Cambridge University Press, 1975.

———, "Invention and Accumulation in America's Economic Growth." In K. Brunner and A. H. Meltzer, eds., *International Organization, National Policies and Economic Development.* Amsterdam: North Holland Publishing Company, 1977.

———, "Clio and the Economics of QWERTY." *American Economic Review,* 1985, *75(2)*, 332–37.

———, "Path-Dependence: Putting the Past into the Future of Economics." Institute for Mathematical Studies in the Social Sciences Technical Report 533. Stanford University, Nov. 1988.

———, "Computer and Dynamo: The Productivity Paradox in a Not-Too-Distant

Mirror." In *Technology and Productivity: The Challenge for Economic Policy*. Paris: Organization for Economic Cooperation and Development, 1991a.

———, "General Purpose Engines, Investment, and Productivity Growth: From the Dynamo Revolution to the Computer Revolution." In E. Deiaco, E. Hornel, and G. Vickery, eds., *Technology and Investment—Crucial Issues for the '90s*. London: Pinter Publishers, 1991b.

———, "Path-Dependence and Predictability in Dynamical Systems with Local Network Externalities: A Paradigm for Economic History." In D. Foray and C. Freeman, eds., *Technology and the Wealth of Nations*, Chap. 4. London: Pinter Publishers, 1993.

———, "The Evolution of Intellectual Property Institutions." In A. Aganbegyan, O. Bogomolov, and M. Kaser, eds., *System Transformation: Eastern and Western Assessments*. London: Macmillan for the International Economic Association, 1994a.

———, "Why Are Institutions the 'Carriers of History'? Notes on Path-Dependence in Conventions, Organizations and Institutions." *Structural Change and Economic Dynamics*, 1994b, 5 (2), 205–20.

David, Paul A., and John L. Scadding, "Private Savings: Ultra-Rationality, Aggregation and 'Denison's Law.'" *Journal of Political Economy*, Mar./Apr. 1974, 82 (2), pt. 1, 225–49.

David, Paul A., and Theo van de Klundert, "Biased Efficiency Growth and Capital-Labor Substitution in the U.S., 1899–1960." *American Economic Review*, June 1965, 55, 357–94.

David, Paul A., and Gavin Wright, "Resource Abundance and American Economic Leadership." Center for Economic Policy Research Publication No. 267. Stanford University, Aug. 1992.

DeLong, J. Bradford, "Productivity Growth, Convergence and Welfare: Comment." *American Economic Review*, Dec. 1988, 78:5, 1138–59.

DeLong, J. Bradford, and Lawrence Summers, "Equipment Investment and Economic Growth," *Quarterly Journal of Economics*, 1991, 106 (2), 445–502.

Denison, Edward F., *Why Growth Rates Differ*. Washington, D.C.: Brookings Institution, 1967.

Denison, Edward F., and William Chung, *How Japan's Economy Grew So Fast*. Washington, D.C.: Brookings Institution, 1976.

De Tocqueville, Alexis, *Democracy in America*, vol. II. 1840. Reprint, New York: Vintage Books, 1945.

Dosi, Giovanni, "Technological Paradigms and Technological Trajectories: A Suggested Interpretation of the Determinants and Directions of Technical Change." *Research Policy*, 1982, 11 (3), 147–62.

———, "Sources, Procedures, and Microeconomic Effects of Innovation." *Journal of Economic Literature*, 1988, 26 (3), 1120–71.

Dosi, Giovanni, and Silvia Fabiani, "Convergence and Divergence in the Long-term Growth of Open Economies." In G. Silverberg and L. Soete, eds., *The Economics of Growth and Technical Change: Technologies, Nations, Agents*, chap. 6. Aldershot, Hants.: Edward Elgar, 1994.

Dougherty, John C., "A Comparison of Productivity and Economic Growth in the G-7 Countries." Ph.D. dissertation, Harvard University, 1991.

Dumke, Rolf H., "Reassessing the *Wirtschaftswunder*: Reconstruction and Postwar Growth in West Germany in an International Context." *Oxford Bulletin of Economics and Statistics*, Special Issue, Nov. 1990, *52(4)*, 451–91.

Durlauf, Steven, and Paul Johnson, "Local Versus Global Convergence Across National Economies." National Bureau of Economic Research Working Paper No. 3996. Cambridge, Mass., 1992.

Earle, Edward Meade, ed., *Modern France: Problems of the Third and Fourth Republics*. Princeton: Princeton University Press, 1951.

Eisner, Robert, *The Total Incomes System of Accounts*. Chicago: University of Chicago Press, 1989.

Emmerson, George S., *Engineering Education: A Social History*. New York: Abbot Newton, 1973.

Fagerberg, Jan, "Technology and International Differences in Growth Rates." *Journal of Economic Literature*, 1994, *32(3)*, 1147–75.

Ferguson, Eugene S., *Engineering and the Mind's Eye*. Cambridge: MIT Press, 1992.

Foreman-Peck, James, "The American Challenge of the Twenties: Multinationals and the European Motor Industry." *Journal of Economic History*, Dec. 1982, 42.

Freeman, Christopher, and Carlotta Perez, "Structural Crises of Adjustment." In G. Dosi, C. Freeman, R. Nelson, G. Silverberg, and L. Soete, eds., *Technical Change and Economic Theory*. London: Pinter Publishers, 1988.

Friedman, Milton, "Do Old Fallacies Ever Die?" *Journal of Economic Literature*, Dec. 1992, *30(4)*, 2129–32.

Gerschenkron, Alexander, "Social Attitudes, Entrepreneurship and Economic Development." *Explorations in Entrepreneurial History*, Oct. 1953, 1–19.

——, "A Rejoinder." *Explorations in Entrepreneurial History*, May 1954a, 287–93.

——, "Some Further Notes on 'Social Attitudes, Entrepreneurship and Economic Development.'" *Explorations in Entrepreneurial History*, Dec. 1954b, 111–19.

——, "Social Attitudes, Entrepreneurship and Economic Development." In Leon H. Dupriez, with the assistance of Douglas C. Hague, eds., *Economic Progress: Papers and Proceedings of a Round Table Held by the International Economic Association*, pp. 307–29. Louvain: Institut de Recherches Economique et Sociales, 1955. Reprinted as chap. 3 in Gerschenkron (1962).

——, *Economic Backwardness in Historical Perspective*. Cambridge: Harvard University Press, 1962.

Harris, Donald J., "A Model of the Productivity Gap: Convergence or Divergence?" In Ross Thompson, ed., *Learning and Technological Change*, chap. 7. New York: St. Martin's Press, 1993.

Harvard Entrepreneurial Research Center, *Change and the Entrepreneur*. Cambridge, 1949.

Hounshell, David A., *From the American System to Mass Production, 1800–1932*. Baltimore: Johns Hopkins University Press, 1984.

Inkeles, Alex, "Convergence and Divergence in Industrial Societies." In M. O. Attir, B. Holzner, and Z. Suda, eds., *Directions of Change: Modernization Theory, Research and Realities*, chap. 1. Boulder, Colo: Westview Press, 1981.

Inkeles, Alex, and Larry Sirowym, "Convergent and Divergent Trends in National Educational Systems," *Social Forces*, Dec. 1983, 62(2).

James, John A., and Jonathan S. Skinner, "The Resolution of the Labor Scarcity Paradox." *Journal of Economic History*, 1985, 45(3), 513–40.

Katz, Lawrence F., and Kevin M. Murphy, "The Changes in Relative Wages, 1963– 87: Supply and Demand Factors." *Quarterly Journal of Economics*, 1992, 107(1), 35–78.

Kendrick, John W., *Productivity Trends in the United States*. Princeton: Princeton University Press for the National Bureau of Economic Research, 1961.

———, *The Formation and Stocks of Total Capital*. New York: National Bureau of Economic Research, 1976.

———, "Total Capital and Economic Growth." *Atlantic Economic Journal*, Mar. 1994, 22(1), 1–18.

Kindleberger, Charles P., *Europe's Postwar Growth: The Role of Labor Supply*. Cambridge: Harvard University Press, 1967.

Kravis, Irving, Alan Heston, and Robert Summers, *World Product Income: International Comparisons of Real Gross Product, Phase III*. United Nations and World Bank. Baltimore: Johns Hopkins University Press, 1982. Also see earlier and later volumes in the same series.

Landes, David S., "French Entrepreneurship and Industrial Growth in the Nineteenth Century." *Journal of Economic History*, May 1949, 45–61.

———, "French Business and the Businessman: a Social and Cultural Analysis." In Edward M. Earle, ed., *Modern France, Problems of the Third and Fourth Republics*, pp. 334–53. Princeton: Princeton University Press, 1951.

———, "Social Attitudes, Entrepreneurship and Economic Development: A Comment." *Explorations in Entrepreneurial History*, May 1954, 245–72.

Lazonick, William, "Social Organization and Technological Leadership." In W. J. Baumol, Richard R. Nelson, and Edward N. Wolff, eds., *Convergence of Productivity*, chap. 6. New York: Oxford University Press, 1994.

Lucas, Robert, "On the Mechanics of Economic Development." *Journal of Monetary Economics*, 1988, 22, 2–42.

Maddison, Angus, *Phases of Capitalist Development*. Oxford: Oxford University Press, 1982.

———, "Growth and Slowdown in Advanced Capitalist Countries: Techniques of Quantitative Assessment." *Journal of Economic Literature*, June 1987, 25(2), 649–98.

———, *The World Economy in the 20th Century*. Paris: Development Centre of the Organization for Economic Cooperation and Development, 1989.

———, *Dynamic Forces in Capitalist Development*. Oxford: Oxford University Press, 1991.

———, "Explaining the Economic Performance of Nations, 1820–1989." In William Baumol, Richard Nelson, and Edward Wolff, eds., *The Convergence of Productivity: Cross-National Studies and Historical Evidence*. Oxford: Oxford University Press, 1993.

Mankiw, N. G., D. Romer, and D. N. Weil, "A Contribution to the Empirics of Economic Growth." *Quarterly Journal of Economics*, 1992, *108(2)*, 407–37.

Miller, W., ed., *Men in Business.* Cambridge: Harvard University Press, 1952.

Mitchell, B. R., and Phyllis Deane, *Abstract of British Historical Statistics.* Cambridge: Cambridge University Press, 1962.

Mokyr, Joel, *The Lever of Riches.* New York: Oxford University Press, 1990.

Mowery, David, and Nathan Rosenberg, *Technology and the Pursuit of Economic Growth.* Cambridge: Cambridge University Press, 1989.

Nelson, Richard R., "Diffusion of Development, Post–World War II Convergence Among Advanced Industrial Nations." *American Economic Review*, 1991, *81(2)*, 271–75.

Nelson, Richard R., and Sidney Winter, "In Search of a Useful Theory of Innovations," *Research Policy*, 1977, *6(1)*, 31–42.

Nelson, Richard R., and Gavin Wright, "The Rise and Fall of American Technological Leadership." *Journal of Economic Literature*, 1992, *30(4)*, 1931–64.

Ohkawa, Kazushi, and Henry Rosovsky, *Japanese Economic Growth.* Stanford, Calif.: Stanford University Press, 1972.

Parker, William N., "Productivity Growth in American Grain Farming: An Analysis of Its Nineteenth Century Sources." In R. W. Fogel and Stanley Engerman, eds., *The Reinterpretation of American Economic History*, pp. 175–86. New York: Harper and Row, 1972.

———, *Europe, America and the Wider World.* Vol. 1, *Europe and the World Economy.* New York: Cambridge University Press, 1984.

———, *Europe, America and the Wider World.* Vol. 2, *America and the Wider World.* New York : Cambridge University Press, 1991.

Perez, Carlotta, and Luc Soete, "Catching up in Technology: Entry Barriers and Windows of Opportunity." In G. Dosi, C. Freeman, R. Nelson, G. Silverberg, and L. Soete, eds., *Technical Change and Economic Theory.* London: Pinter Publishers, 1988.

Prados de la Escosura, Leandra, Teresa Dabán, and Jorge C. Sanz Oliva, "'De le Fabula narrative?' Growth, Structural Change and Convergence in Europe, 19th & 20th Centuries." Dirección General de Planificación, Ministerio de Economia y Hacienda (Spain), Documentos de Trabajo, Dec. 1993.

Romer, Paul, "Increasing Returns and Long-run Growth." *Journal of Political Economy*, 1986, *94*, 1002–37.

———, "Endogenous Technological Change." *Journal of Political Economy*, 1990, *98(5)*, pt. 2, S71–S102.

Rosenberg, Nathan, "The Direction of Technological Change: Inducement Mechanisms and Focusing Devices." *Economic Development and Cultural Change*, 1969, *18(1)*, pt. 1. Reprinted in Rosenberg (1976).

———, *Perspectives on Technology.* New York: Cambridge University Press, 1976.

———, "Why in America?" In Otto Mayr and Robert Post, eds., *Yankee Enterprise: The Rise of the American System of Manufactures*, pp. 49–81. Washington, D.C.: Smithsonian Institution Press, 1980.

———, "Learning by Using." In *Inside the Black Box—Technology and Economics*, chap. 6. Cambridge: Cambridge University Press, 1982.

Rosovsky, Henry, *Capital Formation in Japan, 1868–1940*. New York: Free Press of Glencoe, 1961.

Sahal, D., *Patterns of Technological Innovation*. Reading, Mass.: Addison-Wesley, 1981.

Sawyer, John E., "Strains in the Social Structure of Modern France." In Edward Mead Earle, ed., *Modern France, Problems of the Third and Fourth Republics*, chap. 17. Princeton: Princeton University Press, 1951.

———, "The Entrepreneur and the Social Order, France and the United States." In Miller (1952, pp. 293–312).

———, "In Defense of an Approach: A Comment on Professor Gerschenkron's Social Attitudes, Entrepreneurship and Economic Development." *Explorations in Entrepreneurial History*, May 1954, 173–86.

Schultz, Theodore W., "The Declining Economic Importance of Agricultural Land." *Economic Journal*, Dec. 1951, 725–40.

Schurr, Sam H., Bruce C. Netschert, et al., *Energy in the American Economy, 1950–1975: Its History and Prospects*. Baltimore: Johns Hopkins University Press for Resources for the Future, 1960.

Solow, Robert M., "A Contribution to the Theory of Economic Growth." *Quarterly Journal of Economics*, Feb. 1956, 70(1), 65–94.

Summers, Robert, and Alan C. Heston, "A New Set of International Comparisons of Real Product and Price Levels." *Review of Income and Wealth*, 1988, 34, 1–25.

Taylor, Alan M., and Jeffrey G. Williamson, "Convergence in the Age of Mass Migration." National Bureau of Economic Research Working Paper No. 4711. Cambridge, Mass., 1994.

U.S. Bureau of the Census, *Historical Statistics of the United States, from Colonial Times*. Washington, D.C.: GPO, 1960.

Van Ark, Bart, and Dirk Pilat, "Productivity Levels in Germany, Japan and the United States: Differences and Causes." *Brookings Papers on Economic Activity: Microeconomics*, 1993, 2, 1–69.

Van de Klundert, Theo. C. M. J., and S. Smulders, "Reconstructing Growth Theory: A Survey." *De Economist*, 1992, 140(2), 177–203.

Veblen, Thorstein, *Imperial Germany and the Industrial Revolution*. New York: Augustus Kelly, 1915 [1964].

Verspargen, Bart, "A New Empirical Approach to Catching Up or Falling Behind." *Structural Change and Economic Dynamics*, 1991, 2(2), 359–80.

———, "Endogenous Innovation in Neoclassical Growth Models: A Survey." *Journal of Macroeconomics*, 1992, 14(4), 631–62.

White, Lynn, Jr., *Machina ex Deo: Essays in the Dynamism of Western Culture*. Cambridge: MIT Press, 1968.

Wiener, M. J., *English Culture and the Decline of the Industrial Spirit, 1850–1980*. Cambridge: Cambridge University Press, 1981.

Wolff, Edward N., "Capital Formation and Productivity: Convergence Over the Long Term." *American Economic Review*, 1991, 81(3), 565–79.

———, "Productivity Growth and Capital Intensity on the Sector and Industry Level: Specialization among OECD Countries, 1970–1988." In G. Silverberg and L. Soete, eds., *The Economics of Growth and Technical Change: Technologies, Nations, Agents,* chap. 8. Aldershot, Hants.: Edward Elgar. 1994.

Wright, Gavin, "The Origins of American Industrial Success." *American Economic Review,* 1990, *80(4),* 651–68.

Lau, Sources of Long-Term Economic Growth

Abramovitz, M., "Resource and Output Trends in the United States Since 1870." *American Economic Review,* 1956, 46, 5–23.

Boskin, M. J. and L. J. Lau, "Post-War Economic Growth of the Group-of-Five Countries: A New Analysis." Center for Economic Policy Research Technical Paper No. 217. Stanford University, 1990.

———, "Capital Formation and Economic Growth." In *Technology and Economics: A Volume Commemorating Ralph Landau's Service to the National Academy of Engineering,* pp. 47–56. Washington, D.C.: National Academy Press, 1991.

———, "Capital, Technology, and Economic Growth." In R. Rosenberg, R. Landau, and D. Mowery, eds., *Technology and the Wealth of Nations,* pp. 17–55. Stanford, Calif.: Stanford University Press, 1992a.

———, "International and Intertemporal Comparison of Productive Efficiency: An Application of the Meta-Production Function Approach to the Group-of-Five (G-5) Countries." *Economic Studies Quarterly,* 1992b, 43, 298–312.

———, "The Contribution of R&D to Economic Growth: Some Issues and Observations." Paper presented at the Joint American Enterprise Institute–Brookings Institution Conference on the Contribution of Research to the Economy and Society. Washington, D.C., Oct. 1994.

Christensen, L. R., D. W. Jorgenson, and L. J. Lau, "Transcendental Logarithmic Production Frontiers." *Review of Economics and Statistics,* 1973, 55, 28–45.

Delong, J. B., and L. H. Summers, "Equipment Investment and Economic Growth." *Quarterly Journal of Economics,* 1991, 106, 445–502.

Denison, E. F., "United States Economic Growth." *Journal of Business,* 1962, 35, 109–21.

Hayami, Y., and V. W. Ruttan, "Agricultural Productivity Differences Among Countries." *American Economic Review,* 1970, 60, 895–911.

———, *Agricultural Development: An International Perspective.* Baltimore: Johns Hopkins University Press, 1985 (revised and expanded edition).

Kim, J.-I., and L. J. Lau, "Human Capital and Aggregate Productivity: Some Empirical Evidence from the Group-of-Five Countries." Stanford University Department of Economics working paper. Sept. 1992a.

———, "The Importance of Embodied Technical Progress: Some Empirical Evidence from the Group-of-Five Countries." Center for Economic Policy Research Working Paper No. 296. Stanford University, June 1992b.

———, "The Sources of Economic Growth of the Newly Industrialized Countries on the Pacific Rim." Paper presented at the Conference on the Economic Development of the Republic of China and the Pacific Rim in the 1990s and Beyond. Taipei, May 25–28, 1992c.

———, "The Role of Human Capital in the Economic Growth of the East Asian Newly Industrialized Countries." Paper presented at the Asia-Pacific Economic Modelling Conference-94. Sydney, Aug. 24–26, 1994a.

———, "The Sources of Asian-Pacific Economic Growth." Paper presented at the Annual Meeting of the Canadian Economic Association. Calgary, June 1994b.

———, "The Sources of East Asian Economic Growth Revisited." Stanford University Department of Economics working paper. 1994c.

———, "The Sources of Economic Growth in the East Asian Newly Industrialized Countries." *Journal of the Japanese and International Economies*, 1994d, 8, 235–71.

———, "The Role of Capital in the Economic Growth of the East Asian Newly Industrialized Countries." In B. Kapur, E. Quah, and H. H. Teck, eds., *Festschrift in Honour of Professor Lim Chong Yah*, forthcoming 1995.

Kuznets, S. S., *Economic Growth of Nations*. Cambridge: Harvard University Press, 1971.

Lau, L. J., D. T. Jamison, and F. F. Louat, "Education and Productivity in Developing Countries: An Aggregate Production Function Approach." World Bank Working Paper WPS 612. Washington, D.C., 1990.

Lau, L. J., and P. A. Yotopoulos, "The Meta-Production Function Approach to Technological Change in World Agriculture." *Journal of Development Economics*, 1989, 31, 241–69.

Romer, P. M., "Endogenous Technological Change." *Journal of Political Economy*, 1990, 98, S71–S102.

Solow, R. M., "Technical Change and the Aggregate Production Function." *Review of Economics and Statistics*, 1957, 39, 312–20.

Tsao, Y., "Growth and Productivity in Singapore: A Supply Side Analysis." Ph.D. dissertation, Harvard University, 1982.

———, "Growth without Productivity: Singapore Manufacturing in the 1970s." *Journal of Development Studies*, 1985, 18, 25–38.

World Bank, *The East Asian Miracle: Economic Growth and Public Policy*, Oxford: Oxford University Press, 1993.

Young, A., "A Tale of Two Cities: Factor Accumulation and Technical Change in Hong Kong and Singapore." In O. J. Blanchard and S. Fischer, eds., *National Bureau of Economic Research Macroeconomics Annual*, pp. 13–54. Cambridge: MIT Press, 1992.

Rowen, World Wealth Expanding

Abramovitz, Moses, *Thinking About Growth*. Cambridge: Cambridge University Press, 1989.

———, "The Elements of Social Capability." Prepared for the International Conference on the Economic Development of LDCs During the Five Decades, 1940s to 1980s, Korean Development Institute, Seoul, July 1–2, 1991.

Ahmed, Akbar S., *Discovering Islam*. London: Routledge and Kegan Paul, 1988.

Alesina, Alberto, Sule Ozler, Nouriel Roubini, and Phillip Swagel, "Political Instability and Economic Growth." National Bureau of Economic Research Working Paper No. 4173. Cambridge, Mass., Sept. 1992.

Alesina, Alberto, and Roberto Perotti, "Income Distribution, Political Instability and Investment." National Bureau of Economic Research Working Paper No. 4486. Cambridge, Mass., Oct. 1993.

Alesina, Alberto, and Dani Rodrik, "Distributive Politics and Economic Growth." National Bureau of Economic Research Working Paper No. 3668. Cambridge, Mass., Mar. 1991.

Babst, Dean, "Elective Governments—A Force for Peace." *The Wisconsin Sociologist*, 1964, *3*.

Banfield, Edward, *The Moral Basis of a Backward Society*. Chicago: Free Press, 1958.

Barro, Robert J., "Economic Growth in a Cross Section of Countries." *Quarterly Journal of Economics*, May 1991, *106*.

Barro, Robert J., and Jong-Wha Lee, "Losers and Winners in Economic Growth." National Bureau of Economic Research Working Paper No. 4341. Cambridge, Mass., Apr. 1993a.

———, "International Comparisons of Educational Attainment." *Journal of Monetary Economics*, Dec. 1993b, *32*.

Bhagwati, Jagdish, *India in Transition*. Oxford: Clarendon Press, 1993.

Birdsall, Nancy, "Virtuous Circles: Human Capital, Growth and Equity in East Asia." Paper presented at Conference on the East Asian Miracle. Stanford University, Oct. 25, 1993.

Birdsall, Nancy, David Ross, and Richard Sabot, "Inequality and Growth Reconsidered." Paper presented at the annual meeting of the American Economic Association. Boston, Jan. 1994.

Borner, Silvio, Aymo Brunetti, and Beatrice Weber, *Institutional Obstacles to Latin American Growth*. San Francisco: International Center for Economic Growth, 1992.

Brinegar, Claude S., talk presented at the Food Research Institute. Stanford University, Apr. 15, 1994.

Campos, Jose Edgardo, and Hilton Root, "Rethinking the Asian Miracle: Institutions, Leadership and the Promise of Shared Growth." Background paper for the World Bank's Asian Miracle project (processed). Washington, D.C., 1993.

Chenery, Hollis, and T. N. Srinivasan, eds., *Handbook of Development Economics*, vol. 1. Amsterdam: North Holland, 1988.

Corbo, Vittorio, and Patricio Rojas, "World Bank-Supported Adjustment Programs: Country Performance and Effectiveness." In Vittorio Corbo, Stanley Fischer, and Steven B. Webb, eds., *Adjustment Lending Revisited*. Washington, D.C.: World Bank, 1992.

Doyle, Michael, "Liberalism and World Politics." *American Political Science Review*, Dec. 1986, *80*.

Easterly, William, Robert King, Ross Levine, and Sergio Rebelo, "Policy, Technology Adoption and Growth." National Bureau of Economic Research Working Paper No. 4681. Cambridge, Mass., Mar. 1994.

Easterly, William, Michael Kremer, Lant Pritchett, and Lawrence Summers, "Good

Policy or Good Luck? Country Performance and Temporary Shocks." National Bureau of Economic Research Working Paper No. 4474. Cambridge, Mass., Sept. 1993.

Freedom House, *Freedom Review*, Feb. 1993, 24.

Grossman, Gene M., and Alan B. Krueger, "Economic Growth and the Environment." National Bureau of Economic Research Working Paper No. 4634. Cambridge, Mass., Feb. 1994.

Hale, David, *The World Economy After the Russian Revolution or Why the 1990s Could Be the Second Great Age of Global Capitalism*. Chicago: Kemper Financial Companies, 1991.

Helliwell, John F., "Empirical Linkages Between Democracy and Economic Growth." National Bureau of Economic Research Working Paper No. 4066. Cambridge, Mass., May 1992.

Huntington, Samuel P., *The Third Wave*. Norman: University of Oklahoma Press, 1991.

Inkeles, Alex, and David Smith, *Becoming Modern: Individual Change in Six Developing Countries*. Cambridge: Harvard University Press, 1974.

Israel, Arturo, *Institutional Development*. Baltimore: Johns Hopkins University Press, 1987.

Kahn, Herman, *World Economic Development*. Boulder, Colo.: Westview Press, 1979.

Kahn, Herman, William Brown, and Leon Martel, *The Next 200 Years*. New York: William Morrow, 1976.

Karatnycky, Adrian, "In Global Vacuum, Tyranny Advances." *Wall Street Journal*, Dec. 16, 1993, p. 16.

Krueger, Anne, *Political Economy of Policy Reform in Developing Countries*. Cambridge: MIT Press, 1993.

Lal, Deepak, *The Hindu Equilibrium*. Oxford: Clarendon Press, 1988.

Lau, Lawrence J., "The Chinese Economy in the Twenty-First Century." Asia/Pacific Research Center Working Paper Series No. 103. Stanford University, Jan. 1994.

Lau, Lawrence J., Dean T. Jamison, and Frederic F. Jouat, "Education and Productivity in Developing Countries." Background paper for the *World Development Report 1991*. Washington, D.C.: World Bank, 1991.

Lau, Lawrence J., Dean T. Jamison, Shu-Cheng Liu, and Steven Rivkin, "Education and Economic Growth: Some Cross-Sectional Evidence from Brazil." *Journal of Development Economics*, June 1993, 41.

Lau, Lawrence J., and Jong-Il Kim, "A Simple Model of Growth." Manuscript, Stanford University, 1994.

Levine, Ross, and David Renelt, "A Sensitivity Analysis of Cross-Country Growth Regressions." *American Economic Review*, Sept. 1992, 82+.

Lipset, Seymour Martin, *Political Man: The Social Bases of Politics*. Rev. ed. Baltimore: Johns Hopkins University Press, 1981.

Lipset, Seymour Martin, Kyoung-Ryung Seong, and John Charles Torres, "A Comparative Analysis of the Social Requisites of Democracy." *International Social Science Journal*, May 1993, 45.

Londregan, John, and Keith T. Poole, "Poverty, the Coup Trap, and the Seizure of Economic Power." *World Politics*, Jan. 1990, 42, 151–83.

———, "The Seizure of Power and Economic Growth." In Alex Cukierman, Zvi Hercowitz, and Leonardo Leiderman, eds., *Political Economy, Growth and Business Cycle*. Cambridge: MIT Press, 1992.

Lucas, Robert E., "On the Mechanics of Economic Development." *Journal of Monetary Economics*, July 1988, 22.

———, "Making a Miracle." *Econometrica*, Mar. 1993, 61.

Manne, Alan, and Richard Richels, "The Costs of Stabilizing Global CO_2 Emissions—A Probabilistic Analysis Based on Expert Judgements." Feb. 19, 1993.

Masters, C. D., D. H. Root, and E. D. Attanasi, "Resource Constraints in Petroleum Production Potential." *Science*, July 12, 1991, 253, 146+.

Nordhaus, William D., "Reflections on the Economics of Climate Change." *Journal of Economic Perspectives*, Fall 1993, 7, 11–25.

North, Douglass C., *Transaction Costs, Institutions and Economic Performance*. San Francisco: International Center for Economic Growth, 1992.

Olson, Mancur, *The Rise and Decline of Nations*. New Haven, Conn.: Yale University Press, 1982.

———, "Dictatorship, Democracy and Development." *American Political Science Review*, Sept. 1993, 87.

Persson, Torsten, and Guido Tabellini, "Is Inequality Harmful for Growth? Theory and Evidence." National Bureau of Economic Research Working Paper No. 3599. Cambridge, Mass., Jan. 1991.

———, "Growth, Distribution and Politics." *European Economic Review*, Apr. 1992, 36.

Polachek, Solomon W., "Conflict and Trade." *Journal of Conflict Resolution*, Mar. 1980, 24.

Population Information Program, *Population Reports*. Johns Hopkins University, Dec. 1992.

Przeworski, Adam, and Fernando Limongi, "Political Regimes and Economic Growth." *Journal of Economic Perspectives*, Summer 1993, 7, 51–69.

Putnam, Robert, *Making Democracy Work*. Princeton, N.J.: Princeton University Press, 1993.

Rummel, R. J., "Libertarianism and International Violence." *Journal of Conflict Resolution*, Mar. 1983, 27.

Russett, Bruce, *Grasping the Democratic Peace*. Princeton, N.J.: Princeton University Press, 1993.

Schultz, T. Paul, "Educational Investments and Returns." In Hollis Chenery and T. N. Srinivasan, eds., *Handbook of Development Economics*, vol. 1. Amsterdam: North Holland, 1988.

———, *Human Capital Investment in Women and Men*. San Francisco: International Center for Economic Growth, 1994.

Singer, Max, and Aaron Wildavsky, *The Real World Order*. Chatham, N.J.: Chatham House Publishers, 1993.

Sirowy, Lawrence, and Alex Inkeles, "The Effects of Democracy on Economic

Growth and Inequality: A Review." *Studies in Comparative International Development*, Apr. 1990, 25.

Smil, Vaclav, *China's Environmental Crisis*, Armonk, N.Y.: M. E. Sharpe, 1993.

Starr, Chauncy, Milton F. Searl, and Sy Alpert, "Energy Resources: A Realistic Outlook." *Science*, May 15, 1992, 256, 981.

Summers, Lawrence H., and Vinod Thomas, "Recent Lessons of Development." *World Bank Research Observer*, July 1993, 8, 241–54.

Summers, Robert, and Alan Heston, "The Penn World Table (Mark 5): An Expanded Set of International Comparisons, 1950–1988." *Quarterly Journal of Economics*, 1991, no. 2.

Webb, Steven B., and Karim Shariff, "Designing and Implementing Adjustment Programs." In Vittorio Corbo, Stanley Fischer, and Steven B. Webb, eds., *Adjustment Lending Revisited*, Washington, D.C.: World Bank, 1992.

Weingast, Barry, *The Economic Role of Political Institutions* (manuscript). Stanford, Calif.: Stanford University, 1993.

Westhoff, Charles F., *Reproductive Preferences: A Comparative View*. Columbia, Md.: Institute for Resource Development, 1991.

Weyant, John P., "Costs of Reducing Global Carbon Emissions." *Journal of Economic Perspectives*, Fall 1993, 7, 27–46.

Williamson, John, ed., *The Political Economy of Policy Reform*. Washington, D.C.: Institute for International Economics, 1993.

World Bank, *World Development Report 1991*. Washington, D.C.: World Bank, 1991.

———, *World Development Report 1992*. Washington, D.C.: World Bank, 1992.

———, *The East Asian Miracle*. New York: Oxford University Press, 1993a.

———, *World Development Report 1993*. Washington, D.C.: World Bank, 1993b.

———, *Global Economic Prospects*. Washington, D.C.: World Bank, 1994.

Taylor, Stabilization Policy and Long-Term Economic Growth

Bryant, Ralph, Peter Hooper, and Catherine Mann, eds., *Evaluating Policy Regimes: New Research in Empirical Macroeconomics*. Washington, D.C.: Brookings Institution, 1993.

Caballero, Ricardo, and Mohamad L. Hammour, "The Cleansing Effect of Recessions." National Bureau of Economic Research Working Paper No. 3922. Cambridge, Mass., 1991.

Davis, Steven, and John Haltiwanger, "Gross Job Creation and Destruction: Microeconomic Evidence and Macroeconomic Implications." *NBER Macroeconomic Annual*, 1990, 5, 123–68.

Friedman, Milton, "A Monetary and Fiscal Framework For Economic Stability: A Formal Analysis." In *Essays in Positive Economics*. Chicago: University of Chicago Press, 1948.

Motley, Brian, "Growth and Inflation: A Cross-Country Study." Paper presented at Center for Economic Policy Research–Federal Reserve Bank of San Francisco conference, Stanford, Calif., Mar. 1994.

Poole, William, "When Is Inflation 'Low'?" Paper presented at Center for Economic Policy Research–Federal Reserve Bank of San Francisco conference, Stanford, Calif., Mar. 1994.

Schumpeter, Joseph A., *Business Cycles: A Theoretical and Statistical Analysis of the Capitalist Process.* New York: McGraw-Hill, 1939.

Taylor, John B., "Fiscal and Monetary Stabilization Policy in a Model of Endogenous Cyclical Growth." Econometric Research Program, Research Memorandum No. 104. Princeton University, 1968.

———, "Estimation and Control of an Econometric Model with Rational Expectations." *Econometrica,* Sept. 1979, 47 (5), 1267–86.

———, "Discretion Versus Policy Rules in Practice." *Carnegie Rochester Conference Series on Public Policy,* 1993a, 39, 195–214.

———, *Macroeconomic Policy in the World Economy: From Econometric Design to Practical Operation.* New York: W. W. Norton, 1993b.

Schieber and Shoven, Population Aging and Saving for Retirement

Ballantyne, Harry C., "Long-Range Projections of Social Security Trust Fund Operations in Dollars." Social Security Administration Actuarial Note No. 117. Washington, D.C., Oct. 1983.

Board of Trustees of the Federal Old-Age and Survivors Insurance and Disability Insurance Trust Funds, *1993 Annual Report.* Washington, D.C., Apr. 1994.

Congressional Budget Office, Congress of the United States, *Baby Boomers in Retirement: An Early Perspective.* Washington, D.C., 1993.

"Death, and Taxes," *Economist,* Aug. 13, 1994, pp. 19–21.

EBRI, *Quarterly Pension Investment Report.* Washington, D.C., various years.

Ibbotson Associates, *Stocks, Bonds, Bills and Inflation, 1993 Yearbook, Market Results for 1926–1992.* Chicago: Ibbotson Associates, 1993.

U.S. Bureau of the Census, *Historical Statistics of the United States, Colonial Times to 1970,* Bicentennial Edition, Part 1. Washington, D.C., 1976.

———, *Statistical Abstract of the United States.* 111th ed. Washington, D.C., 1991.

U.S. Bureau of Economic Analysis, Department of Commerce, *National Income and Product Accounts of the United States.* Washington, D.C.: GPO, annual.

Wyatt Company, *The Compensation and Benefits File.* Vol. 3, No. 11. Washington, D.C., Nov. 1987.

———, *Survey of Actuarial Assumptions and Funding,* 1992, Washington, D.C., 1992.

Spence, Science and Technology Investment and Policy

Hatsopoulos, George N., and James M. Poterba, "America's Investment Shortfall: Probable Causes and Possible Fixes." In the conference volume of *Investing for Productivity and Prosperity.* Washington, D.C.: National Academy Press, forthcoming 1994.

Landau, Ralph, "From Analysis to Action." In the conference volume of *Investing for Productivity and Prosperity*. Washington, D.C.: National Academy Press, forthcoming 1994.

National Research Council, *Investing for Productivity and Prosperity*. Washington, D.C.: National Academy Press, 1994.

Porter, Michael, "National Investment Systems." In the conference volume of *Investing for Productivity and Prosperity*. Washington, D.C.: National Academy Press, forthcoming 1994.

U.S. Department of the Treasury, *Integration of the Individual and Corporate Tax Systems: Taxing Business Income Once*. Washington, D.C.: U.S. Government Printing Office, Jan. 1992.

Krueger, Threats to 21st-Century Growth

Baldwin, Robert E., *Nontariff Barriers to International Trade*. Washington, D.C.: Brookings Institution, 1970.

———, *Trade Policy in a Changing World Economy*. Chicago: University of Chicago Press, 1988.

Bhagwati, Jagdish, *The World Trading System at Risk*. Princeton, N.J.: Princeton University Press, 1991.

Boltuck, Richard, and Robert E. Litan, eds., *Down in the Dumps: Administration of the Unfair Trade Laws*. Washington, D.C.: Brookings Institution, 1991.

Council of Economic Advisers, *Economic Report of the President*. Washington, D.C.: Government Printing Office, 1992.

Diebold, William, *The End of the ITO*. Princeton, N.J.: International Finance Section, Department of Economics and Social Institutions, Princeton University, 1952.

General Agreement on Tariffs and Trade (GATT), *International Trade*. Geneva, various years.

———, *International Trade 1983/4*, Geneva, 1984.

———, *Trade Policy Review, United States, 1990*. Geneva, Mar. 1990.

Hecksher, Eli. *Mercantilism*. 2 vols. Rev. ed. London: George Allen and Unwin, 1955.

Hufbauer, Gary C., and Kimberly Ann Elliott, *Measuring the Costs of Protection in the United States*. Washington, D.C.: Institute for International Economics, 1994.

International Monetary Fund, *International Financial Statistics*. Washington, D.C., various years.

———, *World Economic Outlook*. Oct. 1990.

———, *International Financial Statistics Yearbook*. Washington, D.C., 1991.

Keesing, Donald B., and Martin Wolf, *Textile Quotas Against Developing Countries*. London: Trade Policy Research Centre, 1980.

Kenwood, A. G., and A. L. Lougheed, *The Growth of the International Economy 1820–1980*. London: George Allen and Unwin, 1983.

Krueger, Anne O., "Global Trade Prospects for the Developing Countries." *World Development,* July 1992, *15(4),* 457–74.

———, *American Trade Policy: A Tragedy in the Making?* Washington, D.C.: American Enterprise Institute, 1994.

Marshall, Alfred, *Principles of Economics,* 8th ed. 3rd printing. New York: Macmillan, 1950.

Moore, Michael. "Political Economy of Administered Protection: Steel." Paper presented at NBER Conference on Political Economy of Trade Protection. Cambridge, Mass., Feb. 1994.

North, Douglass C., "Ocean Freight Rates and Economic Development, 1750–1913." *Journal of Economic History,* Dec. 1958, *18(4),* 537–55.

———, *The Economic Growth of the United States 1790–1860.* New York: Norton, 1966.

Rugman, Alan M., and Andrew D. M. Anderson, *Administered Protection in America.* London: Croon Helm, 1987.

World Bank, *World Tables.* vol. 1. Washington, D.C., 1983.

———, *World Development Report 1987.* Washington, D.C., 1987.

———, *World Tables.* Washington, D.C., 1992.

———, *World Development Report 1993.* Washington, D.C., 1993.

McKinnon, Dollar and Yen

Balassa, Bela, "The Purchasing Power Parity Doctrine Reexamined." *Journal of Political Economy,* 1964, 72, 584–96.

Bayoumi, Tamin, "Saving-Investment Correlations." *IMF Staff Papers,* June 1990, 360–98.

Dominguez, K., and J. Frenkel, *Intervention Policy Reconsidered.* Washington, D.C.: Institute for International Economics, 1993.

Economic Planning Agency, *Bukka [Price] Report 1992.* Tokyo, Oct. 1992.

Frenkel, Jacob, and Michael Mussa, "The Efficiency of Foreign Exchange Markets and Measures of Turbulence." *American Economic Review,* May 1980, *70(2),* 374–81.

Gertler, Mark, and S. Gilchrist, "Monetary Policy, Business Cycles, and the Behavior of Small Manufacturing Firms." Mimeographed. Federal Reserve Bank of New York, 1992.

International Monetary Fund (IMF), *International Financial Statistics.* CD-ROM. June 1993.

———, *International Financial Statistics.* CD-ROM. June 1994.

McKinnon, Ronald I., *Money in International Exchange: The Convertible Currency System.* London: Oxford University Press, 1979.

———, "The Exchange Rate and Macroeconomic Policy." *Journal of Economic Literature,* June 1981, 531–57.

———, "Currency Substitution and Instability in the World Dollar Standard." *American Economic Review,* June 1982, *72(3),* 320–33.

———, *An International Standard for Monetary Stabilization.* Washington, D.C.: Institute for International Economics, 1984.

———, "Monetary and Exchange Rate Proposals for International Financial Stability: A Proposal." *Journal of Economic Perspectives,* Winter 1988, 2 *(1),* 83–103.

———, "The Rules of the Game: International Money in Historical Perspective." *Journal of Economic Literature,* Mar. 1993, 33, 1–44.

———, "From Plaza-Louvre to a Common Monetary Standard." Mimeographed. Stanford University, Aug. 1994.

McKinnon, Ronald, and Kenichi Ohno, "Getting the Exchange Rate Right: Insular Versus Open Economies." *Seoul Journal of Economics,* 1988, 1:1, 19–40.

———, *Dollar and Yen: Resolving Economic Conflict Between Japan and the United States.* Cambridge: MIT Press, forthcoming.

Maddison, Angus. *The World Economy in the 20th Century.* Paris: OECD, 1989.

Meade, James E., *The Balance of Payments.* London: Oxford University Press, 1951.

National Research Council, *Investing for Productivity and Prosperity.* Washington, D.C.: National Academy Press, 1994.

Ohno, Kenichi, "Estimating Yen/Dollar and Mark/Dollar Purchasing Power Parities." *IMF Staff Papers,* Sept. 1990, 700–725.

———, *International Monetary System and Economic Stability.* Tokyo: Keizai, 1991 (Japanese).

———, "Dynamism of Japanese Manufacturing: Evidence from the Postwar Period." Institute of Socio-Economic Planning, University of Tsukuba, Japan, Jan. 1993.

Organization for Economic Cooperation and Development, *Purchasing Power Parities and Real Expenditures: EKS Results 1990.* Paris, 1992.

———, *Economic Outlook.* June 1994.

———, *Monthly Statistics,* various issues.

Robinson, Joan, "The Foreign Exchanges." In *Essays in the Theory of Employment.* New York: Macmillan, 1937.

Taniguchi, Tomohiko, "Japan's Banks and the 'Bubble' Economy of the Late 1980s." Princeton University Center for International Studies Monograph Series No. 4. Princeton, N.J., 1993.

Tavlas, George, and Yuzuru Ozeki, *The Internationalization of Currencies: An Appraisal of the Japanese Yen.* International Monetary Fund Occasional Paper No. 90. Washington, D.C., Jan. 1992.

U.S. Bureau of Labor Statistics, *Handbook.* Washington, D.C., 1989.

———, *Employment and Earnings.* Washington, D.C., various issues.

Aoki, International Organizational Diversity

Aoki, M., "Comparative Advantage of Organizational Conventions and Gains from Diversity: Evolutionary Game Approach." Mimeographed. Stanford University, 1993.

———, "The Contingent Governance of Teams: Analysis of Institutional Complementarity." *International Economic Review*, Aug. 1994a, *35*, 657–76.

———, "The Japanese Firm as a System of Attributes: A Survey and Research Agendas." In M. Aoki and R. Dore, eds., *The Japanese Firm: Sources of Competitive Strength*. Oxford: Oxford University Press, 1994b.

Chandler, A., *The Visible Hand: The Managerial Revolution in American Business*. Cambridge: Harvard University Press, 1977.

Cremer, J., "Common Knowledge and the Coordination of Economic Activities." In M. Aoki, B. Gustafsson, and O. E. Williamson, eds., *The Firm as a Nexus of Treaties*. London, Sage Publications, 1990.

Fujimoto, T., "On the Origin and Evolution of the So-called Toyota Automobile Production and R&D Systems." Mimeographed (in Japanese). University of Tokyo, 1994.

Gordon, R., *The Evolution of Labor Relations in Japan*. Cambridge: Harvard University Press, 1986.

Hayami, Y., "The Role of Rural-based Entrepreneurship in East Asian Development." Mimeographed. Aoyama Gakuin University, Tokyo, 1993.

Helpman, E., and P. Krugman, *Market Structure and Foreign Trade*. Cambridge: MIT Press, 1985.

Itoh, H., "Cooperation in Hierarchical Organization: An Incentive Perspective." *Journal of Law, Economics, and Organization*, 1993, *8*, 321–45.

Krugman, P., "History Versus Expectations." *Quarterly Journal of Economics*, 1991, *56*, 651–67.

Matsuyama, K., "Increasing Returns, Industrialization, and Indeterminacy of Equilibrium." *Quarterly Journal of Economics*, 1991, *56*, 617–50.

Rothwell, G., "Organizational Structure and Expected Output at Nuclear Power Plants." *Review of Economics and Statistics*, forthcoming 1995.

Campbell, Kessler, and Shepherd, Liability Reforms and Economic Performance

Abraham, Kenneth S., "The Causes of the Insurance Crisis." In Walter Olson, ed., *New Directions in Liability Law: Proceedings of the Academy of Political Science*, pp. 54–66. New York: Academy of Political Science, 1988.

American Bar Association (ABA), *Report of the ABA Action Commission to Improve the Tort Liability System*. Chicago, 1987.

Campbell, Thomas J., Daniel P. Kessler, and George B. Shepherd, "Liability Reforms' Causes and Economic Impacts." Center for Economic Policy Research working paper. Stanford University, May 23, 1994.

Carlino, Gerald A., and Richard Voith, "Accounting for Differences in Aggregate State Productivity." *Regional Science and Urban Economics*, 1992, *22*, 597–98.

Epstein, Richard A., "The Political Economy of Product Liability Reform." *American Economic Review*, May 1988, *78(2)*, 311–15.

Galanter, Marc, "Reading the Landscape of Dispute: What We Know and Don't

Know (and Think We Know) About Our Allegedly Contentious and Litigious Society." *UCLA Law Review*, 1983, 31, pp. 4–71.

———, "News from Nowhere: The Debased Debate on Civil Justice." Unpublished manuscript delivered as Martin P. Miller Centennial Lecture, University of Denver College of Law, Oct. 2, 1992.

U.S. Department of Justice, Tort Policy Working Group, "Report on the Causes, Extent, and Policy Implications of the Current Crisis in Insurance Availability and Affordability." Washington, D.C., 1986.

Scholes, *Financial Infrastructure and Economic Growth*

Black, F., and M. S. Scholes, "From Theory to a New Financial Product." *Journal of Finance*, May 1974, 29, 399–412.

General Accounting Office, *Financial Derivatives, Actions Needed to Protect the Financial System*, GAO/GGD-94-133. Washington, D.C.: U.S. Government Printing Office, 1994.

Jensen, M. C., and W. Meckling, "Eclipse of the Public Corporation." *Harvard Business Review*, Sept./Oct. 1989, 67, 61–74.

Loomis, C. J., "A Whole New Way to Run a Bank." *Fortune*, Sept. 7, 1992, p. 76.

———, "The Risk That Won't Go Away." *Fortune*, Mar. 7, 1994, p. 78.

Merton, R. C., "Operation and Regulation in Financial Intermediation: A Functional Perspective." Harvard Business School Working Paper No. 93-020. Cambridge, 1993.

Miller, M. H., "Financial Innovation: The Last Twenty Years and the Next." *Journal of Financial and Quantitative Analysis*, Dec. 1986, 21, 459–71.

———, "Financial Innovation: Achievements and Prospects." *Journal of Applied Corporate Finance*, Winter 1992, 4, 4–11.

National Research Council, Board on Science, Technology, and Economic Policy, *Investing for Productivity and Prosperity*. Washington, D.C.: National Economic Press, 1994.

Sanford, C., Jr., "Financial Markets in 2020." *Economic Symposium, Federal Reserve Bank of Kansas City*, pp. 1–12. Kansas City, 1993.

Scholes, M. S., and M. A. Wolfson, *Taxes and Business Strategy: A Planning Approach*. Englewood Cliffs, N.J.: Prentice-Hall, 1992.

Cohen and Noll, *Privatizing Public Research*

Abramovitz, Moses, "Resource and Output Trends in the United States Since 1870." *American Economic Review*, 1956, 46, 5–23.

Advanced Research Projects Agency, *Technology Reinvestment Project: Program Information Package for Defense Technology Conversion, Reinvestment and Transition Assistance*. Washington, D.C.: Advanced Research Projects Agency, U.S. Department of Defense, 1993.

Advisory Committee on Industrial Innovation, *Final Report*. Washington, D.C.: U.S. Department of Commerce, 1979.

Clearinghouse for State and Local Initiatives on Productivity, Technology and Innovation, *Research and Development Consortia Registered Under the National Cooperative Research Act of 1984*. Washington, D.C.: U.S. Department of Commerce, 1993.

Cohen, Linda R., and Roger G. Noll, *The Technology Pork Barrel*. Washington, D.C.: Brookings, 1991.

———, "Research and Development." In Henry J. Aaron and Charles L. Schultze, eds., *Setting Domestic Priorities: What Can Government Do?* Washington, D.C.: Brookings Institution, 1992.

Congressional Budget Office. *Using R&D Consortia for Commercial Innovation: SEMATECH, X-ray Lithography, and High-Resolution Systems*. Washington, D.C.: Congressional Budget Office, 1990.

Council of Economic Advisers, *Annual Report and Economic Report of the President*. Washington, D.C.: U.S. Government Printing Office, 1994.

Demski, Joel S., and Robert P. Magee, "A Perspective on Accounting for Defense Contracts." *Accounting Review*, 1992, 67, 732–40.

Denison, Edward F., *Trends in American Economic Growth*. Washington, D.C.: Brookings Institution, 1985.

Griliches, Zvi, ed., *R&D, Patents and Productivity*. Chicago: University of Chicago Press, 1984.

———, "Productivity, R&D, and Basic Research at the Firm Level in the 1970s." *American Economic Review*, 1986, 76, 141–54.

———, "The Search for R&D Spillovers." *Scandanavian Journal of Economics*, 1992, 94, 29–47.

Intersociety Working Group, *Research and Development FY 1993: AAAS Report XVII*. Washington, D.C.: American Association for the Advanced of Science (AAAS), 1992.

———, *Research and Development FY 1994: AAAS Report XVIII*. Washington, D.C.: AAAS, 1993.

———, *Research and Development FY 1995: AAAS Report XIX*. Washington, D.C.: AAAS, 1994.

Jewkes, John, David Sawers, and Richard Stillerman, *The Sources of Invention*. 2nd ed. New York: Norton, 1969.

Kernell, Samuel, ed. *Parallel Politics: Economic Policymaking in Japan and the United States*. Washington, D.C.: Brookings Institution, 1991.

Kline, Stephen J., and Nathan Rosenberg, "An Overview of Innovation." In Ralph Landau and Nathan Rosenberg, eds., *The Positive Sum Strategy: Harnessing Technology for Economic Growth*, pp. 275–305. Washington, D.C.: National Academy Press, 1986.

Larson, Jean A., *Technology Transfer: A Selected Reference List*. Washington, D.C.: Office of Technology Commercialization, U.S. Department of Commerce, 1993.

Lawrence Berkeley Laboratory, *Highlights 1993*. Berkeley: University of California, 1994a.

———, *1993 Report*. Berkeley: University of California, 1994b.

Mansfield, Edwin, *Industrial Research and Technological Innovation*. New York: Norton, 1968.

————, "Basic Research and Productivity Increase in Manufacturing." *American Economic Review*, 1980, 70, 863–73.

————, "Industrial R&D in Japan and the United States." *American Economic Review*, 1988, 78, 226–28.

Markusen, Ann, and Joel Yudken, *Dismantling the Cold War Economy*. New York: Basic Books, 1992.

Mowery, David, and Nathan Rosenberg, *Technology and the Pursuit of Economic Growth*. Cambridge: Cambridge University Press, 1989.

National Institute of Standards and Technology, *Advanced Technology Program: Proposal Preparation Kit*. Washington, D.C.: National Institute for Standards and Technology, U.S. Department of Commerce, 1994.

National Research Council, *The Government Role in Civilian Technology*. Washington, D.C.: National Academy Press, 1992.

National Science Foundation, *National Patterns of R&D Resources*, NSF-92-330. Washington, D.C.: GPO, 1992.

————, *Science and Engineering Indicators, 1993*. Washington, D.C.: GPO, 1993.

Nelson, Richard R., "Aggregate Production Functions and Medium-range Growth Projections." *American Economic Review*, 1964, 54, 576–605.

————, ed., *National Innovation Systems: A Comparative Analysis*. Oxford: Oxford University Press, 1993.

Nelson, Richard R., and Sidney G. Winter, *An Evolutionary Theory of Economic Change*. Cambridge: Harvard University Press, 1982.

Nelson, Richard R., and Gavin Wright, "The Rise and Fall of American Technology Leadership." *Journal of Economic Literature*, 1992, 30, 1931–64.

Nordhaus, William D., *Invention, Growth, and Welfare: A Theoretical Treatment of Technological Change*. Cambridge: MIT Press, 1969.

Office of Management and Budget, *Historical Tables, Budget of the U.S. Government*, Fiscal Year 1994. Washington, D.C.: GPO, 1993.

Office of Technology Assessment, *Defense Conversion: Redirecting R&D*. Washington, D.C.: U.S. Government Printing Office, 1993a.

————, *Contributions of DOE Weapons Labs and NIST to Semiconductor Technology*. Washington, D.C.: U. S. Government Printing Office, 1993b.

Office of the White House Press Secretary, "The President's Industrial Innovation Initiatives: Fact Sheet." Washington, D.C., Oct. 31, 1979.

Rogerson, William, "Overhead Allocation and Incentives for Cost Minimization in Defense Procurement." *Accounting Review*, 1992, 67, 671–90.

Rosenberg, Nathan, *Inside the Black Box: Technology and Economics*. New York: Cambridge University Press, 1982.

Scherer, F. M., *Innovation and Growth: Schumpeterian Perspectives*. Cambridge: MIT Press, 1984.

Solow, Robert M., "Technological Change and the Aggregate Production Function." *Review of Economics and Statistics*, 1957, 39, 312–20.

U.S. General Accounting Office, *University Research: Controlling Inappropriate Access to Federally Funded Research Results*. GAO/RCED-92-104. Washington, D.C.: U.S. Government Printing Office, 1992.

Rosenberg, Uncertainty and Technological Change

Bilby, Kenneth, *The General: David Sarnoff and the Rise of the Communications Industry.* New York: Harper and Row, 1985.

Brock, Gerald W., *The Telecommunications Industry.* Cambridge: Harvard University Press, 1982.

Ceruzzi, Paul, "An Unforeseen Revolution: Computers and Expectations, 1935–1985." In Joseph J. Corn, ed., *Imagining Tomorrow*, pp. 188–201. Boston: MIT Press, 1987.

David, Paul, "The Dynamo and the Computer: An Historical Perspective on the Modern Productivity Paradox." *American Economic Review Papers and Proceedings*, May 1990, 355–61.

Devine, Warren, Jr., "From Shafts to Wires: Historical Perspectives on Electrification." *Journal of Economic History*, June 1983, 43(2), 347–72.

Douglas, Susan, *Inventing American Broadcasting, 1899–1922.* Baltimore: Johns Hopkins University Press, 1987.

Du Boff, Richard, "The Introduction of Electric Power in American Manufacturing." *Economic History Review*, Dec. 1967, 509–18.

Fogel, Robert, *Railroads and American Economic Growth.* Baltimore: Johns Hopkins University Press, 1964.

Gelijns, Annetine, *Innovation in Clinical Practice.* Washington, D.C.: National Academy Press, 1991.

Maclaurin, W. Rupert, *Invention and Innovation in the Radio Industry.* New York: Macmillan, 1949.

Martin, James, *Future Developments in Telecommunications.* Englewood Cliffs, N.J.: Prentice-Hall, 1977.

Rosenberg, Nathan, *Perspectives on Technology.* New York: Cambridge University Press, 1976.

Rosenbloom, Richard, and Michael Cusumano, "Technological Pioneering and Competitive Advantage: The Birth of the VCR Industry." *California Management Review*, Summer 1987.

Schurr, Sam, et al., *Electricity in the American Economy.* New York: Greenwood Press, 1990.

Townes, Charles, "Quantum Mechanics and Surprise in the Development of Technology." *Science*, Feb. 16, 1968.

U.S. Navy, Bureau of Ships, Technical Bulletin No. 2. Jan. 1941. As cited in James Martin, *Future Developments in Telecommunications*, p. 11. Englewood Cliffs, N.J.: Prentice-Hall, 1977.

Wriston, Walter B., *The Twilight of Sovereignty.* New York: Charles Scribner's Sons, 1992.

Bresnahan and Greenstein, Large-Scale Commercial Computing

Allen, Thomas J., and Michael S. Scott-Morton, *Information Technology and the Corporation of the 1990s.* New York: Oxford University Press, Research Studies, 1994.

Ambrosio, Johanna, "Client/server costs more than expected." *Computerworld*, Oct. 18, 1993, p. 28.

Berndt, Ernst, and Zvi Griliches, "Price Computers for Microcomputers: An Exploratory Study." In Murray F. Foss, Marylin E. Manser, and Allen H. Young, eds., *Price Measurements and Their Uses*. Chicago: University of Chicago Press, 1993.

Berndt, Ernst, Zvi Griliches, and Neal Rappaport, "Econometric Estimates of Prices Indexes for Personal Computers in the 1990s." NBER Working Paper No. 4549. Cambridge, Mass., 1993.

Berndt, Ernst R., and Catherine J. Morrison, "Assessing the Productivity of Information Technology Equipment in U.S. Manufacturing Industries." NBER Working Paper No. 3582. Cambridge, Mass., Jan. 1991.

Berry, Steven, Jim Levinsohn, and Ariel Pakes, "Automobile Prices in Market Equilibrium: Parts I and II." NBER Working Paper No. 4264. Cambridge, Mass., Jan. 1993.

Besen, Stanley M., and Garth Saloner, "Compatibility Standards and the Market for Telecommunications Services." In R. W. Crandall and K. Flamm, eds., *Changing the Rules: Technological Change, International Competition and Regulation in Telecommunications*. Washington, D.C.: Brookings Institution, 1988.

Boughton, Andrew, "Power Play." *Computerworld*, Nov. 22, 1993, *27(47)*, 97–102.

Bresnahan, Timothy F., "Measuring the Spillover from Technical Advance: Mainframe Computer in Financial Services." *American Economic Review*, Sept. 1986, 742–55.

Bresnahan, Timothy, and Shane Greenstein, "Technological Competition and the Structure of the Computer Industry." CEPR Discussion Paper No. 315, Stanford University, June 1992.

Bresnahan, Timothy, Shane Greenstein, and Harumi Ito, "The Irreversibility of Large Investments in Computer Systems." Mimeographed. Stanford University, 1994.

Bresnahan, Timothy, and Garth Saloner, "Large Firms' Demand for Computer Products and Services: Competing Market Models, Inertia, and Enabling Strategic Change." Mimeographed. Stanford University, Feb. 1995.

Bresnahan, Timothy, and Manuel Trajtenberg, "General Purpose Technologies: Engines of Growth?" *Journal of Econometrics*, Jan. 1995, *65*, 83–108.

Brown, Kenneth, and Shane Greenstein, "Measuring the Economic Benefits for Innovation in Mainframe Computers, 1985–1991." Mimeographed. University of Illinois, 1994.

Brynjolfsson, Eric, "The Productivity Paradox of Information Technology." *Communications of the ACM*, Dec. 1993, *36(12)*, 67–77.

Caldwell, Bruce, "Client-Server Report: Looking Beyond the Costs." *Information Week*, Jan. 3, 1994, pp. 51–56.

David, Paul A., and Shane Greenstein, "The Economics of Compatibility Standards: An Introduction to Recent Research." *Economics of Innovation and New Technology*, 1990, *1(1/2)*, 3–41.

Dixit, Avinash, and Robert Pindyck, *Uncertain Investments.* Princeton, N.J.: Princeton University Press, 1994.

Dulberger, Ellen R., "The Application of a Hedonic Model to a Quality-Adjusted Price Index for Computer Processors." In Dale W. Jorgenson and Ralph Landau, eds., *Technology and Capital Formation.* Cambridge: MIT Press, 1989.

Farrell, Joseph, and Garth Saloner, "Installed Base and Compatibility: Innovation, Product Preannouncements, and Predation." *American Economic Review,* 1986, 76, 940–55.

Flamm, Kenneth, *Targeting the Computer: Government Support and International Competition.* Washington, D.C.: Brookings Institution, 1987.

Friedman, Andrew L., and Dominic S. Cornford, *Computer Systems Development: History, Organization and Implementation.* New York: John Wiley and Sons, 1989.

Gordon, Robert J., "The Postwar Evolution of Computer Prices." In Dale W. Jorgenson and Ralph Landau, eds., *Technology and Capital Formation.* Cambridge: MIT Press, 1989.

———, *The Measurement of Durable Goods.* Chicago: University of Chicago Press, 1990.

Greenstein, Shane, "Lock-in and the Costs of Switching Mainframe Computer Vendors: What Do Buyers See?" Faculty Working Paper No. 91–0133, Political Economy Series No. 48. University of Illinois, 1991.

———, "Did Installed Base Give an Incumbent any (Measurable) Advantages in Federal Computer Procurement?" *Rand Journal of Economics,* 1992, 24(1), 19–39.

———, "From Super-minis to Supercomputers: Estimating Surplus in the Computing Market." In Timothy F. Bresnahan and Robert J. Gordon, eds., *The Economics of New Products.* Chicago: University of Chicago Press, 1995, forthcoming.

Grove, Andrew S., "The Future of the Computer Industry." *California Management Review,* 1990, 33(1), 148–60.

Hall, Bronwyn, "Industrial Research in the 1980s: Did the Rate of Return Fall?" *Brookings Papers on Economic Activity,* Microeconomics 1993, pp. 289–343.

Hammer, Michael, and James Champy, *Reengineering the Corporation.* New York: Harper Business, 1993.

"Hardware and Tear." *Economist,* Dec. 19, 1992, pp. 61–62.

Inmon, Robert, *Technomics, The Economics of Technology and the Computer Industry.* New York: Dow Jones-Irwin, 1985.

Kador, John, "Downsizing Is Ready for Prime Time Midrange Systems." *ComputerWorld,* May 12, 1992, 5(9), 50–51.

Keefe, Patricia, "The aroma is appetizing . . . but the client/server main course is still simmering." *Computerworld,* Jan. 1, 1990, pp. 35–37.

Klemperer, Paul, "Competition when Consumers Have Switching Costs: An Overview." 1992 Inaugural Lecture to the Annual Conference on Industrial Economics, Madrid, Spain, 1992.

Loveman, Gary W., "An Assessment of the Productivity Impact of Information

Technologies." In Thomas J. Allen, and Michael S. Scott-Morton, eds., *Information Technology and the Corporation of the 1990s*. New York: Oxford University Press, Research Studies, 1994.

Lucas, H. C., Jr., "Organizational Power and the Information Services Department," *Communications of the ACM*, Jan. 1984, 27, 58–65.

Mansfield, Edwin, *Industrial Research and Technological Innovation*. New York: Norton, 1968.

Oliner, Steve, "Constant Quality Price Changes, Depreciation, and Retirement of Mainframe Computers." In Foss et al., eds., *Price Measurements and Their Uses*, pp. 19–62. Chicago: University of Chicago Press, 1993.

Radding, Alan, "Size is Beside the Point—All that Really Matters is Fit." *Computerworld*, June 12, 1989, pp. 69–71.

Ray, George F., "The Diffusion of Mature Technologies." National Institute of Economic and Social Research Occasional Paper 36. Cambridge: Cambridge University Press, 1984.

Rogers, Everett M., *The Diffusion of Innovations*. New York: Free Press, 1983.

Rosenberg, Nathan, *Inside the Black Box: Technology and Economics*. Cambridge: Cambridge University Press, 1982.

Rotemberg, Julio, and Garth Saloner, "Interfirm Cooperation and Collaboration." In Michael Scott-Morton, ed., *Information Technology and Organizational Transformation*. New York: Oxford University Press, 1991.

Scott-Morton, Michael, *The Corporation of the 1990s, Information Technology and Organizational Transformation*. New York: Oxford University Press, 1991.

Stavins, Joanna, "Modelling Entry and Exit in a Differentiated-Product Industry: The Case of the Personal Computer Market." *Review of Economics and Statistics*, Feb. 1996, forthcoming.

Stoneman, Paul, *The Economic Analysis of Technological Change*. New York: Oxford University Press, 1988.

Trajtenberg, Manuel, *Economic Analysis of Product Innovation, The Case of CT Scanners*. Cambridge: Harvard University Press, 1990.

Triplett, Jack E., "Price and Technological Change in a Capital Good: A Survey of Research on Computers." In Dale W. Jorgenson and Ralph Landau, eds., *Technology and Capital Formation*. Cambridge: MIT Press, 1989.

Landau, Lessons from the Chemical Industry

Bernal, J. D., *The Social Function of Science*. Cambridge: MIT Press, 1939.

Board on Science, Technology and Economic Policy, National Research Council, *Investing for Productivity and Prosperity*. Washington, D.C.: National Academy Press, 1994.

Bosworth, Barry, "Unemployed in Europe Versus Poor in America." *International Economic Insights*, Mar./Apr. 1994, 2–5.

Chandler, Alfred, *Scale and Scope*. Cambridge: Harvard University Press, 1990.

Cohen, Linda R., and Roger G. Noll, *The Technology Pork Barrel*. Washington, D.C.: Brookings Institution, 1991.

DeLong, J. Bradford, and Lawrence H. Summers, "Equipment Investment and Economic Growth." *Quarterly Journal of Economics*, May 1991, 445–502.

Durlauf, Steven N., "International Differences in Economic Fluctuations." In Nathan Rosenberg, Ralph Landau, and David Mowery, eds., *Technology and the Wealth of Nations*, pp. 121–147. Stanford, Calif.: Stanford University Press, 1992.

Farrell, Christopher, and Michael Mandel, "Why Are We So Afraid of Growth?" *Business Week*, May 16, 1994, pp. 62–72.

Hatsopoulos, George N., and James M. Poterba, "America's Investment Shortfall: Probable Causes and Possible Fixes." Report to the Board on Science, Technology and Economic Policy, National Research Council, Washington, D.C., 1993.

"How America Sees the World." *Economist*, editorial, Oct. 30, 1993, pp. 5–6.

Landau, Ralph, "U.S. Economic Growth." *Scientific American*, June 1988, 258(6), 44–52.

———, "The CEO and the Technologist." *Research-Technology Management*, May/June 1992.

Landau, Ralph, and Nathan Rosenberg, "Successful Commercialization in the Chemical Process Industries." In Nathan Rosenberg, Ralph Landau, and David Mowery, eds., *Technology and the Wealth of Nations*, pp. 73–119. Stanford, Calif.: Stanford University Press, 1992.

Lau, Lawrence J., and Jong-Il Kim, "Human Capital and Aggregate Productivity: Some Empirical Evidence from the Group-of-five Countries." Center for Economic Policy Research Working Paper No. 318, Stanford University, July 1992.

McKinnon, Ronald, and David Robinson, "Dollar Devaluation, Interest Rate Volatility, and the Duration of Investment in the United States." In Nathan Rosenberg, Ralph Landau, and David Mowery, eds., *Technology and the Wealth of Nations*, pp. 281–325. Stanford, Calif.: Stanford University Press, 1992.

National Science Foundation, *Research and Development in Industry*. Washington, D.C., annual.

Phelps, Edmund, *Structural Slumps: The Modern Equilibrium Theory of Unemployment, Interest, and Assets*. Cambridge: Harvard University Press, 1994.

Porter, Michael E., *The Competitive Advantage of Nations*. New York: Free Press, 1990.

———, *Capital Choices*. Washington, D.C.: Council on Competitiveness, 1992.

Rosenberg, Nathan, and Richard Nelson, "American Universities and Technical Advance in Industry." Center for Economic Policy Research Working Paper No. 342, Stanford University, Mar. 1993.

Solow, Robert, "Europe's Unnecessary Unemployment." *International Chemical Insights*, Mar./Apr. 1994, 10–11.

Spitz, Peter H., *Petrochemicals—the Rise of an Industry*. New York: John Wiley and Sons, 1988.

Wolff, Edward N., "Capital Formation and Productivity Growth in the 1970s and 1980s: A Comparative Look at OECD Countries." In American Council for Capital Formation, *Tools for American Workers: The Role of Machinery and Equipment in Economic Growth*, Washington, D.C.: Center for Policy Research, 1992.

Index

In this index an "f" after a number indicates a separate reference on the next page, and an "ff" indicates separate references on the next two pages. A continuous discussion over two or more pages is indicated by a span of page numbers, e.g., "57–59." *Passim* is used for a cluster of references in close but not consecutive sequence.

Library of Congress Cataloging-in-Publication Data

The mosaic of economic growth / edited by Ralph Landau, Timothy
Taylor, and Gavin Wright.
    p.   cm.
Includes bibliographical references and index.
ISBN 0-8047-2599-3 (cloth).—ISBN 0-8047-2604-3
(pbk.).
    1. Economic development. 2. Economic policy. I. Landau, Ralph.
II. Taylor, Timothy. III. Wright, Gavin.
HD75.M674 1996
338.9—dc20
95-22572   CIP

∞ This book is printed on acid-free, recycled paper.
It was typeset in 10/12.5 Galliard by
G & S Typesetters, Inc.

Original printing 1996

Last figure below indicates year of this printing:

05 04 03 02 01 00 99 98 97 96